MW01534317

H

THE
HERMANS
STALKING AMERICA

THE JOURNAL OF AN UNKNOWN ROCK AND ROLL BAND

CHRIS, BILL, DAVE, DERK

ACKNOWLEDGEMENTS:

The authors of this book would first and foremost like to thank the other two hermans: Bill Pfeiffer, our impeccable bassist, and Chris Entz, our amazing lead guitarist, without whom, this entire venture would not exist. Although these two upstanding Americans did not physically write this book, they contributed equally to this band and this book. Thank you, Bill and Chris. We love you.

In addition, the hermans would like to thank, and in no particular order, mind you, everyone else who has contributed to this band, and this book. If we missed anyone, you have not really been missed, since we appreciate everyone who has supported us since our conception in the winter of 2003. So, thank you to Gregory Edward Jones (our glorious editor and manager), Jason Kernevich (our book designer), Dave's parents and family, Derk's parents and family, Bill's parents and family, Chris's parents and family, Mattie Taco Swanson (our web designer and multi-media manager), Jeff Ament, Colin Alton Hickey (Monty Carlo), Nyree Schmidt, Sophia Grace Gettings, Jessa Gettings, Nate Walters, Christopher David Knudsen (the Count), Mike Gill, Jon Amadeus Markley, Megan Helm, John Fleming, Justin Lawrence (Hell House Sound), Jeffrey Joseph Jones, Rick Parnell (aka Mick Shrimpton), Cameron Kerr and Blake Bickell of Habbilis Records, LLC, Cap'n Sextastic, Joe Danger, Chris Bacon, Bryan Hickey, Shane Hickey, Pat Gill, Aaron Bolton, Adelaide Every (The Mermaid), Kevin Pierce, Joseph Gary, Jennifer and Tarn Rackley, Jill Dieser, Maureen McCourt, O'd, Jeff Kapp, Beverly Walters, Rick Grillo, Amanda Engledrum, Samantha Crumley, Amy Mohr, Tara Turner, Krista Schmidt, David Pierce (Crocodile pics), John Falch, Karen Smith and the Crazy Daisy, Damon Metzner, Chet Smith, Andrea Harsell, Wes Duncan, Craig Roth, Tommy Pertis, Brent Kilburn, Rick Gulman, Cameron and Alley, Scotty's Table crew, Finn and Porter crew, Montana Ace folks, Chad (Jester's Bar), Stewart (Ritz soundman extraordinaire), Gavin and Rose (owners of the Raven), Rainy Shasta Miranda (Portland pics), Joe Kusy for his great drawings, Ear Candy Music, The International Playboys, Victory Smokes, Oblio Joes, Akron/Family, JBOT and his robots which captured him, Green Milk from the Planet Orange, The Icicles, Arrows to the Sun, Marshall Plan, Quiet Jack, Apples of Discord, The Krooks, Bacon and Egg, Volumen, Reptile Dysfunction, Riddilin Que, The Monolators, Friends of Rock and Roll, The Birthday Suits, Get Set Go, The Thermals, The Peelers, Claire DeLune, Pocket Lobotomy, Danny Bobbe and his Dilemma, Daphne Starburst, JC Auto, Chevy Chase, Pope J.P.II, Rowe Factor Five, KBGA, The Trail, The Blaze, The Old Post (esp. Jeanine, former booking agent), The Loft (Higgins Alley), Al's & Vic's, MONTPirg, Missoula Boys and Girls Club, Missoula Downtown Association, Red Light Green Room, Missoula Ale House, The Ritz, The Raven, The Elks Club, The Union Hall, Flipper's Bar and Casino (esp. Donny, Aspen & Ginger), The Other Side, The University of Montana, Vagina Monologues, The Crocodile, Tonic Lounge, Le Voyeur, Mootsy's, The Badlander, Snowbowl, Jon Tester (for coming), Conrad Burns (for going), The Missoula Independent (esp. Skylar Browning, Sarah Daisy Lindmark, Jonas Ehudin, Jason Wiener), The Entertainer (esp. Jamie Kelly, Joe Nickell, Daniel Person), the good people of California (San Berdu), the city and all inhabitants of Missoula, Montana and Running Press/Perseus Book Groups.

Additionally, the hermans would like to thank our photo contributors to this fine book: Mattie Taco Swanson, Nate Walters, Nyree Schmidt, Greg Jones, David Pierce, Krista Schmidt, Megan Helm, Rainy Shasta Miranda, Sarah Spaetzer, Christina Wernikowski, Jason Kernevich

and ourselves, who took the rest of the damn pictures. Thank you all. We love you.

-David E. Jones and Derk K. Schmidt

(with additional text from William Barnes Pfeiffer, Christopher Michael Entz and Gregory Edward Jones)

FOREWORD

BY JEFF AMENT OF PEARL JAM

310.555.1801

You will pay by ~~ ~~ or ~~ ~~
but only by ~~ ~~illing ~~ ~~

BUSINESS VIOLATION
CITY OF LOS ANGELES
VIOLATION

THE HERMANS

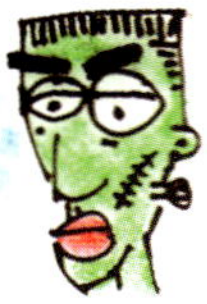

Postage
Required
Post Office will
not deliver
without proper
postage.

PLAYING ROCK N ROLL MUSIC WAS JUST AN EXCUSE
TO GET OUT OF MONTANA ... ANY EXCUSE TO GET OUT AND
SEE THE WORLD. WHAT COULD BE BETTER THAN WRITING
PUNK ROCK SONGS WITH YOUR FRIENDS, MAKING A RECORD
AND SLEEPING ON STRANGER'S FLOORS ACROSS AMERICA?

NOTHING.

CITY OF LOS ANGELES (DON'T MOVE TO)
PO BOX ████
LOS ANGELES CA ████-████

STARTING IT ALL UP IN A SMALL TOWN LIKE MISSOULA IS
THE ONLY CHANCE A YOUNG BAND HAS TO DO SOMETHING
SPIRITED AND ORIGINAL ...
TO HAVE A PROPER START, ~~████~~ ~~████~~

THE HERMANS KEPT A DIARY, SO THEY WON'T HAVE
TO BE TIRED OLD ROCK STARS TELLING ANYONE WHO'LL
LISTEN, WHAT IT WAS LIKE "BACK IN THE DAY."
THEY CAN JUST GIVE THEIR KIDS THIS BOOK.
GENIUS.

Jeff Ament

MISSOULA, MONTANA APRIL 1, 2007

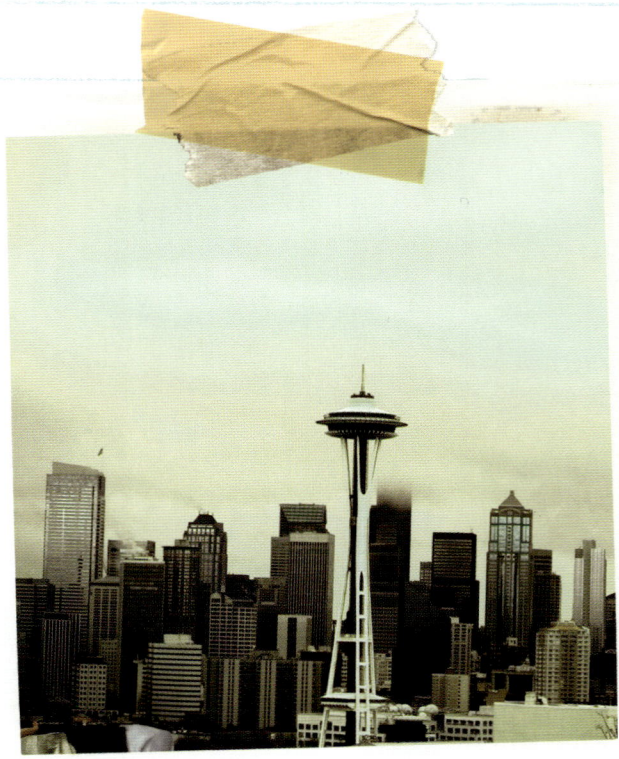

Dearest Sis,

Just got back from our trip to Seattle, probably one of the better weekends in the history of me. Derk, his bitch fiancé Liz (the actress we didn't invite but bitched and moaned so we let her go just to shut her up) and I got to Pioneer Square in time for five hours of prime drinking. We would have ventured all over what is becoming one of my favorite cities but I needed to piss, went down an alley and discovered the Owl and Thistle bar. As I marked my scent on the Pikes Market district I over heard some Irish accents and saw them going in the bar. It turned out to be a pretty cool joint.

Anyway, in between the Eagles/Seahawks game and the Pearl Jam benefit (you would have dug Steve Earl) we were at the Owl n' Thistle and Derk and I decided to start jamming together when we get back. It probably had something to do with the energy and all the music that was going on downtown that night…we saw some shitty bands that rocked! I have five or six riffs I have been fucking with since high school and I think they are lonely and need some heavy drumming and screaming guitars…my guitar playing doesn't scream, it whines.

Derk played in this really lame folk-rock band that played the Old Post Pub here in Missoula all the time but the singer was a clichéd douche bag and the songs sucked. Derk's piano was kick-ass, however, and he says he drums a little (he is a multi-talent musically) so if he is as amateur at drums as I am guitar, we should do just splendidly. AND his drum set is cow printed so even if we suck our drum set will still be cooler than any other band's.

Well, we will see what happens with that idea. I have never played with anyone except for Greg and, obviously, he is our brother so I wouldn't be nervous around him, but playing with an accomplished musician freaks me out. They get all technical like and think they are cool and will probably give me shit. Seriously, I am anxious to hear what his opinion is of these "songs." It is funny that he has no idea that I don't know what the fuck I am doing!

Pearl Jam were slicker than whale shit and the Eagles destroyed the Seahawks, even with our third string quarterback who I believe is twelve years old. I saw some asshole (probably from North East Philly - he had the accent) get kicked out of the stadium for starting a fight: it was fabulous! We almost got decked but Seahawks fans are not like us; we are an entirely different breed of sports fans all together.

Talk to you soon,

Love,

SCALE AND CHORD CHART

Chords are given in *1st* Position only. Accidentals in parentheses indicate *lowered 3rd* deg
ing the Minor chord, and *lowered 7th* degree, forming the Seventh chord.

MAJOR SCALES

Middle

C

G Scale

CHORDS
(MAJOR, MINOR AND S

G — A — B — C — D — E

G   Gm

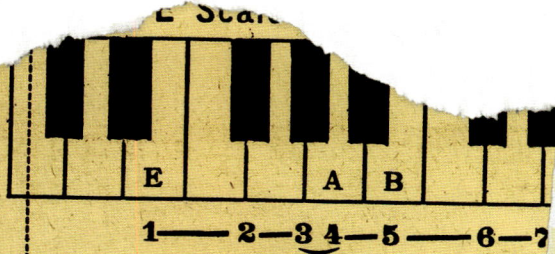

Roger Podactor,
I will be home around 7:30; the time I kick you in
the face and then we jam. Tune my guitar. I tried and it
sounds like a bus accident.
oh, I won "safety bingo" at work (If the "team members" don't
trip over their own shoes and spike ~~them~~ themselves, the pot grows) so the
Heineken in the fridge is band beer... so it's for us.

E Scale

E   A B

1 — 2—3 4—5 — 6—7

B Scale

B

1 — 2—3

PECKER —

I HAVE TO WORK TONIGHT UNTIL
9:00. IF YOU GET A CHANCE, RUN
TO ESP ON HIGGINS AND GET SOME STICKS
OR I WILL HAVE TO USE BROKEN NUBS
AGAIN. GET THE CHEAP-ASS $7 ESP
BRAND STICKS, SIZE 5A — AND MAKE SURE
THEY HAVE WOOD TIPS, NOT NYLON. THOSE
ANGER ME. DO IT. NOW!

— HAMMER

F# Scale

F#   F#m

-----Original Message-----
From: dudejonz@yahoo.com
To: Jones, Greg
Subject: Practice? We talkin' bout practice?

Greg,

Derk and I just had our third practice and this shit is fucking cool. He is a pretty good drummer for a piano player turned guitar player turned drummer and daft weirdo. We are practicing three nights a week and it also serves as a good way to get away from the lady and little lady for a few hours a week to drink a few beers and go deaf…hey, she thinks it is cooler than football. She is a great momma and thank god she loves rock and roll.

We finally turned this riff I've been playing since I was a sophomore in high school into a song called "Tidal Wave." It's pretty dynamic (that is musician lingo for "all over the fucking place) and goes up and down…like a tidal wave.

Not bad for a punk with no lessons, thanks a lot family. Just kidding.

So we are going to do an open mic in a few days. The Ritz (the bar across from Red's Bar where we watch the Eagles beat up on everyone and their mother) has them on Tuesdays and we are going to play our three songs that actually sound cool with just drums and a dirty, raw guitar sound. Oh, we are also playing Yoda (Weird Al's version of Lola) and Around the Bend (CCR) where Derk will come off the drums and do guitar with me.

I sing like shit…I think I may have heard donkeys fucking with more harmony at one time. I am going to fuck this up!

Dave

9

ASSWIPE —
    IF WE ARE GOING TO PLAY OPEN MIC
TUESDAY @ THE RITZ, WE HAD BETTER CALL
OURSELVES SOMETHING. TRY TO THINK OF SOME
BAND NAMES AND WE'LL GO TO FLIPPER'S
LATER AND "BRAINSTORM," AS THEY SAY IN
THE CORPORATE WORLD. I'VE GOT A FEW
IDEAS. LATER, LOSER.
        —HAMMER

DAVE

DERK

And so we ended up at Flipper's bar and grill. Or bar and casino. I don't know what the fuck it is called I just know it is a cool spot. There is no liquor served which allots for more room for less assholes. The assholes can keep going to the meathead bars downtown on Front Street that I would not stop to take a leak in. I don't even like to walk by because usually some douche with his North Carolina hat meticulously placed sideways in order to alert the general public of his doucheness has something negative and neolithic to say. Jesus, these people! You are in fucking Montana! You get off any exit on the highway and you are pretty much assured to find an awe inspiring place…except for maybe Billings! I don't get the chip on the shoulder thing with these tough guy idiots. I guess they are pissed because the Back Street Boys broke up.

Anyway, back to Flipper's. The bartenders only serve beer and wine which makes them have to move less so when they do, they still do it slow because why rush a good beer? They are always in a good way and they've always interesting notions contrary to the usual mundane bullshit that comes prevalently with your run of the mill public houses. Although this bar is a double wide (not being a native of this state the term double wide is new to me and I imagine it means two trailer park domiciles positioned mutually for the purpose of contributing more space) it is dark but alluring, sparse but content, flinty yet appealing and it also smells like an ashtray convention with complimentary Heineken. Yes, I love this bar. The regulars are a meager but noble lot and I think that comes with the nature of being a true beer drunk without the whisky. Most whisky drinkers I have come across here do the reverse change from sweet friendly butter-flies into fire breathing dragon bitch slugs except dragons are cool because they breath fire and these idiots just curse, spit and drool…and fall down head first after they stagger their incoherent dummy dance. Nay, the true beer drunkard will start off friendly, become an even better friend, ask you for a ride home to smoke pot and then maybe remember who you were to buy you a beer three nights later. They are the garlic of the earth.

Lo, Flipper's is a modest joint; a true watering hole. And I love it. It is a very good spot to go and write song lyrics in the afternoon over a beer. Even if it is sunny and beautiful out it will still be dark at Flipper's so if you feel that spur in the but-tocks writers sometimes encounter to write about crazy chicks or cool chicks or chicks you would kill or die for or your kids or the Pope or the nature of this stranded nation, Flipper's is the place for me.

DERK & DAVE'S AWESOME 2-PIECE BAND NAMES

JERKSTORE
BROWNFINGER
POPE ON STRIKE
KFCIA
MR. SQUISHY
MR. MIYAGI
MAYWOOD STREET
SHRINKAGE
COWFLOP
BODY BAG BREAKFAST
THE THUMBS
LIFE OF BRIAN
THE SILLY SODS

CHAPTER ELEVENTEEN
THE GERMANS
THE SHERMANS
THE HERMANS
THE IRWINS
PIPING LUCY
SUBURBAN TURBAN
FREE LUNCH TAXIDERMY
BACKFAT
THE ANWAR SADATSUN
FUNNYFUCKER
FUCKTUNSTEIN
THE RAMRODS

-----Original Message-----
From: gregjones99@yahoo.com
To: Jones, David
Subject: rock star

Hey Dave,
So you're finally going to get up on a stage somewhere? You know we've all been expecting this day since your daily performances of "She's So Cold" on the living room table as a 7-year-old punk-in-training. You were fucking relentless with that song!
Still using that ratty old guitar chord and scales sheet I drew up for you in your bedroom with a No. 2 pencil back in like '87? You know, I was surprised by your playing last time you were home -- much cleaner sound than I've ever gotten out of the ax. But what's with playing that same riff over and over again?!! Mom knows what I'm talking about...
Anyway, have fun up there and don't sweat it if you puke on yourself. Once you get going I'm sure you'll be fine. Or not, heh heh.
Looking forward to hearing your stuff! Do you guys have a name or anything yet? Give me a call after your "show."
Greg

From: dudejonz@yahoo.com
To: Jones, Greg
Subject: peewee munster blume

Greggor,

You vile moth-like creature, allowing society to change you into a corporate whore like a damned wretched insect! Anyway, Kafka, we are calling ourselves "the hermans." It is short and to the fucking point. Kevin (you remember Kevin from Divine Lorraine and my high school, yes?) in Philly liked it as he said it tells one nothing about our style, genre, music, what-have-you and it is pretty much open ended. I like it because it was Bill Murray's name in Rushmore and he rejected a lay up by a ten year old punk out of the blue.

The original idea is from a friend of Derk's fiancé in Michigan who shaved her head and left only a long clump in the front as if she were in Anthrax but really worked at the mall. Derk called it a herman but since that story involves that fake plastic woman of his (this is not going to last) I am telling people we got the name from Rushmore…because that is my reasoning behind it so I guess it is a half truth, heh heh. She wants to sing with us but I'd rather have my hand turn into a chainsaw like the guy from Evil Dead. I want her to have nothing to do with this band. Fucking Yoko.

I am going to school then taking Sophie to the carousel. She is getting big (I think she is getting big, she is the only one and a half year old I know!) and more beautiful by the day and will be smarter than both of us by the time she is seven. Smart and beautiful. God bless the NRA. Dirty apes!

Dave

BABY SOPHIE...
DAVE'S BEST CONTRIBUTION
TO THE WORLD.

3

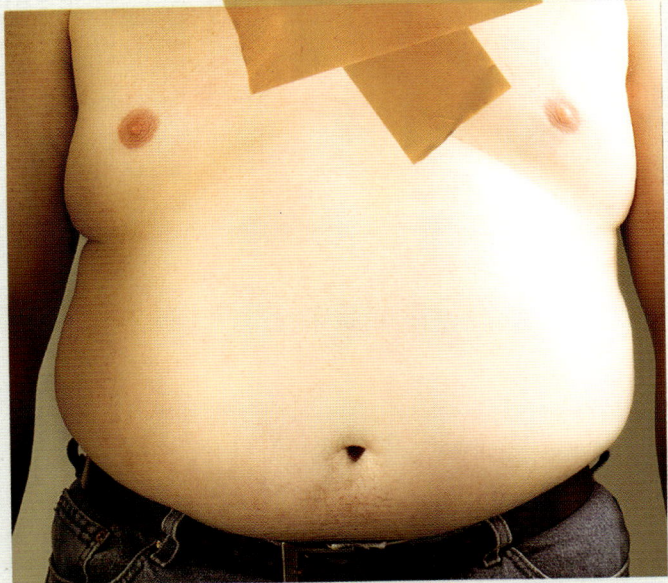

February 10 or 30 or so, 2004

Dave and I played at the Ritz open mic last night as "the hermans." I like the name.
I think it says absolutely nothing about us or our music. It is silly and presumptuous.
I lugged my stupid cowprint-laden drums down there and spent about as much time setting
them up as we did playing - 20 fuckin' minutes. We have been jamming in my basement for
several weeks and could only come up with one song with lyrics, "Headache," along with
an asinine cover of "Angie" by the Rolling Stones which we mauled into a waltz rhythm
for a spell and cleverly brought back to end it with at least some shred of dignity, and
our perpetual "hippie jam song" that is, for now, a mere instrumental. Then I strapped
on my guitar and we played "Yoda," a parody of "Lola" by the Kinks as re-performed by
"Weird" Al Yankovic. We also did "Around the Bend" by CCR. Surprisingly, no one told us
to get the fuck off stage. In fact, many cheered and caroused along with our musings. I
think one guy may have even removed his shirt.

I thought Dave was going to shit in his trousers backstage before we went on. I have
been on stage in front of real people for some ten years, so I didn't really care, but
he had never played anything in front of anyone ever. He was scared. What a loser. I think
halfway into the first song he forgot he was on stage and let the music take over. That's
what should happen. Fuck people. If they don't want to listen they can leave. I mean, it
is only an open mic for Christ's sake. I think we will do it again soon. Hopefully I will
not have to play the guitar again. We'll have to write a couple more songs so we can rock
it out as a two-piece on guitar and drums. Maybe someone will dig it and
want to play bass for us. It happened once to me before back in Michigan when I was
fifteen playing guitar in my first real band called "Bent." We played our first show with
two guitars, drums and vocals. After the show, a guy we all knew came up and asked if we
wanted a bass player. He started playing for us that night. Dreams can come true. I loved
that band. We probably suck. I am not really a drummer. I miss my guitar.

The fucking EAGLES just lost in the playoffs and this is my BLOOOOOD!!

NO, really, this is my Blood because my DumBASS punched the Dumpster outside of Flippers. FLip's is like the EDEN to my SNAKE (but I only offer people cigarettes and Beer and am not trying to piss ANYONE OFF) But I will never watch an EaGles game there again! Two years in a Row we watched the whole season @ RED'S Bar and then the playoffs at Flippers so Fuck this!

I am selling my Danelectro HODAD Hotrod mother Fucker, Flying to TAMPA Bay (Go Scientology!) and tar + Feathering Rhonde BaRder ... I'll get his brother next year.

Dearest journal,

You heathenous bastard. Thanks for not coming to the open mic. It is always nice
to play in front of a bunch of drunks. So, yeah, we played our third open mic last
night at the Ritz and kicked some ass. Playing live has quickly surpassed my other
most cherished things to do like hamster juggling, giving random dental checks to
strangers and lighting G.I Joes on fire. In all honesty, I have never felt anything
like it before. It probably has a lot to do with undergoing drunken screaming in my
direction, the smell of sweat, beer, cigarettes and things undiscovered in the bar,
bad dancing and me and Derk experiencing all of these things because of our songs.
It is hard to describe. I have never jumped out of a plane, surfed big waves or
slayed any dragons so I have nothing to compare it to but to say it is like a natural drug and better than cocaine, kind of.

Back to the point. Bill, from Hot Action (another Pennsylvania native) approached
us after our set and wants to play bass with us. In the last week we had two people
jam with us but they just didn't gel. The one girl was really sweet and an o.k.
bass player but I think she only said two and a half words in the hour we played.
People like that give me the willies and the sensation that they are plotting my
fucking death so she was out. The other guy worked at the gas station behind our
house and asked to sit in. He brought a patch cable that was about two feet from
bass to amp and I think he lied about being able to play. He must have been high
because he was incessantly giggling about fucking up a simple three chord song.
Bill, however, is a great guitar player and has a good voice as well. He's been in
bands and has confidence (as he does open mics a lot) and in watching him do the
open mics it is obvious he wants more.

We are practicing this week and Bill is coming over. I have a feeling about this
guy and, being from PA, he can't be totally off. I am somewhat anxious as Derk is
the only other musician I have played with so I will most likely end up spiking
myself. But, as long as he likes to drink some brews, digs rocking out and enjoys
watching the Eagles beat the snot out of guys with other jerseys on, we will surely
be the next Beatles. Or the next Shitty Beatles…or the Rutles.

Davey

Journal, you hooker…

First of all, I hate you. Second, this band practice space shit has
taken its toll on me. Not only is this basement ridiculously small and
dingy, but I think my entire kitchen is being held at bay by a two-by-
four and a couple of shims. I believe that in the near future, Dave,
Bill and I will rock out so hard that the stove will crash through the
ceiling and kill me. The fridge will kill Bill. Dave will narrowly
escape, covered in pipe sludge and with a significant knot on his melon,
which is sad since he should surely be the first to go. In addition to
this ridiculousness, I have my woodworking shop down there, and we have
to move all of the tools upstairs to make space to play music, then
reverse the process afterwards so I can work again. It takes a half an
hour both ways just to be able to set up the room for practice. I should
just quit this woodworking shit, but I got a sweet deal supplying Brent
the redneck European taxidermist with the oaken plaques on which he
mounts the taxidermy trophies he makes for his stupid redneck clients
that like to hang dead shit on the walls to display to their wife-
beating friends. It pays pretty well, though, and Brent gives me free
elk meat, which tastes like jellybread. Needless to say, journal, whore,
I think this whole thing stinks and I want to have a studio to practice
in so my musical equipment is not covered in saw dust, which can't be
good for anything. Fuck you, journal. You have been no help whatsoever.

Dave —
NYREE GOT US A SHOW AT THE MISSOULA ALE HOUSE
BECAUSE THE BARTENDER THERE USED TO GO TO HER
HIGH SCHOOL IN HELENA. THIS IS TOTALLY AWESOME — I
ONLY MET HER A FEW MONTHS AGO AND ALREADY SHE IS THE COOLEST
GIRL I'VE EVER BEEN WITH. AND HER NAME IS COOL, TOO.
SHE GOT US OUR FIRST REAL SHOW! WE ARE PLAYING IN
2 WEEKS SO YOU'D BETTER BE READY, MOTHERFUCKER!
WE NEED SOME COVER SONGS TO FILL TIME SO THINK OF STUFF
THAT WILL BE COOL AND NOT LAME LIKE YOU. NO .DEVO!
YOU ARE NOT THAT GOOD.
— HAMMS

DERK... MOMENTS BEFORE BEING DEMOLISHED
BY THE KITCHEN STOVE

COVER SONGS FOR ALE HOUSE

MELLENCAMP MEDLEY
FOLSOM PRISON BLUES
500 MILES
DEAD FLOWERS
ROLLER COASTER (BUDDY HOLLY)
↳ BILL CAN SING THIS B/C HE HAS GLASSES
LEAVE THE BIKER
SLIVER
PUMP IT UP

Last night we played our first show that was not a 20 minute open mic...

at the Ritz, compliments of the Missoula Ale House. This is such a crazy, crazy fucking thing: playing live music in front of fifty people. People were standing on tables, on the bar and, at one point, on my feet as that bar is like a shoebox.

Greg and Dad were in town from Philly, and most of the staff from the restaurant were there, so it was an overall comfortable show and I didn't yak on myself.

Looking in the crowd and seeing my dad rocking next to my brother (who is responsible for my taste in music) was something inexpressible. I had a feeling of certainty for the first time doing this.

On the other hand, Bill and Derk didn't know it, but I was nervous as hell and wasn't ready and wanted to smash my guitar. The originals, the covers, and just talking into a microphone to a bunch of people made me sick in the stomach, but it turned into a good pain especially when they responded with laughter and screams - and without "fuck you!" or "you suck!"

The show seemed to last forever, but in the end it was one of the coolest things I have ever done. I didn't think I'd be the type to jump around like an idiot for two hours but then again, I only play power chords and need to supplement.

I've been wanting to do this since I lived in Philly with Divine Lorraine, but I really don't want to do it that way—those guys never really leave the city and they play the same places a lot. Missoula's rock scene is different. These bands get the fuck out of here as much as possible - they have to - and Seattle and Portland are right down the street. We also, in return, get a lot of touring bands coming through Missoula, and it all seems connected. I am hoping we land a gig at Jay's Upstairs with this band the International Playboys. We watch football with the singer and he is a little off, which is good for a rock guy. He also has cool hair...which is also good for a rock guy. He books the shows at Jay's, which is a cool little shit hole, a perfect seedy dump that smells like my grandfather's old-person bar in Wildwood, NJ, but with a rock and roll twist: it smells like cigarettes, whisky and ass but the old person smell is substituted with an aroma of sweat and vomit. I have only been to Jay's five or six times but I feel right at home even though the patrons and workers have a friendliness that makes you feel like they already have enough friends. Fuck 'em, the hermans will kill that place. Even though this music is only a few months old, Derk and Bill are helping me create a style that is far more hard rock than what it sounded like in my room with an acoustic broken piece of shit guitar. There is much more energy which makes me feel like Jay's will be a perfect place for us to play, especially because we won't have to fill three goddamned hours with cover songs that I don't really know. No, instead we will probably play our hardest shit for forty five minutes and then I'll go puke.

I gotta go now and get some Pepto Bismol...so I don't puke.

David Eric Joseph (confirmation Name) Jones

WE TACKED UP **150** OF THESE FUCKERS ALL OVER TOWN

THE
HERMANS

THURSDAY APRIL 8
MISSOULA ALE HOUSE
ladies night

LIVE!
ROCK & ROLL

the
ermans

PEE WEE HERMAN
SARASOTA COUNTY
SHERIFF'S DEPARTMENT

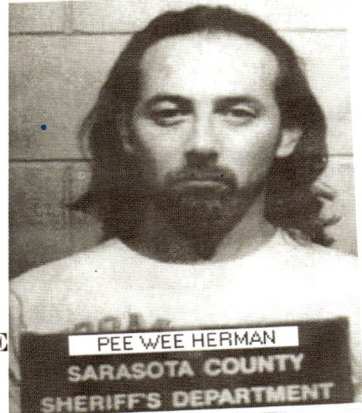

missoula ale house
thursday april 8

Dr Rosenpenis,

Jay's is DEAD! Just talked to Colin (Colts fan w/ lame moustache and cool hair - singer o' the playboys). Jay's is closing so he can't book us there. He will try to get us on a real show at the Ritz. We should probably quit rock and roll, turn into goth people, get mascara and play depressed crap music at the Boys + Girls club. We can do a Boys + Girls club tour and wear black all the time and sing about how cool it is to be pissed off at our parents. By the way, I know you secretly like Good Charlotte you fucking queerball!

Harry S. Truman
San Burque.

2nd July, 2004

HEY...YEAH YOU FUCKFACE JOURNAL ASSHOLE BITCH HEAD—

Thanks again for showing up to another show. I am truly tired of your repetitious bullshit. You haven't even seen one show. In fact, you have only made a couple appearances at practice—solely because I left you sitting on the workbench, and even then you were closed! Closed emotionally as well. You must really hate me. Don't you want me to succeed? Do you even know what a show is like? Well, I will tell you, and since you are open, I will force you to listen. The Top Hat has one of the best stages in town, including a pretty good sound system. I played there several times a few years back when I played piano for a band called Pronto but that band sucked and I did not like the songs. Or the songwriter, for that matter, and I ultimately had to quit to save my musical integrity. But I liked playing there. Now I don't because the owner is somewhat of a jerk and he does not like our band. The clientele also sucks, and many of our friends will not even set foot in the place because they don't like the owner either. But if you could see this place, if you weren't such a waste, you would notice that the stage is big and carpeted and about two feet off the ground. It has four monitors in the front for the guitarists and such and then another raised platform in the back for the drummer. That is me, dickwad. There is even a large monitor up there so I can hear the vocals and whatnot. And it sounds pretty good. Too bad we won't be playing there anymore because the crowd sucks and we don't fit in there at all. And the owner screwed us by paying us next to shit. Most of the bands there are old-guy cover bands or bluegrass bullshit bands or stupid hippy-stinky-Grateful Dead wannabe bands that I cannot tolerate. So now where are we going to play, journal? Where? Probably just in our basement again, inhaling saw dust and hoping the kitchen doesn't collapse on us. What fun! Missoula's rock scene is dying and we are just getting started. We should've begun doing this shit two years ago when we would've had a chance to play in front of people who actually like rock and roll music. Now Hip-Hop and bluegrass have taken over and no one has any taste in good music. You don't care, though. Just like them. You are nothing but a turd on a pulp sandwich. I don't even know why I bother telling you anything.

the hermans

THURSDAY JULY 1ST 10:30
FREE **TOP** **FREE**
HAT
LIVE ROCK N ROLL   LIVE ROCK N ROLL
www.thehermans.net

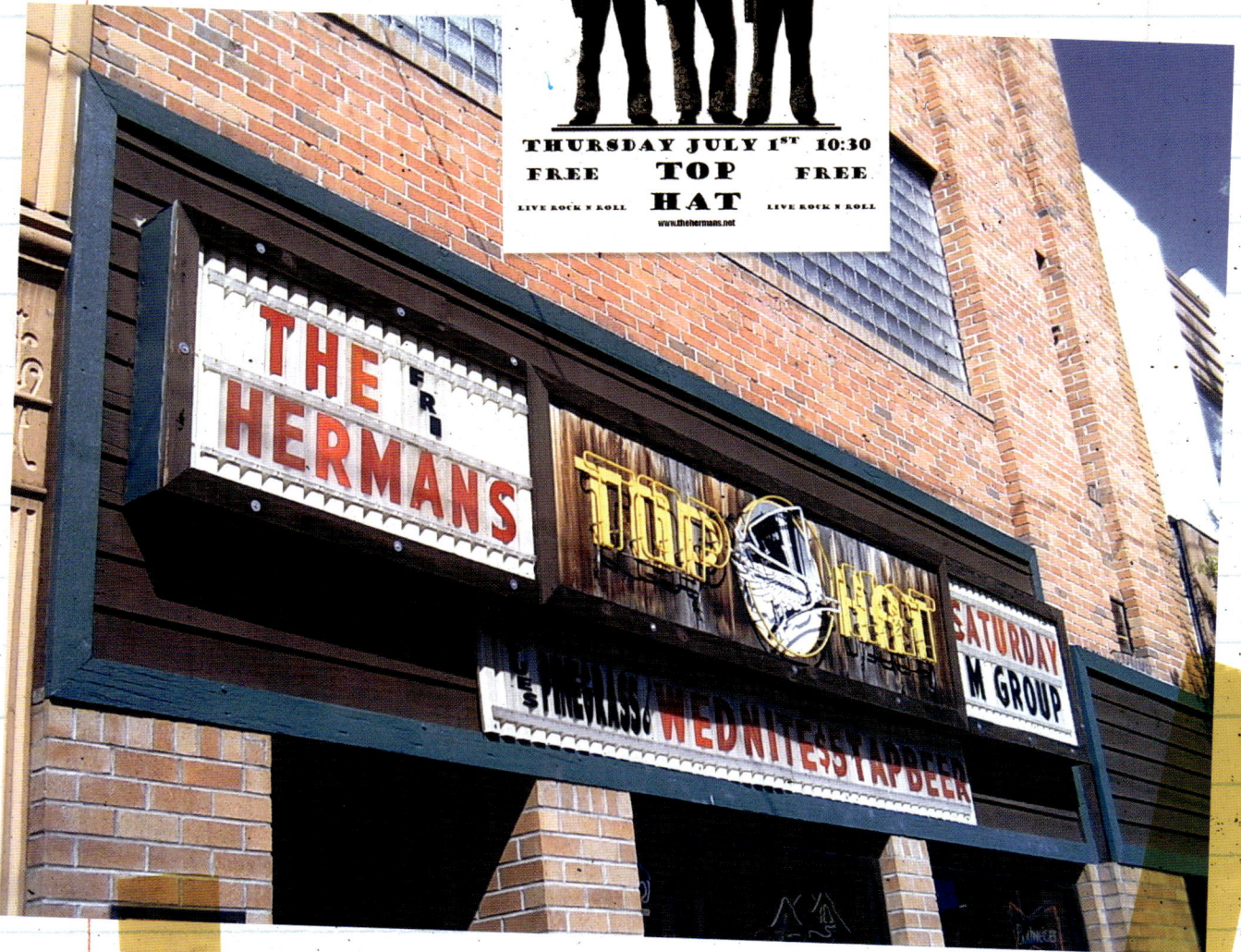

Item No.	Description		Total Count
		4	

Apart from getting bamboozled and hoodwinked at the Top Hat, I think the hermans are moving in a good direction. The only problem I have is that I am not even sure I would come and watch this band play for one hour let alone three. There is seriously something missing and I think it is probably talent and lead guitar. I have been working on my third and fourth robotic arms so I can play lead while I drum, but it is slowly not at all happening. I was thinking of calling Angus Young and Trey Anastasio to see if either of them might be interested, but I can't find their phone numbers. I was also thinking of quitting this piece of shit band and going to live on an island somewhere but as I have no moneys since we never get paid worth a shit I suppose this will not happen either. People say they like the music but I think it is mostly because we have a lot of friends between the three of us and they must be nice and supportive \people for fear I flog them publicly. Something must happen soon. We sound like the repetitious droning of whales fucking. I wonder what Steve Vai is up to? I hate myself. And Dave, too. Lousy beatnick.

Cock sleeve,

If you are going to sing over "TIDAL WAVE" it would be in yo' best interests to write some fucking lyrics, dumbbell. I only have that one line and that is all I want to do for that: Fell in love w/ a tidal wave. She crashes down and that was it for me. Now I'm dead but I'm not sorry.

I think that sums up Jess and I right now. Speaking of which, thanks for letting me crash. Your couch rules.

Ahh relationships. I hope I am better at this music thing than I am w/ people. People suck, anyway, since I hate love songs, and some "fuck" words to it so our christian mothers disown us. It's funny that grown people still believe in a bearded guy who lives in a magical cloud place and loves everyone including Hitler and Rick James.

David Eric

COCK AND BALLS —

I THINK THESE LYRICS, WHICH I AM SURE WILL SUFFICE, HAVE ALREADY BEEN WRITTEN, BITCH. I WENT ON THE THEME OF WRITING ABOUT HOW AWESOME PEOPLE LIKE MY EX FIANCÉ ARE. YOU REMEMBER LIZ, SHE WAS YOUR BEST FRIEND. SHE DID ALL KINDS OF THINGS FOR YOU, INCLUDING MAKING YOU HAPPY DAY IN AND OUT. ☹ HERE ARE THE WORDS — YOU HAVE TO WRITE THE BRIDGES... AND SING THEM. MY DRUM PARTS THERE ARE TOO AWESOME FOR ME TO BE SINGING ON THEM.

— DERK

TIDAL WAVE

V1 SHE BELIEVES IN REVELATIONS
BUT OF ANIMALS AND GHOSTS AND SUCH
BECAUSE SHE KNOWS THEY TALK TO HER

V2 OH, SHE'S A TIDAL WAVE
AND SHE BELIEVES IN BETTER DAYS
BUT IT'S BECAUSE OF ME SHE'S GOT IT MADE
AND I CAN'T STAY

CHORUS: SHOULD I SAY I'M SORRY
'CAUSE I'M NOT FUCKIN' SORRY
SHE SAYS "THERE'S ONE AND ONLY ONE"
WELL, LET IT NOT BE ME. ...

BRIDGE:

V3 I WANT TO GO, SHE WANTS TO STAY
AND WATCH THE TV SET ALL DAY,
AND BITCH ABOUT WHAT SHE CAN'T TAKE
— WHICH IS EVERYTHING

....but there were about 70 people at that first show. And I think we all got laid, like true rock and roll assholes. So, it went from seventy people watching us to about seven people and whatever bugs flew in the door. And I didn't have sex with any people or bugs. But I talked to John Flemming from Oblio Joes and he was very reassuring and said that was the nature of the way these things go. A lot of bands play in front of no one until they break up so at least we put an imprint on a lot of folk right away.

More importantly, I can't stop writing songs; they are just happening. I don't know if that is normal or how anyone else goes about writing songs but, shit man, all I seem to need to do is turn on CNN or think about my ex or just have my own riffs stuck in my head at work and the shit comes to me. We started bombing Baghdad on television the other night and it was hard for me not to write this new song called "Desert Island" which is basically a laundry list of problems I have with our present monarchy...fucking morons. It is like a top ten list of things I hate, but then I turn it into a love song....

"ON A Desert Island"

ONE, two, three, four
I Don't want your fucking war!
I don't need your malls and stores
I Don't like your internet.
I don't like humans ... period
I don't like your tele-V.
I Don't care if you like me
I don't like your politic.
I Don't like me cause I'm a Dick.....

   But I Do like you!
   oh I think I Do, I think, I think,

I don't like your ~~(_____)~~ History
I don't like any racial integrity
I don't mind some protest
But on the other hand I love watching the government.
                                              (fuck it up!)

   oh But I Do like you!
   All the pretty things you Do
   only want to be with you
   on a Desert Island!

I don't like pollution
I fucking hate todays ADministration
I don't like the media
I don't like being spoon fed information.

   ✳ AGAIN (?)
        x 2

I only want to be wy you
on our Desert Island
only want to trust in you
you're my Desert Island.   Bye

Yo,

Cameron, the guy ~~that~~ that did our sound @ the
Ale House, wants us to play at his wedding, the creep.
I think that marraige will last until we rip through Desert
Island and then his wife will kill him and then kill us.
I was simply astonished but they are giving us $225... $225
that could have went to a better DJ.
   Once again, we have to play a few cover songs to ~~fill~~ fill time.
I am tired of this shit and we need to get on a bill w/
some other bands like us. I asked him to get a list of
covers they would want but told them we wouldn't ever
learn "Achy Breaky Heart" because that song is the epitome of
sucking and that guy ~~should~~ should be sent to Siberia and pelted
with tacks.
   They'd better have a hot tub at Snow Bowl (where the
wedding is, moron). Eat me

                              Djones

...well journal, as I said, before, the hermans are clearly not a wedding band. It is silly for
three loud rock guys to play original rock songs no one knows in front of a bunch of old people
and children, while the groom who booked us and his friends (the only ones who even liked us)
sat over at the bar and got toasted. Everyone kept asking us if we knew this or that cover song
so finally we ended up playing "Wonderful Tonight" for about a half an hour until I got up in
the middle of the song, said "Fuck this" and went up to the bar. Then Dave and I got wasted. At
least we got paid, though. And drank for free. And there was a hot tub which was great until
Bill got in and decided it would be perfectly acceptable to not wear any underpants.

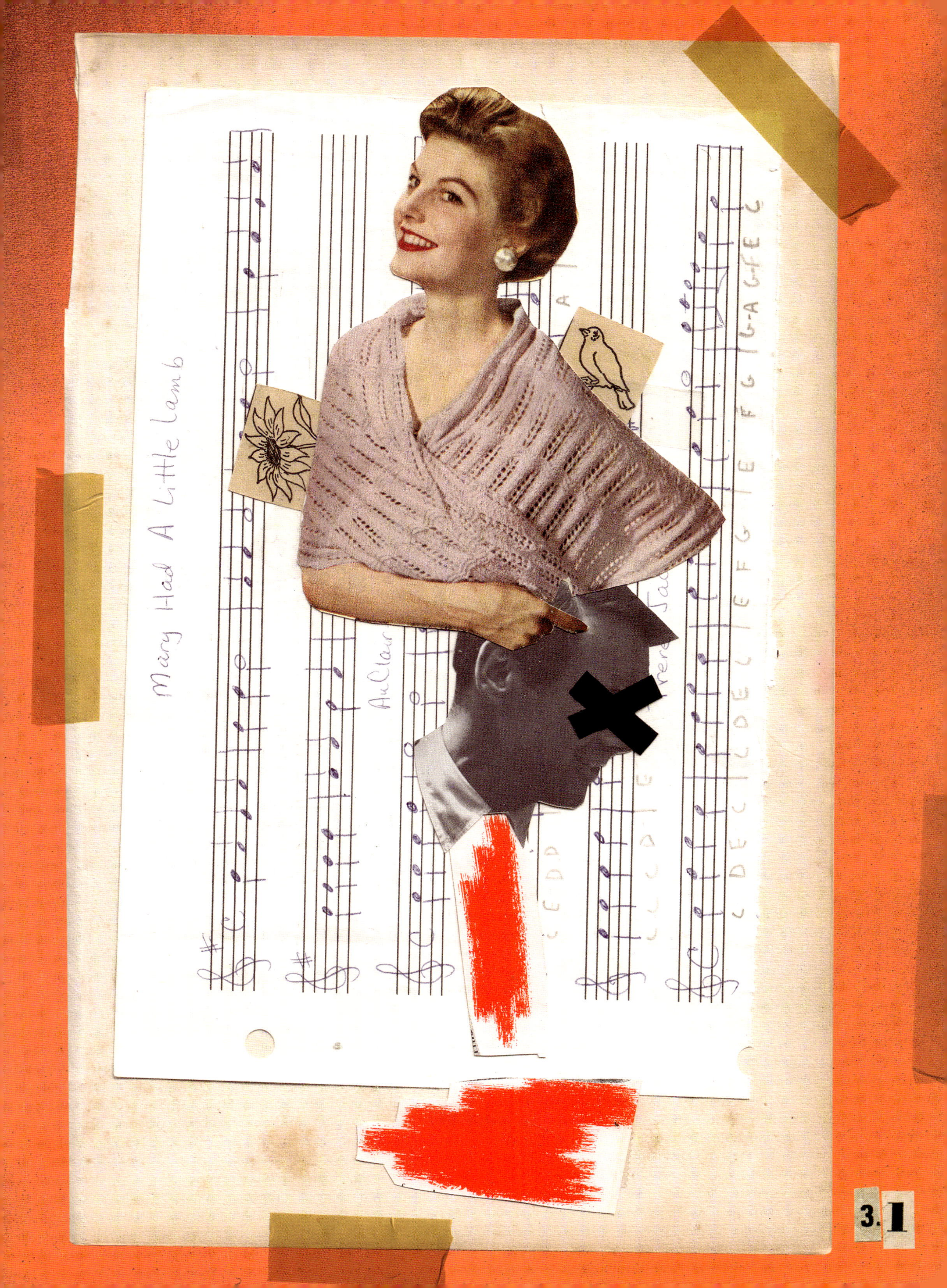
Mary Had A Little Lamb
Au Clair

-----Original Message-----
From: dudejonz@yahoo.com
To: Jones, Greg
Subject: the hermans first REAL show ever…

Greggor~

Don't go changing, we like you just the way you are.

Hey, man, finally got a real show for the hermans. Colin from the International Playboys hooked us up with a band called Bacon and Egg (two guys from the Volumen) and another band from Great Falls called Bridgebuilder. It is at the Other Side which is connected to the Bucks Club. I think Fugazi played there once when it was a pool hall or some shit.

Now it is a full club dedicated to rock shows and there will be a PA and lights and all that rock and roll crap. Should be interesting to hear the music while I play it instead of just hearing Derk's ride cymbal destroying my hearing and will to live. The only problem with this joint is that it is about a mile from our main street…yes that is right: people here mock the notion of driving, or maybe even walking a mile to see a show! Shit, I used to walk forty city blocks in Philly to get to South Street to see bands I'd never heard of.

Anyway, the Phillies suck really fucking bad and I heard rumors of the Eagles getting T.O. Who cares if he is a Sharpie happy lunatic, the guy catches everything and laughs at double coverages.

I will see you in a few weeks. Oh, the sound guy at the Other Side said he could record us for twenty bucks so maybe you'll be able to hear how far we have come since the spring. Now I am trying to sing a little instead of screaming everything and losing my voice after the first two songs.

See ya' jerky.

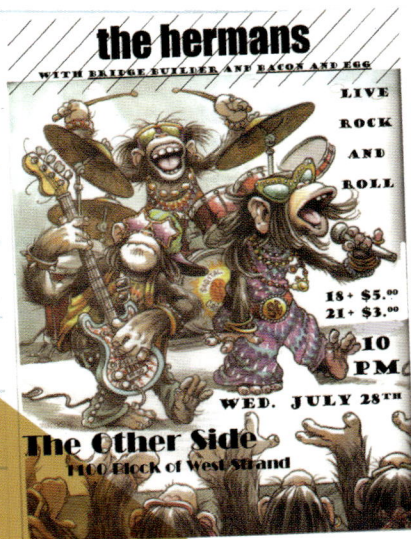

the hermans
WITH BRIDGE BUILDER AND BACON AND EGG

LIVE
ROCK
AND
ROLL

18+ $5.00
21+ $3.00

10
PM

WED. JULY 28TH

The Other Side
1100 Block of West Strand

only 25¢

A FREE GIFT FOR YOU

Journal,

Thanks for not coming to the show, jerk.

Anyway, we played a few shows at the Other Side in the last month and a half and, as usual, good and bad things came throughout and I am starting to sense that musicians are not as cool as THEY fucking think they are. We played with two folk-rock-emo-indie-arrogant dicks (Elephant Michael and some other punk) from Indiana or somewhere like that who are on tour and unfortunately stopped in Missoula. They seemed cool at first but in the end were all about the money. We were asked to play a longer set as the one guy only had about a half hour's worth of material (who the fuck goes on tour with a half an hour of songs?) and then he got wasted, had to have the other guy come on the stage to retune his guitar and got hammered during his own set….what an asshole. Then the mother fucker demanded a third of the door for each of them. Two single performers vs. a band of three. Maybe I am so pissed because they both sucked and we played our asses off.

But, good prevailed when the sound guy became very reassuring. We hung out after the show, had some beers and he told us he digs our sound. He used to do the sound at Jay's Upstairs and was in a few bands and knows Colin and his bros and all the musicians who watch football at Red's so we had some mutual stuff to talk about aside from how cool Kiss rocks.

The sound is always good there but it is hard to get people to drive a mile outside of town to see a rock show. The Bacon and Egg show had a good turn out (maybe 30 or so) for that but this last one had about fifteen people and most left when that second dildo started his emotional bullshit ranting and then proved that his limit is four lagers before he starts acting like the sun shines out his ass. Fucking amateurs.

Well, the music feels good and the stage is becoming a comfortable haven instead of being a zone of unfamiliarity. I find it easy to lose myself in that energy and jump around like an idiot. Some girl at the show asked me why I exert so much in front of only fifteen people (I think she was on some weird drug) and I had to tell her that in my lack of musical ability I had to find some way to entertain her dumb ass. Jumping up and down to the music only seemed natural. Bill laughed at her.

Schlomo —

BILL GOT US A GIG PLAYING AT CARAS PARK DOWNTOWN! IT
IS FOR A THING HE HAS GOING THROUGH MONTPIRG CALLED
"VOTESTOCK" WHICH GETS PEOPLE TO SIGN UP FOR THE
MILITARY OR VOTE OR SOMETHING. I THINK IT SHOULD
BE COOL, EXCEPT THE GUY BOOKING IT, FROM WHAT I'VE
HEARD, IS A TOTAL DOORKNOB AND HE LIKES HIP-HOP
MUSIC AND SMELLS FOUL. WHATEVER. IT SHOULD BE
COOL, AT LEAST PLAYING OUTDOORS AT THE "BUM"
PARK. I THINK IT IS THIS SATURDAY. I DON'T KNOW,
MAYBE NEXT. CALL BILL IF YOU GET A CHANCE. I
HAVE TO GO TO WORK.
— HAMMER

REGISTER TO VOTE!
VOTESTOCK
SEPTEMBER 25
0 PM CARAS PARK FREE
FOR ALL!
OWN CITY ROCKERS
VER SINCE THE ACCIDENT
ASS-END OFFEND
LOCKE AND NASTY
JAZZFILL
& THE HERMANS
PLUS SPEAKERS, FOOD, BEER AND MORE!
PRESENTED BY
HPG ■ MontPIRG
"ENCOURAGING THE YOUTH TO VOTE"

$0.00

³6

-----Original Message-----
From: dave@thehermans.net
To: Jones, Greg
Subject: fucking douche bags

My brother,

Oh brother. The list of douche bag musicians we get to play with continues as we played a show on Election Day eve with a band straight out of the how-to-be-a-rock-star manual for asswipes. These guys were the poster boys for coolness and the prototypes for all the shit that is polluting the airwaves today. First off a disclaimer: you are in Philly and I know if you still lived here you would be hanging out at our shows taking mental notes because that is what good writers do. So you would see that Derk and Bill and I make it a point to be cool to everyone no matter what the circumstance unless they are total dicks because why would you want to burn bridges in a business that seems to rely on personal connections and networking (as much as I loathe and detest that goddamned word and its concept)?

The Blakes, from L.A. (could have been from Indiana like those other pimples) certainly did just that: burned the only bridge into Missoula. We played our set, just like we always do – as if it were our last – and the bastards took the money and fucking ran. About ten people showed up; they came up with some lame excuse about one of their girlfriends being sick, grabbed the door money from the bartender and split WITHOUT PLAYING at all. Once again, they seem like nice people but then are all about the fucking money. Anyway, if they ever play in Philly, give them a true Philly welcome as if they were the Dallas Cowboys without security and bring some mustard and eggs…and batteries. Until then, we will wait for Karma or just continue to support our local scene and the touring bands who are cool and are in this for the same reasons we are: to take over the world through rock and roll. And if the hermans ever disrespect a hosting band (if we ever get the fuck outta here) may the fleas of a thousand camels infest our underwear.

~The Iron Sheik~

SCHMEGMA —

MY FRIEND MATTIE TACO FROM WORK AND I ARE WORKING
ON A TOP-SECRET PROJECT TO PUBLICLY DISPLAY OUR MUSIC
AND BAND OVER THE VAST TECHNOLOGICAL HIGHWAY KNOWN AS
THE "INTERNET." I AM SURE YOU'VE HEARD OF IT. I THINK AL
GORE OWNS IT OR SOMETHING. ANYWAY, HE HAS NEVER DONE
IT BEFORE BUT HE THINKS HE CAN DO IT AND WANTS TO LEARN
HOW TO DO ALL OF THAT NERDY SHIT. IT HAS TO BE "WWW.
thehermans.net" SINCE APPARENTLY SOME JEWISH FAMILY IN
NEBRASKA HAS THE ADDRESS "www.thehermans.com" ALREADY AND
HAS DONE ABSOLUTELY NOTHING WITH IT. I THINK FOR THE
HOME PAGE WE SHOULD HAVE YOU, BILL AND ME PLAYING
SUPERGIGANTIC INSTRUMENTS ON A FOOTBALL FIELD OR SOME
SHIT. MAYBE WE COULD USE THAT FIELD BACKGROUND YOU
GOT FROM THOSE RANDALL CUNNINGHAM STATIC CLING
DEALS. THINK ABOUT IT. IT MAY BE A BIT PRE-
MATURE SINCE WE HAVEN'T RECORDED AN ALBUM YET
OR ANYTHING, BUT IT IS A STEP IN THE
RIGHT DIRECTION. LATER FUCK-O.

— DERK HAMMER

MATTIE TACO

OUR FIRST HOMEPAGE...

the hermans

Upcoming Events

Photos

Contact Us

Band Biography

Show Flyers

000603

Designed by 27 Publishing. M. Swanson, Prop. www.27publishing.com

LOOKS LIKE SOMETHING OUT OF THE
HELEN KELLER SCHOOL OF WEB DESIGN.

Hello fans or friends or those who went to the wrong site,

It is an arduous thing, this thing that we do. Since the hermans began to slowly stain Missoula like a teeming drip of ale upon the shirt of the village idiot, we have played for crowds of fifty to that one lonesome village idiot. On that note, I now thank those of you who have been there since The Ritz and continue to come and watch us defile what sounds pretty fucking good in our basement in places like The Other Side and (this week end) Caras Park. There is no better sound than the screams of sanction from any crowd of any size after we crash through a song that was most likely written through pain, happ ness, angst, defilation or spontaneity, or all of these emotions in amalgamation. If you keep coming, we will not stop exerting ourselves in what, for me personally, is the best feeling on this planet far under a hug from my baby girl.

the hermans cannot pledge a perfect combination of sounds for you. We can't offer three hours of concrete music without err. We most likely will not be able to save Missoula's music scene...even though it is in our utmost interest to do just that. With that said here is what we can do: I will give every ounce of energy and truth that this body can give to make you laugh, cry, punch a wall, jump into the fucking ceiling or just say "yo, go see this band" at work the next day. We will offer our music to you and allow you to take it like puddy and decide for yourself what we are trying to do and say. You can criticize if you like (especially those who don't make music) but just remember that I have never or will ever write anything unless it is wholly decent and pure in integrity; no cliches, nothin held back in fear of misinterpretation and no deception. Why do those things that are so prevalent in music today? It has already been done and it is bullshit! This music is strictly for us for reasons I will not tell you because you don't fucking need to know! But, it is als for you to listen to, hear and interpret, and hopefully make yourself move around in any given fashion....as long as you don't get any on me.

Our shows have been blissful because of you...and us...and these together. For without that combination, we stay in a cold, bitter, asshole of a basement that Derk uses as a stinkin' woodshop so you can imagine how clustered the goddamned place is. But you seem to learn something new about yourself every time you are down there. See you at the Battle of the Bands (@ The Other Side) and at Caras Park for Votestock.

Love,

David Eric Joseph J. Herman

(guitar, vocal and numero uno bastard)

Greggor,

GET OFF THE FLOOR, TAKE OFF THAT MOTHRA OUTFIT AND GET BACK TO WORK YOU IMPIOUS BASTARD! Anyway, I am sick as a doggie this morning so this will be brief. the hermans played our first (and last) battle of the bands yesterday. Note the no capitalization of "battle of the bands" because battles of the bands are fucking trite and don't deserve to be capitalized. Needless to say, we lost and lost bad. And not "bad" in the sense that we played bad; we lost to a new-age, neo-gothic, typical teenage we-are-pissed-and-angry-and-we-don't-know-why "heavy metal" band who actually make Bon Jovi look like the poster boy for talent. I would have rather lost to a band with the likes of Richie Sambora than these mascara wearing satanic cheerleaders.

Actually, Satan would not have these people, they are far too predictable.

We also lost to a punk band who had the brass cajones to cover Baba O'Reilly….a song I have seen, oh about 1,000 punk bands cover, none of them doing it well. Their original shit was pretty good, however, so I don't mind that we lost, not to mention we don't have a lead guitar player.

I don't know what this was for, we just heard about it on the radio so I wish I would have kept on Walk This Way, Stairway to Heaven, Daughter or whatever other classic song modern radio has annihilated with it's over playing that day.

This soiree of sodomites was put on by none other than 96.3 "The Blaze" which is the equivalent of any shit sandwich of a radio station. You know: they only play top 40 crap that is played at the gap, Hot Topic and during most fraternity parties that I wouldn't be caught sniffing paint at. So I suppose I now understand why we lost: THEY DON'T LIKE ORIGINAL ROCK AND ROLL!!!!! I am glad I will not be associated with these people.

Goddamn this email is angry.

Well, I think we are going to ask Chris (from Williamsport and Finn and Porter) to join the band as his guitar playing wails like an alley cat high on angel dust who wants to turn every face he sees into a puddle with his high notes.

Yours,
Igor Stravinsky

Ladies & Gentlemen …..
CHRISTOPHER ENTZ

41

Dear jernyl,

I have spent the last week sitting on my fucking ass in my stupid house watching stupid tv and eating soup. You know why? Of course you don't you stupid whore. It was because my otherwise totally awesome girlfriend Nyree made me go dancing and so I drug Dave along, too, and when I was rocking out the sweetest dance move ever, my patented totally amazing Bill Cosby dance, I was magically flung backwards into a couple of 33 gallon garbage cans and went straight back on my ass, completely fucking my ankle in the process. I am sure it had nothing to do with the fact that I was totally schnockered. I had to go to the hospital with no insurance and get X-Rays and found that it was a severe sprain. I cannot work for at least a week. And I am not getting paid. And the hospital bill will be a whore. Now I get a call today from Colin of the International Playboys that we could open for Captured! By Robots in two days and I can't imagine how horrible it would feel to hit the kick drum with my ankle right now. So naturally I told him absolutely we would do it. This is because I am a total fucking idiot and I hate myself. I will figure it out. Robots are cool and I guess these ones play their own instruments and enslaved some crazy fuck named J-BOT. It should make all of my wildest dreams come true. I have also decided that I will never dance again and if someone asks me to I will shove a spatula into his or her eye socket. Then I will rip out his or her still-beating heart and pee on it, then put it back. Why am I such a pathetic waste of time? Thanks a lot, jernyl. You suck.

CAPTURED! BY ROBOTS

photo by snapcult

THE GREATEST ONE-MAN-EIGHT-ROBOT
BAND IN THE WORLD.

Dearest diary,   11/07/04

Thanks for being there for me last week when my pen exploded on me, you vicious prick! I heard you laughing inside the spine. Anyway, the hermans added a fourth member yesterday and I think we officially have "something." I don't know what we had before because the three-piece thing was pretty damned powerful but now that Chris has jammed with us it felt over night that we were lacking something obvious that was completely hidden before. This guy is goddamned good.

Chris has been to a couple shows and the notion was always there that he should jam with us but I have been too nervous to play with someone who easily dissects our songs while wasted at the shitty Top Hat bar. I think Derk's progressive side has finally had enough and he felt we need another mind to add structure and stability. Jesus, in one fucking practice this guy nailed three songs. We did Desert Island and he went into the solo exactly where I imagined it and exactly how I imagined it. I think I once said that Cinderblock had a Gossard/McCready sound. I must have said that because after Chris did his first solo over it, he told me he was intentionally thinking about that style. It was frickin' bizzaro.

Anyway, I was nervous at first just because I thought he was too good. But I guess that pessimism is the same rat bastard that showed up when I was nervous about ever playing with Derk just a wee eight months ago. I think this dude will make our sound what it was supposed to be from the beginning. My shitty, dirty, haphazard guitar disability should match well with his genius…like Boss Hog and Roscoe.

Peace out.

Davey

DAVE—

WE NEED TO WRITE SOMETHING ABOUT PIRATES, BECAUSE THEY ARE COOLER THAN YOUR EX-GIRLFRIENDS!

DO IT NOW. —H—

"MODERN DAY PIRATE"... Arrrgh!

① Hail all y'all to the I~
Patch on my eyeBall, Rum's
Feet hit Land and I start ~
could have went to college but I ~

Be a pirate. He ~   ~tho — into chorus again for
(CHORUS) modern day pirate (rep~   4 Bars)

② Got no ship so I do my sailing.   So hail all y'all to the skull & crossBones
on the strip of my 8 track wailing.   ~ a poster of Kevin Sorbo (Hercules?)
Sailing to a game of Dungeons & Dragon~   ~that packets insides on a summer day.
could have had a lover But I'd rath~   ~ have Been cool But I'D
    (Bridge) — girl was everything I ~   ~le Be a pirate.
         I could never ~   ~or break at end of verse
         a normal guy wh~   ~e than   ~~rvier Bridge?
            play video g~   ~ know what you
         girl was ev~   ~A But I   ~think]
         choose
         "I'd rather ~   ~te, a pirate,   Brid~   ~o !!
            a pirate ~   ~DAY?

③ Got no parro~   ~sparrows on my shoulder   mate'p,
got no woma~   ~uarters are colder
heavi~   ~to pillage and play   I just figured you
could hav~   ~ancer But I'd rather be a   to read these lyrics befo~
        PIRATE HEY!!   brought them to the ta~
                                                      Because I think they are
    Solo — (Chris goes SHIT House)   of funny. Just picture ~
                                                     as you read.
                                                            Love,
                                                            Cat Litter

47

December 1, 2004

So Chris has played a couple of shows with us now and the missing link has been, well, linked. In other terms, he fucking blows my mind while at the very same time melting my face and soothing my inner musical soul. He has learned enough songs already in a few weeks to play full sets, or at least 40 minutes or so, and is catching the newer ones like "Parade" very quickly. It is what we needed, journal, no thanks to you. You would rather have seen us play in front of no one, wouldn't you? Well, as long as he digs it and wants to move forward with the hermans, I see us in the realm of unstoppable followed by immediate recognition as the greatest rock and roll band, perhaps, ever. Hey, I can dream, fuckstick—you don't help us book shows. You don't even know how. We played Jesters Bar in Helena over the weekend and it was frickin' great you dick. We debuted our new pirate song which is called "Modern Day Pirate" and it was a true crowd pleaser. At least I think it was. I am pretty sure the whole band was fairly drunk, but it sounded great to us. You didn't do anything to make it great. I am glad you weren't there, since it was our first show ever outside of Missoula. Who cares if we got lucky getting the show? Unfortunately, around here it is who you know. Well, at our last show at the Other Side I was talking with my new favorite person of the month Justin Lawrence and he gave me the number of the guy who runs Jesters, Chad. So I called the bastard and told him Justin, who also does sound at Jesters certain weekends, said that we would fit in great at Jesters and we must play there post haste. He took Justin's word and gave us a show right away. It was so fuckin' easy that I am sure it will never happen again. But we had a pretty good crowd and Nyree came with us since a lot of her family still lives there and they came to the show and it was pretty fucking rad, journal. The stage was immeasurably tiny, but it was just cozy enough to fit us all up there. I think Chad liked it, since he told us to come back any time. So we will, journal, and you will not stop us you lazy prick! I must go now and practice. You stay here and be a worthless puddle of shit as you are accustomed to.

CHAD

THE HERMANS AT THE JESTER'S BAR

HELENA, MT 2004

Journal,

The unthinkable has become thinkable and I can think about it because it actually happened. We played a show last week with two bands that meshed with us like potatoes. Colin Playboy asked us to play a show with them at Area 5, a cool newer venue that used to be an old garage but now houses rock shows a few times a week as well as the artist freak that runs the place. He lives in the back in a plastic bubble eating government cheese and preserves out of unmarked silvery cans and never ever leaves. You can bring your own beer as this place is not a bar nor do they have a liquor license. I don't even think there is a fire escape so the next hermans show will surely cost the lives of thousands.

We got to play between the Krooks, a Missoula punk rock staple who kicked ass, and the Playboys who also kicked ass. Between the three bands that played that night, we could have taken on China. It was something I didn't think would happen and was such a fucking joyous night. Colin said "you passed" but I don't know if we passed with an A minus or a D plus. We played that new song about pirates which had the crowd in a frenzy but I couldn't remember all the lyrics so I made them up…come on, how hard is it to improvise about the coolest group of humans to walk, hobble, pillage or sail the face of this planet? On top of that, no one can hear what the fuck you are saying in that place anyway as the bands have to run their own sound and the PA system is from 1958.

All in all it was fucking great to see a bunch of people get into the hermans who have been involved in this music scene for a long time and who were really there to see their friends play. It was also reassuring in that I felt I can now trust that this town is genuine, honest and prone to curiosity and will not stick its nose up to new music.

They also like a lead singer who throws in a jumping rock kick now and then.

I think it will be easy to be successful here as long as we write honest rock music that is far from cliché and as long as Chris doesn't quit and join a monastery because the way he plays guitar he will most assuredly get laid quite often and leave the remains for the rest of us dorks.

THE INTERNATIONAL PLAYBOYS

LADIES (& GENTLEMEN)

← CAP'N SEXTASTIC

← JOE DANGER

← MONTE CARLO

← THE COUNT

november, 2004

Folks and folkeses,

This is number two in a series of correspondence we write to you, which will hopefully never stop as long as we breathe, to thank you or just communicate with you post-show. As a spokesperson for the band, I just wanted to thank those of you who came out to Votestock, those who registered to vote in this, the most important election of our life time, and those who are going to be with us on November 2 to oust that greed mongering, money-driven oil-hick from Texas. Votestock was a decent show for us and a soothing after-shock to the Battle of the Bands which I will candidly talk of now. The Battle of the Bands was neither a success nor a failure due to the fact that a lot of our friends showed up to be there for us and cheer for us and drink with us and laugh with us...especially at the expense of, well, other human beings. Chris did not play as he still needs to learn some of the songs we played in the set...and he was working. Though the hermans did not move on in the rounds, we were extremely happy afterwards with the responses that we received, not only from the crowd, but from the fellow musicians who also exerted them- selves that night as well as the bartenders at The Other Side who were more angered with our demise than we were. We are still tremendously optimistic and ecstatic about our music and simply feel that perhaps our style is too raw and original for the three judges who went with bands that don't sound much different from what you hear on the radio today. There is nothing wrong with this and we accept that pop-culture is reality. But we just don't enjoy or listen to cliche driven sound. Freedom of choice is what we got and it is such a beautiful thing to be able to hit a button and force away shitty music! So, we accept that we lost and we think it is funny; adversity is absolutely nothing new to this band. the hermans will never compromise or conform to what "they" want to hear...we just want to play what we want to play and what YOU want to hear. "They" are controlled and owned, and their minds and opinions were fortified by some external entity before they could understand the notion of self-reasoning. Or, we suck. However, most strangers who have had the decency or curiosity to approach us after a performance and share their views of our songs or style or stage dynamics or just want to shoot the shit about music tend to make me feel otherwise. So I suppose we will just keep doing what we do, as promised, and see what comes next. With the talent I surround myself with and the confi- dence they allot me, I am curious to see where this music goes when we start writing more. See you again on the flip.

DAviX Jones (Soda Pop pilot and crooning vagabond, the hermans)

P.S.
Special thanks to Andrea at The Other Side for being so cool and for agreeing, in paper on legal document, to name her soon-to-be-born baby, either Herman or Hermanette

DEAR GOD:

WHY DOES MY BAND KEEP GETTING THESE CRAPPY SHOWS THAT NO ONE SHOWS UP TO? WHY DO WE CONSISTENTLY PLAY IN FRONT OF NO ONE? ADDITIONALLY, WHY CAN'T WE SEEM TO EVER GET PAID FOR THESE PIECES OF SHIT THAT TURN OUT MORE LIKE A PRACTICE THAN AN ACTUAL GIG? IS IT BECAUSE WE DON'T SING ABOUT WALKING ON WATER AND CURING LEPERS? BECAUSE HERE IS THE THING: I'VE HEARD A LOT OF THESE "CHRISTIAN ROCK" GROUPS AND I'VE GOT TO TELL YOU, I THINK YOU OUGHT TO SUE SOME OF THESE BASTARDS FOR COPYRIGHT INFRINGEMENT. BASICALLY, HALF OF THEIR LYRICS ARE STOLEN AND PLAGIARIZED RIGHT OUT OF YOUR BIBLE! I JUST THOUGHT THAT MAYBE YOU WOULD RATHER PREFER BANDS SANG ABOUT WHAT'S GOING ON RIGHT NOW DOWN HERE ON EARTH RATHER THAN ALL OF THOSE RE-HATCHED STORIES ABOUT MIRACLES AND THE THE DAUNTING HEROICS OF YOUR SON. I JUST FIGURED MAYBE THAT WAS WHAT CHURCH WAS FOR.

I GUESS WHAT I WAS HOPING FOR WAS MAYBE A COUPLE OF SHOWS WHERE MORE PEOPLE SHOWED UP THAN EIGHT OF OUR FRIENDS. I SUPPOSE I WAS HOPING FOR MAYBE A TOURING BAND— YOU KNOW, LIKE THE TIME WE OPENED FOR CAPTURED! BY ROBOTS. WE MUST HAVE PLAYED IN FRONT OF A HUNDRED AND FIFTY PEOPLE. THAT WAS FANTASTIC. HERE'S WHAT I AM THINKING: I KNOW WE WON'T BE OPENING FOR RUSH ANY TIME SOON, BUT MAYBE YOU COULD SEND A MID-MAJOR BAND THROUGH MISSOULA AND PUT US ON THE BILL. WE DON'T EVEN NEED OUR NAME ON THE MARQUEE —AND WE WILL MAKE OUR OWN FLYERS. YOU KNOW, ANYTHING WOULD HELP. THIS IS STARTING TO BLOW DONKEY BALLS.

I HOPE YOU CAN TAKE SOME OF YOUR INFINITE TIME TO CAREFULLY CONSIDER THIS HUMBLE REQUEST. WE NEED TO DO SOMETHING SOON OR I MAY HAVE TO START STEALING LYRICS FROM THE BIBLE. IN THIS CASE, PROBABLY FROM JOB SINCE HE WAS ALWAYS GETTING SCREWED, TOO. THANK YOU FOR YOUR TIME AND CONSIDERATION.

HUMBLY YOURS,

DERK SCHMIDT (OF THE BAND the hermans)

P.S. IF INDEED YOU ARE A BIT TOO BUSY AT THE MOMENT, I AM SENDING A FACSIMILE OF THIS LETTER TO SANTA CLAUS AS WELL. I ASSUME HE WILL BE PROMPT IN RESPONDING, SO LET'S NOT GET SHOWN UP BY A JOLLY FAT MAN. SOUND GOOD?

P.P.S. I AM ALSO A CONFIRMED CATHOLIC. IS THAT THE GOOD ONE? I HOPE SO. MY CONFIRMATION NAME IS SEBASTIAN IF THAT MAKES IT EASIER FOR YOU TO FIND MY FILE.

PEACE.

january,2005

Punk butts,

Yes, yes it has been a while but can't a man be busy goddamnit!? Anyway,
I blame it, like most hermans problems where the beat lies: on the drummer.
It is Derk's fault there has been no letter and he should stand up and take
his caneing like a man.

Well, we have played too many show to count since the last I wrote and
these are our sins: Helena was a great experience. The bar was something
out of a Hunter Thompson daydream but was missing the bikers. No one in
the place had ever seen, or probably even heard of us but it was obvious
they were thankful that an original rock band was there to exert all of their
energy just for them. Let's see...I don't really remember much before this
past weekend so I will now thank The International Playboys (Missoula's
best group of mother fucking rock bastards) for getting us in with them and
The Krooks this past Saturday night at Area 5. It was minus fifteen degrees
outside but plenty of Missoulianites and their kin folk still showed up to
brave the smoke and ear drum shattering melodies put forth from the three
bands. the hermans feel it was our best show yet and I must also now thank
and welcome Chris Entz to the band whose guitar sounds sexier than Lando
Calrissian and Indiana Jones combined.

Well, since the Sixers are on in five minutes I must go now and say a quick
Rosary. Come see us this Friday at the Other Side (unless, of course, a five
minute drive from Higgins is too far) and again at Jester's Bar in Helena on
Feb. 12th.

Go Eagles.

CHRIS AKA ANALOGATRON

Journey (short for "journal" not the coolest rock band ever),

So we had this show booked for us from Johnny Flemming, the guy that owns Ear Candy Record Store (and bass player for the Oblio Joes - probably the most solid band to ever come out of Montana). On the day we were to play, the show was cancelled, re-booked, cancelled, put back on and scheduled again for the standard 10:00 time slot.

John asked us to play with The Icicles, a touring band from Grand Rapids, Michigan, at Area 5 a few weeks ago. To shorten a very long story and make it less boring, we will go about this in a police blog method (this is also because you are a dense, half-witted nincompoop of a journal and need things spelled out for you like a youngster);

1:53 (in the p.m.) Dave hears rumor Area 5 is shutting its doors today - the day of the show!

1:55 Dave freaks out and calls Area 5 while eating a burger - the day of the show.

1:59 Area five guy (let's just call him Mr. Smith) tells Dave "the show will most likely go on tonight." Dave knows this person is a renowned fraud and then…

2:00 - 2:05 Deviant thoughts go through Dave's head - the day of the show.

2:06 Dave decides that continuing banter with Mr. Smith would be as resourceful as eating a handful of tacks so he hangs up…on the day of the show!

2:08 Dave begins his expedition to find a new venue (did I mention this was the day of the show???) going to every goddamn bar in town except one…this comes in later.

3:37 Dave comes home to find Derk watching porn…er…a Pete Yorn video and tells him the show is probably off as he couldn't find a venue. (editors note: meanwhile, Dave had to call the Icicles - who were told earlier that morning the show was cancelled and were two hundred miles east of Missoula on their way home - to promise a venue and tell them to come back…yeah, I took a chance! On the day of the show!)

3:42 Derk listens attentively to his pal, waits for a short silence, slaps Dave in the face (the day of the show) and asks why he didn't stop at the Elk's Lodge.

3:42.55 Dave is on the phone with the bartender of the Elks Lodge; some sort of Veterans Club where members gather to confer about business and bitch about rock and roll assholes like Dave and his cohorts. The bartender tells young David she would have to speak with her boss (who is no one to be trifled with) about the current impasse and would have to get back to him.

3:50 (yes, she was quite astute!) the bartender calls Dave back and says "Bring your shit down and let's have a rock and roll show tonight!"

Dave replies (in his take-off of Ted Knight from Caddyshack) "I don't believe it…really?!"

"Oh, yes," she says "we don't have shit going on Wednesday nights and the three regulars are already drunk so give us a dollar off every head and we'll call it a deal…ON THE DAY OF THE SHOW!"

You still with me, idiot?

3:55 Dave is on the phone with The Icicles (who were playing this show on this date, by the way) and found them more than happy to turn the van around to end their two month long tour in Missoula.

4:15 Dave, Derk and Bill proceed to put up makeshift flyers around town, hang a sign on the door of Area 5 instructing people to reroute to the Elks, and place calls to local scenesters who would sequentially make similar calls to spread the word.

9:30 The Icicles arrive at the Elks and do not kill Dave or Mr. Smith. People begin to swarm in and the show goes splendidly well taking into account all the bullshit that you just read.

We played for free, again, and the Icicles made enough money to make it worth while. Or, at least to Billings.

So, here we are today: unsung heroes. To sports fans, those are people who go above and beyond and rarely receive credit. What do I speak of? The huge fucking article in the Missoulian about how now the Elk's Lodge is the new hip venue harboring constant exhibitions and we are barely mentioned!!! AM I SALTY?! no. In fact, I get in for free a lot because Colin works the door and this kid Mike Gill is booking some shows in the spring that he is going to put us on with his new band. On top of that, I get freaked out when people ask me questions and I probably would have said something obtuse and lame.

Well, that is that I guess. Justin has been doing the sound there so the shows will continue to get better. And the beer will hopefully get cheaper because it is always freakin' packed. God bless the Romans...terrific race.

april, 2005

Hey punks,

Yeah, whatever, it has been a while but when is the last time you were on here? You don't care about our feelings. You have no heart, do you? You just move on with your life and pretend we never existed. Just strangers in the night that pass briefly in the early morn where night and day glance fleetingly at each other before turning away without a bye or leave, goddamnnit!

Anyway, that is enough insight into personal lives. The hermans have played a few shows since the last I have written, some to talk of, some to put in an urn and blasted into space Leary style. We opened for the Icicles out of Grand Rapids who were frickin' awesome and it may or may not have opened up a new venue for Missoula at the Elk?s Club. If you get the chance, go there for a show as it reminds me of a banquet room out of The Shining. We thank The Icicles for coming to town (it was the last show of a two month tour) and all the people who showed up even though it was cancelled that afternoon and then put on again at a different venue at about 7:15 later that evening. And thanks again to all of you who have requested demos and to those who continue to watch Derk, Bill and Chris play good music and watch me defile myself on stage?.it is actually quite fun.

So we have been getting a lot of guff for not having lyrics on our site and I think that may stem from the fact that we have yet to play with a decent PA and no one knows what the fuck I am saying?..that or I just constantly mumble. So, here you go. You have beat me. I have been bested by YOU so you can dance now, or high five your pals, or jump in the air, or point and laugh or do whatever it is that you do when you best someone with the high and mighty amounts of power that I alone possess, you faceless wretch! Thank you for listening.

D. Jones

Soda Pop's pilot

Pope goes on Strike!!

① He was just a lad in Poland
   running around as if mad Believing everything.

   Oh just a lad: never sad
   then again he's just a Boy
   But now and again he thinks Back to those Days
   when he was young and strong of his hand thinking
   'bout girls and things...
              never could be bad — we never gave him a chance!

   Take him back before he starts to tremble
   to youthful days anyone would remember: (chorus)

        Back to times your pain
        Before we made him God's right hand man.

② what were you like as a boy, what did you play?
   Did you pretend to bless and pray for all us sinning ones?
   what did you ponder, what did you say?
   Ever have thoughts of a girl?

   I'll bet he sometimes thinks back — those days when he was
   young and strong of his hand thinking 'bout pew bound women.
   But now he's just a man .... of God in his hand!

   He was just a (   ) lad w/out funny hat not yet
   forced to be the church's middle-man
   oh just a lad, not yet sad, w/out sins of all in his head
   WHY can't he ever wear Black, or hit back
   WHY they make him change his name?
   mayhem is coming down the pike But I'll Be
   alright if the Pope goes on strike!!!!

[other chorus, maybe]
Here he comes again on his own, Bass?
God's right hand man! Robed + empowered oh yeah!
Or it's own Baby? God's right hand man!!

what would they say?
what would they do?
when the pope goes on strike?
for a month or two?,
who would bless you
on strike?

....so I figured if these Christian nut jobs are going to come down on the Pope for being
too liberal I would question it in a song. Besides, does anyone really know what the Pope
was like as a child? Do these lunatics ever look at him as a real person instead of being
just a guy who could get them farther up on the line into heaven? Do they give a shit
what he thinks about when he is taking a smoke break from being the Pope?

I am writing this to Chris' new song that is sort of pop-rockish; his second installment
as a herman and his second installment that is just fucking cool. I hope he doesn't mind
the Pope thing...

Bill Speaks
Part I

Well, my new band is getting a chance to play with the greatest band in the world, and I'm scared shitless.
First of all, I used to be a bad guitar player. Then in a bold move, I decide to switch instruments in mid-stream. Brilliant.

My best friend Seth is probably the greatest musician I've ever met. The first time I was introduced to
him, I was a senior in high school and he was still in 8th grade. Usually seniors in high school and mid-
dle-schoolers don't hang tight. So I meet this kid who is only 14 and can rip off Jerry Garcia licks like
nothing. Not only that but he is wicked smart and kind of an asshole, in the way that the hermans are
assholes to each other. But we hit it off. My parents were like, "Why are you hanging out with this
little kid?" I said, "Because he's a genius, Mom."

So all through college I did whatever I could to help Seth and his musical ventures. First I tried to
play in a band with him. We were called Another Roadside Attraction after the famed Tom Robbins hippie
epic. We called ourselves a blues band, probably because except for Seth we were sad. Seth used to say,
"We were so bad we didn't know how bad we were." My friend Mike played rhythm guitar with a right hand
that sounded like he had a brick tied to it—a little heavy on the downstroke. I tried to play bass. We
had this straight-edge kid Aaron Barner on the drums. He was lazy and liked to ride the cowbell for
entire songs. He also drank milk like it was water. Our friend Chris Franklin sang vocals and improvised
amazingly well. At some point Seth decided that we had to kick Mike out of the band. The downstroke was
just too much. Soon after I quit the band because I knew if anyone else would get kicked out it would be
me and I wanted to save myself the humiliation.

It wasn't long before Seth was playing with another group of guys, including present hermans lead guitarist, Chris Entz, Akron/Family drummer Dana Jansen, and Justin Miller of Monkeypod on bass. They started
a little thing called Buka Mongra and the Outhouse Funk, a jam band with Franklin as the front man. They
were a teen sensation. ll the high school kids for miles around thought they were the shit and would
show up on all kinds of drugs and dance at their home base, My House Café. I got them to play a show at
my college's house party weekend at a fraternity at Bucknell. They were only 16. These three gangsters
from Philly jumped on stage and started freestyle rapping, until one of them passed out into the drum
kit. Seth looked at me with fear in his eyes but I was so fucked up I thought everything was just fine.
I was like, "Keep playing! This is awesome."

So eventually Buka dissolved when most of the band went to music school in Boston. Chris and I moved out
here to Missoula to catch trout and find ourselves. We found the hermans instead. Super.

Seth and Dana went on to form Akron/Family and holed up in an apartment in Brooklyn for two years, making
recordings and sending them to various avante-garde record people. Eventually, former Swans frontman Michael Gira heard their stuff and signed them to his label, Young God Records. They've toured Europe and

PART II

The Akron show was bitchin' and they even played before us! The boys got to town and we went to check out the Historic House to see what the sitch was. To not mince words, the place was a shithole. It looked like there had been a month-long continuous keg party in the place. Your feet stuck to the floor in every room. The main room was barely big enough to hold a band much less an audience. Seth had the same look on his face that we had. Our friend, Danny Bobbe, opened the show with his weird, spinning folk songs. It was interesting to say the least. Then all of sudden people started showing up in droves. As Akron took "the stage" people started packing into the house, spilling out into the kitchen and the foyer. The boys had been getting some radio play in town, but this was really unexpected...

6v

4/24/05

Dear Diary,

It has been a while but the last time we spoke you were drunk and spit in my face after throwing up on my shoes, you wretch. Anyway, the hermans played with a young lad named Danny Bobbe and Akron/Family last night at a house party on 3rd street in Missoula. Danny B. started the show with a very interesting set list. His style is utterly unique and to say he is a typical folk-singer/song writer would be comparable to calling Robert Goulet a typical lounge act. This lad's humor is very Alaskan and I haven't figured it out yet.

Akron/Family went second and if you ever the chance I suggest you see them, diary. Just one hour and a half set will not enable me to justifiably speak of how impressive this band is. I guess, on such short notice and slightly still hung over, I could say Akron is Radiohead going through a subtle heart attack that will get you close to over load but leave you smiling disjointedly like you just watched the Grateful Dead cover Metallica. I don't know what to say except that I wanted to go straight home and play with myself instead of following them.

Alas, oh diary, the hermans did indeed follow. It was one of our better sets and we must thank all who stayed and opened their minds and ears to our forty five minutes to an hour long piece of lunacy. The energy remained intact and the B.M.M.S. house continued to sway and flutter in a happy panic all night.

I am happy that Bill and Chris were able to not only watch their friends from Williamsport kick ass but also share the stage and crowd with them. I think I can also speak for Derk when I say that we were honored and excited and soaked with sweat as well. So, thanks to Danny, Akron/Family, Mike from the house and everyone that showed or at least intended to go as long as the excuse is creative.

the hermans will be playing at the Union Hall upstairs in a few weeks with The Krooks and Pocket Lobotomy. We will keep you posted even though you are just a depressed diary who struggles with alcoholism and the notion of self-worth.

Love,

David

Hey Asshead,

Going to work tonight to fill in for some scumbag who isn't really sick but told our gullible management otherwise. We need to go on tour! If those hippies in Akron slash Family can do it, we can do it! Soon! Now! Damn it! and get on with your life.

Dave

DOUCHE —

I AM PRETTY SURE THAT AT LEAST TEN PEOPLE HAVE TO KNOW WHO YOUR BAND IS, LET ALONE THINK YOU ARE GOOD ENOUGH TO GO ON TOUR. IT WOULD BE FUCKING GREAT TO TOUR, BUT I DON'T THINK IT IS VERY REALISTIC AT THIS POINT. PERHAPS WE SHOULD RECORD A DEMO SO PROSPECTIVE VENUE BOOKERS OR WHATEVER COULD HEAR US. YOU ARE DUMB AND I DON'T WANT TO TALK TO YOU ANY MORE.

— DERK

Shit Bag,

Yes, you are a bag that is half full of dog shit sitting in a corner waiting to be filled w/ more shit. Playboy's Colin books tours and will help us if we even record so you are right... for the first time in your miserable existance. How can we record w/out money? Perhaps you should go back to sucking pole in alleyways and take one for the band, you good-for-nothing land mass!

As you wish,
Wesley

THERE ARE NO WORDS TO DESCRIBE YOUR PATHETIC EXISTENCE. MAYBE YOU COULD PULL YOUR HEAD FROM YOUR RECTUM AND THINK FOR ONCE. LAST TIME WE PLAYED THE OTHER SIDE I WAS TALKING TO JUSTIN LAWRENCE AND HE SAID HE HAS THE EQUIPMENT AND WHATNOT TO RECORD LIVE SHOWS. ASK COLIN IF SOMETHING LIKE THIS WOULD WORK. IF NOT, GET A REAL FUCKING JOB AND RAISE MONEY SO WE CAN FIND SOMEONE TO RECORD US FOR MONEY OR WHATEVER. OTHERWISE, MAYBE YOU COULD BOOK US A SHOW WHERE WE ACTUALLY GET PAID MORE THAN $30 AND THEN WE WOULD HAVE CASH MONEY TO SPEND. I AM TIRED OF WASTING MY TIME DICKING AROUND. LET'S DO SOMETHING! LATER, LOSER.

— HAMMER

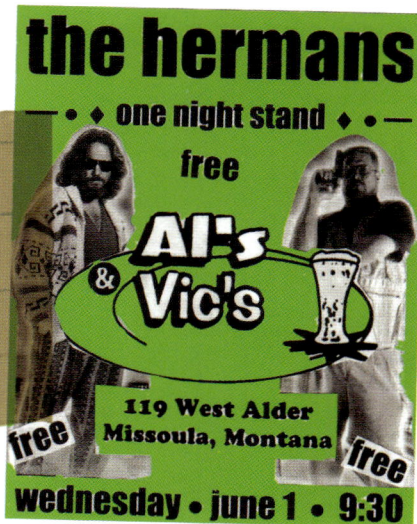

the hermans
— • ◆ one night stand ◆ • —
free

Al's & Vic's

119 West Alder
Missoula, Montana

free   free

wednesday • june 1 • 9:30

-----Original Message-----
From: dave@thehermans.net
To: Jones, Greg
Subject: Al's and Vic's (don't fucking forget Vic!)

Yo bro,

Did you used to go to Al's and Vic's (Alcoholics and Victims as we call it here in Mizootown) to write your articles for the Independent or did you do them at Charlie B's? I remember you saying something about writing at the bars and I don't know if they had music then but we landed a show at Al's! My friend Tiffany, a manager at Finn and Porter, is dating a waiter there (so they will probably both get axed soon) and plays for Al's pool league team. She finagled them to let us play for his birthday party and they said we are the first rock and roll band to play there since before I was born, according the bartender. I guess I look younger than 28. Fuck, this town needs a goddamn venue like a hooker needs penicillin so why not? I am ecstatic to play a favorable dive like Al's and hopefully we can go back. Damn that bar has a "home" feel to it only there is scattered drunks, piss on the floor and no blankets.
Are you busy next week and itchin' to get out of Philly for some rock?

Dave

...and so we were officially the first rock band to be allowed to play this bar in something like 30 years. I guess they have had some jazz band play recently but, being that most of the hermans have problems with drinking and spend a lot of time in Al's, I don't recall seeing any jazz bands, let alone hearing anything but AC/DC or Metallica coming from the juke box… Fucking great show. We had a blast and we covered a song each by Wilco and the Pixies for all the broke ass Missouliants who couldn't go to the Gorge to see that show last week. Everyone knew what we were doing and people thanked us for those songs afterward. It seemed like the right thing to do as I am still pissed I couldn't go to that. Fucking Pixies and Wilco together. That is like peanut butter and bananas, carrots and broccoli (I hate peas) and…well…Wilco and the Pixies! Outta Mind Outta Site and Gigantic. Thank heavens Derk sounds like a chick, or, Geddy Lee. It was fun and we all got laid. One girl told us she was going to make tee shirts that say "everyone gets laid after a hermans show" as it is apparently becoming a prevalent thing…

CRAIG THE BIRTHDAY BOY

ADELAIDE AKA "THE MERMAID"
— KBGA DJ

69

70

"Ladies and Gentlemen, from parts unknown…

THE ULTIMATE SOUNDMAN!!!"

Justin is a fine individual who knows how to turn any crappy, shit-hole venue or stage into the sound of the Rolling Stones on tour. He also knows how to make a cool, high energy rock and roll band sound like Jesus through an eight track and he can also make shitty touring bands seem not so fucking lame. Today's scene of the "emo"tional ties and style-before-creativity approach to music envelops some bands while others still just sweat buckets of rock and roll bile. Justin makes the first sound tolerable and the latter sound like lightning. Other bands sound good regardless (like the hermans) so he just sets up the mics and gets drunk standing off to the side and watches us reach the heights of rock and roll heaven just by showing up to the gig and then plugging in.

We owe our souls to Hell House Sound (Justin's company) and we love that man. He is a fine, fine man even though he only wears black…he has the only black hermans tee shirt in the world without sleeves. That is cool even in Hatboro, PA, the town I grew up in, and there are a lot of sleeveless tee shirts there. With dragons on them.

We hope one day to go on tour and have Justin do our sound. If he does it for free, this will happen because we are fucking broke. Go Justin. We love hell.

5/19/05

To one, to all, or both of you:

This is your Bovine Balladeer checking in to divulge and rant pertaining to recent misgivings and suspicions. True, I don't post newsletters, Dave usually takes care of that once and a while, (and I hear he has been spreading rumors of sorts about me of the impolite and evil persuasion) but I must post this newsletter, or perhaps I will christen it a "debriefing." Listen, I have been in receipt of a considerable amount of pressure from the Christian/Religious Front. (They are everywhere, and if I don't step in here and offer words of warning, they may come for you next when you least expect it!) I capitalize "Front" because "They" do it all the time: "God" & ?"Jesus" & "Holy Water" and so on. Look, not only am I being told that band practice on Sunday is a sin, but these totemistic monkeylords are trying to recruit me to watch Christian Rock concerts and go to Church with them in weird places that I can't spell. Herein lies the quandary: I have been asking these overzealous humps to come watch the hermans? shows in the midst of all these monkeyshines. That said, I need a damn good reason not to go to their what-have-yous if I expect them to come to mine. Do you see what absolute donkey shit this whole conundrum has turned in to? Of course I have absolutely no intention of attending their Power Hour or watching a band that sings about cliched Bible verse or other various horsepuckey, but how do I convince these weirdoes that they should still consider showing up to support the hermans instead? Well, this is what I have been able to come up with so far: I have been telling them that in no way, no how could I possibly join a Church at this juncture since I know as well as any God-fearing American that one must tithe (for those of you whom did not go to Catholic school for 12 years, tithing means you give like ten percent of your monthly wages to the Church via putting it into a basket with a long stick attached to the side of it that some smelly old gabardine-clad codger waves in front of your face until you drop in a little envelope or a wad of cash money each Sunday) in order to properly belong to a Church. Since I neither possess, nor earn any of said moneys by playing my bovine-clad Holstein wonder kit aptly dubbed "lemonade," I could not contribute to their basket-on-a-stick each Sunday to aid in their righteous cause. Thus, therefore, hence et cetera, I have requested that they not only come support the hermans very soon (perhaps at the Old Post on June 9th) but to pay extra moneys so that I may gather enough to tithe to their Holy and Grand Royal Ballyhoo of weekly assembly. Now, I understand that many of you, most of you, do not attend such ceremonies, but you must do your part as well. Come to the shows, support the hermans, so that I may join their Fraternally and Sisterly institution and get these constipated minions off my goddamned back. With this, I bid you adieu. Until next time, stay away from the ones that fall down and speak in tongues---Charismatic, I believe they are called. Fuckin' weirdoes.

Peace out,

---derkhammer herman

P.S. Thanks to all who showed up down at Caras Park for the weird-ass graduation party for people we didn't know on Saturday, May 14th. Sorry we started a bit late, but it turns out we were lucky to get a chance to play anyways. So to all of you who came down: We had a blast and rock and roll lived in Missoula for at least one more day. To you, my beloved hermanites, I offer these words of advice the next time you find yourselves in Church: I always found it best to put empty envelopes in the money basket, that and make sure you sign the name of some tumbleweed or ding-dong you don't like all that much.

Jrnl,

I think it is very acceptable that I finally got to play a show with a progressive rock band. This is my deal, journal, I live for this shit. They were from Tokyo, called Green Milk from the Planet Orange. They spoke broken English and the only things we could understand were Rush, Yes, and Dream Theatre. This is ultimately cool because I love the first two, and the third isn't bad if you are a total music weirdo and appreciate insanity from instruments and talent. I have never seen three guys make such beautiful noise together. Their drummer and bassist were completely insane, and never missed a beautifully syncopated beat. I didn't even mind that the drummer took his shirt off, which is usually reserved for redneck cover bands who think they are about to open for Whitesnake next show. Not that there is anything wrong with Whitesnake, except they totally suck ass. And don't get me wrong, I like rednecks, too. They keep America mediocre. And stupid. Nonetheless, this band was great and we were good, too. Especially when we rocked out for Japanese folk who thought we were cool. Or maybe they said we had nice shoes. I am not sure. All I know is that it is a shame that the show was not promoted well, and not enough people showed up, and all the moneys (which, unfortunately for them, was probably not very much) went to the Orange Planet, but we are used to not getting paid. That is also stupid and should be noted that once and a while we would like to at least make enough to cover the beer we drank during the show. I still think this one was tops, and I am finally happy to join another band on stage that appreciates good music. Those guys have soul. And talent—dangerous combination. Until next time, jrnl, go fly a kite!

-derk herman, fellow Rush and Yes lover.

GREEN MILK

FROM PLANET ORANGE

Dearest Diary,

Today in between second and third periods Morgan and Tanner (cunt) had it out over Taylor (duh, what a loser) and then Josh (dork) and Constance (ugly) broke up because Josh screwed Becca (bitch) in his dads Mercedes. It would have been cooler if he fucked Mercedes (slut) in the Mercedes….

Anyway, that is kind of what it is like working at a restaurant and I think my head will indeed explode soon if I do not get out of this industry. And I am writing a fucking journal and that is how most journals go, no? We played the Old Post for the first time and joined an elite group of Missoula bands; bands who are on the invited list! The Volumen (cool), the Oblio Joes (awesome), Russ Nasset (oh boy!) and Janesville (retired...but they were cool) are some who have played there and it was a hot show. It is funny but I was nervous dropping off our demo because Janine (rad) the booking person looked as though she were going to head butt me when I gave it to her and then called the next day and booked us for last week. We were psyched, especially Bill because I think he has a bed in their basement, and rocked the packed bar all night. You get three hours for three hundred bones. That's a hundred bucks an hour to you and me, Russ.

We also got the invite back so you other losers can eat it!

Gotta go—my new girlfriend is here and she looks crazy…why do most of my girlfriends get the same look after a while?

7.5

10/12/05

Friends, fans and whomever,

Well, it has been some time and we are sorry about that but who the fuck really reads this anyway? I am not even going to edit out the misstakes or "fuck" words this time! See that! We do whatever the hell we want because we are Griswolds...HA HA!

So there have been some shows since the last we were in communicae; some good, some at a ghost town an hour north of Helena, Montana. The hermans were the lone rock and roll band at the Ear Infection Festival put on by our pal Chad from Jester's bar. The feeling just as one would imagine rolling into a ghost town to play a show an hour north of Helena, Montana. However, the tides turned for the better and the hermans got to play in front of about a hundred people who normally would not get to see us. Most of the other bands were new age or heavy metal acts from around the West coast and kind of stared at us during our set like deer in the headlights of a truck much bigger than any semi about to send them to deer heaven forever...without being able to bring their Metallica records with them. They were nice folks in the end and of course very stylish.

Other than that, we did the Old Post a few times which always brings out the looneys and we also are very proud to say we played a benefit show for Hurricane Katrina relief which raised over $18,000 thanks to fellow musicians, business owners and volunteers from Missoula. On that note (since that show was at the Wilma building), does anyone have about $4.5 million laying around so we can purchase that historic Montana landmark? It is for sale and the Red Light/Green Room where we played is a kick ass venue. If you would like to make a donation, or uh, contribute one of your children's college funds, send a check to the hermans and we will take care of business.

Well, it is time for me to go and vacuum Chris's head as he smells like cat pee. Congrats to Derk and Nyree as they are taking the plunge next summer...want to see me get reaaallllly wasted? ha ha ha ha ha. November 4th at the Old Post again.

Until then, I remain yours but with clothes on...unless you are Russian but with the last name Jones.

DAvE the Pilot of the Pop

11

-----Original Message-----
From: dave@thehermans.net
To: Jones, Greg
Subject: Radio Radio

Greggor~

Get your damned legs off the door and let me in so I can spray your face with RAID. Anyway, Derk and I went on the radio today (Swimming With the Mermaid on KBGA) and made asses out of ourselves. We played the Old Post last night and were still whacked. It was our friend Adelaide's show, she plays everything from earth-trance to Eartha Kitt which fortunately for her but unfortunately for us, is listened to by most of Missoula....that is, until we came on and spiked ourselves. It was just strange knowing that a lot of people I know (and probably many I don't know) were listening to a DJ interview two guys in a band they have never heard and we were still drunk and showing it. Well, it was my first interview and Adelaide saved us: trained DJs know how to kill unnerving moments of silence and she knows us well enough to pull questions out of the air. I think Mattie Taco will put it on the web site so you can go listen to your little brother and his asswipe drummer sound like average idiots who happen to be in a band. The good thing was that we got to plug the Benefit for Katrina that we are playing. The Red Light Green Room is a cool place to play; it is situated under the Wilma building and most shows there are packed just because it is a cool place to get drunk and watch music. Justin is doing the sound which means we will sound like we know what we are doing...unless we play as bad as we interviewed.

I can't believe the devastation there. I saw some pictures from a guy from Missoula who went to observe the aftermath and it is awful. Hopefully, we will raise enough for them to build more voting booths to get this asshole out of office and get a president who might act on something this massive instead of shrugging it off and hitting from the next tee. Fucking douche bag.

All right, I am going to go beat Derk at ping pong and then rip some hair from the dog who bit the hermans in the ass last night.

Davix

RUNNING PRESS
BOOK PUBLISHERS

David Jones
102 E. Central Ave.
Missoula, MT 59801
November, 2005

Dear David,

As I mentioned on the phone, Running Press is interested in the book idea we talked about and would like to make an offer to you and Derk. As we discussed, the book concept is to follow an unknown rock and roll band from Anytown, USA (i.e. the hermans) from when they first start out to when they start touring – and all the details in between. I know you guys have been documenting many of the things that have happened so far, and we could use that material plus new original text to create the manuscript. The book would also include a lot of photos and art. We want to publish in Fall 2007. Sounds like a long ways off, but you'd really need to get started right away.

Here's what we can offer:
Advance: ███████████
Royalty: ███████████

Running Press will hire a designer, cover some photo costs, and of course print, market, and distribute the book. Everyone here thinks it's an original idea that could appeal to anyone who's in a band, or who's ever been in a band, or who has always wanted to be in a band.

Please let me know asap if you guys are interested in doing this. If you have any questions or would like to discuss terms, please call me.

Regards

Greg Jones
Editorial Director

125 SOUTH TWENTY-SECOND ST.
PHILADELPHIA, PA 19103–4399
215–567–5080 FAX 215–568–2919

Pile of Duke,

Greg wants us to write a book about the hermans. I am going to work...

again... so call me there (fuck my boss, my bitches needs to get ahold of me, sucka!) sos
I can tell you about the worst idea since they moved a hockey team from
Minnesota to fucking Texas, totally lame-o!

D-Rock Bizzle Jizzle

YO, SNOOP,

WHAT YOU BEEN SMOKING? I WOULD CALL YOU AT WORK BUT SINCE WE
DON'T HAVE A PHONE YET, I WILL STOP IN. I DON'T EVEN UNDER-
STAND WHAT YOU ARE TALKING ABOUT. GREG IS PROBABLY FUCKING
WITH YOU BECAUSE YOU ARE A GULLIBLE TURD. SEE YOU TONIGHT, LOSER.
—DERK, THE PRACTICAL

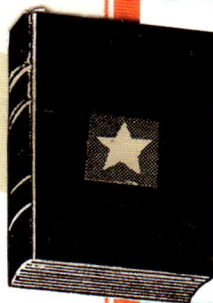

Bird Brain,

where the hell were you? It was ~~Dead~~ dead at
work so we watched the Sixers at the bar all night and it
was genious. Anyway, working nights is for the birds: the
~~Brainless~~ ones who fly into windows.

So, Greg's publishing co. is jumping on the "reality" craze so they want
to use the journal stuff we have been keeping, web site letters, and any
other correspondance so they can put it in book form, send it all over the
world and then wait patiently for the world to fall asleep to our lame
story. They wanted a NO-NAME band from "Anytown USA" which I
thought was in Oklahoma but I guess it is here.

I told him to go fuck himself and their corporate agenda and
figured you would agree. I'll tell you more when you STOP fucking
AROUND w/ THAT WELSH TART AND COME TO FINN +
PORTER SO WE CAN TALK AND STOP THIS NOTE-
PASSING SH*T !!! you idiot.

                            J-Lones

PENIS,
I DON'T LIKE YOU OR YOUR RESTAURANT. SO THERE. I THINK THIS IDEA
IS SILLY, PRETENTIOUS AND ARBITRARY. WHAT'S IN IT FOR US BESIDES
~~KITTEN~~ HUMILIATION? IF HE IS SERIOUS ABOUT THIS, PERHAPS THE
IDIOTS AT HIS COMPANY SHOULD MEET US AND WATCH OUR BAND BEFORE
THEY WASTE EVERYONE'S TIME. I HAVE BETTER THINGS TO DO THAN
PUBLICLY ~~EMBARRASS~~ MYSELF IN OTHER PLACES BESIDES A STAGE.
WE NEED TO TALK TO GREG AND FIND OUT WHAT THE FUCK HE THINKS
SOMETIMES. BESIDES, NO ONE HAS EVER HEARD OF US. EVEN OUR PARENTS
WOULDN'T ADMIT TO IT— ~~ESPECIALLY~~ YOURS. MAYBE IF THE "BOOK"
(STUPID IDEA) INCLUDED A CD OF THE HERMANS AND THEY WANT TO
PAY FOR IT TO BE RECORDED, THEN WE COULD TALK. STOP WASTING
MY TIME. YOU PHILADELPHIANS ARE ALL THE SAME. FUCKIN' LOONY.
                            DKS

Dear Publisher,

After excessive discussion, harsh but thorough argument, multiple head slaps and questioning my four-year-old daughter (our final attempt to figure out whether or not to sell our souls to you), we accept a large fraction of your terms for this book, but feel we need to haggle.

We deem this book will not work unless we can include a CD, because no one besides a small fraction of people in Missoula know who the fuck we are, and even they don't seem to give a rat's tuchass about our career because they cannot listen to us at home, in the shower, in the car, while making sweet passionate cha-cha, or doing whatever it is Missoula people do when not out riding their damned mountain bikes and kayaks. Actually, we think the advance is a little low (Derk wants to fly to Philly to spit on your building), but if Running Press agrees to pay for a demo we will let you use our rock and roll journal, pictures, web site items and underwear.

There is a brand new, state-of-the-art recording studio right here in called Habbilis Records, which we can use. We can make the CD in four days, and it will cost your company a mere $████ The necessity for beer, on your tab, is also required.

This notion of adding music to the book completes an idea whose main concept we are still unsure of. To use the parlance of our times, we are a little freaked out. Honestly, who would want to purchase a book by a band and about a band from the middle of nowhere who aren't very well known in their own peanut shell of a town? If you people turn on us and market us as the next biggest boy band so you can make a lot of money, I will definitely send Derk to Philly to spit on your building. We want no association with those flagrantly unoriginal douche bags. We will not be your monkey boys. Or The Monkees, for that matter—even if my name IS David Jones.

Alas, if you will leave the editing and design to us and allow us to be totally honest in what we do and have done, and especially in what we think about everything from politics, religion, popular culture, love, sex, violence, death, and fucking rock and roll, you have got a band to fornicate with on this project. Allow us those things, and a recording session, and the hermans can work with you.

Now we wish good wishes and heart-felt gratitude for this opportunity. If you were here, I would bow, but instead I just gave a salute.

Good night and good luck,

the hermans

Liberace,

Greg called. We got the ~~a deal~~ Fucking Deal! Besides

the ADVANCE $ (which wouldn't be enough for us to buy enough

Red ink to spell "Romani Ite Domum" 100 times all

over Running Press' Building), we will be getting some

Dough to make a demo CD that will go in the book.

Let's make a whole fucking ALBUM! They asked if

XXXXX would be enough for four or ~~five~~ five songs and I

had to pull the phone away so they wouldn't ~~hear~~ hear me

laughing at them! These guys are better than a record

company! Let's go to Flippers, get hammered, figure out

what songs to throw on ~~three~~ the Demo and watch Jeopardy.

I Don't have Sophie tomorrow (or work) so I can tie

one on ... and it's Friday you Scum Bag!   — D —

P.S. the Contract is in the Mail

8 4/4

HERMANS: HERE ARE SOME ALBUM TITLES WE HAVE CONJURED UP. LOOK THEM OVER AND WE WILL ALL PICK A NAME FROM THE LIST OR OTHERWISE AT PRACTICE ON SATURDAY.
— DERK & DAVE

TIDAL WAVE   THE HERMANS ALBUM ONE

STALKING MATILDA   KARL'S DREAM

THE HERMANS—WILL MELT YOUR FACE

                    THE HERMANS — ALBUM ZERO

WHO THE FUCK ARE THE HERMANS?

          CENTRAL AVE.   POPE ON STRIKE

YOUR FAVORITE BAND SUCKS.

                              NUMBER FIVE

THE HERMANS URGE ALL Y'ALL TO GO FUCK YO'SELVES

SONGS ABOUT STUFF   SONGS ABOUT CRUD

       POOP   PALINDROME

              MODERN DAY PIRATES

SONGS FROM THE BISMARK

...but after the session the artwork for the CD will be fun to work on. I think we have a friend of ours (little Megan the cool hottie rock girl who can't eat fucking gluten) who is willing to pose nude as "Matilda." We will either put her on the cover or on the back or whatever as well as pics of us in handcuffs or outside her window or something with us being freaks to go along with the whole sick "stalking" thing. What a stupid crime! When I got dumped (however many times that was), as the dumpee, the last human I want to see is the dumper. And as far as getting laid, or even a date, showing off your climbing skills late at night outside someone's window is hardly the way to go about it. Get them drunk!

So, hopefully we will be recording soon....

Dearest Readers of this here book

At this point, since our terms have been accepted and we are all aware that we are writing this and you are reading this, we would like to be the first to thank you for reading this, and we would even like to thank ourselves for writing this. In fact, we first would like to thank you for noticing this book, buying it, then reading it, then assuredly wiping your ass with it—as long as whilst you wipe you have our included demo CD blaring from a small, shitty stereo in your shit-stained bathroom.

This is fun. You see, now that I know I am writing this and you, hopefully, know you are read-ing it, we can both agree that things are being both written and read. Before, Dave and I knew we were writing, but we didn't know why and were growing to not like each other very much. Now that we know why we are writing this, and you know as well, we can agree that Dave and my re-lationship should improve immensely. Or we will kill each other. Don't worry: you're safe. Either way, at least we know who is doing the reading and who is doing the writing. That would be you, and us, respectively. So, children, if we have learned one lesson today, let it be known that if you do anything that is even remotely important to you, keep a journal of it. Some idiot may want to use it to profit from your aspirations.

Sincerely,

Derk Kenneth Schmidt, drummer extraordinaire of the hermans.

p.s. from the singer: why the fuck are you reading when you could be watching reruns of crap, buying crap at Wal-Mart, or eating crap at your favorite fast food chain like a true American? Didn't you listen to your president? Buy more crap! Eat more crap! Indulge in more crap! That moron drummer was right: this is fun!

-----Original Message-----
From: dave@thehermans.net
To: Jones, Greg
Subject: Habbilis and Us

Greggor,
You are a vile, old-fashioned wretched moth and need to be squashed into modernity.
Anyway, thanks for the go ahead on this book thing. The demo was good to give out, but it will be nice to send a professionally made CD to clubs in other towns. I haven't admitted this before, but the money to make the CD was the only reason we accepted this book deal. We may be writers, but we never wanted to write a book about the hermans – we just want to rock the fucking world.
Anyway, the CD will help because I suppose club managers like to see and hear what you look and sound like before they book you. This country is fucking great.
We are gonna start recording in about three weeks at Habbilis and have about thirty hours or so to rock out a kick ass album. Next step is to figure out what songs to put on it, which I am sure will end up in a fist fight at Red's after the Eagles second string blow another game out of their asses. Fucking McNabb. Fucking hernias.
I can't wait to do this, to hear what we really sound like. I talked to Blake about how we will record and he thinks a band like ours should do it all live, which means we play the songs together as we would on stage and let the magic of technology make it sound less raw and fuzzy and without drunk chicks behind us screaming. Neat-o.
Thanks again, man. We can now at least sell some albums when we maybe go on a tour of the northwest. The northwest is cool. These people like rock music. And hopefully, for Running Press'sake, they like to read books about rock too, heh heh heh!
By the way, I broke up with that Russian lass…caught her fucking half naked with a teenager who is of some relation. Woe is me and the crazy freaks I decide to date.

Devox

Diary of a Hitman,

the hermans are now recorded and henceforth engraved into history unless some fascist militia desecrates and breeches our secure lines, overthrows our premiere, obtains a stranglehold around the capitalistic vertebrae of our pure and pristine nation-state and presses a malevolent Pinko regime upon our children whose first order of business is to carry out mass burnings of American rock and roll albums starting with the hermans' first.

Yeah, it was so cool recording these songs that we have been playing for over a year now; especially being that I have never heard them other than live or at practice, neither of which count. Where to start?

The studio, as an absolute place, is an imposing locale for a rookie like myself in that I feel like if I happen to slip and lean into one of the 7,892 knobs or buttons or doo hickeys, Missoula will ignite in a paradoxical blast that will start Armageddon. I have no idea what the fuck I am doing there, I feel like a stupid grazing cow most of the time and I certainly ask no questions. We did thirteen songs in the last two days and I need to get over this cold before Blake and Cameron will let me sing. Thirteen songs in two days. It is unreal how good it sounds and these guys haven't even mixed the thing, whatever that means. To me it simply means "make my fucking album sound better!" And I am certain they will. Chris and Bill and Derk started speaking Boobot from planet X-9 language as soon as we got in there (you know, music lingo) so I began drinking in this cave of a building. I guess the narrow construction has something to do with sound waves and...I have no clue, man. Anyway, Jess agreed to take Sophie for four days so we could have this "experience" and, of course, we blew it by getting hammered. Then again, Eddie Van Halen apparently doesn't remember recording some of 1984 so fuck it! Actually, it was more like a slow, constant and natural buzz as we didn't have time to sit around and slam beers even though we were there from ten a.m. to midnight for two days. Well, even when we did do that, for some reason, it didn't phase us a bit.

So on and on the other hand, the studio as an abstract thought is something even more colossal. Some songs we nailed in one or two takes and others, like Parade for instance, took forever. All you have to do is take a break, look around and remember where you are and a smile instinctively forms...even when you fuck up a song you have played a hundred times! We could hardly see each other and were only connected with mics and headphones but the communication sparked regardless; for me, the magnitude of finally doing this was unreal. I felt like I had drunk some absinthe-tonic-potion like Kurt Russell in Big Trouble In Little China that made me invincible but it was really just Pabst and the mighty buzz.

Chris made his guitar fly and I got to watch him over-dub a few solos from outside the glass room he was in. That was kugot.

When the dust settled (the studio is still in construction) I felt like moving in. I knew this shit was for real and everyone shared the same look that needed no words. And then someone said "Got the balls to sing in a studio, asshole?"

HERMANS: HERE'S A LIST OF ALL OF OUR SONGS THAT WE KNOW WELL
ENOUGH TO PUT ON THIS ALBUM. I THINK THE RECORD SHOULD BE
AROUND 50 MINUTES AND CONTAIN 12 OR 13 SONGS. EVERYONE CIRCLE
3 OR 4 EACH AND HOPEFULLY THAT WILL FILL IT. WE WILL HAVE TO
NARROW IT DOWN TO 3 OR 4 THAT WILL BE ON THE CD THAT GOES
IN THE BOOK, BUT WE CAN FIGURE THAT OUT LATER. LET'S FIRST
CONCENTRATE ON THE WHOLE ALBUM.

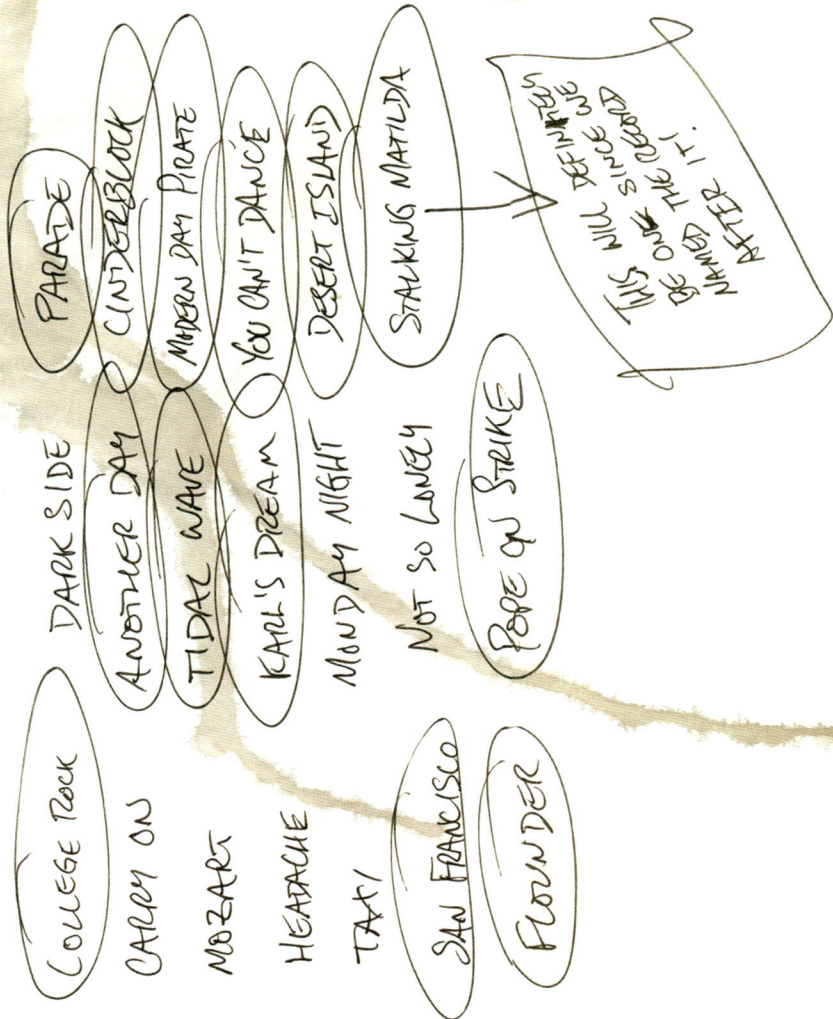

PEACE, HAMMER

DARK SIDE

(PARADE)

(COLLEGE ROCK)

CARRY ON   (ANOTHER DAY)   (CINDERBLOCK)

MOZART   (TIDAL WAVE)   (MODERN DAY PIRATE)

HEADACHE   (KARL'S DREAM)   (YOU CAN'T DANCE)

TAXI   (MONDAY NIGHT)   (DESERT ISLAND)

(SAN FRANCISCO)   (STALKING MATILDA)

(FLOUNDER)   NOT SO LONELY

                (POPE ON STRIKE)

THIS WILL DEFINITELY
BE ONE SINCE WE
NAMED THE RECORD
AFTER IT.

...SO WE DECIDED TO GO WITH THE "STALKING" THEME FOR OUR ALBUM ARTWORK. WE TALKED IT OVER AT FLIPPER'S AND DECIDED THE ALBUM ART SHOULD TELL A STORY. SO WE GO GET SOME BINOCULARS AND START STALKING HER. SHE KNOWS WE'RE WATCHING, PERHAPS EVEN LIKES IT, AND SINCE SHE HOLDS THE KEY TO OUR FATE, WE END UP IN FUCKING HANDCUFFS!

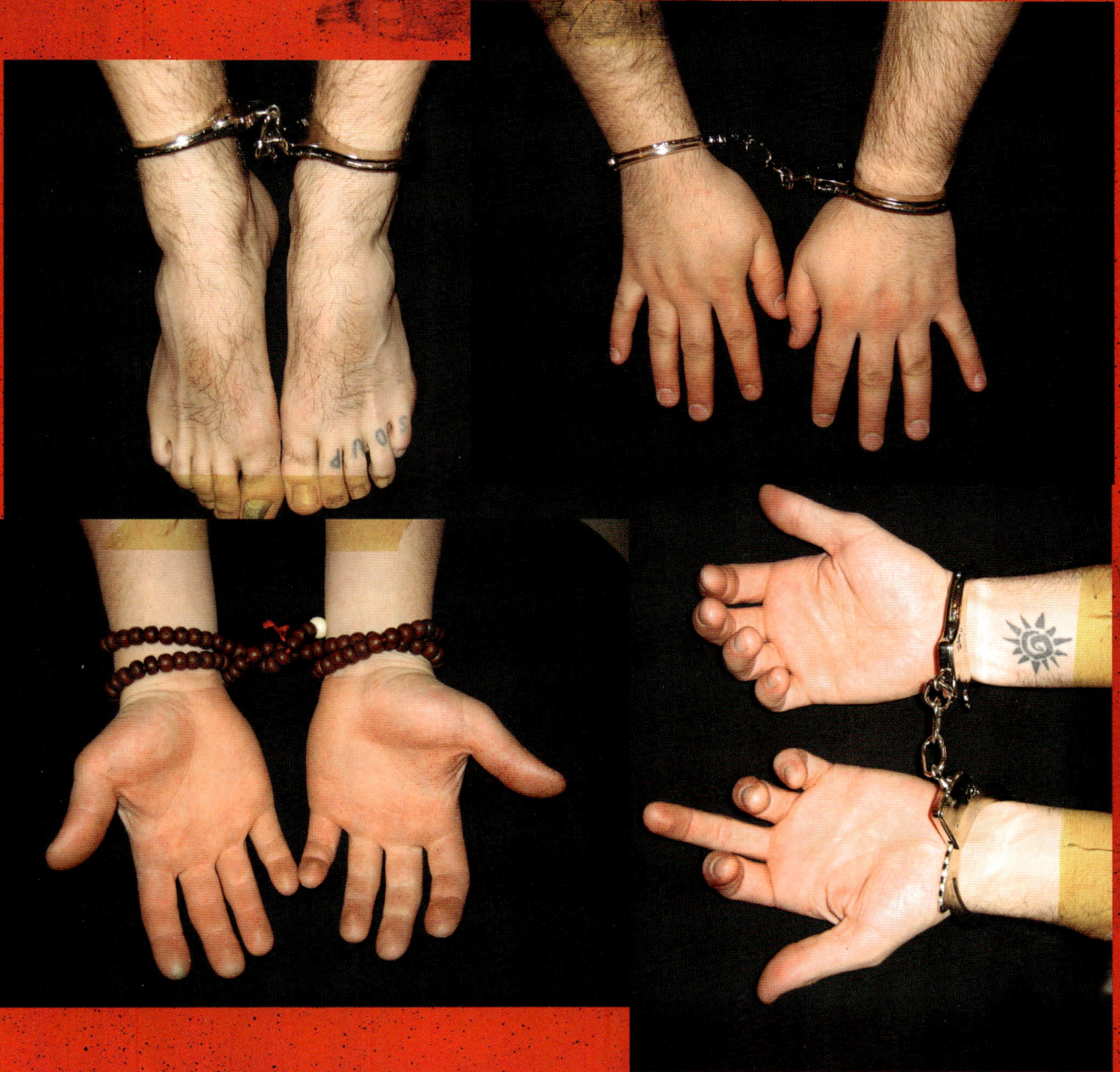

STALKING MATILDA
RECORDED NOV-DEC, 2005

January 03, 2006

People who read this,

Again, I must apologize. Sorry I've been neglecting you: I'm a dick. There, that is settled.

So, since the last I have written some very important things have happened that need serious discussion. I am very proud to say that we were in Montana for most of that shit and if you want to wax philosophic about why George's war is a shit-brick of bull dung, we'll be at the Old Post Friday, January 13th and then at the Raven on Friday the 3rd of February with the Victory Smokes, a band yet to be determined and Jackrabbit's Laugh.

The later is a new band who we are very proud to say we shared the stage, or little area that usually has two tables, some pool cues, and a drunken lush, at Al's and Vic's with on December 8th. They are a three-piece band that do absolutely nothing but rock out on stage. You will be hearing and seeing more of this band unless your idea of fun involves a T.V., a DVD player and the first season of Benson with some root beer on a Saturday night. Jackrabbit's laugh could kill Benson. They could probably kill B.J. McKay and the bear as well.

Anyway, the Al's show was insane as usual. After begging, pleading, grunting, crying, bellowing, chanting, mopping, brownnosing, tap dancing, falconing (where you have a big hawk that flies off, you take a nap, it comes back to land on your arm, then you go home), weeping, praising, bribing and finally just asking; the manager allowed us to bring in an opening band. Who better to share the iconoclastic stage of Al's and Vic's with than a brand new Missoula band? Yes, Pearl Jam is correct but they were playing in Tibet that night. Jackrabbit's Laugh proved to be a decent and sufficient alternative. Come see them play at the Raven show and you will not be let down. You can also ask them about the war and I am sure Gavin will give you plenty of reasons why war sucks.

See you later, you little rat finks you!

David

P.S. never mind that Russian thing...I must have been on acid again...probably the Beavis and Buttheads; those were insane!

The cow says mooo

the hermans

Home

Upcoming Events

Photos

Contact Us

Listen

Band Biography

Show Flyers

Merchandise

Mattie Taco

W3C HTML

Al's & Vic's
"Where the elite meet"

YO — SHITFACE —

CHECK OUT THE WEBSITE
IF YOU GET A CHANCE. I
WAS TALKING TO MATTIE TACO
AND WE DECIDED THE SITE
NEEDED A MAKEOVER. IT
IS NOW MUCH COOLER AND
FEATURES A COW AND WHAT
NOT IN AN INTERROGATION
ROOM. IT IS MUCH BETTER
THAN BEFORE AND I AM
SURE WE WILL GET AT LEAST
300,000 HITS IN THE
FORTHCOMING DAYS. OR
MAYBE AT LEAST ONE
IF YOU LOOK AT IT.
TACO IS GRANDE.
MUY GRANDE.

HAMMER

119 West Alder, Missoula, MT

the
hermans

Friday
the 13th
of January

All I said was,
"It's Free"

Old Post Pub 10 PM

01/16/06

Uuuuuuuhhhhhg,

To all those at the Post for Friday the 13th: thanks for coming, sorry I was late, sorry I played like a fuckin' amateur, thanks for being so cool and receptive, thanks for drinkin? with us, and thanks for coming this Thursday when we really need you the most.

We are probably going to put the Post on the back-burner for a while and stick to doing shows with other local bands. We are a little loud for that venue and, aside from that, the hermans have a lot of exciting things coming up within the next two months.

First of all, our first album should be released by spring, which in Montana could mean anywhere from late February to June depending on mother nature, that bitch. Secondly, we are starting to plan our first tour. We don't really know where we are going or how we are going to get there but if you want to someday say "I saw that band play at that shit-hole Al's and Vic's one time" while watching Conan O'Brien or the View, we need to get this band to bigger cities and larger venues. We are also proud to say that we are adding to our venues-played list next month with a show at the Raven. Thanks to Mike Gill of the Victory Smokes, we will be infiltrating and throwing a coup upon the small cafe and turning it from a respectable little coffee shop into a miserable, trashy rock and roll dump...then we'll have tea and strumpets in the morning.

Enough about us. We need to thank Blake and Cameron of Habbilis Records for putting up with us for five long days in the studio. With endless cases of Miller Genuine Draft, Pabst Blue Ribbon, and a haze that would choke a Clydesdale, we managed to track thirteen songs in two days and then make them sound bearable with an additional two days of mixing and mastering. I don't remember what we did on the fifth day...we probably got baked and played video games. Anyway, between them they have four magnificent ears and a tolerance level that would make Ghandi look like a spoiled brat on Ritalin. So, thanks again, the album sounds great.

I must go now and play with Rachel's robotic monkey...wow...that may be a concept for a new song.

Love and kisses,

Davey

01/29/06

Folks and Folkesses,

So to those of you who came to the Other Side for the Pabst Blue Ribbon Battle of the Bands Extravaganza, we would like to whole heartedly thank you for coming out to support your home-town boys, the hermans, kick the shit out of every other band that had the brass cajones to show up?unfortunately, we lost

But, the "kick the shit out of" thing is mostly true being that I don't recall seeing anyone else move, shudder, breathe, dance, disco, dip, doniker, flip, flack, flutter, freak-out, feather, funk, twirl, whirl, jitter, jang, jump, bump or even fucking fall down on the stage. I must take that back: J.C. Auto kicked some ass and I didn't see the last band. However, the winners of the first round actually sounded o.k. but I just wish the powers of the Pabst would have told us it was a battle of the fucking cover bands.

If we would have known that, we would have done our cover of the theme to Pee-Wee's Big Adventure (by Danny Elfman), Neil Diamond's "Forever In Blue Jeans" followed by a twenty minute version of "Bitches Ain't Shit" medley with "Fuck the Police" and we would have obviously ended with a cover of Tears For Fears "Shout."

People's heads would have exploded. Their knees would have buckled at the sight of the Chuck Norris mask Chris would have been wearing. Ladies would have fainted at the sight of the tee-shirt I would have worn stating "I humped Martha Washington. 13 stars. 13 inches. Coincidence? I think not." Derk would have shit his pants, rubbed it on his face and punched a judge drunkenly and we still would have won. Bill wouldn't have shown up because if he were a part of that, the hermans would have been a complete entity and then Missoula would have suffered spontaneous combustion as a fucking town. Enough ranting.

We did have a fun set after all and attained a few things out of it. A lot of people got to hear original rock and roll and, hopefully, we will play with J.C. Auto from Bozeman again soon. Andrea Harsell and her dad are cooler than ice in a fine 12 year McCallen, by the way.

So, we may be playing a big show next week and if it happens you will know. Until then, we are definitely at the Raven next Friday night for the Vagina Monologues benefit concert with the Victory Smokes, Hail Man Well Met and Raise Your Hands!. There will be belly dancers, fire eaters, sword jugglers and hopefully some midgets so we can get stoned outside and then come in to something completely fucked up and obscene.

Dave

Disclaimer, I am only speaking for me on this one and not the rest of the band.

Red Cabs'll do that to a man.

O.k. so we lost "Montana's Best Band" PBR, battle of the bands thing, it is a few weeks later (as far as you know), and we are over it, right? Fuck no! Well, yes….kind of.

The International Playboys won (if you don't know who they are yet, start the fuck over and pay the fuck attention) and proud we are of all of them. We will be especially proud if they buy The Count some damned deodorant. This is kind of neat-o because their singer is brothers with the Volumen bass player so I am sure there were fights. The show was a regal one as the Playboys, Joes and Volumen shared the stage, something that probably hasn't happened since a real club existed here. Playing with them would be a warranted test as these three bands are the last from the Jay's era; a time lost and reverential to naïve, callow punks like us only to be rekindled through oral tradition. Anyway, the point here is that we think it is about time to introduce the rest of the world (or whoever the fuck lost a bet and had to buy this book) to Missoula's other bands; some of whom we have shared shows with, some we are still waiting to share shows with (look up) and some who might only exist in folklore by the time you read this.

In any case, up until now, this has been a very, very cool ride. Sure the venues have been coming and going like the cheap sluts they are, but we use them as such (coming and going heh heh) and others will arise in their wake…and we hope to do the same. The same goes for Missoula bands. What is it now, early spring 06? This "myspace" do-hickey has introduced us to four or five new Missoula bands and we have only been on it since December. This says a lot because this town is the size of Rhode Island's left nut and we didn't know these people were doing what we are doing and it will be fucking great when we play with them.

We look forward to playing at the Raven, even though it is a coffee house and I am not that guy who plays in coffee houses.

Oh well, whatever, nevermind.

the
international
playboys

....if The International Playboys were a car they would be a silver and black 69 Charger with machine gun turrets, grenade launchers, 120 watt speakers on top and a sharpened chrome Ibanez on the front designed for impaling...the hermans would be a matching van from the early 80's with a jolly roger on the back...

MIKE GILL

...when I saw the Volumen at the Raven last week. My girlfriend doesn't remember this amazing show and I think she has not been sober for a decade. Anyway, Volumen are such a concentrated collaboration of dynamics and imposing lyrical scheme. What do you call it? Nerd rock and electric roll? They are a thug in an alley who will steal your wallet and then solve rigid formulaic equations for you. It is not fair....

THE VICTORY SMOKES

...so they changed their name from Good Guy/Bad Guy to Victory Smokes. This was a very, very good idea. They are an Indie Rock band but are creative and not consistent to that overly unswerving genre. The same goes (with the name changing thing) with Jackrabbit's Laugh who changed their name to Hail Man Well Met. Well, perhaps something else has to happen on that one as that is just plain out hard to say or remember...especially if you are my drunk girlfriend. But this is also a good new Missoula band. It is dark electric surf rock.

...and there are a couple good punk bands still in Zoo town and I saw the Reptile Dysfunction last night and they kick some serious buttocks. The Ass End Offend played at the punk rock prom last year but they played Volumen songs so I never got to see them as themselves. The Reptile rules, however, and I think we will have a good show together...

And finally there is somewhere cool to play in Missoula: the Raven Café! And we desecrated it. With our vaginas. And it is also cool that the Independent finally wised up and put our picture in the spotlight for the V Monologues show. It is wonderful to see four grown men, naked in a shower, next to a write-up about Women and their Vaginas, and how wonderful it must be to have a vagina, and how belly dancing (which some lovely women performed between sets) is apparently a celebration of the vagina, itself. Yet none, not one herman has a vagina in our naked shower picture. Nor are we homosexuals (not that there is anything wrong with that). We just think that there is no better way to promote band unity than to watch Eagles games together, drink together, play together, and shower together. And celebrate vaginas together. I am still not sure what our relation to the vagina is, but we were kindly asked to play this fundraiser to promote vaginas. And to stop acts of violence again women. And the Raven is very cool. Vagina. It is kind of like what Area 5 was supposed to be (a cool, BYOB and rock out venue) except the owners, Gavin and Rose, are cool and don't make me really uncomfortable when we are the only ones in the room like that creep from Area 5 did. And they aren't completely full of shit. I draw the Area 5 comparison because you can bring your own beer and drink a shitbasket of it, or you can be any age and just not drink. It has a cool stage Mike Gill and John Markley and crew built, and good sound (well, with the hiring on occasion of Justin Lawrence, Satan's loyal servant and KISS aficionado). This place is cool, and just may save the Missoula music scene. As long as we play there a lot since our band is cool. We must be since a ton of people showed up to rock out and celebrate you-know-what. It is a very cozy atmosphere, and an intimate setting for locals to get very close to bands, and since there is no bar, people actually watch the bands instead of sitting at the bar and bullshitting or hitting on the bartenders. Yes, perhaps the pendulum has swung the local musician's direction and rock and roll in Missoula shall be saved. Vagina. Those are cool, too.

SPOTLIGHT

stage the word

The Raven Cafe invokes V-Day on First Friday with a flurry of events to include belly dancing, art displays, fire juggling, dance; and a surprise appearance by the latest addition to The Raven's floor plan.

V-Day, conceived by *Vagina Monologues* author Eve Ensler, is not actually a day but a movement in which annual performances of Ensler's play are used to raise funds for local groups working to prevent violence against women. Though this year's performance of the *Monologues* doesn't take place until February 14, the University of Montana Women's Center is mining the movement for all it's worth in order to raise funds for their mission promoting "greater responsiveness to the needs of university women."

As for the entertainment to solicit your support, event organizers are offering dance performances from A Whole Pile of Hips and Flaming Hand of Eris as

The Hermans, one of the bands that will be celebrating V-Day on Friday.

WHAT: Vagina Goldmine: Benefit Concert, Dance and Art Show

WHEN: Fri., Feb. 3, 6 PM

WHERE: The Raven Cafe, 130 E. Broadway

HOW MUCH: $5 donation

well as music by The Hermans, Victory Smokes, Hail Man Well Met and Raise Your Hands—all on a new stage that's just been constructed in the space.

—Aaron Young

Yeah, fucking yeah. This is what I'm talking about. The Raven is becoming a haven but if I hear another Edgar Allen Poe reference I'm going to puke on my own loafers.

The venue is coming into its own and is no longer a "coffee shop where they let us have shows." Instead it is now an indie rock club that has good breakfast during the day and coffee that makes you crap a lot.

Mike and John Markley are working their asses off booking shows into the next three months and everyone is pretty amped to play or even just to hang out and see who is coming to town. We played a few shows in the last week back-to-back—one good, one last-second, which always pisses me off, doesn't fucking pay and seems to be prevalent for us. The first show, a Saturday night, consisted of the hermans and Sharktopus (the two Missoula reps.) and Claire D'Alune and Dream End (who hail from Minneapolis and Chicago).

A good amount of people showed up and keep showing up at this new spot. The bring-your-own-policy is something I never saw in Philly and seems to work here. Then again, in Philly it would probably cause hockey fights at rock shows. We will see how long this lasts, however, as the cops here in Missoula run the other way when there is real street violence but will grant a buzzed scenester a free proctology exam with the decisiveness of an angry pit bull. Poor scenesters; just trying to have a good time hanging out drinking beer while working so hard to look cool and hip telling you "how it is" when it comes to music and art. Then some cop gives them a breathalyzer anally. Ironic that most of the shit that comes out of their mouths is just that. Fucking music Nazis.

PISS ON
THIS BOOK.

DERK DIDI

...so we played a few shows but I am tired of being asked to play last minute which leaves us off the flyer. I was talking to Brian Volumen and he said something to the effect of, "you guys have come a long way in such a short amount of time....my band was playing in front of fucking nobody for a year or two before people started coming. You guys never paid your dues. That ain't fair" And I thought, what fucking dues? What the fuck is this guy talking about, man? Two years is a long time.

But I think he was basically telling me to shut the fuck up and stop bitching because a lot of people don't get to do what I do and not that many musicians get a response like we have been getting this early or at all. I have heard of some bands here that used to get booed. That must be weird in a place like this as it is so diminutive and constrictive.

The point being that I think we were moving too fast there and need to stop and look at what is around us and appreciate it because he was right: I know a lot of musicians who want to play in bands, or even who do, but don't have what we have in the way we are gelling as a band. I guess we don't really think about it because it honestly just fucking happens and there is no control. I guess we are lucky in that. Maybe B Hick was right and I should just shut the fuck up and go with it...

$1.00 4

The KROOKS
the hermans
LIVE ROCK AND ROLL
JAN 15TH PM
AREA 5
the hermans
at the PBR Party, the Other Side, Missoula
Jan 19
$6
the hermans
LIVE ROCK AND ROLL
THE OTHER SIDE
18+ $5
21+ $3
FREE w/ Griz Card
WITH THE TRILLIONAIRES AND SPECIAL GUEST
The Raven, Missoula
with the Victory Smokes
and two other bands
the hermans
8 pm
live rock and roll
ermans
WITH GUESTS
LIVE ROCK AND ROLL
esters
Helena
PM February 12th
the hermans
Ever Since The Accident
Joey Butta and The Fuctones
AREA 5
9 PM
CHUCK NORRIS
PRIVATE LESSON
How to Rock and Roll
Listen to:
the hermans
Masterful Martial Arts Demonstration
9:45 PM Sunday, March 5th @ the Raven
with Clair d'Alune, Team Owl, and Sharktopus
THREE LESSONS IN ONE!
CD Release Show
the hermans
Rocket Lobotomy
Chuck
Ribs
Short Loin
Sirloin
Round
Brisket
Plate
Flank
@ the Union Hall
(upstairs of Union Club)
E. Main St
9 PM
March 12
ALL AGES $4
THE ICICLES
(RAD FEMALE POWER POP)
THE HERMANS
ROCKGARAGEROCKPOPROCK)
MY PAL GHOSTY
(WILL KILL YOU)
WED. MARCH 23RD
AEREA 5 732 S. 1ST W.
the hermans
DAS GEHEIMNIS DER LAGUNE
SATURDAY APRIL 8
10 PM
THE RAVEN
the hermans
live rock & roll
free
free
thursday april 29
missoula ale house
hermans
live rock and roll
Old Post Pub
November 4th. 9pm.
the hermans
Monday, 8/22
9PM
Elk's Lodge
Higgins Alley upstairs
the hermans
benefit concert!
FREE!
THURSDAY DEC 8TH
Al's & Vic's
Celebrate The Season With:
the hermans
9:30pm
FREE!
the hermans
the hermans

There is somewhere else in town to play!!! That is two places now. Go Missoula! The Loft, or Higgins Alley, or The Loft Above Higgins Alley Downtown in Missoula on the Main Street that is called Higgins, or something to that tune, has shows and beer. And lights and a pain in the ass fire escape out back up which you have to bring your equipment. And they have bathrooms, too! We just had the proverbial fortune to play there with local band, the Turnoffs. Don't be alarmed by the name. They fuckin' mean it. We played with them last summer for a graduation party of sorts at Caras Park, and they refused to leave the stage. This angered me. They played for over an hour and it got late and then we got shut down after like four songs 'cause the cops or some lame-ass said "It is too late and it's past ten o'clock and you can't play rock music because babies are sleeping" or some shit. Bunch of horsecock, I say. I also say that we got to play another benefit for some fucking thing (I think it was put on by Outdoor Montana which is a magazine or something to promote the kayak wavepool thing or whatever the fuck it is out by Caras Park downtown in the middle of the Clark Fork River) at the Loft and that was pretty cool except when Dave jumped sideways in mid-song and fucked everything up. He landed on somewhat of a run-jump and divided the stage into sections like the Red fucking Sea and sent half of my drumset into the abyss. For now, the Loft only has a portable stage that is not fixed to the ground so when people jump wrong like Dave's dumb ass the fucker splits apart at the sections and, apparently, has the propensity toward sucking in my still-fairly-new drumset. Other than that, it was cool. Even though a bunch of old drunk people kept asking us to cover songs thirty years old that we didn't know because we are NOT A FUCKING COVER BAND! If you want to book us for a show or benefit or bar mitzfuh or what ever it is, know that we play original rock and roll and that is it. If you want a cover band, go scope out the bowling alleys. You will find several worthy adversaries. And a bunch of totally shitty bands, too. Stinky, shitty bands. Like us. Well, we are stinky, but at least we have the balls to play our own music. Goddamnit. Now I am angry, and I am going to go drink now. Probably rum. Mount Gay. And then maybe some beer. Pilsener Urquell. And whence I am drunk, I will probably dial five or six numbers until one brings me a pizza. This is because I am a total loser. I don't know how Nyree puts up with me. She must like our band, since she has likely been our biggest supporter since we started playing real shows. And she is going to marry me in June.

Hopefully.

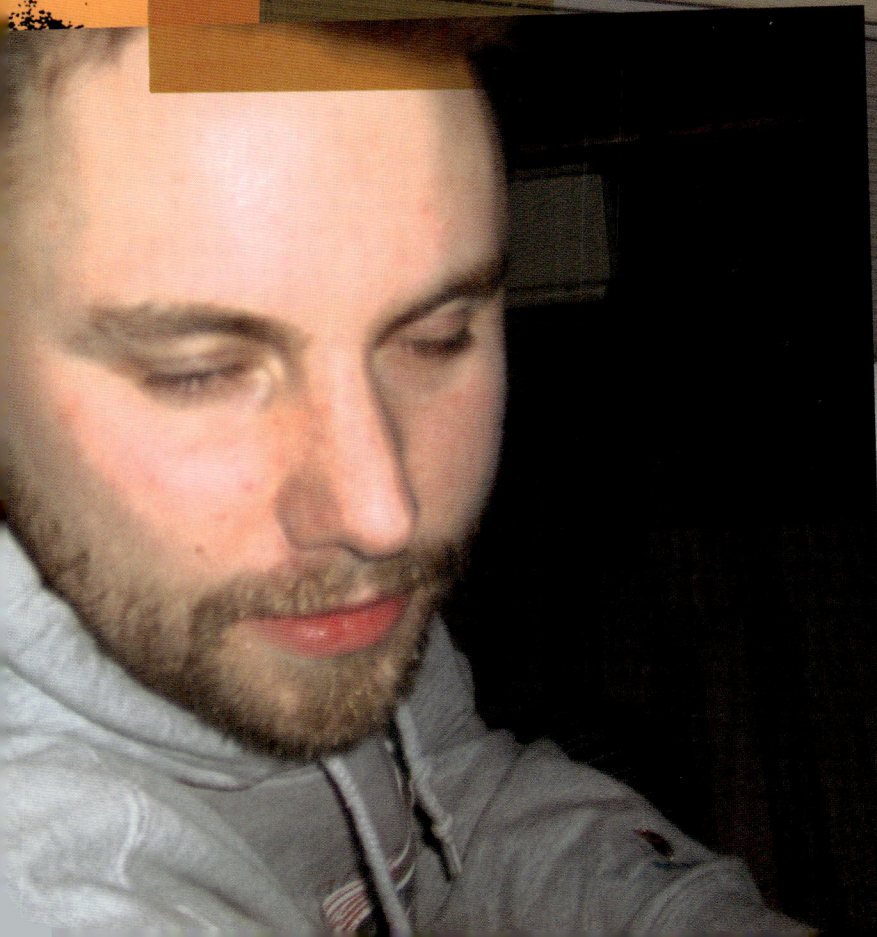

-----Original Message-----
From: dave@thehermans.net
To: Jones, Greg
Subject: you are kafka's muse

Greggor,
You maggoty mass alone in your room.

We played a show at the Raven last night with a band called Racetrack. It is a cool name. They are from Bellingham, Washington which I hear is a good rock and roll town. We wish to play there so give us some fucking money so we can go on tour, you damned Gypsy. We also played with a band called Speaker Speaker! who are also from the Seattle area, I believe, and were fucking awesome. It was a good combo. Racetrack had a sound as if they were from, uh, the Seattle area but that shit (three power chords-muted/ratt pedal/Telecaster) will be good forever. The guitar player/singer was a girl of about five feet two inches and I was hoping Chris would get wit' her because it would be like a hobbit wedding.
So, the bands keep rolling in to this Raven of ours and we are getting consistently better shows from Mike Gill of the Victory Smokes who I told you about. We are also very excited, proud, delighted, hungry and fucking overjoyed to tell you we are having our first album CD release party (at said Raven) in late April. Those are usually followed with a tour so discussions are definitely in the works.
We were asked to play Missoula's annual Brewfest at Caras Park in May a few weeks after the CD release party but there is too much alcohol and people that like to rock out at those events so we will probably not accept it, heh, heh. We were invited to play the Old Post in between but that may be a little much. Someone asked us to play at a frat party but we told them to go fuck themselves because you can't drink at the ones here in Missoula. We need to get this band the fuck out of here and play a city…one with buildings you could actually die falling from unlike our peanut shells. Anyway, it seems that there are highs and lows but right now, with all this new shit, we seem to be moving in a good direction…like a sideways Beck dance slide.

Davey

TRANSCRIPT OF VOICEMAIL
from Dave to Greg

March 19th, 2006

"Dude, call me immediately. I don't know what the hell is going on. I
think Derk cut off his hand. FUCK!! WHY NOW!?! THIS SUCKS!! Call me! I'm
heading to the hospital..."

```
MR#:M000456154        Acct#:M0000891912
SCHMIDT,DERK K                         PRE SDC
01/07/1980   26   M  Adm:
ATT/ER: Peterson MD,Steven L
ADMIT:
```

-----Original Message-----
From: dave@thehermans.net
To: Jones, Greg
Subject:

Yo,

This is really bad. Really fucking bad. Just got back from the hospital and you are probably out, so here you go:

Derk was working in the basement today and got his hand caught in his table saw. It ripped the tip off the index finger and went through the other three in an angular motion to the bottom of the pinkie (I think) and I am pretty sure it is bad. Well, I know it is bad he went to fucking surgery right away. I stopped home after getting Sophie from school and we were on our way to the playground but saw Rachel called so when I called her back she told me where she was and what happened. He called everyone and finally got a hold of her so she drove him there. She said it wasn't too bad but when I got there I saw the look on Nyree's face and I new right away it wasn't just a couple of stitches. Then the nurse came out and told us. Kind of harrowing to say the utter fucking slightest about my best friend and a hell of a musician.

Where the hell were you today? Anyway, I won't be at home, Joe from Scotty's Table went to St. Pat's then just came over to watch Sophie so I can go be at the hospital for a while.

I am going back to the hospital right now so I'll call you tomorrow or later tonight.
Dave

p.s. you are probably wondering how she drove him to the hospital: she has been sober for three days now. Whoopeee! Tell ma and pa what is going on and keep him in your thoughts.

I cannot believe the inauspicious turn my life has taken. It is as though I just went on the Price is Right and got spayed and neutered by Bob Barker. Thanks a lot, you son of a bitch. What is it with really old men with bright orange, leathery tans? It makes them look older. And like jerks. I digress. My well-being is not good right now. I am tired of taking drugs, which I would usually enjoy, except these are for pain, not pleasure. When my pain-killers start to wear off, I start shaking and freak out like an ape with a permanent electric shock entering his ass. Bill, Chris and Dave have taken turns coming over to my house a lot to help me cope, and Nyree has been amazing, though she probably hasn't slept much in two weeks since I usually wake up screaming in pain four or five times a night. Plus, I am still looking forward to another surgery to possibly save the end of my index finger, or amputate it. At least I won't know the result until after I wake up. What fun! Yes, in case you were wondering, I did request to be put under for this second operation, as I was in the first. Fortunately, this time I will be able to not eat or drink for 12 hours before-hand so they don't have to choke me when I go to sleep. You see, last time, hours after my loss to the table saw (heartless cocksucker), I had eaten right before I made my fingers look like shredded wheat covered in tomato sauce. Therefore, the doctors told me I had to wait until like 11:00 pm (this was at 5:30, the accident at 2:30) before they could administer anesthesiology. My on-call surgeon, Dr. P. (god bless his heart) said that if we waited that long, I could lose one, maybe two fingers and increase the loss and/or recovery potential dramatically. So they offered me a second option, and I believe it went something like this:

"Yeah, Derk, here's the thing: Right before you go "under" we will have two of us with our hands like this (he wraps his hands around my neck in B-movie stranglehold fashion) and we will be choking you to close your esophagus as to not allow any food or fluid to enter your lungs when you go to sleep."

"What happens if something does go in my lungs?" I said.

"Oh, well, then you will die instantly."

Well, kids, I am happy to say that thanks to sister Morphine and Brother whatever the hell they had me on at the time, I agreed and signed a waiver stating that the hospital staff and so on would not be liable if I died during the procedure. Very persuasive stuff, I tell you. Obviously it worked, since I am writing this right now, but my fiancé, the trooper that she is, was pretty goddamned scared, and I think I probably was too. The only two reasons I agreed were the drugs and the idea of keeping my fingers so I could continue to play rock and roll music with my fellow hermans. I often second guess if they are worth it, but personally, my talent is unsurpassed and it simply wouldn't be fair to the rest of the world to deprive it of me and my mad skills. See what drugs can do to you!!! I am such a dick! Look at me go! What ever. I am tired of all of this and want my hand back. Yes, drugs also make you a whiny bitch. Like me. Waaaaaaaahhhhh. Fuck this. I wish I could be excited about the potential that I could still play the drums nearly the same as before, but two things bother me about this notion. The first is that I haven't even seen my hand out of this cast yet, and thus, do not even know how bad it really is. The second is that I am not really a drummer. I have played piano and guitar since I was five years old. I used to be pretty good, my mother tells me. Now I may be confined to just the drums, which blows. Good thing I switched instruments when I started jamming with Dave! Thanks, Dave! You are my hero. Actually, you are a shitball. Oh well. Poor me. Yeah, yeah, yeah, I should just be happy I will hopefully still be able to play in my favorite band I have ever been in, even if it is on the drums. Well, the good news is that my mom says I am pretty good on those, too, so there. I need better drugs.

1. —10"

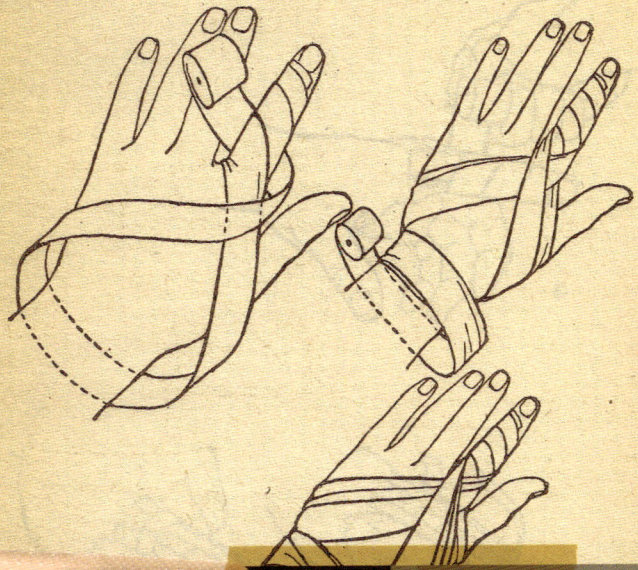

ZOO REVIEW

NOTES FROM MISSOULA CULTURE

Bizarre table-saw accident

What is it about drummers that makes them such tragedy hounds? Whether they're getting offed in fictional bizarre gardening accidents, or real bizarre gardening accidents (Toto's Jeff Porcaro), or losing their arms in car accidents (Def Leppard's Rick Allen) or having all their gear stolen from the back of a 1973 rusted-out Datsun, these poor mutts are always taking one for the team. Enter **Derk Schmidt** of the local band **The Hermans,** who sliced up his hand on a table saw a few days ago, a pretty serious injury that required surgery. Derk's out of commission for a while, but meanwhile the band hobbles on. Their gig at the Old Post on Friday is still a go, though it'll obviously be a more acoustic-sounding set, featuring jazz and supplemented by members of the Victory Smokes. The band is also making the evening an open-mic night. No cover charge, but the (remaining) Hermans are passing around the tip jar for Derk and his injured paw. Give a little, will ya?

He can still hold a beer. But Derk Schmidt, far right, of The Hermans, is out of commission on the drums for now.

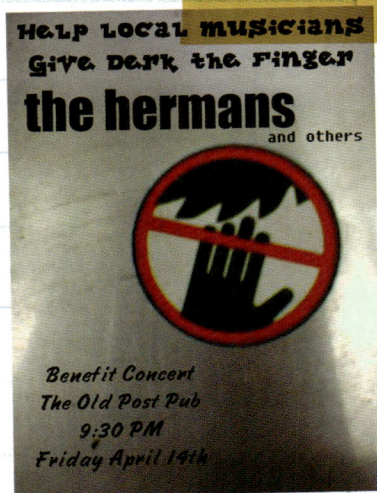

Help Local Musicians Give Derk the Finger

the hermans and others

Benefit Concert
The Old Post Pub
9:30 PM
Friday April 14th

Jazz and eggs

The Blue Canyon Kitchen & Tavern, which is adjacent to the new Hilton Garden Inn on North Reserve, is opening up its breakfast Sundays with live jazz starting at 10 a.m.

Debuting on Easter Sunday will be a group consisting of saxophonist Chuck Florence, bassist Beth Lo and guitarist David Horgan.

The restaurant plans to host live jazz every Sunday.

– *Jamie Kelly*

So Derky Poo cut his fucking hand off and it would look like we have to cancel our CD release party, the Brewfest, and an Old Post show. Derk's hand is nothing compared to what that Janine girl, the tattooed booking agent, will do to me whence I tell her we are canceling a show at the Post this Friday. She's gonna take Chris's and Bill's and I's heads and clunk them together like Moe!

But guess fucking what, we are not canceling the CD release party, we are moving it back. We are not canceling the Brewfest, we are just going to get Derk a Darth Vader hand. We are not canceling the Old Post, we are using it as a benefit for Derk because he has no health insurance. Our President is no Canadian and is, in turn, a giant Ram Rod.

The accident was a day ago and we have it set up already. Pat Gill (Victory Smokes drummer) is replacing Derk on the drums, and the hermans plus Pat will hopefully be able to get through four or five songs. He is a tenacious little monkey on the drums but better not do that disco shit to our rock sound or I'll force him to eat glue.

I know what you are thinking, you are thinking to yourself "self, why is he so jokey right now, his drummer just lost his entire arm." Don't be so naïve. Fact is, we jumped right on the motherfucker and are sending in the Wolf: the hermans in disguise. We do not quiver, we fucking rally to help a friend in need. And what is cooler: a bake sale or a fucking rock show?! We will be doing both, of course, but the rock show comes first.

The Old Post is so cool for letting us do this. They could have, should have, cancelled as the Victory Smokes have never played there (they are playing after the hermans with Patrick) nor have they sent a demo, which is required when playing new venues. Lo, Janine did no head clunking, nor did she poke us in the eyes. She said there would be no way she would stop us from doing this for our fallen comrade.

Derk said he would try to play in his powder blue, gay cast (he asked for that color; nothing wrong with that) but as he is jacked on Morphine, Sudafed, Lithium, Vicatin, Tap Water, Soup, Crank, Xanex, Viagra and Hybernol, he spiked himself trying to get down the steps…like an asshole. He is all fucked up anyways. The last time I saw him he was shaking uncontrollably so I took the wolfman mask off and reassured him it was me. He then told me, although the mask was scary, the shaking was from the pills.

Obviously, Derk can't go to the benefit because he rented wolfman movies and is stuck to the couch all week - doctor's orders. So Nyree is allowing us to use her digital video camera to film three idiots and a Victory Smoke hacking away at five songs Derk worked so hard at so they wouldn't sound like shit. Pat is pretty damned good, though, and has really good hair.

I took a break this morning to go to Butterfly herbs coffee shop, because the coffee at my work tastes like it came out of a rhino's penis, and I could not believe what I heard. There it was like a snot out of a farmers nose: Pope On Strike coming out of my speakers and into my unbelieving ears....AND I don't have a CD player in my car yet so I'm talking radio here, mother fucker! F mother fucking M. And not the college radio station KBGA but right on the Trail 103.3, a corporately owned radio station who caters to the likes of John Mayer, Jack Johnson, Ben Harper and any other artist who might have some spunk if they'd just smash their acoustic and pick up a fucking Fender.

We dropped off a CD a few weeks ago but I didn't think I would hear the hermans on regular or corporate radio...ever. We are too hard, too rock and roll, and not commercial-pop enough. These things, plus we are not a signed band.

Anyway, it was pretty cool. I found out it was for the Brewfest, some kind of advertisement, but they still used our band. There are a few bands playing, by the way, but I don't know who they are yet. Because they weren't on the radio heh, heh.

God bless Missoula and please hold off on the rain until we are done...unless the first band decides to do a cover of Journey's "Anyway You Want It" then bring rain, lightning, thunder, tidal waves, no, we'll cover that one, and the fucking plague.

Dave

05/03/06

To everyone who reads this,

First of all, the Def Leppard jokes have to fucking stop. You need to be more creative with the time you have doing whatever mindless things you do to come up with something that will make Derk laugh and not wince. He does enough of that when I pour sugar on his left hand. Uuugh. Anyway, thanks for the support and the thoughts and the whatever. You can stop the praying, though, as Derk is convinced that god hates us and only did this to see what we would come up with next. What is it that Mel Gibson says in Lethal Weapon? When god hates you, hate 'em back? Well, that would be rude and we already wrote a song about the Pope. So, I suppose we can use this time to be creative, write new material, change direction, hone our talents and create a buzz about the comeback. Or we will just drink and enjoy the sun and when we do play our first show we will set the damned room on fire and smash an old table saw to pieces in front of the crowd. Whatever we do, you probably won't want to miss it. On that note, we will indeed be playing our final show, for now. Missoula's Annual Brew Fest is this Saturday the 6th of May. We are playing for two hours from 3 to 5:00 in the afternoon. Rick Parnell (a.k.a. Mick Shrimpton from Spinal Tap) will be sitting in on the drums for a spell. Don?t ask, just buy the fucking book next year. Derk is going at this head strong and steadfast with one goddamned arm. You don't want to miss this!

Well, folks, that is all for now. Oh, yeah, we aren't playing at Total Fest this year because...uh...here is the one time where I bite my tongue...as I know some of the "bands" who are playing this "rock music" festival thing. I guess I will write back after this show and after that we will be silenced for a while.

Goodnight and good luck,

David E. Jones

FIG. 1 115

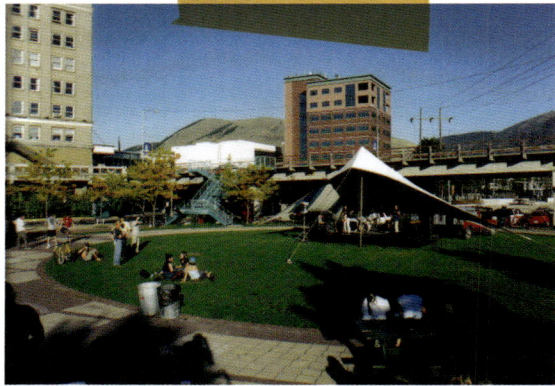

Ok, so I have to play Brewfest tomorrow with one hand because Dave told them we would because, apparently, I told Dave to tell them that I said I could but I was all fucked up then and I thought I could but now I know that it probably will suck because I do and so does everything right now. Hopefully Caras Park will look like this tomorrow, because this could get embarrassing….

I know what you are thinking. You are thinking "this punk mentions the guy from Spinal Tap playing with his band at a huge venue and does not dwell on it whatsoever." Well, now I shall dwell.

We all know by now what happened to Derk. Yeah, the moron was thinking about porn and chopped his bits off and everyone is sad. He is not a lizard and that sucks for him and us and Nyree. Unless, of course, she is into that weird necrophilia shit. I digress. Anyway, a few weeks ago, the week the accident happened, an older guy from the opening band called to berate me for cancelling the Brewfest. I suppose this chap was told by the Missoula Downtown Association, who put the whole thing on, about our withdrawing. His one-way conversation commenced with a story about Viet Nam (I guess the fact that this man is a veteran is vital to us playing the Brewfest) and how many local bands he has played with since the fall of pinko tyranny in southern Asia. He refused to believe a table saw accident was getting in our way of playing the festival and I told him we would not play without our drummer. What the fuck does anything have to do with Viet Nam, Walter?

Consequently, the name dropping began (how many drummers he knows, who he has played with, how illustrious these socialites are, etc.) so I told him I was the crown prince of Dork and do not know or care about virtually anyone but Dr. Who, hoping to throw him off. Impossible. The list of names swelled like the dial on my how-pissed-off-I-can-get gauge. I was almost in the red (as he kept telling me that any of these mysterious drummers could "easily sit in with the hermans"…fuck you) when he mentioned R.J. Parnell. That rang a tower bell in my head. "You mean the guy from Spinal Tap?" Oh yeah. I threw my current viewpoint in the toilet and accepted the offer without even asking Derk…Derk owns three copies of that movie. I put my hand over the phone and told Derk about Mick Shrimpton possibly playing and he said "hang up on that mother fucker, I'll play one armed."

We had about four days to get a hold of Parnell, set up a practice, teach him four or five songs and possibly learn a Tap song and play Brewfest. Did we do it? Keep reading.

.... Didn't I tell you the hermans will never be fucking stopped?

welcome to the Brew fest!

I came home from work a little late Thursday and there was an old guy with long grey hair, glasses, a tie-dye shirt and a plastic bag full of tall boys on my back porch smoking and coughing as he obviously had a bad cold. He apologized a few times (I didn't know what for as he didn't say) then asked me if he was at the right place. I said I didn't know because I am not his attorney and asked him if he was Rick Parnell. In his fabulous British accent he said "Oh, yeah, man, are you Dave from the hermans." I said "Oh, yeah, man, I'm Dave already." Then we had a beer, talked about

music for about fifteen minutes then Derk showed up and the conversation continued. Spinal Tap did not come up right away as I am sure it does in every conversation this poor guy has with new people. In fact, we let him bring it up which he did after a while and it was lovely...you know...because he was in fucking This Is Spinal Tap!

Bill and Chris got there after about a half an hour and Rick wanted to watch us jam with our one handed drummer before he sat down, just to get an idea of what we sound like. I must be honest, I did not think this was going to work. As I had been to Brewfest before and know what kind of crowd we were going to be dealing with, I was nervous for the first time in a long time. We are talking two-to-three thousand on and off throughout the day, with roughly half of which paying attention to the music at any given time. I was not nervous about the people because none of them were asked to play by the Missoula Downtown Association nor were they asked to play with a guy from one of the best films ever made. No, I was nervous because we had one fucking practice with this guy (who, by the way, was drinking faster than we were and we already knew the goddamned songs) and he is not the average Missoula punk-drummer who has seen and heard us several times before.

To make a long, long fucking story not as long, this limey bastard nailed every song after two or three runs, was totally ecstatic about it, forced us to go upstairs and watch Spinal Tap with him, and then decided (remember, we were all drinking a lot by this point) that it was mandatory to cover a Tap song - this was his fucking idea! So, we decided on "Bitch School" after much arguing, inhalation, and giggling. Then we went downstairs and nailed it...and kept drinking.

The practice lasted about five hours, mostly because we watched half of the movie with Rick....did I say he was from Spinal Tap yet?... and also had a twenty minute jam session on one of Bill's new songs which is fucking sweet, may I add. Rick turned out to be a pretty cool guy which is pretty much what I'd imagined. He also likes to get his drink on. Which is also what I imagined. Damned soggy English.

Anyway, the show was insane. Rick was impeccable as he is a super tight and talented drummer, and Derk flew off the handle playing one-handed as there is a big white mitten on his other hand cause he chopped it off. But you know that story already.

I have to say that when there is a gargantuan audience fueled with ever-flowing kegs of stiff, stiff ale in front of you, your drummer was slain by a wood saw, you have a guitar player who melts face, and your bass player is an oak tree, the only thing you can do is put your head down and fucking rock. So that is what I did. It was one of the craziest afternoons I have seen. I can't wait till Derk gets better so we can do it again.

RICK PARNELL AKA MICK SHRIMPTON OF SPINAL TAP ⟶

WE GOT STARTED BEFORE THE CROWD DID.... THE HERMANS AT 3 PM

MICK SHRIMPTON ROCKS

THE HERMANS + CROWD ..... 3:15 PM

123

At least one good thing came out of this injury: the hermans finally got some press. Yeah, it was totally worth it. My left hand is a useless piece of shit, I am flat broke, I have no insurance and will probably owe a million dollars for this shit, I am moving in two weeks and getting married in four. But we got an article in the Indy! If you could see me right now you would see me at my desk jumping joyously like a fairy or minstrel! Hopefully next time we get press it will be because our band is totally fucking awesome and we are bringing rock and roll back from the dead. For now, I guess I will take it. Brewfest was great, but I do not wish to play one-handed ever again because it totally sucks and is hard and sucks really bad. Now we are supposed to release our debut record two days before my wedding, so our CD release party has turned into my official bachelor party. Cool. I hate strippers. I would much rather play a rock show in front of my family and friends (my parents are seeing me play in a band for the first time) than go get drunk at a strip club. This will likely be the best bachelor party ever. At least for a musician. Other people would think this bachelor party needs strippers and hookers and all kinds of other lame shit that meatheads think is important. For me, I care only about my family, my band, my friends, and the fact that I should be able to play two-handed at this show. Thank heavens, as a man once said. This man was probably drunk. And, since this is a CD release show, the glorious Independent has promised us an album review. They will probably say we sound like the Meat Puppets but with no talent and an inferior name. Either that or they will be honest and explain that it is the greatest rock and roll album in history since "Sticky Fingers" by the Rolling Stones. Either way, maybe some people will show up and buy an album or two. And if there are strippers, hopefully the crowd tips them well enough to buy the album to play behind them next time they take their clothes off for money in front of lonely truck drivers. Again, I digress. At least our mothers will see our picture in the paper. And it doesn't involve handcuffs or police officers. Not yet, anyway. Check me out, ma! I'm famous! Kind of! Whoopee!!!

June 08, 2006 - Missoula Independent

the hermans
stalking matilda
i like you, betty records

the hermans

The next time you take the '88 Cutlass Sierra down to the gravel bar for a bonfire party, take along the hermans' stalking matilda, an album heavy on power chords and frenetic drum fills that's best listened to loud, not to mention drunk. It's just the thing to drain a keg to.

The album's first song, "desert island," introduces the band's compulsively confrontational persona by ripping through a list of items offensive to the singer's sensibilities, including some paired opposites. That song, mixed with the whimsy of "pope on strike," which imagines a pre-pontifical pope "thinking 'bout pew-bound women," proves good times and gut-rock riffs can carry an album.

Forays into more earnest fare, however, like the anti-trustafarian tirade "college rock," turn the sound sour. Lines like "you're all the same and I won't play your game" threaten to bum out listeners whose attitude is going to have a lot to do with how much they enjoy an album that's raw enough to irritate if picked at persnickitously.

Those inclined to crack the case without attitude, however, can expect to enjoy the aural equivalent of a cold canned beer—a swig of something to slake the thirst of the unpretentious. (Jason Wiener)

the hermans play The Raven Cafe Wednesday, June 14, at 9:30 PM. $5.

Return to top.

SOUNDCHECK

A leg up
Shorthanded hermans release debut CD
by Skylar Browning

In a birth typical of so many aspiring rock bands, the hermans began life as a couple dudes jamming together in a basement. Since that beginning, however, the local prog-rock outfit has experienced a string of luck—good and bad—that qualifies as anything but typical: releasing of a debut album, inking a national book deal and having their drummer suffer a career-threatening table-saw accident that's left the quartet's immediate future in question.

"This band is full of peaks and valleys," says lead guitarist Chris Entz, "and right now, it's about as deep a valley as you can imagine. But, again, I think we're coming out of it."

The hermans (the lower case being the band's preference) started in August 2003 when novice guitar player Dave Jones, a native of Philadelphia, and pianist Derk Schmidt, a Michigan native who happens to be a huge Philadelphia Eagles fan, became fast friends playing Neil Young covers in Schmidt's Missoula basement. The sessions were spirited, but as Schmidt says, "It was a guitar and a piano—I mean, what are you gonna do with that? We sucked as rockers." So Schmidt picked up the drums and he and Jones recruited Bill Pfeiffer, another Pennsylvania transplant, to play bass. The three started writing together and playing 15-minute open-mic sets at the Ritz to practice, but it wasn't until a year later, when the band added Entz, formerly of the power trio Hot Action and yet another Keystone State ex-pat, that the hermans were complete.

"Our songs went from being a little improvisational and jam-based and, basically, boring the shit out of everyone—when the bass player's doing your solos, that's bad—to the sound it was supposed to be when Chris joined," says Pheiffer. "Chris is a real lead guitar player; he was the missing piece."

But even after Entz signed on, the band needed additional seasoning. Schmidt and Pfeiffer were both playing new and unfamiliar instruments and Jones had never been in a band before. In fact, Jones, now the hermans' lead singer, had never played guitar for anyone outside his bedroom before launching the band. He remembers screaming so hard during one live performance of the band's "San Francisco" at the Elk's Lodge that he passed out mid-song. Until just recently, he required help tuning his guitar on stage.

"Chris introduced me to the concept of harmonics when I thought that was just something Victor Wooten did," says Jones.

The basement sessions, open-mic shows and onstage test-runs finally paid off last year when Jones' brother Greg, an editor with Philadelphia's Running Press (now owned by Perseus Books), thought of the hermans during a proposal meeting. The discussion centered on "reality books" about average people struggling to make it in competitive fields, and Greg mentioned his brother's basement band in the middle of nowhere Montana.

"It was a pretty cool thing to have offered," says Schmidt, "but we didn't really get it. I mean, who would care about a year in the life of us? We wrote a letter back to Greg saying we think your whole company is full of shit…We slammed the company, we slammed the idea, we slammed us, and they still jumped on it."

The modest book deal included enough of an advance to pay for the hermans' debut CD, *Stalking Matilda*, which was completed earlier this month. The 13-track effort, full of original songs written by Jones, Entz and Schmidt, was supposed to be followed by a local CD-release party and the band's first tour this summer and completion of the book's manuscript by September, but the hermans literally hit a snag.

"Bob Villa here had to go chop his hand off," Jones says, joking about an otherwise serious situation. "We're waiting now to see what happens with Tool Time."

Schmidt's left hand is still discolored from his recent bout with a table saw—his pinkie gnarled and his index finger wrapped in thick gauze. Working at home on his woodworking business two days before the CD's release, Schmidt had a thin piece of wood stick in the saw and flip his hand into the blade. His index finger was almost completely severed and, following surgery to reattach nerves and insert a pin to align the digit, his surgeon remains optimistic that amputation will not be necessary.

"I remember asking him, am I going to play guitar again? Play piano again? Play drums again?" remembers Schmidt, who has no health insurance. "He said no to the guitar and piano, but I had a chance with the drums…That's all I needed to hear. As soon as I can hold a stick with this hand, we're playing."

Schmidt is already pressing forward. He played one-handed during the band's pre-scheduled gig at Brew Fest last week and he's insistent the band continue scheduling its summer tour. "We're coming back full force," he says defiantly, and his bandmates have every reason to believe him.

"It was really scary when it happened," says Pfeiffer. "We had no idea about the band, but even more we were just worried about Derk. Then, a few weeks later, I got this call from Chris, and I figured we were going to be all right."

The call? Despite his injury, Schmidt was wrapped up in a basement jam session with Jones; he was calling to invite his bandmates to join in. 🔥

The hermans' debut CD, *Stalking Matilda*, is available now at Ear Candy Music. The band's CD-release party is tentatively re-scheduled for June 14 pending doctor approval.

arts@missoulanews.com

25c

I would personally like to thank two people in reference to my totally awesome bachelor party and CD release blowout. The first is my phenomenal guitar player, Chris Entz, for being so incredibly talented and remarkable to learn the lead to "Thunderstruck" by AC/DC. We had this song down for our encore and it was going to be sweet. The second is International Playboys' bassist, Chris Knudsen for playing with his band, Daphne Starburst, to open the show, and then later for being way too incredibly wasted to come even remotely close to singing "Thunderstruck" on stage with us. I think I died, along with the crowd, after the third "thunder" that was not anywhere near to being on cue. Chris played the intro for what seemed to be a half an hour before Dave jumped in and sang the song. It was the closest thing we had to salvation. Thanks, chaps, for making it a memorable night.

--derk

Ah the lovely Missoula Independent; such sweet, sweet vernacular rock and roll testament for a blatantly kick ass fucking album. Captain Calendar done good! I also love the wording, especially "persnicketously," which, according to Webster, is not a word. Then again, the Indy does a lot of hard work for a lot of bands who don't do hard work so they can say whatever the fuck they want. The guy (Jason Weiner) is also an English teacher so rock on, bro.

It was cool to read an outside perspective from someone who is not a musician but is nevertheless a lover of good music. I have heard that most singers or songwriters don't like to read reviews, probably because they are so used to smoke of grandeur enveloping their asses in a cloud of bullshit, but I see things a little differently…mostly because Stalking Matilda is my first goddamned album. This reviewer is evidently the Mako shark of album critics around here which led me to believe he was going to take it in like a cheap stake and then spit it out before sending it back and slapping the cook: ME. He took it for what its aesthetical value is (to me, anyway): a hard rocking album that is consistent and tight and very good to drink to. True, we are not AC/DC, but when was the last time you heard Brian Johnson sing about the Pope or Pirates or George W. Assclown?

Anyway, there are flaws on it and there are frequent pieces that make me cringe but with songs you wrote, play and know better than anyone, you are the only person who hears those stains that make you cringe and I usually do so with a smile. So, in summation, I haven't been more proud of anything I have been a part of since witnessing Sophie come to grace this planet. I just hope people find our songs, style, rigidity and energy as cool and cute as they find her because our music is just as real…but not as beautiful.

--dave

To my wife, my band, my family and my dearest friends:

Most men spend their bachelor party entertaining strippers, occupying bars and tittie joints, and usually finding that after the drunken loser-fest is over, the night is remembered as somewhat disappointing and quite lame. I took another approach. I could not imagine a better way to spend my bachelor party than with my band, family and friends. Fuck strip clubs; we played a show. This was significant in many ways for me, and I want to thank you all for making it a wonderfully memorable night. Not only did the hermans melt faces at the Raven Café, but I was able to play for my best friend, my closest family and friends, and most of all, my parents. I have been playing music in bands for over ten years, and finally, two days after my final surgery, my parents were able to see me play for the first time. Additionally, it was great that the girls hosting Nyree's bachelorette party brought her down for the show as well. Unfortunately, my sister got stuck in Salt Lake City overnight and missed the show, but thankfully Mike Gill and the Victory Smoke boys added us on to a show at the Elks the day after my wedding with the Peelers, and my sister will finally be able to see the hermans for the first time as well. In addition to this wonderfulness, I went against my better judgment, not by getting rather sauced, but by playing the drums for the first time with both hands since I mangled my fingers in April. I hurt like hell at first, but the pain wore off with the adrenaline and energy coming from the crowd. The only hindrance was the band-aids on my fingers. They kept sliding off and exposing the fresh stitches on my index and middle fingers of my left hand. That sucked goatballs. But I played and somehow I think I got even better since the last time, over two months ago. This may have been the booze, however, but I felt, pain aside, about as good during that show as I think I have ever felt in my life. The hermans are back, bitches!!!

Love,

Derk herman.

SOPHIE..... DAVE'S LITTLE ROCK AND ROLL ANGEL

Nothing is better than marrying the one you love than to have the rest of the people you love around you. This went down as the best "rock and roll wedding" Missoula has ever seen, according to all who attended, or at least what they remembered from it. The party went all night and everyone was jolly. And drunk (thanks, Dad, for taking care of that tab). Thanks to my beautiful wife, Nyree, her dad, Bruce Walters (for giving her to me, and the financing, of course) to her family: Nate, our band photographer and wedding photo man, Chris for the speech (Nate gave one too, it was awesome) her sister Stephanie for being the maid of honor, and traveling with her family from Boston, Bev, Nyree's mom, and Nick, her brother and Grand Exit Coordinator (the man in charge of the cool sparklers) Nyree's hot bridesmaids for making my groomsmen, especially the band, look better as they walked down the aisle, the other three hermans (not so beautiful), my best man, Rick Grillo, who came all the way from my homeland of Michigan to kick everyone's ass with his speech, to Joseph Gary, who made the wedding actually happen, I think, Justin Lawrence and "Hell House" for doing the sound, Kevin Pierce for being M.C., my awesome parents for everything, which was a lot, and my family(especially Krista who came from New York) and friends, to "Father Tom" and the minister's wife, Connie, and to all who attended. Getting married is fun. What a fucking hoot!

6/25/06

So here I am, a lonely herman.

No lady, no band, no money, no clean socks, no beer, no smoke, no upcoming shows, and nothing but the blues. My drummer's on vacation in Michigan (where any logical newlywed would go for a honeymoon), the other hermans started a side project called Sisyphus and the Big Rock which I believe has something to do with Moses, the Catskills and Silly Puddy, and I am alone in my apartment with only an orange guitar and a slight hangover. What a great time to write a new song.

Mike and Pat Gill and Amadeus Markley want me to write a song about getting laid, rocking out and drinking beer (specifically after a hermans show) and, as easy as that sounds, I am just not feeling it…even though two of those things happened two nights ago. But, she left like piss in the wind and took my beer.

So, maybe I'll inscribe a tune about that insignificant sloth that I used to romp with, R. I could use that clever idea derived by Carly Simon where it kind of is about someone who is utterly vain but the song really isn't about them even though it is…kind of like a paradox within itself. Mine will be called "You're So Drunk…you probably think this song is about Whisky."

Fuck her, she really doesn't deserve it. Besides, how many rock songs have been about ex girlfriends…on that note, how many of the first hermans songs were written about ex girlfriends!?

Burt Reynolds is cool. Perhaps it'll be about Burt Reynolds. Or Sam Elliot. They both had really cool moustaches and I don't recall any rock songs about moustaches.

Actors are really fucked up as they seem to thrive on duality. The man behind the moustache. There is a notion.

Well, we have no shows booked but it looks as though the Playboys will reunite in September and tour to back the release of their new album. I will poke around, as we await the return of our lopsided drummer, and see if we can't make it a double come-back show as the Playboys drummer has been in one of the Carolinas with his lady friend for the last six months. Derk should be playing with two hands by then, and who knows what will happen in the mind set of this band in the meantime. Chris and Bill and I are very impatient and need the rock so perhaps some ballads will ensue.

Missoula is such an exquisite place this time of year and if we are not playing music the doom of a long, drawn out summer looms ahead. I am not complaining, however, as Missoula is second to only nothing throughout this season. Derk and Nyree will have fun being married and healing his flipper. Chris and Bill will catch a lot of fish and lie about it. I will go on the hunt and be merry. Cheers.

Missoula is such an exquisite place this time of year

08/30/06

Listen up, hermanites: This is your bovine balladeer checking in once again, this time typing with a mere nine digits since my left index finger is being a total whore and not registering any nerve stimulation whatsoever. It's kind of like having a cold piece of steak for an index finger with the consistency of a miniature punching bag. Anywho, listen: THE HERMANS ARE BACK, BITCHES. Yes, indeedy, that crazy, cuddly lovable band is back and we are ready to rock your miniscule world with rock and/or roll music. Chris is ready to melt your face. Dave is ready, again, to scream like a careless idiot with nothing to lose. Bill is prepared to lay down a solid groove. And I, your fearless balladeer, am ready to play the fuck out of my aptly-named drum set, Arnold Palmer. You see, long before I cut my hand to smithereens, I played a MAXX piece-of-shit kit called Lemonade. Then it broke a lot and I had to acquire my beautiful Yamaha fully-functional rock demon which I originally titled Iced Tea. However, when I sold Lemonade to my friend Danny Bobbe, I kept the massive floor tom and added it to my faded black rock monster, Iced Tea. Considering the combination I had created in mine own image, a new mischievous sprite was born: Arnold Palmer. (Since we all know, boys and girls, that Arnold Palmer instantly shows up every time you mix Iced Tea and Lemonade. He is somewhat of a busybody) So there you have it. Arnie and I are recovered (enough) to once again conspire to bring you the Rock of Ages. In this glorious rebirth, the hermans have set out to play more shows, new songs, and bring joy and pure rock to your disenfranchised lives. Here is what is going on soon: This Friday, September the 1st, 2006, we have been invited to rock by our favorite KBGA disk jockey, The Mermaid, aka, Adelaide. Her superb artwork (including a rather precarious cloud made of garbage) will be on display at the Crazy Daisy, downtown Missoula, kicking off another First Friday art walk. Ryan Bundy and Purrbot will play for your listening pleasure starting around 6:00 in the p.m. Then the hermans will lay down some jazz for you later before we totally rock out. It is a scene not to be missed. Next, save the date for September the 9th, as Victory Smokes and the hermans join The International Playboys at the Raven Cafe, downtown Missoula. Yes, Joe, the Playboys' infamous drummer has returned and the Playboys will be launching their comeback show / CD release party / tour kickoff show. It is sure to be the best show you have ever seen, minus that time you saw Journey and fell in love for the first time during "Don't Stop Believing." Victory Smokes are sure to be great. the hermans are considering this show our own "comeback show" since it is the first real show for us since my bachelor party last June. We?ve prepared some songs that will make your colon swallow your face, including a hot new tune and possibly a Playboys cover in which we will show them how to play their own song. This show is an absolute skip-your-sister's-wedding-and-your-mom's-funeral-to-come-to-this-show type of event. Then, on September the 22nd, the hermans will once again be flying solo at the Old Post Pub, downtown Missoula, for three hours of mind-bending, face-melting madness. Although I won't be able to play "Punk Rock Girl" for you (since my guitar-playing days are on indefinite hiatus) I think I will bring the piano this time and see if we can't play that again, though I haven't tried since the accident. So look out! the hermans are fucking back, and we are ready to face-melt full force.

For those of you who read the last entry I made, yes, the Christians are still on my ass. However, it doesn't look like I will be able to join any churches any time soon. As you know, to join a Christian church, you have to tithe. Well, sorry, bitches, but my medical bills rounded out to around $16,000 cash money and I see no way I will be able to tithe to anything but my grandiose medical loan. But you Christians can help! Send me money. That would be great. In addition, come support the hermans and that will bring me closer to my goal of joining the fraternal order of ding-dongs that take your money to bring in air conditioning to their devout places of worship where they meet once a week to ask God for stuff. Until we meet again, peace, love, and harmony from your bovine balladeer. Hope to see you soon at a rock show near you.

Peace out,

the hermans

the hermans have gone... *mobile!* Grab your phone or PDA and GO!

Groovy!

the hermans

stalking matilda

WAP Mobile Browsers go to: http://thehermans.net/wap/index.wml

HTML Mobile browsers go to: http://thehermans.net/mobile

the first album is out! buy it here!

So we returned to our old house on Central Ave. yesterday and played in the shitbox of a basement. We haven't played since the day after my wedding, but it sounded good to me. My cousin came to Missoula yesterday from Ann Arbor, MI, where she attends the University of Michigan medical school. She came here last year as well to work at Camp Mak-a-Dream, some groovy new age camping excursion for kids with horrible diseases like cancer. I guess she helps them forget about how awful cancer is for a week and has fun with them and such. What a soldier. Anyway, I had to go pick her up from the airport at like 10:30 pm and then go straight to the old house where Dave, Sophie, Nyree and me used to live. We played late and she was a real trooper, since she had been up since very early and then lost two hours in the time zone trap. I think she had fun. We had quite a turnout, considering Mike and the other Victory Smokes (who currently occupy our old house) didn't really advertise except through word of mouth. We sounded pretty good for being fairly fresh, not having played in some time. This, of course, was until Dave somehow had the old boozer switch flip to the mentally incapacitated position, and was falling all over himself for our last four or five songs. Bill and Chris and I kept playing because the atmosphere was very fun, but if it hadn't been for that and my cousin being there, we probably would have dragged Dave out in the alley and stuffed him in a garbage can. What an asshole. He couldn't even remember how to play the songs he wrote himself. Then he tried to jump or some fucking thing and fell down and cracked his head on the concrete floor. He got up slowly and started yelling about how someone pushed him or hit him. Accordingly, when his back was turned to me, I threw broken drumsticks at his head. He still doesn't know what was happening to him, but he seemed very disturbed and drunkenly angry. Fuck him. That's what happens when you decide to get wasted before your set. We have a few real shows coming up, so I suppose it was good to get this fiasco out of the way. My cousin probably thinks Dave is a mental patient. Sometimes I do, too.

Dear Puke Face,

Sorry, cherished journal, I recognize it has been some time. As you know, we were compelled to take the summer off for medicinal and therapeutic reasons but as the Earth plummets and casts on its inane route the seasons wane and come to an end...and idiots who chop their fingers off luckily heal.

What have we been up to you ask? the hermans have been quite busy keeping ourselves occupied with various hobbies, recreational activities, side projects, house chores and all of the other things normal people do. Chris has taken up knitting and has just completed a fine oval yarn weave of a man catching a giant trout. The inscription reads "Got Trout?" It made us snicker and it beautifully matches the red, white and blue coverlet that he fashioned to go over his tan Davenport. Bill, meanwhile, joined a bowling league and has been busy speaking at old age homes about the dangers of geriatric Methamphetamine abuse. He also plays bingo and makes casseroles. I am still at the Shady Acres Relaxation Communtiy and currently hold the tupperwear throwing championship. I hit Leonard with a tapioca pie Tuesday and grabbed the nurse's buttocks when she went to pick up my pills that I "dropped." Group time is my favorite. Dr. Broboban asked us all to share briefly what we want out of life. I told him I was a dolphin and tried to jump through a giant hoop which was really the nurses' station. I think Dr. Broboban is trying to kill me.

Derk came to visit yesterday and we had a wheelchair race. As I made my way past him down the final stretch of Ward 7, Dr. Rosen was coming out of the shock therapy room (I like to call Lightning Land!) and was tripped by the leg braces of my rocket ship. I knocked him down the stairwell and he smashed through the glass door at the bottom. To make a long story short, I am now in hiding at Derk's house. I tried to convince he and Nyree that in order to stay completely hidden, I need to go incognito as a pineapple. Derk said this was only temporary and that he only busted me out to play our first show since his accident. It was at the Crazy Daizy Clothing Shoppe last night.

Back on Earth, the show was a sweet success. It was First Friday downtown (every First Friday coffee shops, galleries, museums, and porn dens free their walls for local artists to showcase their substance for the socialites of town who drink free wine and pretend to comprehend negative space and linear function) and we played an acoustic set to open Adelaide's (our favorite KBGA DJ) art exhibit. It was a wonderfully photographed cornucopia of the artist with a massive bag of garbage she entitled her "clowd." It was black and white; dualism at its best. Anyway, we had not practiced this unplugged set list and, once again, we had to "wing it." This seems to be a prevalent function of the hermans and so goes the fact that we nail these unpracticed shows without a thought. I know not how this happens and I don't recommend bands play shows without a practice. But, I suppose it is the adrenaline stemming from these droughts or just that we have been playing these songs for a long time now. Either way, it was fun and I was shocked and thrilled to hear the songs in a mellowed alteration and with a vocal style I had to improvise. The crowd (mostly Missoula folk who don't frequent rock and roll shows) was into the set and let us know it. Some met us afterwards to grant us their opinions (sorry folks, we will never tone it down even thought we appreciate the gratitude you gave) and that is always very cool. So, we figured we will do it once and a while for fun...but without practice like Allen Iverson.

Hence, the VH1 Unplugged Story Tellers night was fun but I can't wait to get back to the Raven to fuck shit up hermans style: raw, dirty, vigorous and utterly rocking enthusiasm on a small wine soaked stage...and with the Victory Smokes and Playboys. EEOOOOGH!

My envy builds as I think about the Playboys going on a thirty day tour. It is not a negative jealousy as I wish them well (so they can take us with them next time) but I also want to leave Missoula to rock out for a month. Bastards.

Anyway, we are fucking back. We played between them and the Smokes last night and it was insane. Joe Danger, their drummer, hasn't been in Missoula for something like six months and they nailed it. The Smokes opened up to a full house and got the crowd up and rocking. Then we came on, knocked them the fuck over and then the Playboys decanted them with gasoline and lit it up. There is something to say about the energy of two local bands who have not played together in a long time coming back and ripping it up. I just don't know what those words are but I am sure they would be laced with obscenities. And people screaming.

For our finale, I put on an afro wig, Derk sketched a sharpie moustache upon my lip and we erupted on the Playboys song "Pucker Shots For Everyone" which was not going to be played by them according to the Count. I did my best Colin impression but I unfortunately had to play guitar so I couldn't put the Mick-Jagger-from-Louisiana act on.

It was a great heavy evening and if there was a soul in Missoula who wasn't satisfied, they were probably on the other side of Higgins Bridge eating hot pockets and watching American Idol or drinking alone at Charlie B's. Who could that be?

-----Original Message-----
From: dave@thehermans.net
To: Jones, Greg
Subject: stalking hermanos

Bro,

Get this shit. Rachel came into the Raven last night (dude, this is getting crazy) probably looking for me knowing the hermans were playing with the Thermals (Sub Pop band – Dustin did their new album cover – maybe he can pass on a CD, huh?) and grabbed me right away wanting to talk. I don't get it: if I dump someone I want it to be over. I don't go around spreading bullshit lies about false abuse. Poor me!

Anyway, the show was great, the Thermals are a cool band, but I went out for a cig and was followed and accosted. I guess she was pissed because I wouldn't talk to her but before I knew it she was punching and kicking me! ME! All I have done was, oh, maybe save her life a few times, and trying to avoid the situation, had to take that shit! It was actually very, very funny. Bill grabbed her like a disgruntled parent screaming "What the fuck is wrong with you?" (even though we all knew) and Chris grabbed her forever-falling-down-trousers by the belt loop and quipped "And would you pull up your goddamned pants woman!" It was the highlight of Derk's night since he has been tired of seeing her butt crack for the last year. Derk dragged me in and we went back to watching the show. I was insanely pissed but then realized who I am to Sophie and that I never did anything wrong. My bros at the Raven told me they deal with her a lot and it is never pleasant. Personal shit should never get in the way of a show but I guess some people thrive on drama.

The rest of the show was great. Unfortunately, we are losing another venue.

The Raven will be shutting down in a few weeks so I suggest you invest in it right now so we can still play shows and get beat up by drunk chicks in the Zoo Town. It will make a good story for the book, heh, heh.

Pimpbot 9000

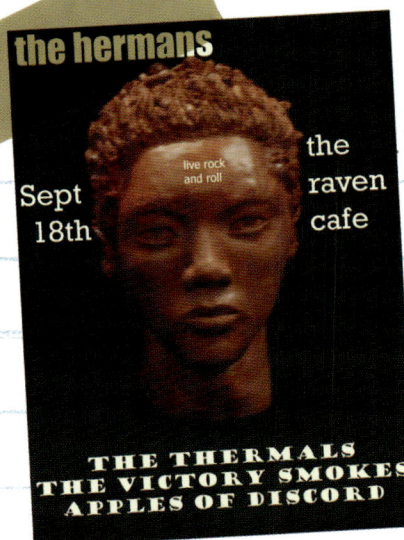

the hermans

live rock
and roll

Sept
18th

the
raven
cafe

THE THERMALS
THE VICTORY SMOKES
APPLES OF DISCORD

138

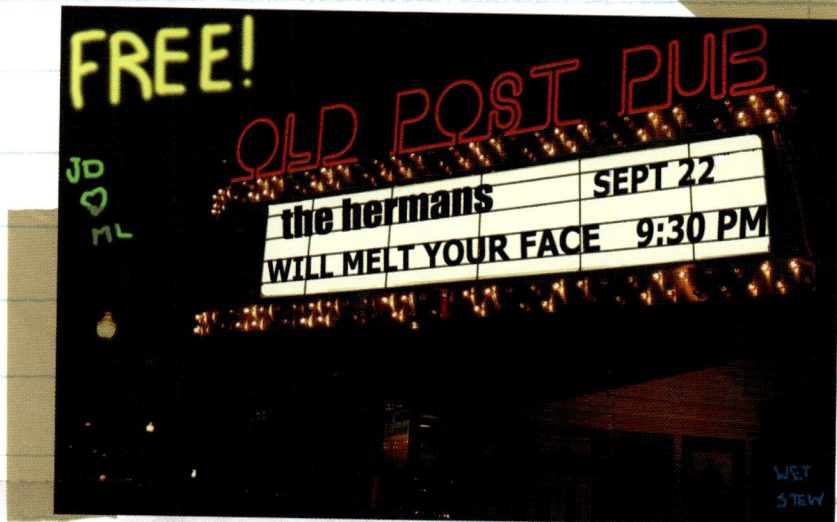

Journal,

We haven't talked in a while. How was solitary confinement in a box with old hermans flyers and newspaper articles? Hope you enjoyed your hiatus. Actually, I hope it was miserable like the wretch that you are. Did you know we are playing again? Did you know that we are going back to the Old Post for the first time since the benefit for my accident? Well, I am sure you are not helping to advertise, either. Do you know what I go through before every show? Well, I will bring you up to speed so next time you can help me through it. The illustrious Mattie Taco, or "Grande," as we have referred to him of late, has made a glorioso (I don't care if you don't think that is a word. Fuck off!) flyer, as usual, and now I have to go to Kinko's and make copies on colored 11X17 paper product and go around town and staple the fuckers to sign boards and poles and store windows (like Ear Candy) and in and around the Old Post, etc. Sound fun? Next, we have to email the Independent and the Entertainer and tell them to write stuff about our show in the nightlife section or otherwise so that the peeps in Zoo Town know we are playing and then they automatically come down to the show because we are so beloved (this is in Marx's Utopian society, of course). Then we make some smaller flyers called handbills and we go to bars and pass them out or leave them on tables or whatever so more people know about it. How many handbills have you passed out you worthless pile of shit?

What else, you ask? Well, Chris, since his recent joining of the fine University system we have here in Missoula, my alma mater, UM, as the kids say, has gained access to screen printing know how and whatnot and thus, has created a tee-shirt design. It, as you can imagine, is totally badass. I have been saying for years now that everybody loves pirates, and so pirate imagery is where it's at. He, unlike some people we know, listens well and made a kick ass pirate shirt with the hermans on the top and the Jolly Roger (skull and crossbones, or in this case, cross-swords) and underneath it says, "hail all y'all to the jolly roger" which is from our hit single, er, uh, song from our album, "Modern Day Pirate." He and Dave and Bill made up a bunch of shirts and hottie girl shirts for the ladies which we will be presenting at the Post this Friday. He also gained access to button-making and has a hundred or so one-inch black and white hermans buttons to give out at the show with tees and records. This is so very exciting, journal. I wish you would show a little emotion, you prick. To hell with you. You will feel like a turd when you see Missoulians walking around with hermans' pirate shirts, won't you! Hail!

Diaryah,

I am making this entry a brief one as I am happy and sad. The Raven closed. One more in the books, one more empty shell. A lot of good times and great bands in our memories. Gill and Markley and Colin and Josh Vanek and Nikki and whoever the fuck else brought us a summer of fun and we thank you all. We are so proud looking back on that place to be etched in with friends and strangers who came together to watch, listen and perform music. I made out in the bathroom after the Thermals show! That after being stricken! Derk's bachelor party was there. Our CD release party. Clare D'alune. The Vagina Monologues when we handed out eye patches for the first time AND christened the stage with alcohol and blood (Bill hit me with his head stock in the lip). Playboys come back show. Victory Smokes and Pleaseasaur - hilarious. Racetrack playing for Missoula right before breaking up. Volumen and the Joggers who covered the Yes song Long Distance Run Around (my personal favorite highlight of the Raven...besides the hermans)! That fucking bum throwing the owner through the window during Bacon and Egg's set, who didn't miss a beat. The Japanese rocket ship known as The Birthday Suits - awesome.

Finally, a few nights ago, we closed it down with the Smokes, Get Set Go! and the Obs. It was fucking about time we got to play with the Oblio Joes and in great fashion, may I add: the last show at the Raven, ever. For some reason, we played after them. Get Set Go were stuck in Spokane only to arrive three minutes into our set (luckily for us - had they gotten there any sooner, we wouldn't have played until three am) so I was happy they got to see us play. Playing with the Joes was something I day-dreamed about at Finn and Porter two years ago after seeing them at the Old Post before Chris joined our band. I felt strange going onstage after them, that feeling you get like no one will stick around because they just saw what they needed to see. In the end, Felix (their drummer) gave me a wink right before we ripped into our first song and it felt almost as good as the bottle of wine I just tanked. Red Cabernet will crush any butterflies and permeate the confidence any artist should have in their original rock music.

Well, I fucked up. This wasn't short but the Raven deserves correspondence. So do the bands that played there. But not you journal, fuck you. You missed the show, again.

Diary, Journal, and Pecker Wood,

My brother Jeff is the coolest mother fucker on this planet. You know why? First of all, you hear people talking about "that guy who walks into a room and everyone wants to talk to him" right? Well, he is cooler than that douche bag and he probably owns the room! Jeff came out to take his little brother, me, to the Rolling Stones. Oh, yeah, the Stones came to Missoula the other night and played at Washington Grizzly Stadium where our beloved (whatever, go Nittany Lions!) Grizzlies kick ass on a weekly basis. No big deal right? No, our town turned upside down and then did the robot, the monkey and broke out the fucking cardboard and breakdanced for two months beforehand. It was incredible but if I hear Wild Horses on Missoula radio ever again I will put Mayor Kadas in the Camel Clutch. Anyway, my brother is so cool because seeing the Stones wasn't good enough for him. He went and rented out our old favorite bar, The Top Hat, to see the hermans play a show for...well...himself. The owner, even though my brother gave him a wad of cash, still douched out and gave us shit for charging a cover. Some fucking people, man. Déjà vu? We probably won't play there again.

It turned out to be a good night and, I think for the first time ever, they allowed two bands and we asked our pals the Victory Smokes to help us bust that fucker up.

Jeff had a great time but probably paid for it on the plane the next day. And he didn't tell me to quit and try to get a real job. He instead told me to go for it, as the hermans rock.

Some people have it all and don't give a shit. Others obviously make a life for themselves and aren't happy until those around them are. What a great bro.

SEE WHAT HAPPENS... THE HERMANS COVER ONE OF YOUR SONGS AND YOU GET TO PLAY A STADIUM IN MISSOULA!

45

....so I have to fucking move again because my landlord is a bitchy fuckin' jerk. She is selling the house Nyree and I moved into only four months ago. Now we have to move to a house without a full basement because moving in October in Missoula is crap, and overpriced, and nothing at all is available. Now we won't have band practice space at my house anymore, which is also shit because the jam room in my current basement is fucking great. Hopefully the V-Smokes will let us jam at their house, my old house two houses ago. Chris lives there, so I suppose this shouldn't be a problem, at least while he is still there. Everything sucks sometimes. This is my second move in five months, third in fifteen! Fuck this! So now what am I doing? I am having a fucking garage sale like the poor white trash I have become. Nyree and my friend Rick from work are outside right now operating the massive shit sale. I am in here writing this because I was scared inside by what appeared to be a Hutterite (Montana Amish, I think) family of 29 or so just showed up and invaded my garage. Two of them were looking at picture frames, but were much more interested in the pictures inside of them rather than the frames. Two of them are on the treadmill and elliptical machine. One is inside a dog cage and the other 20 or so are running around in circles screaming. They are all dressed like lumberjacks and characters from "Little House on the Prairie" and I had to get the hell outta there before they cornered me and captured my soul. Garage sales bring the worst people out of the woodwork to pillage and frighten poor folk like me who are simply looking to unload some worthless shit for profit due to moving issues. I am not going to lie to you. I am literally scared for my life right now. Thank god Dave and Colin Playboy are coming over soon to discuss our first tour in January. I need some semblance of normalcy, like rock and roll discussion, soon before I drop acid and go hide in my closet wearing one of Nyree's old dresses. Colin says he should be able to book a five show tour over the Pacific Northwest. This would be grand. Right now, I need to get the fuck out of Missoula as soon as possible, even if it will be in a small van with three dudes....

Journeyman,

I am late for work so you can eat it…you are lucky I am talking to you at all.

Played a Halloween benefit for Forward Montana (a progressive Non Profit group that is working to change the world for the better and get Conrad Burns' racist ass out of Congress) at the Loft last night. Benefits are cool, especially when they give us free drink.

The V. Smokes opened dressed as English Soccer fans. We played second as dead rock stars and, once again, played a great set after having not been in the same room together for a month. Chris had the best costume ever as James Marshall Hendrix and we rocked Cross Town Traffic. Billy pulled off a superb Buddy Holly and even sang a totally unrehearsed, unpracticed, we-learned-this-backstage-before-the-show version of Roller Coaster. Derk winged a Keith Moon outfit (which I was nervous wouldn't sail) that turned out to be perfect and hilarious and I was Johnny Cash. So it wouldn't have been right to not play Folsom Prison…also unrehearsed. I wish Maureen could have been there but if she weren't home babysitting Sophie, I would not have been there…and I am the fucking singer! T'anks Mo, you rule.

Anyway, the show was awesome, at a maxed capacity so we made them some money, and we were told the floor was bouncing….

SPOTLIGHT

phat phalanges

The hermans have given Missoula more than just the temptation to begin a sentence without capitalization. Their fans have a legend to follow, an evolution not only to witness, but in which to participate. With the near-behanding of drummer Derk Schmidt last year, their first tour into the wilds beyond Helena was cancelled. Fortunately, the amphibian Schmidt has regenerated his percussive digits and the band is ready to get on with its life.

The weeklong tour of the Pacific Northwest, which includes shows in Seattle, Portland, Olympia

photo by Sarah Daisy Lindmark

WHO: the hermans

WHAT: Tour Kickoff Party

WHEN: Sat., Jan. 13, 9:30 PM

WHERE: The Loft, 424 N. Higgins Ave.

HOW MUCH: $5/$7 under 21

and possibly Bellingham, will be a crash course in life on the road for the hermans. Guitarist and lead singer David Jones reports that the band is "fucking psyched" to begin the tour, especially on the heels

of a send-off party with the International Playboys and Retardo Montalbon.

The band is broadening its horizons in several ways, from releasing a new album last June to closing the deal on their soon-to-be-released reality book. Running Press, an East Coast publisher, is putting together a volume based on Jones' journal entries that will chronicle the struggles a small-town band faces on the road to greater exposure. While it may not be a live concert video, local music lovers will want to be at The Loft for a chance to be immortalized in print.

—Jonas Ehudin

Dearest Diary,

If you don't know what it is to have your wildest dreams come true, start a band with your best friends, write cool songs that people in your town can lose themselves to, get a book deal that will get you to other parts of the country and hopefully world, and then do just that: TOUR!!! Unless your dream is to go to school, get married, have a few kids and lose your mind in middle America.

The notion of departing on a rock and roll circuit, a.k.a. touring, to the lay person, is completely unreal and fantastical. We left Missoula on a cold and shitty Tuesday morning. To reiterate, it was bitter fucking cold! We rented a white mini-van and found the weather even shittier in the Cascades, a series of mountains that blocks the dead tundra of Eastern Washington from the great and soggy golden lights of Seattle. White mini vans are the new symbol of rock and roll, by the way. Derk had to do 25 mph in an otherwise 65 mph area and it took us an hour and a half to best a route that normally takes about twenty minutes. We didn't think we would make it and almost ditched the Seattle show to try to get to Portland for the next night. Portland is a great town but the fucking tradition and idea of playing at the Crocodile Café in Seattle was worth this risk. And it was a risk: when we stopped to get chains in Ellensburg, WA, a small, rural desert town, the lady peered at our pallid chariot, guffawed and told us we'd better head south towards Oregon. How dare she torment the beast! Lo, we continued like rock and roll combatants and knocked down the Cascades to find Seattle at forty five degrees and humid and three hours to spare. Good driving, Hammer man.

The sweet aroma of a welcoming Seattle I cannot describe in text. I am sorry but neither can I describe the feeling of pulling our car into town and finding the venue. The night employees of the Croc were as I suspected: not rude but not welcoming. Bands come and go but that mattered not to us, we owned this place. They weren't mean but just went about business and told us who to talk to and where to go. Damn if Missoula had a venue that this bar could even shadow! We could have driven through twenty Cascades at this point and wouldn't have had any less electricity going through us.

They wanted us to set up and play a song to sound check. We were immediately puzzled as sound checks in Missoula come right before your set, not three hours previous. We figured Stalking Matilda would be a good one; dynamic, rocking, utterly hermanesque. The five workers present were smiling. So were we, uncontrollably.

After the check we couldn't stand still. This is Grohl country. Mudhoney. Sub Pop. Sleater Kinney. Visqueen. Mookey Blaylock. All of whom have some ties to the Crocodile in one way or the other. So, we went and got some coffee. Bill drank about seven.

Capitol Hill has a cool brewery/restaurant with hearty beer and decent burgers. Not enough grease for Derk and I but Chris ate a plate of wings with his burger and tried to eat the menu afterwards. Before we knew it we had to get back to the venue and made it for the first band, the Braille Tapes from Bellingham, WA. We found that we had been pushed fom the opening slot to the last which would normally piss us off as no one ever sticks around for the last band unless they are Foreigner. Alas, this gives us more time to drink local beer, see local Seattle bands and take in every fucking second of this evening.

By the time we played (after two other bands, Child Bride, local, and Indonesian Junk - really nice dudes) we were drunk in every aspect of the word, but without drinking heavily to get us there. Without conveying it to each other through words, we were ready and had been waiting for this forever. Fucking Seattle, man.

Again and unfortunately, there are no words to describe this. All I can say (to give a slight idea to the reader) is that during Chris' solo in Desert Island I found myself paralyzed staring at the ceiling. In that moment it dawned on me that McCready sometimes stares up during solos and that PJ played here. It was an eerie feeling. My feet felt weird. It also hit me that though the crowd had dispersed from fifty to about fifteen (the bouncer punched the singer's dad from Braille Tapes and kicked out about ten of their friends!), this was real. Absolute. Bands want to play the Crocodile; it is a first choice and here we were rocking this stage. After the show, we were invited back to "show Seattle what we got" according to one of the sound guys. What can I say? You got a few hours?

So here I am a few weeks later in hindsight. Usually that word means that regret is coming but for us it means the opposite. Chris called me the other night. My daughter was asleep like a weary angel and I was watching a movie like an exhausted turd…I think For A Few Dollars More. Anyway, I could tell he was baked and when he told me what he was watching I fell victim to his feeling. It was an early Nirvana DVD. They were playing the Crocodile.

He said "yo, Novaselic was just staring at the ceiling like you were, you retard. Thought you might like to hear that." It was a little heavier than "like."

I kiss my baby girl all the time. The one I gave her as she slept that night I will never forget.

ONE WAY →

photos by david pierce

5

Tour. Day 2, which seems, somehow, like day 20.

Apparently, people in Portland, Oregon, have never seen snow. It's as if the entire town shut down and collapsed. And I am not certain, but I think shovels and DOT snow-removal machines are a foreign concept in this town. We arrived downtown around noon and had some coffee, etc. Then we went over to the Hawthorn district near the Tonic Lounge to pretty much fuck off and wait for the show to start. Nyree drove out here to stay with her friends who happen to live in Portland, and she met up with us in the evening for beers. Then we went to the Lounge. I am not sure if it started here, or after we did sound check, but Dave proceeded to get unprecedently wasted, akin to the show in our old basement when my cousin visited Missoula. We had to play first, and I think ten or so people watched us, three of which being Nyree and her two friends. We had a beautiful merch table Bill set up. I think I was the only one who looked at it. After us, three indie bands played and no one seemed to care about them either, except Dave, of course. He decided that the local microbrew, which was about 10% alcohol, called Arrogant Bastard Ale, was his credo for the night, and proceeded to drink about fifty of them. I was watching the third band and he stumbled into the stage room (the other half of the venue was a bar/restaurant with tables and such), watched the band for half a song, looked at me slant-eyed and screamed, "What the fuck is this shit? I'm outta here! These guys can kiss my ass!" Then he left. I think to the bathroom where he filled a urinal with Arrogant vomit. Sometime later I saw him in the lounge room with Bill and Chris, drinking a Pabst tallboy and swaying. I asked him if he had checked out the headlining band, Swim Swam Swum, a local indie outfit whose review in the local independent paper was less than kind, and, without regard, slovenly sauntered into the stage room. About two minutes later he walked back into the lounge and said something like, "I thought this town was supposed to be cool. What the hell is that racket? They sound like every other fuckin' indie band I've ever heard anywhere ever. I want some fuckin' nachos. This place sucks. Who the fuck are these guys anyway. I thought we were going to play last. Where the fuck are we? I hate you." Then I told him to shut the fuck up, lest we never be asked to play in Portland again. Then Bill and Chris told him, repeatedly, to shut the fuck up or they would back over him with the van. Then I probably told him to shut the fuck up again. As the night came to a close, apparently Dave, the booking guy or whatever from the Tonic Lounge, approached our drunken mess, Dave, and handed him forty dollars, put his arm around him and said, "Hey, your set rocked. Don't worry about it, Portland is a tough rock crowd." A minute later, in the stage room where Bill and I, once again, were loading out our equipment, this Dave guy came up to me and said, "Hey, thanks for playing tonight. I enjoyed it. You would probably have better luck next time playing with some rock bands. By the way, I gave forty bucks to your singer, Dave, a minute ago. You should probably go find him and get the money before he loses it. He looks like a fuckin' wreck." Nice guy, Dave was. Total fucking idiot, my Dave was. After Bill and I loaded out our shit I said goodbye to Ny and her friends and we hit the road. Dave is lucky we didn't throw him out of the van on highway 5 heading north. Every once and a while he woke up and started giggling, insulted Chris, said fuck a bunch of times and then passed out again. When Bill and I finally found a hotel that had vacancy about an hour and a half later, if it wasn't for me, Dave would have spent the night in the van, and if he was lucky, died of hypothermia. I finally dragged his worthless ass into the hotel room around 3:45 in the a.m. Then I had to sleep next to the fucking loser in a double bed. I should have killed him.

...Uhh...yeah...sorry about that heh. Fuck it, that is how it goes sometimes.

We left Portland in the morning and I was train wrecked. I just read Derk's account of Portland and am happy it wasn't from Bill as Derk told me our beloved bassist almost killed me. Chris thought it was rather funny in that he has a knack of being able to disassociate himself from drama. God bless him.

So, Portland Oregon was actually a very cool town and up until the blackout I thought the Tonic Lounge very charming and a good venue. I thought the next day I enjoyed the bands but I guess that was my evil twin, Quasar, taking over. We left early and my head was in a cloud. Bill and Chris wanted to fish somewhere on the Olympic Peninsula and Derk didn't care: I was doing a puzzle. It was a twenty thousand piece from the night before and I was failing.

We drove for what felt like a day on Mars and found no good spots.

There was no need to rush, however, as Olympia is about an hour and a half from Portland and I heard it was small and there wasn't much to do. After a few hours of bad angler ju-ju, we blazed on out of the lush green forest and back onto the sullen grey highway. I started feeling a little better when we arrived in mid afternoon in the Capitol. The four of us went to a coffee shop to peruse the local papers in search of our show. No dice. The diner/coffee house/rock and roll bar/cinderblock box venue, Le Voyeur, was a half a block away from the Beanery. The place proved just as odd as we gathered from friends back home but turned out well worth it. The back of the restaurant was a fucking concrete box with a target painted on the floor. They probably used it to sacrifice virgins here. Or whores. Or rock bands. I am not kidding, this place was strange. I didn't think a whole town would be on the same weird drug. We had authentic cheesesteaks (by authentic I mean they had Amoroso rolls shipped from my homeland) and then spent the next three hours smoking in the van listening to Chris deliver the goods on every whack-o that walked by. "This guy has sex with his pets," "That guy don't take care of his kids," "look at the tank on her ass." This is what touring is, for some. What the fuck else are we supposed to do when we don't want to spend money, don't know anyone, are low on sleep and fear that if we did go to the venue, the Druids might come out and eat us.

Pre show time came so we loaded in and hit the bar. It was very cozy and the place was beginning to warm up. I saw a few stickers of Missoula bands in the back so we put one of ours on the circuit box. I told Derk and Bill to get hammered as penance for Portland. They looked at each other, took a sip of beer, and flipped the switch that I left on last night. We played a great set between six and ten people (as that is all that can fit in that back room) and then drank for two hours at the bar. For every beer or vodka the other three hermans disposed of, I sipped a half. The Friends of Rock and Roll were a pretty cool band and the Monolators (from LA) were a couple of really sweet people who knew Get Set Go and Shiloe, another LA band we played with in Portland, so I suppose touring makes the cliché right - it is a small fucking world.

As the legislation session was in, all hotels were booked. I had to call the same Hampton Inn we stayed in two nights ago and beg for a room. Keith (the night manager at the Hampton Inn Sea Tec) rules and hooked it up. On to Seattle! Again.

Chris discovered a nice treat in his cigarette pack so we took a small detour, threw in my Euromotion CD and headed north. Derk was hammered and stoned but wasn't being the asshole that Quasar was. He put in Wilco and started that we-are-going-to-be-famous bullshit ranting about how he "can't wait till we are big enough to have horns." Horns, shit, I want a guitar that costs more than $336 at a pawn shop.

Anyway, drunk people are fucking annoying when you are sober. They think everything is funny when it is not. Well, Euromotion is funny but road signs aren't my idea of comedy. I am obviously a better drunk.

5

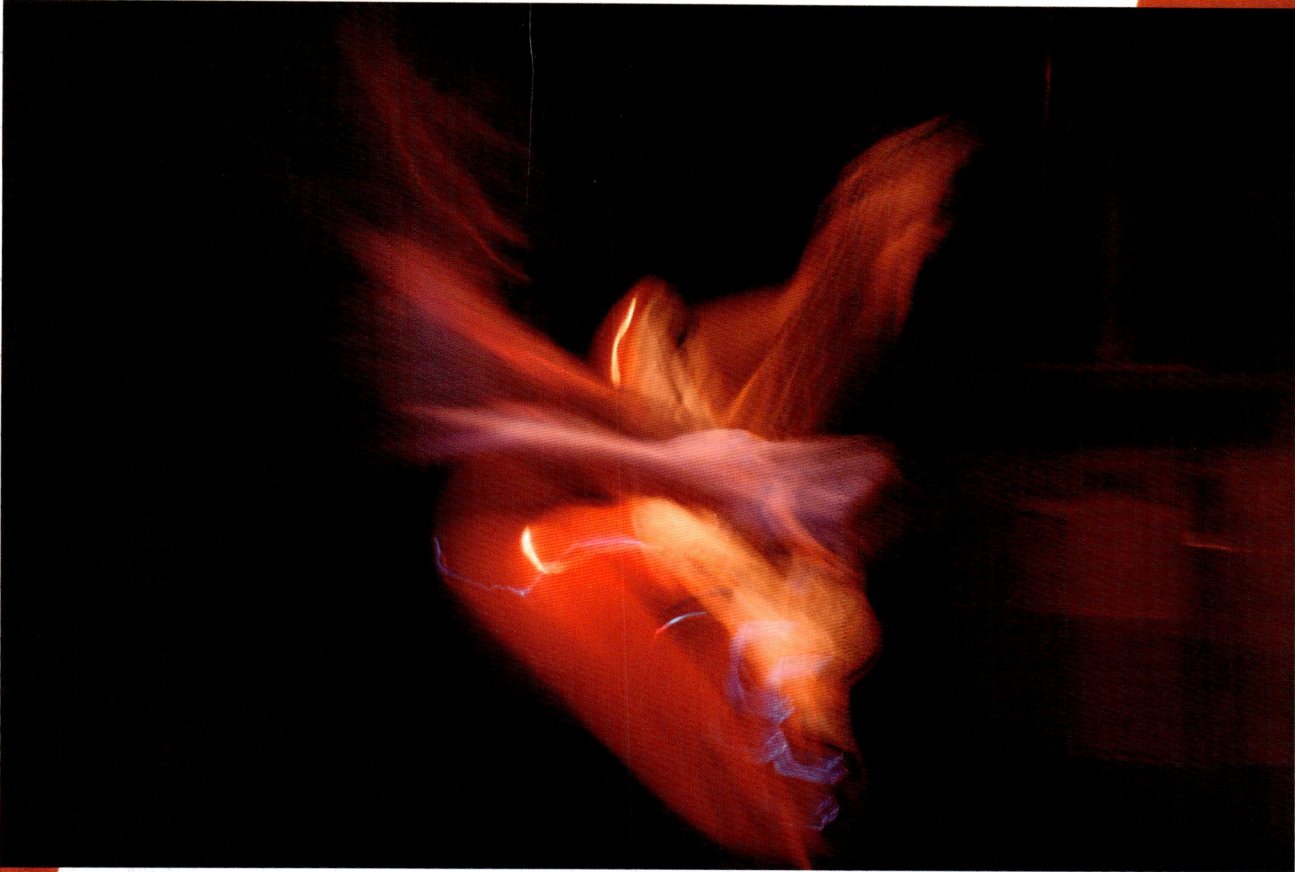

As I am still hungover from Olympia, I will spare you the arduous details of being on tour. I was, however, relieved that we had a long drive from Seattle to Spokane to "bond" as they say, as a band, and to discuss the book, the band, and our future. We are very excited about this book, and about the tours to come in the following months. We are happy, as well, to welcome Greg, our glorious editor, as our band manager. He did, after all, get us last minute shows for this tour, one being in Seattle, and this one, in Spokane. The show was very exciting. A lot of people, apparently, in Spokane, still like good ol' rock music. Our friends from Missoula, Arrows to the Sun, came down to Spokane to split the bill with us for this show. They were amazing, and incredibly fun. We went back and forth for two sets each, and by the end of it, the hermans (during the fourth set) played two long-ass but very fun jam songs, then one great shorter rock song, Desert Island. This is when the bartender came up and said we had to stop, even though it was only 12:30 or so. I guess this is their protocol at Mootsy's (which is a great venue/bar, by the way). This was unfortunate because we had just rocked the fuck out of the joint and had about fifty people there screaming at the top of their lungs for more. I suppose it is better to end on a high note. My only hope is that we make it back to Missoula safely, since it snowed about fifteen feet during our show in Spokane, and the roads are absolute shit. It seems as though we have been on tour for a month, and it has only been four days. At least our next tour to New York will be in the summer time. Touring in January, especially for your first tour is, well, pretty fuckin' stupid.

H

Journal, Screw you, you can continue on-line.

People who purchased this (or borrowed it because you are cheap), friends who got one for free, and family member who deservedly got this for free,

The bastards at Running Press, minus Greg, told us to end the book at page 160 so they could send it to China and get it pressed. So here we are.

Through the course of writing, re-writing, editing and revising this journal/memento, we have found that certain things that have happened to us as a collective were far too paramount and emotional to describe in words. This is one of those times. I will give it a shot:

Although this is the last page of this book, chapters for the hermans will continue to come and go with the shows we play, songs we continue to write and places we wreak havoc on when we tour again. If you turn the page you will find a CD with four early songs we recorded for our album, Stalking Matilda. If you like these songs, thank you so much. If you really like them, there are more that will have already been written by the time you read this. Check them out.

One inimitable factor about our band is that we constantly attempt to view and mingle prevalent social incidents with how they affect the four of us personally and write strong, hard energetic music to wrap around blatant lyrics that present how we feel. Conversely, sometimes songs come to one of us when we are alone watching our goldfish in the act of getting it on.

We take our music very seriously and hope this crass publication does not sway the reader's estimation of how our music fits in the larger scope of this great art form. The events herein are totally true and happened as described (or, how we thought they happened during many a great drunken night in MISSOULA, MONTANA!!!) and the many people (and bands) who were there for those events or who wanted to be but were home with their kids, we thank you and we are also sure you have no idea how much we owe to you. If your story differs from ours, screw you, get your brother to get you a book deal and then tell your side - the hermans will still get free press out of it!

Anyway, music is only part of this book but it is definitely the backbone to what has become a great bond, a great friendship, a family (now Sophie has three more uncles); and a hard rocking fucking proud Missoula based rock band. We sincerely hope you enjoyed this, and if you have made it this far, I assume you have. Or you are probably trying to figure out what it is you just read. Either way, it has been a sincere pleasure. And sometimes pain. Stay tuned! We are far from done. Just done as far as this book is concerned. Keep reading on our groovy website: www.stalkingamerica.com and keep in touch.

Sincerely, and most gratefully,

the hermans.

NOTES

NOTES

NOTES

Analogotron (AKA Chris)

The book is Almost finished.
Are you going to write Anything
for it or what?
— Soda Pop Pilot

Davey Boy,
how about something
like this:

SCREW YOU!

Love,
Chris

CW01466770

THE WHO

MUCH TOO MUCH

MIKE EVANS

THE WHO

MUCH TOO MUCH

PALAZZO

PALAZZO

First published in 2021 by
Palazzo Editions Ltd
15 Church Road
London, SW13 9HE
www.palazzoeditions.com

Text © 2021 Mike Evans
Design and layout copyright © 2021 Palazzo Editions Ltd

All rights reserved. No part of this publication may be
reproduced in any form or by any means — electronic,
mechanical, photocopying, recording, or otherwise — or
stored in any retrieval system of any nature without prior
written permission from the copyright holders. Mike Evans
has asserted his moral right to be identified as the author of
this work in accordance with the Copyright, Designs
and Patents Act of 1988.

Every effort has been made to trace and acknowledge
the copyright holders. If any unintentional omission has
occurred, we would be pleased to add an appropriate
acknowledgment in any future edition of the book.

A CIP catalogue record for this book is available from
the British Library.

ISBN 978-1-78675-115-7

Printed in China

10 9 8 7 6 5 4 3 2 1

Designed by Becky Clarke for
Palazzo Editions

ENDPAPERS The Who, circa 1973. (L–R): Bassist
John Entwistle, singer Roger Daltrey, drummer
Keith Moon,and guitarist Pete Townshend.
PAGE 2 (L–R): John Entwistle, Roger Daltrey,
Keith Moon, and Pete Townshend following a live
performance at Ahoy in Rotterdam, Netherlands
on October 2, 1975

CONTENTS

6 FOREWORD

8 INTRODUCTION

10 1. MY GENERATION
26 2. A QUICK ONE
38 3. THE WHO SELL OUT
52 4. TOMMY
64 5. LIVE AT LEEDS
76 6. WHO'S NEXT
86 7. QUADROPHENIA
100 8. THE WHO BY NUMBERS
116 9. WHO ARE YOU
132 10. FACE DANCES
146 11. IT'S HARD
154 12. WHO'S LAST
164 13. JOIN TOGETHER
180 14. BBC SESSIONS
196 15. ENDLESS WIRE
212 16. QUADROPHENIA LIVE IN LONDON
224 17. WHO

238 DISCOGRAPHY
239 BIBLIOGRAPHY
240 PICTURE CREDITS

FOREWORD

My fifty-year-old love affair with The Who (sixteen as their press agent and twelve as a music journalist) got off to a less than auspicious start at the London Marquee Club in 1964, where I was to interview them in my capacity as a cub reporter for top-selling teen magazine, *Fabulous*.

At the time, these "no hitters" from west London were yet to become chart-makers, but now are regarded by myself and other rock music critics as the best live rock group in the world. With a back catalogue of classic hit singles like "My Generation," "Pinball Wizard," and "Won't Get Fooled Again," plus a flood of hits from the pen of Pete Townshend, they are now established super rock icons justifiably regarded as the most influential band of the twentieth century, having sold more than 100 million albums. They have become the only band to have their own rock opera *Tommy* go to No. 1, three times in the album charts. First, as The Who, then Lou Reisner's orchestrated version, and then their soundtrack to the 1975 Ken Russell film. That was then and this is now, but still they remain a massively significant force in worldwide rock culture. Their two front men still alive and kicking in Roger Daltrey and Pete Townshend, keeping them on course over an unbelievable fifty years.

Back at The London Marquee, The Who came on like desperadoes involved in a musical smash and grab raid led by their passionate, angry, windmilling guitarist known as "The Birdman." Songs like "Zoot Suit" and "I'm The Face" were played to a thunderous volume that hurt your ears, along with a string of ska, bluebeat and R&B covers. I'd had to fork out seven shillings and six pence for the dubious pleasure of witnessing a four-man demolition squad smashing their instruments to bits through clouds of smoke and screeching feedback.

But the demonstrable excitement of the packed crowds of Mods dancing and cheering was infectious.

Even without a hit yet, there was an obvious empathy between the band and their fans—they were in tune with each other. I sensed The Who were something special. They had a vitality and empathetic response that marked them out as something different and dangerous . . .

Following their explosive finale in smoke and splinters onstage, their manic drummer who appeared to be playing with another band on a different planet, managed to reduce his kit to pile of debris after hurling his sticks at his murderous looking vocalist and fell off stage in a cloud of smoke.

Their dapper manager with the public school accent, Kit Lambert, grabbed my arm in a vice-like grip and insisted I stay whilst puffing cigarette smoke all over me. "I expect you would like to interview 'The Boys' now?" he insisted, pulling me into the tiny backstage dressing room.

"What I would really like is to get the last train home and please don't tell them where I live," I whimpered as drummer Keith Moon burst out of the door carrying a short-handled axe.

"Who's that for?" I gulped. "Roger," he replied, large brown eyes revolving from his latest amphetamine intake. "He smashed my last tambourine," snarled their drummer and disappeared into the dark sweaty hell of the club.

Seconds later Roger emerged: "Where is the little shit I am going to kill him—he called me a crap singer live on mike, onstage."

"He went that-away," I pointed helpfully into the sweaty crowd.

Next to emerge from the tiny dressing room was their brilliant bass player John Entwistle whom I asked in my teenage reporter capacity if he had "Any Hobbies?" John volunteered he had to go home as his tarantulas needed feeding the grasshoppers he had bought in an "exotic pets" shop earlier.

"I do wish they would not make that crunching sound at night they make, when they eat them, when I am trying to sleep though," he smiled. I felt our teenage readers would be enchanted.

Finally, the brains of the gang emerged in the shape of Townshend and basically informed me that I was right when I sensed an unique empathy between the band and their audience.

"I think you can use music to express feelings that you can not do in words," said Pete. There is a means of communication open to us through music and recording for our mutual feelings and times that we share. We are trying to tap into that compassion, anger and frustration that lasts through time."

And succeed they have with unprecedented success both live and on record for over half a century, and painstakingly researched in this book with perceptive evaluations of their back catalogue of work. Without peer from the sixties and still relevant today— The Who. The Best Band ever.

Keith Altham, April 2021
Publicity Manager to The Who 1971–1987

The Who, 1974. (L–R): Pete Townshend, Roger Daltrey, John Entwistle, and Keith Moon.

INTRODUCTION

Still making sensational live appearances on the international concert circuit, The Who have been rivalled only by The Rolling Stones as an enduring rock phenomenon, with a career spanning over half a century. Yet The Who, as now represented by Pete Townshend and Roger Daltrey, have surprisingly only released twelve studio albums and a similar number of live sets, in the fifty-six years since their recording debut in 1964. Compared to The Stones—with thirty studio collections to their name, plus as many live recordings—The Who's recorded legacy might be considered somewhat thin on the ground.

Nevertheless, their albums mark key moments in the story of The Who. From their days as Mod standard-bearers in the mid-sixties, through the triumphs of Pete Townshend's ambitious creations in *Tommy* and *Quadrophenia*, the tragic passing of drummer Keith Moon and bass player John Entwistle, and their renaissance with a variety of lineups in recent years, the band's tumultuous history can be traced via these milestone recordings.

In setting an account of The Who in the context of their record releases, I have chosen every studio album as originally released in the UK, notwithstanding variations for the US market and elsewhere. In addition, a number of live releases have been deliberately omitted to avoid needless repetition, while retaining concert recordings of significance—both because of their exceptional content, and as essential markers in a celebration of one of the key names in rock music history.

Mike Evans, September 2020

LEFT At the *Ready, Steady, Go* TV studios, mid-1960s

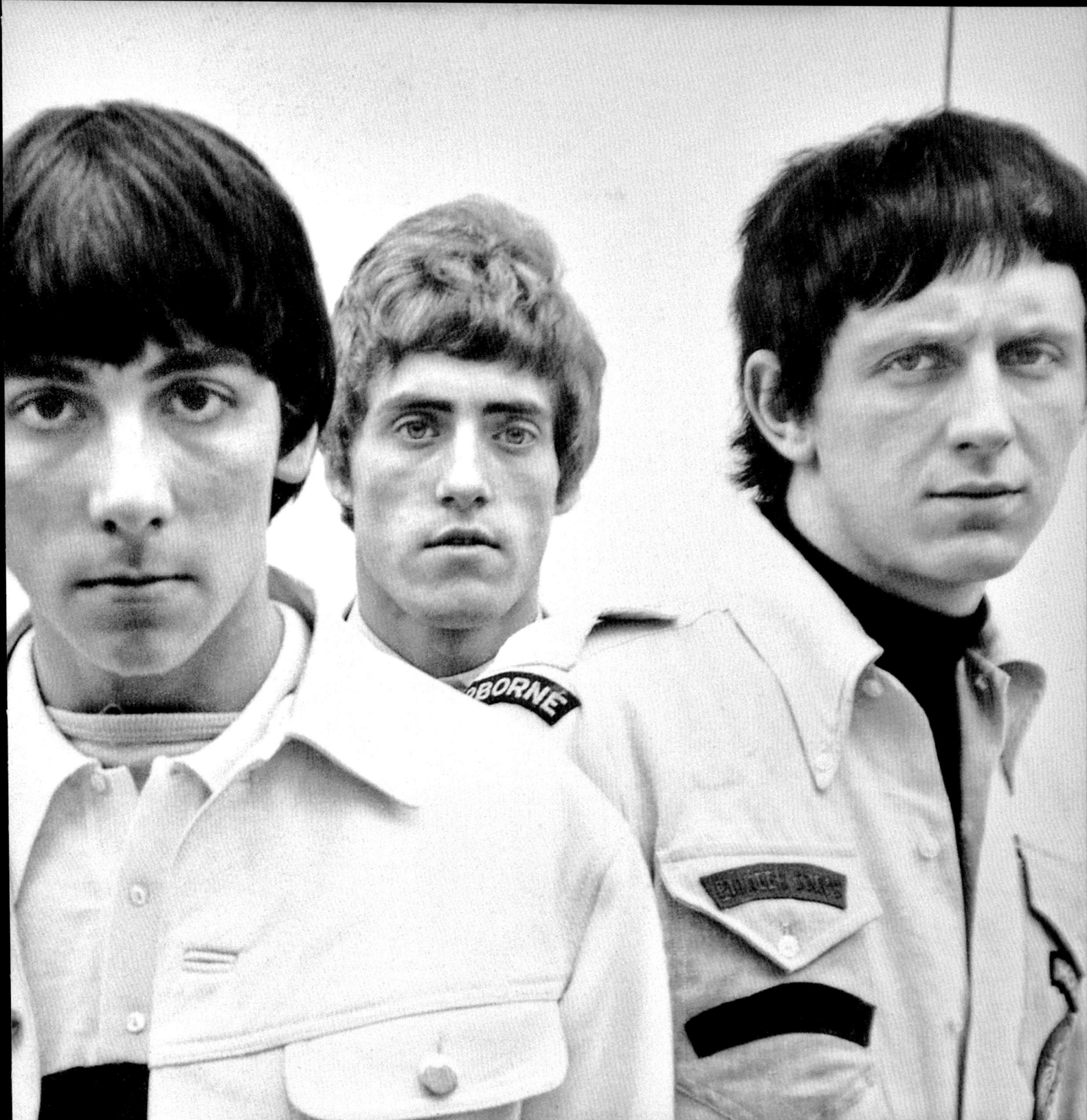

1 MY GENERATION

The route to potential success for any ambitious rock band in the mid-sixties was slogging it out "on the road" for a couple of years, getting an initial record deal that was usually limited to one or two singles, and if one of those took off it became the selling point for an album. So it had been for The Beatles, The Stones and the other big names of the British beat-and-blues boom, and the four archetypal Mods who dubbed themselves The Who were no exception.

Before that crucial debut LP, they had already released four singles, the second of which, "I Can't Explain," made it to No. 8 in the UK charts, but it was "My Generation" that became the title track of their first album after it hit the No. 2 spot in November 1965. It was a well-earned breakthrough that followed the usual rock 'n' roll apprenticeship—both before and after the birth of The Who—for Pete Townshend, Roger Daltrey, John Entwistle, and Keith Moon.

GROWING UP

All four had grown up in west London in the aftermath of World War II. The eldest, Roger Harry Daltrey, was born ("during a heavy bombing raid") in Acton on March 1, 1944. Although he spent his early teens at Acton County Grammar School, Roger had no academic ambitions, and after being expelled from school at fifteen for smoking cigarettes, he got a job as a sheet metal worker. But he had caught the music bug under the all-pervasive influence of Elvis Presley and the UK's "King of Skiffle," Lonnie Donegan; the latter had sparked a craze for do-it-yourself music based on American folk and blues, and like thousands of would-be skifflers across the country, Daltrey spent his spare time practicing the rudiments of guitar. In his

PREVIOUS PAGES The Who, London, 1965. (L–R): Pete Townshend, Keith Moon, Roger Daltrey, and John Entwistle. LEFT The Who, 1965

case it was initially on a home-made instrument, but he soon graduated to performing in public, in local pubs and clubs, emulating contemporary rock names including Elvis, Buddy Holly, and the UK's nearest thing, Cliff Richard.

John and Pete, meanwhile, had already hooked up in their second year at Acton County Grammar School. John Alec Entwistle (born October 9, 1944), unlike Roger was encouraged by his parents to make music; first as a seven-year-old taking piano lessons, then on a trumpet bought for him by his father. Learning to read music (a rarity among aspiring rock musicians), by his early teens he was also playing French horn in the Middlesex Schools Symphony Orchestra.

Alongside rock 'n' roll and skiffle, the big music craze in late-fifties Britain was "trad" (traditional) jazz—the New Orleans-based style better known as Dixieland in the United States. And it was via a mutual enthusiasm for trad jazz (though not exclusively) that Entwistle and Townshend first became friends.

Born on May 19, 1945, Peter Dennis Blandford Townshend was surrounded by music from his earliest days. His father, Cliff, was a saxophone player in the famous Royal Air Force dance band The Squadronaires, while his mother, Betty, was a featured singer with various other professional outfits. During a somewhat fractured childhood, due to his parents' volatile and unstable marriage, Pete discovered rock 'n' roll right at its inception, when in 1957 he was mesmerized by the film *Rock Around the Clock* starring Bill Haley and His Comets. His grandmother bought him his first guitar that Christmas, and it wasn't long before he was also playing rudimentary chords on the banjo.

Soon after they met Pete and John Entwistle formed a short-lived jazz quartet, The Confederates, with Pete on banjo and John on trumpet. The band played what was one of very few gigs at a local

ABOVE Pete Townshend playing an acoustic guitar with his father Cliff, saxophone player with the Squadronaires, and mother Betty at home in London on March 30, 1966

OPPOSITE Keith Moon at the Pavilion, Bath, October 10, 1966

youth club known as the Congo Club, in December 1958, before John felt he couldn't hear the trumpet properly and switched to guitar, which was far more suited to rock music than to trad. Jamming with Pete, who by this time had also decided that rock 'n' roll was the way forward, John moved to bass (his first being a home-made instrument) as he reckoned his hands were "too big" for deft guitar playing. The pair played with several Acton lineups, including The Scorpions, whose repertoire included covers of instrumentals by Cliff Richard's backing group, The Shadows.

DETOURS

By this time Roger Daltrey had helped form a local group called The Detours. Initially, he was lead guitarist, and he was on the lookout for a bass player when he noticed John Entwistle carrying his bass down the street. John was more or less recruited on the spot, and in late 1961 he suggested his friend Pete as lead guitarist, with Daltrey assuming the role of lead singer.

Before he actually joined The Detours in early 1962, Pete had enrolled at Ealing Art College. That was when he began to pick up on American rhythm and blues by the likes of Muddy Waters, Howlin' Wolf, and Ray Charles, music increasingly fashionable in Britain, especially in the emerging Mod culture. The Detours were still sticking with a playlist of reliable pop-rock covers, but were getting some decent local gigs as support to various names including Screaming Lord

Sutch, and one of Pete's seminal influences, Johnny Kidd and the Pirates.

Through 1963, the group's material gradually shifted in favor of blues and early soul, as Pete's influence made its mark, and by the end of the year they were—along with a burgeoning army of like-minded bands across the UK—a bona fide R&B group.

After various permutations of personnel, in early 1964 The Detours, who now consisted of Daltrey, Townshend, Entwistle, and drummer Doug Sandom, decided to change their name when another outfit—Johnny Devlin and the Detours—appeared on national TV. After much deliberation long into the night with his flatmate and fellow student at Ealing Art College, Richard "Barney" Barnes, Townshend (after getting Daltrey's approval) agreed to Barnes's suggestion of The Who. Around the same time, after the sudden expulsion of Sandom (on Pete's instigation) following a failed audition with Fontana Records, the lineup was reduced to just Townshend, Daltrey, and Entwistle, with no regular drummer: Cue the arrival of Keith Moon.

> "From the moment we found Keith it was a complete turning point . . . Before then we'd just been fooling around."

PETE TOWNSHEND

RIGHT March 30, 1964. Mods gather in Clacton on the Essex sea front, on their scooters over the Easter weekend, which was marked by several scuffles between Mods and Rockers. OPPOSITE Carnaby Street, London, pictured in 1965

Keith John Moon was born on August 23, 1946, and grew up in Wembley, a few miles north of Acton. The "class clown" throughout his school years, with a paucity of academic achievement to match, his only interest besides making his fellow pupils laugh seemed to be music. After briefly playing the bugle in the local branch of the Sea Cadets when he was twelve, he turned to the drums, and acquired his first kit in 1961 after leaving school at fourteen. One of his musical idols at the time was Gene Krupa, the flamboyant jazz drummer famous in the thirties and forties, who was the first jazz percussionist to became a star attraction in his own right.

Moon paid ten shillings (fifty pence) per half-hour for drum lessons from Carlo Little, drummer with Screaming Lord Sutch's Savages, and was soon playing with various bands on an ad hoc basis. His first regular gig was with The Beachcombers, a local surf-style covers band, but they were all part-timers with no ambition to turn fully professional. So when he had the chance to join The Who, who were using freelance drummers on a gig-to-gig basis, he didn't hesitate.

In April 1964, The Who were playing one of their frequent dates at the Oldfield Hotel, Greenford, using a session drummer, when Moon offered his services. It was a spontaneous, unplanned audition—and although Keith nearly wrecked the session player's kit, he got the job. It was the last piece in the jigsaw for the fledgling group, as Pete would recall: "From the moment we found Keith it was a complete turning point . . . Before then we'd just been fooling around."

The four began honing what would be a unique sound. Pete was experimenting with some audacious guitar dynamics, bending notes, distorting the sound coming out of the amps, and all at an ear-pummeling volume. Roger's strident, blues-inflected vocals grew more inspired and confident by the day. John attacked the bass guitar like it was a booming, rock-solid version of a lead guitar, and Keith was a whirlwind behind the drum kit, in Townshend's words "battering away like a lunatic."

MOD

The Fontana audition which had triggered the departure of Doug Sandom was arranged by Helmut

Gorden, who for some time had been managing the group; and although his expertise in the music business was limited, Gorden did introduce them to Peter Meaden. Initially, Meaden acted as the banc's publicist, but soon assumed the role of co-manager, and immediately came up with the inspired notion of promoting The Who as *the* Mod group.

The Mods had originally appeared on the London scene in the very early sixties as "modernists," snappily dressed devotees of modern jazz (hence the name) and American rhythm and blues. By 1964 Mod had evolved into a full-blown youth cult, favoring R&B, early Motown, and West Indian bluebeat music, and with its own distinctive look: boys in tight-fitting tailor-made suits or madras cotton jackets, button-down collars, casual shoes, and neat, stylish haircuts; girls adopting faintly androgynous short hairstyles, often wearing men's shirts and pants, or Twiggy-inspired miniskirts.

And it was in 1964 that Mods came under the media spotlight in a series of weekend beach battles with their rivals, the leather-clad Rockers who represented the now-outmoded culture of Teddy Boys and fifties rock 'n' roll. Every weekend of the summer, gangs of Mods on their Italian scooters and Rockers on their motorbikes would descend on UK seaside resorts and battle it out on the beaches. The press had a field day, and suddenly Mod cool had acquired an edgy flavor of potential violence.

Pete was fascinated by Meaden's proposal. With his art school friend Barney he had already been discussing the importance of a unique visual image for the group, a stage presence that adopted some of the avant-garde notions they had picked up at the art college—now Meaden was seeing a way forward via the language and style of the Mod movement.

HIGH NUMBERS

His first move was to get the four kitted out in the latest clothes from London's Carnaby Street, the center of Mod fashion. Then he persuaded them they needed to change their name to something reflecting Mod vocabulary and street slang. He came up with The High Numbers. In Mod pecking order, a "number" was not as elevated as a style-setting "face," but a regular good guy all the same, devoted to the same

The Who as The High Numbers, September 1964

Neither side reflected the group's onstage dynamic, which was by now beginning to attract audiences on the live club circuit, including London Mod meccas like The Scene club in Soho, and the Goldhawk Social Club on Goldhawk Road. The recording sounded insipid, and despite Meaden going all-out on his publicity assault on the Mod-oriented pop press, the single—described as "The First Authentic Mod Record" in its promotional material—sank without a trace, selling a total of about five hundred copies after its release on July 3, 1964.

DESTRUCTION

Prior to the ill-fated release of their debut single, however, on June 30, 1964, a landmark event at the Railway Hotel in Harrow, north-west London, would change the group's fortunes, and subsequently the course of rock history. It was their first appearance at the venue, and the band were in the middle of a frantic R&B set, with Pete doing one of his electric distortion tricks by running the guitar against the metal mike stand, producing a series of bullet-like shots of feedback. He climaxed the aural onslaught by thrusting his guitar into the air, only to realize he'd made a hole in the low ceiling above the stage.

In what he later described as a split-second decision, Townshend continued to thrust the guitar into the ceiling until all that was left of the instrument was splintered wreckage. He held it aloft to the crowd, who roared approval. The mayhem immediately became part of the High Numbers' act, as the next week at the Railway saw Pete overturning their stack of Marshall amplifiers, Roger swinging his mike on its lead like some weapon of war, and Keith Moon kicking over his drum kit. From then on, the orgy of destruction became the band's trademark, a signature wild finale to all their shows.

Delivering their blistering interpretation of raw rhythm and blues with a nervous energy that threatened to spill over into nihilistic violence at any moment, the band quickly achieved what Peter Meaden could only dream of, as they became regarded by their growing legions of fans as the personification of Mod.

Townshend would later link the onstage chaos with the notion of "auto-destructive art," to which he had been introduced by one of his art college lecturers, Gustav Metzger. "We're trying to advance music. To that end we employ physical and visual violence in our

music, the same fashion, and (referencing the "high") the same drugs—mainly amphetamine "pep pills."

Meaden arranged another recording session, at the same label— Fontana Records—who had rejected them prior to Keith Moon's eventual recruitment. Assuming control at seemingly every level, Peter Meaden proceeded to organize the material for The High Numbers' first (and only) single. First, he and the band selected two American R&B discs which they all felt happy with: "Misery" by The Dynamics, and "I Got Love If You Want It" by Slim Harpo. Then Meaden, keeping closely to the originals, rewrote both songs as potential Mod anthems under his own name. The result was "Zoot Suit," (a Mod reference to a clothing item) as the A-side, based on "Misery," and "I'm the Face," which borrowed heavily from the Harpo record.

Pete Townshend smashes up his guitar; a recurring stage antic in The Who's live shows for which Townshend became notorious

act. There's conflict when we play . . . tension. We want to smash everything; it's part of what's happening to us and to our audiences."

But to the group's youthful followers, it had more in common with the amphetamine-fueled mayhem of a bank holiday trip to the coast.

LAMBERT AND STAMP

In what would seem an example of pure serendipity, present in the audience at that first Railway Hotel gig was a young filmmaker, Kit Lambert. Lambert was researching a documentary he was planning with his friend Chris Stamp, showing the youth culture of London through the life of a new, undiscovered pop

group. Amazed by Townshend's guitar-smashing and the audience reaction, he brought Stamp to the band's next gig at the venue the following week.

The two decided the High Numbers should be the subject of their film, but as they got more deeply involved with the band, saw their chance and offered to manage them. This suited the group, who felt they had got as far as they could with Meaden and Gorden, and were impressed by the more dynamic approach of Lambert and Stamp. A deal was struck, and the first move under the new management was to revert to the name the band had chosen for themselves originally—The Who.

Kit Lambert was the son of Constant Lambert, musical director of the Royal Ballet at Covent Garden; Chris Stamp, on the other hand, was from an ordinary working-class family, although there was a performance connection in that his brother was an established film actor, Terence Stamp. The chemistry between the

Chris Stamp (L) and Kit Lambert (R), pictured in 1966

two worked for The Who—Lambert related to Pete's art college background, encouraging his songwriting, while Stamp was the no-nonsense wheeler-dealer. As Townshend would reflect, "Most importantly, the two of them knew how to get things done."

Through the summer of '64, The Who began to get bottom-of-the-bill spots on big pop package shows, headlined by, among others, The Beatles, The Kinks, and Dusty Springfield. Their star was rising, albeit slowly. What they needed was another record release.

The Who's repertoire was still the staple R&B playlist, delivered in their high-octane style. But what became clear, after a couple of failed auditions, was that what record companies wanted from any new pop group was original material. With that in mind, Pete got down to some concentrated composing, while Lambert and Stamp arranged for a meeting with Shel Talmy, the American producer of The Kinks' first hit "You Really Got Me," which had recently topped the UK charts.

Talmy first saw the band live at a gig in Shepherd's Bush, west London, and liked what he heard. At later meetings, they played him what would be their first single as The Who, a new song by Pete called "I Can't Explain," and in November Talmy booked them into a session at Pye Studios.

As with many rock band sessions at the time, producers often arranged for session players to be on hand if they were needed, and Pete was taken aback to find someone there to fill in on lead guitar if need be—by the name of Jimmy Page. Page was already a respected name on the session scene, and Talmy had used him for the guitar solo on the Kinks' hit. In the event, Townshend's performance was strong enough to be retained as part of the lead sound, with Page playing a collaborative role. Also guesting anonymously were The Ivy League, providing Beach Boys-sounding backing vocals.

The band felt the single, with its tougher, bluesy B-side "Bald Headed Woman" featuring Page more prominently, was a move away from their uncompromising style of R&B to something a lot more pop-sounding. Nevertheless, they hoped it was the first step to the rock 'n' roll big time, and when it

was released on January 15, 1965 it was certainly a step in that direction, climbing to No. 8 on the British singles chart by mid-April. Since then the song has been a favorite among fans over the decades, and remained a staple number in live shows by The Who.

MAXIMUM R&B

The progress of "I Can't Explain" up the charts was accompanied by the growing popularity of The Who on the live rock circuit. Key to this, in the London area at least, was the Tuesday-night residency at the Marquee Club in Wardour Street, that Lambert and Stamp had fixed for the group commencing the end of November, 1964.

The Marquee residency continued for half a year, each week breaking the club's attendance records. And it was the booking at the club that prompted one of the all-time iconic images in rock 'n' roll graphics, the famous "Maximum R&B" poster. It was the creation of a designer friend of Kit Lambert, Brian Pike, and pictured Pete, arm aloft after he'd just struck a chord, with the now-familiar Who logo designed with an arrow coming out of the "O," and the "Maximum R&B" slogan underneath.

The Who, perform live onstage at the Marquee Club in Wardour Street, London, where the band had an early residency, circa 1965

Kit and Chris's connections proved invaluable in securing media coverage for the band, not least when Kit managed to get the group on the hippest TV music show at the time, *Ready, Steady, Go!* Lambert knew the show's producer Vicki Wickham, who allowed him to ship in a hundred fans from the regular Marquee crowd, flooding the live studio audience with voluble Who supporters. The program was by then *the* flagship of Mod, and on that night of January 29, 1965—and on their many appearances that followed—The Who had taken over its captaincy.

Just as "I Can't Explain" was hitting its peak position on the Top Ten chart, on April 13, 1965, The Who were in the IBC studios in central London, preparing material for their second single with Shel Talmy. Pete was anxious to achieve the sound they had onstage, and with its use of feedback throughout—a breakthrough in a pop single—"Anyway, Anyhow, Anywhere" did just that. The song, with its jazz-influenced lyrics, a call-and-response structure punctuated by Moon's energized drum breaks, and some keen piano fill-ins

by session player Nicky Hopkins, was co-written by Townshend and Daltrey, the only time the pair ever collaborated as composers. Released on May 21, the single didn't do quite as well as "I Can't Explain," but nevertheless reached No.10 in the UK.

The Who were riding high, and through the summer of 1965 toured British seaside resorts, plus the usual club circuit, and made forays into continental Europe in Holland, Denmark, and Sweden, where their two singles had enjoyed modest success. They had still to make an impression in the United States, where "I Can't Explain" had made a minor impact on the *Billboard* Hot Hundred at No. 93, and the *Cashbox* singles chart at No. 57.

GENERATION

When the band went into IBC Studios on October 13,

1965, it was to record their next single; the song they chose had been gestating for a while in various stages of completion, initially called simply "Generation." Pete Townshend had been working on the number throughout the summer, gradually honing the lyrics to create a song that would become one of the true anthems of rock 'n' roll.

The essence of the recording was Roger's staccato delivery, a stammering enunciation that at the time Townshend claimed was simulating a teenager high on amphetamines: "Yeah, the guy who's singing is supposed to be blocked," he told one journalist. "It's reminiscent in a way because Mods don't get blocked any more. They get drunk or other things. Pills was a phase." Elsewhere, Pete said the stutter was introduced after he'd heard "Stuttering Blues" by John Lee Hooker. Conversely, producer Talmy said it was just a "happy

FAR LEFT
The famous "Maximum R&B" poster. It was created by a friend of Kit Lambert, Brian Pike, and featured the now-familiar Who logo designed with an arrow coming out of the "O". LEFT The Who appearing on TV show *Ready, Steady, Go!*, in 1965

trigger the release of The Who's first album, of which it was the title track.

THE ALBUM

Shel Talmy was well aware that if two or three singles proved successful, an album would be the next step. During the April recording sessions that produced "Anyway, Anyhow, Anywhere," The Who were already laying down some of the R&B-oriented material that was core to their live performances, nine tracks in all. Later in the year, at the "My Generation" sessions, more tracks were produced, this time leaning in favor of Townshend originals.

The album was released in the UK on December 3, 1965, its twelve songs dominated by Pete's compositions, with just three rhythm and blues covers—two by James Brown (a particular Mod favorite), and one by Bo Diddley. For the American version, *The Who Sings My Generation*, which wasn't released until April 25, 1966, the Diddley track was dropped to make way for "Circles" (aka "Instant Party"), a Townshend song recorded in January.

On its release, the band felt that the album sounded like a bit of a rushed job, that they'd moved on since recording some of the tracks eight months earlier, and that it failed to reflect their onstage sound. Whatever, fans loved it, and it was soon hitting No. 5 in the UK album charts.

In retrospect, *My Generation* has been reappraised as one of the strongest examples of British R&B at its most dynamic and original, bridging the gap between the straight-ahead blues bands of the mid-sixties, and the heavier more experimental blues-based outfits that would emerge toward the end of the decade. Not to mention heralding punk and new wave music, still a dozen years in the future.

accident," (confirmed by Daltrey on more than one occasion), when Roger couldn't hear his voice through the monitors, so struggled to fit the lyrics with the music.

In addressing the "them and us" confrontation of youth and maturity, conformist and rebel—even the contradictions of honesty and hypocrisy—what had originally been considered a lightweight song through numerous rehearsals, was now a stark (albeit minimalistic) no-holds-barred celebration of generational conflict. With the line "I hope I die before I get old," Townshend provided a timeless slogan for disaffected youth everywhere.

Released on October 29, just a couple of weeks after the recording, "My Generation" shot up the UK charts to No. 2. Hitting the Top Ten in another half dozen countries—Australia, Austria, Canada, Ireland, Holland, and West Germany—its success would

MY GENERATION

TRACK LIST (original vinyl edition)
[All songs written by Pete Townshend except where indicated]

SIDE ONE
1. Out in the Street
2. I Don't Mind [James Brown]
3. The Good's Gone
4. La-La-La-Lies
5. Much Too Much
6. My Generation

SIDE TWO
1. The Kids Are Alright
2. Please, Please, Please [James Brown, John Terry]
3. It's Not True
4. I'm a Man [McDaniel]
5. A Legal Matter
6. The Ox [Pete Townshend, John Entwistle, Keith Moon, Nicky Hopkins]

RECORDED: April, October–November 1965, IBC Studios, London
RELEASED: December 3, 1965 (UK), April 25, 1966 (US)
LABEL: Brunswick (UK), Decca (US)
PRODUCER: Shel Talmy
PERSONNEL: Roger Daltrey (vocals, harmonica, tambourine); Pete Townshend (guitar, vocals); John Entwistle (bass guitar, vocals); Keith Moon (drums, vocals); Nicky Hopkins (piano)
CHART POSITIONS / AWARDS: No. 5, UK album chart; UK Gold disc

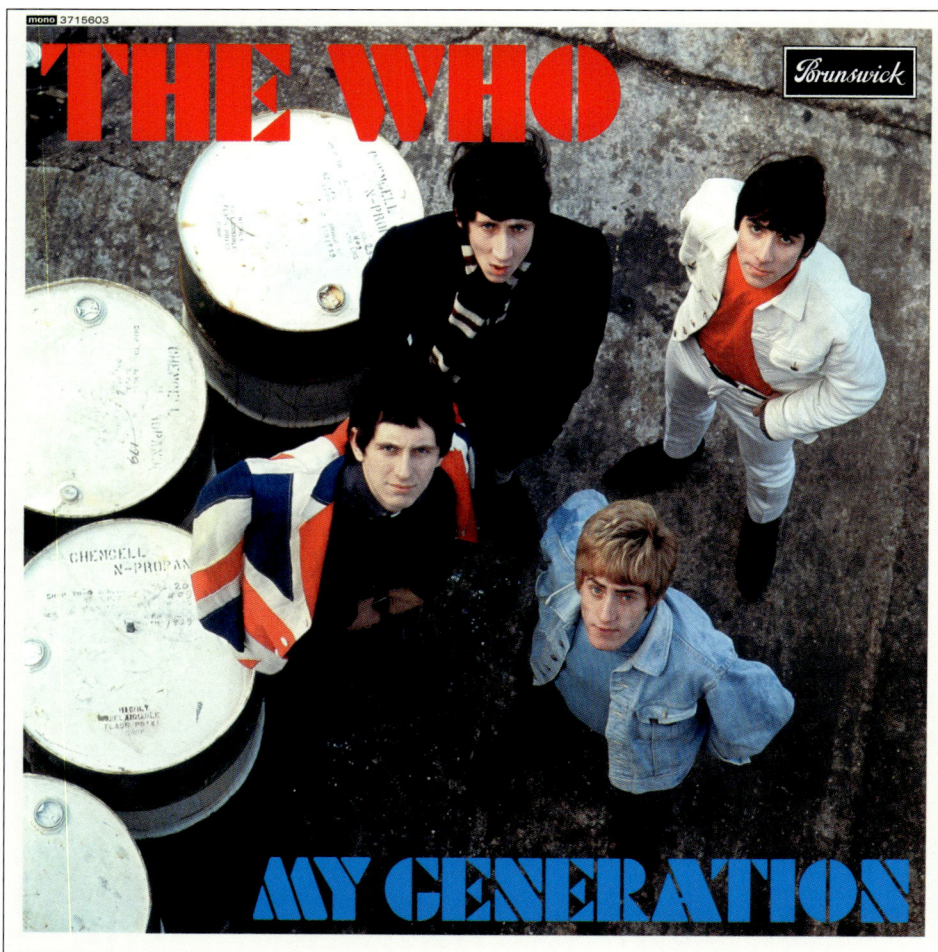

OUT IN THE STREET
What sounds like a false start from Daltrey into the intro soon establishes a strident rock chant, his twenty-one-year-old voice exuding the confidence of a time-served rhythm-and-bluesman.

I DON'T MIND
The first of two numbers by James Brown, reflecting The Who's popularity among the soul-hungry Mod fraternity.

THE GOOD'S GONE
At four minutes, by 1965 rock and pop standards a long track. A great buildup with droning guitar that carries the listener on, almost hypnotically, through the song.

LA-LA-LA-LIES
With its doo-wop backing vocals and great piano from guest Nicky Hopkins, a gem. Released as a single a year after the album appeared, it failed to chart in the UK but made No. 7 in Sweden.

MUCH TOO MUCH
Listening to tracks like this, you can hear where later Brit rockers like Oasis were coming from.

MY GENERATION
Instrumentally, during its three minutes and twenty seconds the now-classic track highlights every aspect of the band's sound. Pete's feedback-laden guitar is ever-present; there are some typically furious drum breaks from Moon; and John Entwistle contributes one of the earliest bass guitar solos in rock music.

THE KIDS ARE ALRIGHT
As sixties-pop as The Who ever sounded—in a blindfold test they could almost be mistaken for The Hollies, among others. Released as a single in September 1966, it made it into the top fifty at No. 41.

PLEASE, PLEASE, PLEASE
Roger totally under the influence of the original, in a nevertheless passionate rendition of the James Brown soul classic.

IT'S NOT TRUE
A jaunty rocker, with some rockabilly flavor from the rich harmonies. It just shows how varied The Who's sound could be, even at this early stage in their recording career.

I'M A MAN
A Bo Diddley R&B standard with some down-home piano from Nicky Hopkins, cosmic riffing from Townshend, and great, raunchy blues delivery by Roger Daltrey.

A LEGAL MATTER
Another hectic rocker, which Shel Talmy saw fit to put out as a single in March '66, after he had parted company with the band. The lyrics, with Pete singing lead, offer a pessimistic view of wedded bliss: "My mind's lost in a household fog / Wedding gowns and catalogues / Kitchen furnishings and houses / Maternity clothes and baby's trousers."

THE OX
A wild improvised instrumental jam, including Hopkins on piano, closes the album—inspired in no small part by the 1963 surf classic "Wipe Out," by the Surfaris. For Moon, it harked back to his time with a surf combo, The Beachcombers.

2 A QUICK ONE

The release of "My Generation," and the titular album just a few weeks later, marked the end of what we might think of as The Who's original Mod period. As early as August 1965, a piece by Nick Jones in the *Melody Maker* describing the cost of the band's instrument-smashing was headed "The Price of Pop Art—The Who Count the Cost" and firmly linked them with the Pop Art movement that Pete had learned about at art college: "The Who stand firmly for pop art. By their terms, pop art means how they behave and dress both on and off stage."

POP ART

As far as The Who's image was concerned, by the end of the year the neat minimalism of Mod had given way to the more flamboyant visual statements of Pop Art. And their music had likewise moved from the purely R&B inspiration evident on *My Generation*, even before the album was released.

The Pop Art movement as such had developed in the late fifties and early sixties, both in the United States and the UK. Celebrating the visual messages of mass culture, it made icons out of the ordinary and the everyday: think Andy Warhol's Campbell's soup cans, Jasper Johns's stars-and-stripes flags, or David Hockney's Typhoo Tea packet.

For The Who it meant a jacket created out of the Union Jack flag (draped over John Entwistle's shoulders on the *My Generation* album sleeve), the iconic Royal Air Force red-white-and-blue roundel that became almost a trademark for the band, and other appropriated symbols. And it wasn't just via The Who that pop art iconography came back into the cultural mainstream where it had originated; the striking graphics that formed the backdrop to *Ready, Steady, Go!* were created by students from the Royal College of Art (where Hockney, Peter Blake, and other UK Pop Art pioneers had studied), specifically recruited to design the sets.

Not long after the release of *My Generation*, a dispute blew up with Shel Talmy. It transpired that the producer had a sub-licensing deal with Decca Records in America—the band's label Brunswick was US Decca's outlet in the UK—so the band themselves ended up with a minimal royalty. A lengthy legal battle ensued, but in the meantime The Who left Talmy and signed with Robert Stigwood's Reaction label.

SUBSTITUTE

The first thing Lambert and Stamp did after signing the band to Reaction was to get them back into the studio for their next single. That was on February 12, 1966, at Olympic Studios in Barnes, south-west London; the single was "Substitute."

Inspired in part by Smokey Robinson and the Miracles' "The Tracks of My Tears," and the Rolling Stones' "19th Nervous Breakdown," by his own admission Townshend addressed a personal crisis of self-identity in the song: "I heard in my own voice the tumult of a young man playing a role, uneasily, repackaging black R&B music from America, relying on gimmicky outfits, and pretending to be wild and free when in reality he needed to be looked after by his mother."

In the absence of Shel Talmy the record was produced by Townshend, and released in the UK on March 4; it immediately charted, rising to No. 5. In the event, the first version, released with "Circles" (which Talmy had intended for the A-side) on the B-side, had to be withdrawn due to Talmy's pending legal action. Then, incredibly, a week later it was rereleased with

PREVIOUS PAGES The Who, while shooting their own TV show in Amsterdam, Netherlands. September 20, 1965
LEFT Pete performing his infamous "windmill" arm live onstage at the Bath Pavilion, October 10, 1966

ABOVE John and Keith enjoying an on-the-road break in June 1966
OPPOSITE Keith Moon at home with wife Kim Kerrigan and daughter Mandy, 1968

the same flip side now renamed "Instant Party." That version too was pulled out of circulation, and a third release appeared with an instrumental "Waltz for a Pig" (the title allegedly aimed at Talmy) on the flip. Credited to The Who Orchestra, "Waltz . . ." was actually performed by R&B group The Graham Bond Organisation, a jazz-oriented lineup including Bond on Hammond organ, Dick Heckstall-Smith on sax, and Ginger Baker on drums (who wrote the number, using the pseudonym Harry Butcher).

FRICTIONS

Prior to "Substitute" entering the charts, The Who were never far from the headlines, and it wasn't just the nightly guitar smashing that grabbed media attention. Early in January, on the BBC TV program *A Whole*

Scene Going, Pete had admitted using drugs——still a shock-horror story for the tabloid press back in the mid-sixties. And some early high-profile exposure in the United States, where they were yet to make an impact on the charts, came that same month when they appeared on the last-ever edition of the influential TV music show *Shindig!*, playing "I Can't Explain" and "My Generation," prerecorded in London.

With the Talmy court case looming over everything they did, personality differences in the band became more focused and, at times, fraught. Moon and Entwistle had bonded in what Townshend would later describe as "a drug fuelled alliance," and were privately talking about leaving the band. Things came to a head on May 20, when the pair were late for a gig in Newbury, Berkshire, after hanging out on the set of *Ready, Steady, Go!* with Bruce Johnston of the Beach Boys. Tempers flared onstage, and during the "My Generation" finale, Townshend attacked Moon with his guitar, the drummer receiving a black eye. Keith and John actually left the band there and then, right after the performance, but were back a week later.

It wasn't the first instance of violence erupting within the group. Back in October 1965, during a short trip to Sweden and Denmark, Daltrey—frustrated by the constant pill-induced, nonsensical banter between the other three—lashed out at Moon, giving him a bloody nose. This seemed to drive a wedge between the drummer and Daltrey, which persisted for some time to come.

Less volatile than relationships within the band, initially at least, was when on March 17, Keith Moon got married at Brent Registry Office. He'd been dating model Kim Kerrigan since January 1965, and when she found herself pregnant Moon did what was then generally considered "the right thing" (under considerable parental pressure) and agreed they would marry. Their daughter, Amanda, was born in July, but their family life was fractious, and after a series of marital traumas, in 1975, Kim sued for a divorce: "He had no idea how to be a father, he was too much of a child himself."

A LEGAL MATTER

When the Shel Talmy case came to court, the result wasn't what The Who, Lambert, or Stamp would have preferred. The court ruled in favor of the American producer, granting him five percent of all the band's recording income for the next five years. He also retained rights to the material he had produced,

> # "I don't know that it was music; it was more like watching violence put to rhythm."

ALAN SMITH, *NME*, MAY 1966

which meant he was able to release any tracks from the *My Generation* album, along with others recorded during his sessions with the band.

Quick off the mark, and much to the band's annoyance, in March 1966 Talmy released (ironically?) "A Legal Matter" without their permission. The move was clearly to challenge the release of "Substitute," although the latter made the Top Five while "A Legal Matter," without the band to promote it, languished at No. 32.

Talmy continued to release singles from the album, with "The Kids Are Alright" appearing in September, making the Top Fifty at No. 41, and "La-La-La-Lies" in December, when it failed to chart in the UK but hit the No. 7 spot in Sweden. The debut album itself was released in the United States in April 1966, as *The Who Sings My Generation*, under Talmy's deal with Decca. In that version, the Bo Diddley track "I'm a Man" was replaced by "Instant Party (Circles)," which Talmy had intended as the follow-up single to "My Generation" before his severance from the band.

I'M A BOY

Through 1966, The Who hardly stopped touring, playing live virtually every night across the length and breadth of the UK, with occasional forays into Ireland, Scandinavia (where they were particularly popular), Holland, and West Germany.

Highlights of their gig sheet included a May 1 appearance at the *NME* (*New Musical Express*) Poll Winners' concert at the Empire Pool, Wembley. Along with an amazing lineup of eighteen acts that included The Beatles (their last-ever concert appearance in the UK), The Rolling Stones, Dusty Springfield, and The Small Faces, the band had time for just two numbers—

"Substitute" and "My Generation." Reviewing the show, *NME* writer Alan Smith commented on The Who's set: "I don't know that it was music; it was more like watching violence put to rhythm."

And on July 30 they appeared at the major UK music festival, the Sixth National Jazz and Blues Festival, held in Windsor. Again their onstage theatrics elicited most attention from reviews, including the "musicians' bible" *Melody Maker*: "The Who enjoyed themselves smashing footlights, kicking over amplifiers, breaking guitars, demolishing drums, throwing buckets of water at the audience, and managed to squeeze in 'Barbara Ann,' 'Heatwave,' and 'My Generation' in between." Even Townshend sensed that the mayhem was becoming a Who cliché, as he reflected in his 2012 autobiography: "The summer dragged on, the band's antics on stage becoming a parody of auto-destruction with smoke and flashes."

The day after the Windsor festival, The Who were back in the studio, this time to record their next single, "I'm a Boy." Lyrically, it demonstrated how far Pete Townshend's songwriting was moving away from conventional pop-tune subject matter. The song was originally planned as part of a mini-opera called *Quads*, set in a future world in which parents can select the sex of their children; in the song, a couple who choose four girls end up with, due to a mistake, three girls and a boy. The mother brings the boy up like his sisters—"I'm a boy, I'm a boy, but my Ma won't admit it"—hinting at all sorts of gender issues which we would recognize today.

Recorded over two days, the single was produced by Kit Lambert (who Pete would describe as "a joy to work with"), and released three weeks later on August 26 with "In the City" on the B-side. John Entwistle featured on the recording on French horn as well as bass guitar, harking back to his days in the Middlesex Schools Symphony Orchestra. Another success story, "I'm a Boy" reached No. 2 in the UK charts, and also made No. 2 in New Zealand, an indication that their popularity was spreading worldwide, though they had yet to crack the United States in any significant way.

John Entwistle at CBS Studios, New Bond Street, London, recording "Don't Look Away", October 3, 1966

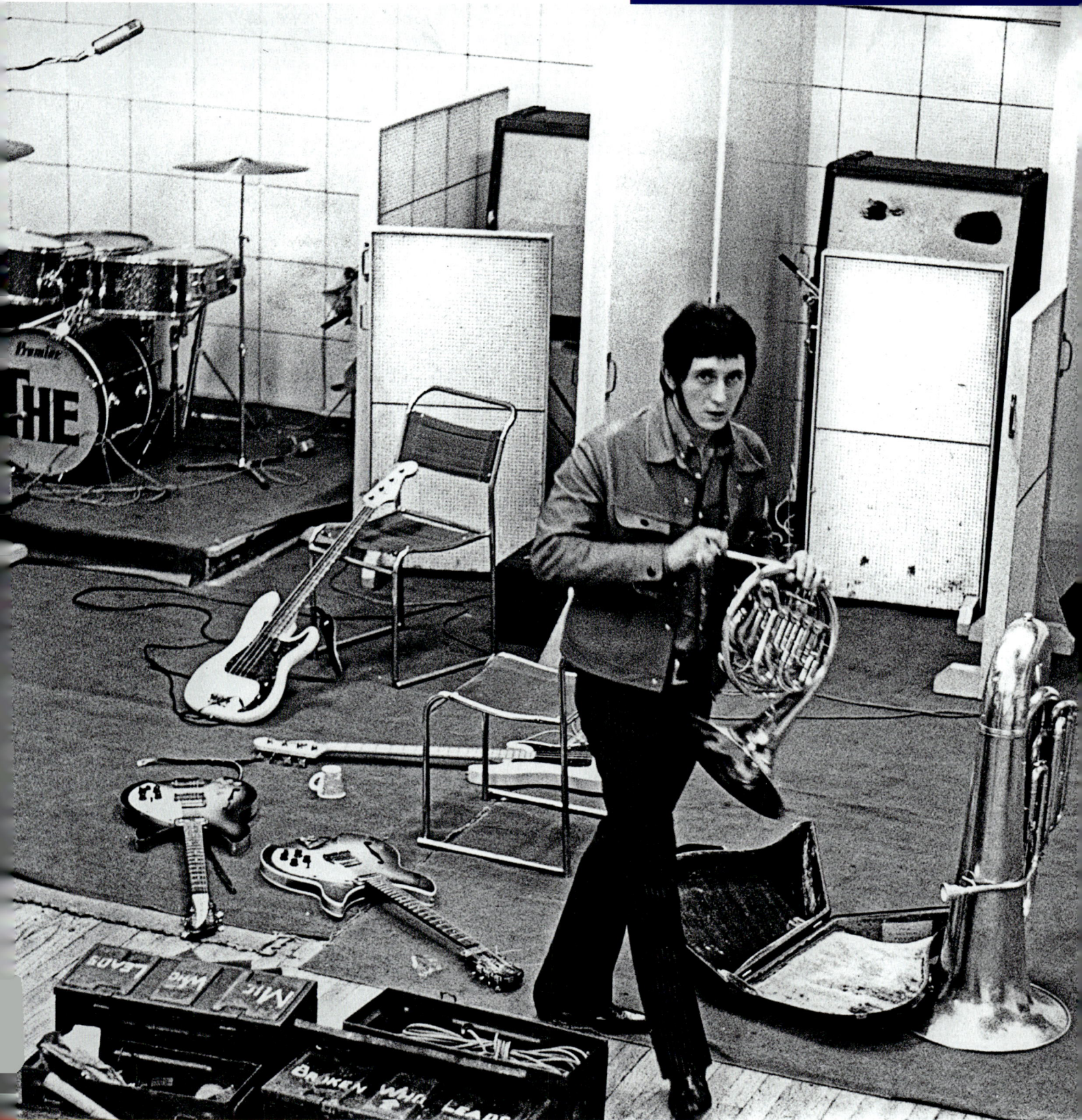

English artist and graphic designer Alan Aldridge, who created the album cover artwork for *A Quick One*

READY STEADY WHO

The "I'm a Boy" sessions also included another song intended for the never-to-be completed *Quads*, "Disguises," which was released later in the year on the *Ready Steady Who* EP.

In the fifties and sixties particularly, the seven-inch vinyl EP (extended play) record was a less expensive alternative to a full-length album. Indeed, many pop albums were also split into two or three EPs, each typically featuring two songs per side. And occasionally big-name rock acts—including The Beatles and The Rolling Stones—would issue an EP of otherwise unavailable material.

Recorded at various sessions between February and early October, 1966, the *Ready Steady Who* EP had no direct connection with the TV show, although there was a close relationship between the band and the program due to the frequency of their appearances.

The record featured two Who originals, the aforementioned "Disguises," and "Circles," which with its alternative title, "Instant Party," already had a complicated history as part of the Shel Talmy dispute. The second side of the EP presented three covers: a short instrumental take on Neil Hefti's theme for the *Batman* TV series; "Bucket T," a Keith Moon vocal excursion part-written by Dean Torrence of the surf pioneers Jan and Dean; and another surf specialty, the classic "Barbara Ann" released by the Beach Boys in 1965.

Ready Steady Who was released on November 11, and topped the British EP charts, but was not made available in any other countries. Many fans and critics saw it as a "filler" of material that otherwise had no home, as they eagerly awaited the band's next album, which would appear on December 9, just a month later.

Before the next album, however, another single was scheduled. Recorded at CBS Studios in London on November 9 and 10, right after The Who's second Scandinavian tour of that year, "Happy Jack" was another Townshend composition spotlighting a social outsider. This time the misfit was based on a mentally challenged character who slept on a beach on the Isle of Man, who Townshend remembered from family holidays there as a child. The song describes how children would tease the harmless unfortunate—apparently on one occasion, kids buried him in the sand—who always responded with just an innocent smile.

"Happy Jack" was intended for release on December 3, a week ahead of the new album, but due to technical problems appeared the same day as the LP. It would be The Who's sixth big seller, hitting No. 3 in the UK charts, and also giving the band their first No. 1 when it topped the chart in Canada. And after its American release in March 1967, it was their first US single to appear in the Top Forty, at No. 24.

A QUICK ONE

Alongside *Ready Steady Who*, recording for the new album had spread across several sessions starting at the end of August, with the bulk being completed in October and November. Managers Chris Stamp and Lambert (who was producing) came up with a publishing deal via their own new publishing setup New Action, whereby the album had to feature at least two songs each from Roger, Keith, and John, in addition to material from Pete.

To that end, Entwistle and Moon supplied two each, and in the event Roger Daltrey wrote only one, while Pete contributed three regular songs plus a nine-minute "mini-opera." The latter was initially instigated by Kit Lambert, suggesting Pete create a linked sequence of several different themes that he was working on. The result was "A Quick One, While He's Away," an innovation that The Who would later expand on in the full-length "rock operas" *Tommy* and *Quadrophenia*. And in the absence of a second track from Daltrey, the album also included a cover of the Motown classic "Heat Wave," a 1963 hit by Martha and the Vandellas.

The Who, in archetypal Mod gear, circa 1966

The cover design of *A Quick One* was certainly more ambitious than the posed "pop group" photo on *My Generation*. Created by the celebrated graphic designer and illustrator Alan Aldridge, the images of the four members, with song titles coming out of their instruments, was in the "psychedelic" graphic style just coming into fashion in late 1966.

Sales-wise, the album went one better than its predecessor in the UK, making No. 4 in the album chart. And it was well received, though not always ecstatically, by reviewers. Certainly, after the underwhelming response to their debut LP in many quarters, critics saw it as a step in a more interesting and challenging direction. In an in-depth *Melody Maker* review, Chris Welch colorfully described their previous ideas as being "smothered in a fog of feuding, and a clutter of broken amplifiers and blitzed drums," but praised *A Quick One* as "a collection of compositions and treatments that captures the Who essence, humour, cynicism, nervous drive, violence, and delicacy."

A QUICK ONE

TRACK LIST (original vinyl edition)

SIDE ONE
1. Run Run Run [Pete Townshend]
2. Boris the Spider [John Entwistle]
3. I Need You [Keith Moon]
4. Whiskey Man [Entwistle]
5. Heatwave [Holland, Dozier, Holland]
6. Cobwebs and Strange [Moon]

SIDE TWO
1. Don't Look Away [Townshend]
2. See My Way [Roger Daltrey]
3. So Sad About Us [Townshend]
4. A Quick One, While He's Away [Townshend]
   I. Her Man's Been Gone
   II. Crying Town
   III. We Have a Remedy
   IV. Ivor the Engine Driver
   V. Soon Be Home
   VI. You Are Forgiven

RECORDED: August 30, November 1966, IBC Studios, London; Regent Sound Studios, London;
              Pye Studios, London
RELEASED: December 19, 1966 (UK), May 1967 (US)
LABEL: Reaction / Polydor (UK), Decca / MCA (US)
PRODUCER: Kit Lambert
PERSONNEL: Roger Daltrey (vocals, trombone); Pete Townshend (guitar, vocals, tin whistle);
              John Entwistle (bass guitar, vocals, French horn, trumpet); Keith Moon (drums, vocals, tuba)
CHART POSITIONS / AWARDS: No. 4, UK album chart; Gold disc, France

RUN RUN RUN
A rollicking Townshend opener that moves just like the title suggests, smoother than typical Who power pop of the time, but a great start to the album.

BORIS THE SPIDER
The first of John Entwistle's two songs on the LP, an amusing ditty about a monstrous spider that he delivers with gusto, singing the chorus in deep-throated unison with his bass lines.

I NEED YOU
A weird contribution from Moon, inspired by an encounter with The Beatles at London's Ad Lib nightclub, reflecting on the communication schisms that can occur between the very biggest stars and lesser mortals.

WHISKEY MAN
A great track from Entwistle, with a strong though doom-laden narrative, and a sound reflecting The Beatles' influence—perhaps unavoidable in the mid-sixties. John accompanies on French horn too.

HEAT WAVE
A terrific, energetic version of the Motown classic that was a long-time part of the band's onstage repertoire, and a nod here to their soul, Mod-friendly roots.

COBWEBS AND STRANGE
Another bizarre track from Keith Moon. According to Townshend, the marching-band instrumental was recorded as the group trooped around the studio playing a variety of unlikely wind instruments, including John on trumpet, Roger on trombone, Pete on a penny whistle, and Keith on tuba.

DON'T LOOK AWAY
Some great harmonies, on a Townshend song that reflected the sound of country rock, being pioneered at the time by the likes of The Byrds and Buffalo Springfield.

SEE MY WAY
Roger Daltrey's one song on the album, a Buddy Holly-inspired number which benefits from some effective French horn and trombone by Entwistle.

SO SAD ABOUT US
The interaction of bass and drums, and typically jangling guitar, adds up to a classic sixties pop sound. The song was originally written by Pete for the Liverpool duo The Merseys.

A QUICK ONE, WHILE HE'S AWAY
Pete Townshend would admit that the nine-minute "mini-opera" was analogous to his own experiences as a child.

I. HER MAN'S BEEN GONE
A girl is grief-stricken as her boyfriend has been absent for a year. All four harmonize unaccompanied, *a cappella* style.

II. CRYING TOWN
Daltrey in Dylan mode, as the girl's constant crying upsets the whole town.

III. WE HAVE A REMEDY
Roger sounding more like himself, as the townsfolk tell her "he's only late."

IV. IVOR THE ENGINE DRIVER
John Entwistle as a dastardly engine driver, who briefly takes the absent lover's place.

V. SOON BE HOME
Again, the whole group harmonize as the absent cowboy turns up, and the girl confesses of her infidelity . . . the backing hinting at a lilting country sound.

VI. YOU ARE FORGIVEN
"Dang, dang, dang" opens . . . prompting a final reconciliation between the two estranged lovers. Townshend takes the lead. The band wanted cellos to play an orchestration, but as Lambert said they couldn't afford it, they sang "cello, cello, cello" instead.

3 THE WHO
SELL OUT

The closing days of 1966 marked the end of one era and the beginning of another, encapsulated in two gigs involving The Who.

On December 20, they recorded their spot for the final edition of *Ready, Steady, Go!*, the show that had put cutting-edge rock on the map, and The Who in particular, over the past three years. Retitled *Ready, Steady, Goes!*, the farewell program included appearances by a dozen or so top names including Mick Jagger, Eric Burdon, Lulu, and Donovan. The Who played short prerecorded versions of Johnny Kidd's "Please Don't Touch," and "I'm a Boy."

Then on New Year's Eve, the band took part in a 10pm-till-dawn extravaganza at London's Roundhouse, billed as "Psychedelicamania: Giant New Year's Eve Freak Out All Night Rave!" Featuring Pink Floyd, The Who, and The Move, it was one of the early manifestations of the "flower power" era that was about to explode in the "Summer of Love" six months later. It included a projected light show (a new innovation, but soon almost obligatory at rock concerts) staged, coincidentally, by Gustav Metzger, who had introduced Pete to the notion of auto-destructive art back at Ealing Art College.

MAKING TRACKS
Sensing the changes apparent all around, in late '66, Lambert and Stamp decided the time was right to launch their own record label. "I've spent my life having rows with record companies," Lambert told *Disc* magazine, "and the only solution was to start my own." Although The Who would have seemed the

natural choice to kick off the label, Track Records, it was a new, little-known American guitar player who had that distinction: His name was Jimi Hendrix.

Hendrix had been around the London scene for a couple of months, managed by Chas Chandler, former bass player with The Animals. When Lambert heard the guitarist for the first time, at a showcase gig at the trendy Scotch of St James night club, he was stunned, and told Chandler there and then he wanted Hendrix to launch the new label he and Stamp were planning.

Hendrix's extraordinary sound astonished all who heard him, not least Pete Townshend. The twenty-four-year-old American's style was steeped in rhythm and blues, but delivered with a phenomenal technique and outrageous theatrics, including much use of feedback, distortion, and playing the guitar with his teeth and behind his back. Townshend sensed that his own trademark gimmicks were being challenged on an altogether different plane: "It was as though he had discovered a new instrument in a new world of musical impressionism."

The debut single by Hendrix was earmarked for Track, but the label was not yet fully operational, so the iconic "Hey Joe" appeared under the banner of Track's distributor Polydor, in December 1966. The first record released by Track, and the second for The Jimi Hendrix Experience, was "Purple Haze," on March 17, 1967—a month before The Who appeared on the label.

The Who, in the meantime, had been making tracks of a different kind. Having spent the early part of the year touring the UK and Europe, on March 21, 1967, they embarked on their first working visit to the United States.

As well as whatever publicity had been secured for "Happy Jack," which was released in the US just a few days before their arrival, the band's live appearances

PREVIOUS PAGES November 12, 1966, Duke of York's Headquarters in Chelsea, London, UK. The group pose leaning on singer Roger Daltrey's car.
LEFT Keith Moon (L) and Pete Townshend (R) of The Who, live onstage at London's Marquee Club, March 1967

were as part of a nine-day-long festival-style series of concerts hosted by celebrity DJ Murray the K. Entitled "Music in the Fifth Dimension," the package of acts ran continuously, five times a day from ten in the morning, at New York's RKO 58th Street Theatre in Manhattan.

Top American names included Wilson Pickett, Simon & Garfunkel, and The Young Rascals; the only other UK act—at the bottom of the bill—was Cream. The crammed lineup meant that The Who were only given ten minutes for their performance on each show, enough time for just two numbers; nevertheless, they went all-out with the pyrotechnics and destruction, trashing mountains of equipment in the course of the week. The crowds loved it, the press publicity was sensational, and The Who's US fan base was born right there and then.

An eye-witness recollection from a fan who was there on the opening day says it all:

Quite frankly, most of the acts I saw that day are a blur to me now, except for the short but riveting performance(s) by The Who. There was something so raw, cool, and aggressive about them and their sound that they stood out miles ahead of the other performers. The Who had "IT," and for a 14-year-old, The Who was the epitome of Rock and Roll. Pete's windmills and guitar smash-ups were astounding, and I remember to this day the pungent smell of smoke when they finished their sets that day—yes, I could smell the smoke bombs from the 5th row!

The band's American debut, at the RKO 58th Street Theatre on March 25, 1967, in New York

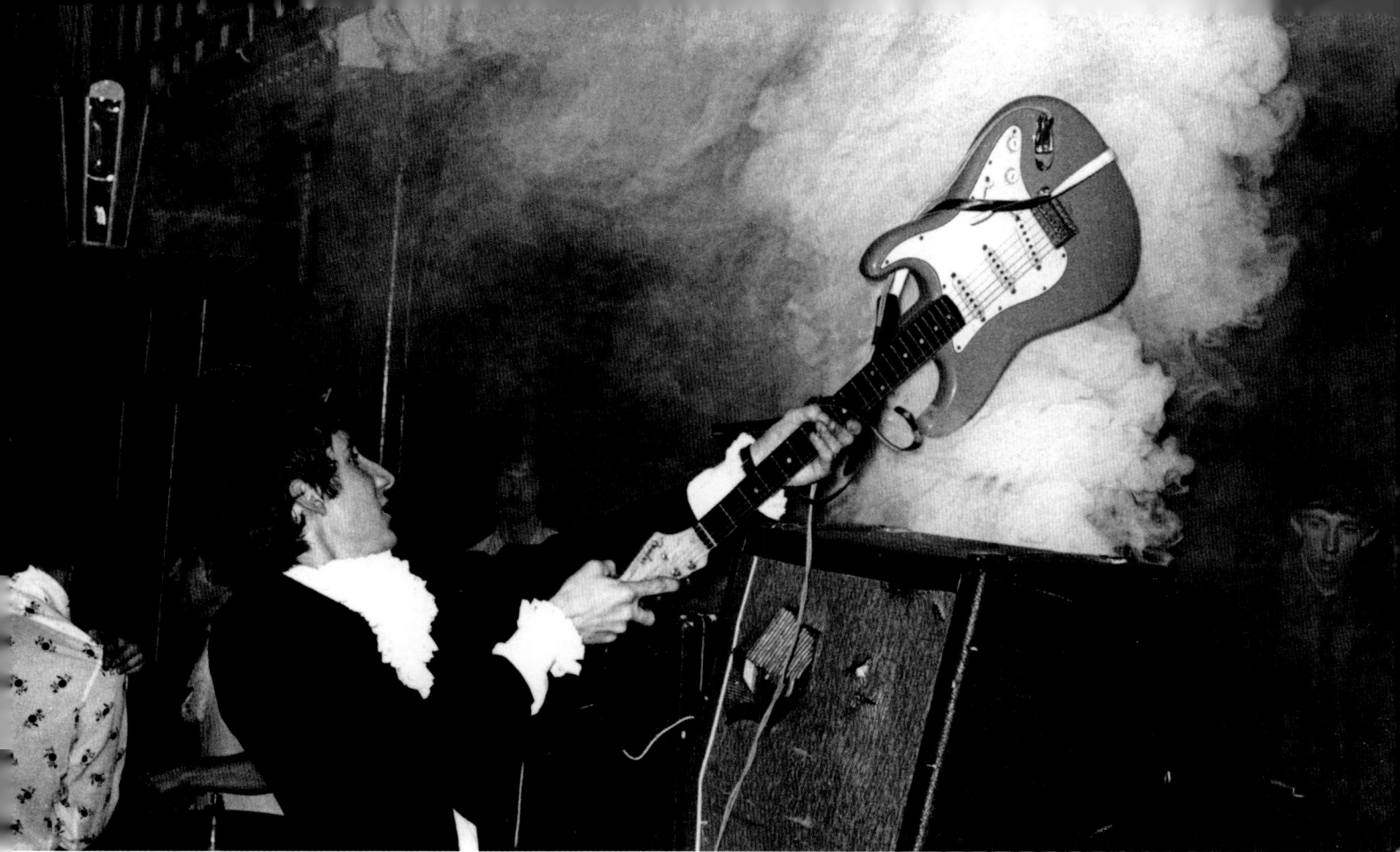

Pete smashes his guitar against an amplifier during a "Rag Rave" at Granby Halls, Leicester, UK, March 13, 1967

PICTURES OF LILY

The band flew back to London on April 3, and two days later were in the studio recording their next single, "Pictures of Lily" and John Entwistle's "Doctor, Doctor." "Pictures of Lily" was another Townshend teen-angst confessional, initially inspired by antique picture postcards of a scantily dressed Lily Langtry—the notorious Victorian-era actress, and mistress of the Prince of Wales—on the bedroom wall of his girlfriend, Karen Astley. In the song, the boy looking at the pictures is informed that the subject died in 1929 (as did Langtry), so has to be satisfied with—implied, but not mentioned explicitly—masturbation fantasies.

With its tight harmonies, energetic delivery, and crisp production values, "Pictures of Lily" was the epitome of mid–late sixties "power pop." Indeed, the term is thought to have been first coined by Pete Townshend in an interview in the *New Musical Express*, just a month after the single's release on April 22. The single became The Who's fifth to make

the UK Top Five, reaching No. 4, but the band had still to make a significant impression on the charts across the Atlantic.

Things were soon to change, however. After another string of gigs across continental Europe and the UK, on June 13 the band flew out to the US again, this time to make more substantial appearances than the short slots on the Murray the K package had afforded them. Now they were booked onto a new emerging rock circuit, closely linked to the "psychedelic" counterculture initially concentrated on the West Coast, and around San Francisco in particular.

MONTEREY POP

Their first two dates were in the Midwest, in Detroit and Chicago, before jetting westwards to appear for two nights at the Fillmore Auditorium in San Francisco. The Fillmore as a rock venue was the brainchild of promoter Bill Graham, and in 1967 was a leading venue on the new scene. Used to fifty-minute sets maximum, it was a baptism of fire for The Who after Graham told them they were expected to play two one-hour spots on each evening. But the pressure of hastily rehearsed material, including songs from their first two albums, paid off. The band rose to the occasion, Townshend praising the venue's PA system and acoustics, describing it as "The best gig we've ever played . . . a rock group's paradise."

Straight after the Fillmore concerts, the band flew down to Monterey, around a hundred miles south of 'Frisco, for the closing day of the Monterey International Pop Music Festival, the first big international gathering of the "beautiful people." Organized by record producer Lou Adler, Michelle and John Phillips of the Mamas and Papas, and ex-Beatles publicity man Derek Taylor, it was staged at the Monterey County Fairgrounds in California on June 16, 17, and 18, 1967—heralding the now-fabled "Summer of Love."

BELOW Performing at the Monterey Pop Festival on June 18, 1967 in California
OPPOSITE With Jimi Hendrix, circa. 1965. (L–R): Roger Daltrey, Pete Townshend, Jimi Hendrix, John Entwistle, and Keith Moon.

As well as featuring key names on the alternative rock scene including Country Joe and the Fish, The Grateful Dead, and Jefferson Airplane, the festival was the setting for the major American debuts of Janis Joplin, Jimi Hendrix, and The Who. On the closing Sunday evening, Pete Townshend was apprehensive about following Hendrix, given the latter's similar guitar-smashing finales. The two decided to toss a coin for it: Pete won, and The Who went on before the Hendrix Experience.

Just as well. Although The Who's instrument-destructing climax left some of the crowd yelling for more, others were just stunned by the sight of the onstage mayhem, and then Hendrix came on and topped even Pete and Keith's antics. Pouring lighter fuel over it and lighting a match, he set fire to his guitar, winning the crowd over completely. Pete Townshend would recall it as a milestone: "When Jimi set his guitar on fire, Mama Cass, who was sitting

next to me, turned and said 'Hey, destroying guitars is your thing!' I shouted back over the cheering, 'It used to be. It belongs to Jimi now.' And I meant every word."

Despite Townshend's fears of being upstaged by his (friendly) rival Hendrix, the event catapulted The Who into the front line of new UK acts ready to take on America, although immediate local press coverage was mixed. The *San Francisco Examiner* called them "The most impressive British group," while the *San Francisco Chronicle* described their set's riotous ending as "nothing at all to do with music. In fact it's really anti-music and disgraceful."

But the Monterey festival also marked the dawn of an all-too-short era—which effectively saw its final manifestation at Woodstock in 1969—of a peace-and-love fellowship among a generation of young people, and a backstage camaraderie often rare at musical events before or since. As Jefferson Airplane's

"When Jimi set his guitar on fire, Mama Cass, who was sitting next to me, turned and said 'Hey, destroying guitars is your thing!' I shouted back over the cheering, 'It used to be. It belongs to Jimi now.' And I meant every word."

PETE TOWNSHEND

Grace Slick remembered: "It was the first time many bands met and saw each other perform, so we were all really marveling at each other. It was just one good group of people after another, and different kinds of music—Jimi Hendrix to Ravi Shankar, The Mamas and the Papas to The Who . . . everybody was wandering around meeting each other. It was amazing."

The film director D.A. Pennebaker, who had made the groundbreaking *Don't Look Back* documentary of Bob Dylan's 1965 UK tour, shot footage of the entire festival; much of it (including The Who's dynamic closer "My Generation") would be included in his subsequent film *Monterey Pop*, released in May 1969.

LOVE IS ALL YOU NEED

Two days after Monterey, the band flew back to London. Their return to the UK was just two days before John Entwistle got married, on Friday, June 23, 1967. John wed his long-time girlfriend Alison Wise, who he had been dating since 1960, in a ceremony at Acton Congregational Church, which all the band attended.

With Keith Moon having married Kim Kerrigan the previous year, this left Pete Townshend as the only single member of The Who. Roger Daltrey had been married since 1964, to Jacqueline "Jackie" Rickman, who he'd wed after she got pregnant: "Pete was going out with a girl called Delores and Jackie was her friend. She was wonderful, but neither of us was ready to have a kid."

Sunday, June 25 saw Keith and his wife, Kim, joining in with The Beatles, at Abbey Road Studios. The occasion was a part of the celebrity back-up choir on "All You Need Is Love," for the first-ever live worldwide satellite broadcast, *Our World*. Others joining the chorus included Rolling Stones Keith Richards and Mick Jagger, both of whom would be appearing in court the following Wednesday.

The two Stones were tried on drugs charges, pertaining to circumstances that many felt were set up with the connivance of a tabloid newspaper, the *News of the World*.

As a gesture of support, Pete, Keith, and Roger (John being on honeymoon) went into De Lane Lea Studios and recorded two Rolling Stones songs, "The Last Time" and "Under My Thumb." In the event, after appealing, neither musician was sent to prison

as they had originally been sentenced, and Lambert announced that proceeds for The Who single—which hit No. 44 in the UK chart—would go to charity.

SEE FOR MILES

Early in July, the band set off again on a trek across the United States. A couple of gigs in New York—and a couple of recording sessions working on tracks for their next album—preceded a full-blown nine-week coast-to-coast tour, in the unlikely role as support act to the out-and-out pop outfit Herman's Hermits. In what Pete Townshend would describe as "our indoctrination into the real America," the group just played a straight twenty-minute warm-up spot at each show, while the largely teenybopper audience screamed for Herman (Peter Noone) and his group. Nevertheless, The Who received some rave notices for their brief but effective contribution.

Throughout the summer, both in the UK and America, the band had been in and out of studios in

ABOVE June 23, 1967. John Entwistle weds Alison Wise. OPPOSITE Keith Moon and his wife, Kim Kerrigan, protesting the prosecution of Rolling Stones' guitarist, Keith Richards, June 1967. Richards was being tried, along with fellow band member Mick Jagger, on drugs charges.

August 25, 1967, St. Louis, Missouri, USA. John Entwistle (front row, left) and Keith Moon (second row, left) traveling to the first of two shows at the Kiel Opera House where The Who are supporting Herman 's Hermits, whose lead singer, Peter Noone is pictured front row, right.

a somewhat sporadic style, preparing tracks for their next album. With the provisional title *Who's Lily?*, it was still nowhere near completion when they arrived back from the American trip in mid-September. One track was ready, however. The day after the final show of the Herman tour, which was in Honolulu, Hawaii, on September 10, the final mastering of "I Can See for Miles" was completed at Gold Star Studios in Los Angeles.

No strangers to drugs of one kind or another, whether it was via the Mod predilection for amphetamines, or the increasing popularity of marijuana, in 1967 it was inevitable that The Who would experience the hallucinogenic wonder of the age, LSD or "acid." "I Can See for Miles," apart from being what Townshend considered the best record they had yet made, and the best he had ever written, encapsulated the acid-tinged "psychedelic" sound of the era—clearly inspired by cutting-edge recordings such as The Beach Boys' "God Only Knows," and The Beatles' *Sgt. Pepper* album.

"I Can See for Miles" came out in the States as a rush-released single on September 18, 1967. It was the band's first American hit, climbing to No. 9 in the chart—aided no doubt by a literally explosive TV appearance on *The Smothers Brothers Comedy Hour*, when Moon had overfilled his bass drum with flash powder, and ignited it to devastating effect. Keith sustained some minor injuries, including a three-inch

wound in his arm, while Pete—who was the nearest to the blast—had a temporary loss of hearing. Released in the UK nearly a month later—where it made No. 10 —it would be the only single to be released from their next album, *The Who Sell Out*.

SELL OUT

There had been a number of songs in gestation over the past few months, and now the band were back in Britain it was time to put finishing touches to them, and decide on the overall structure of the forthcoming album, scheduled for the end of the year. The songs as such were unrelated to each other, with no uniform "concept" connecting them in any way, until the band came up with the idea of linking the tracks with mock advertising jingles—just as records are linked by ad breaks on commercial radio.

Pop radio had an odd history in the UK. Until the early sixties, the only station broadcasting a lot of pop and rock 'n' roll was Radio Luxembourg, beamed from the tiny European country since the thirties.

Pete helps US television host Tom Smothers destroy his acoustic guitar as Roger looks on, following The Who's performance on *The Smothers Brothers Comedy Hour*, September 15, 1967

Mainstream radio meant the BBC, with no advertising, and with pop music low in its priorities. Then in 1964, an offshore "pirate" station, Radio Caroline (named for the ship it broadcast from), challenged the status quo with a non-stop diet of pop records. The "crew" of fast-talking DJs had more in common with their American counterparts, like Murray the K and Wolfman Jack, than their contemporaries at the BBC. More pirate ships followed Caroline's example, until August 1967 when an act of parliament deemed them illegal.

Bands like The Who had been nurtured by the pirate ships, and on its release in December 1967, the album—now called *The Who Sell Out* as an ironic reference to the fact that they had actually made some real commercials themselves—was seen by many as a tribute to the outlawed maritime stations.

The album cover displayed four photographs of The Who plugging products featured on the recordings, two on the front and two on the back, shot by David Montgomery. The front photos were of Pete holding a giant-size stick of Odorono deodorant, and Roger sitting in a bath full of Heinz baked beans; on the reverse was Keith applying an acne cream called Medac, and John in a leopard-skin "caveman" outfit, with his arm around a blonde model in a leopard-skin bikini (one of the fake jingles referred to Charles Atlas's famous bodybuilding course).

Considering that it didn't sit comfortably with the counterculture ethos of 1967, being ostensibly a celebration of commercialism—though tongue-in-cheek, the irony might have been lost on many hippies, particularly in America—the album was generally well received by reviewers. In the US, *Rolling Stone*'s Jann Wenner praised its musicianship, humor, and total originality, while *Esquire* rated the band as "the third best not just in Britain but the world."

Due to disagreements about the running order, and various threats of litigation from some of the companies whose products were being cited without permission, the original British release date was postponed from November 17 to December 15, ahead of its US release on January 6, 1968. The album just scraped into the US Top Fifty at No. 48, while hitting No. 13 in the UK. Perhaps surprisingly, given the pop culture references in much of the material, its best chart position was achieved in France, at No. 3.

THE WHO SELL OUT

TRACK LIST (original vinyl edition)
[All songs written by Pete Townshend except where indicated]

SIDE ONE
1. Armenia City in the Sky [Speedy Keen]
2. Heinz Baked Beans [John Entwistle]
3. Mary Anne with the Shaky Hand
4. Odorono
5. Tattoo
6. Our Love Was
7. I Can See for Miles

SIDE TWO
1. Can't Reach You
2. Medac [John Entwistle]
3. Relax
4. Silas Stingy [John Entwistle]
5. Sunrise
6. Rael (1 and 2)

RECORDED: May–November, 1967, IBC Studios, London; Pye Studios, London; De Lane Lea Studios, London; CBS Studios, London; Talentmasters Studio, New York City; Gold Star Studios, Los Angeles

RELEASED: December 15, 1967 (UK), January 6, 1968 (US)

LABEL: Track

PRODUCER: Kit Lambert, Chris Stamp

PERSONNEL: Roger Daltrey (vocals); Pete Townshend (guitar, Hammond organ, vocals); John Entwistle (bass guitar, horns, vocals); Keith Moon (drums, vocals); Al Kooper (organ, "Rael 1," "Mary Anne with the Shaky Hand"); Speedy Keen (vocals, "Armenia City in the Sky")

CHART POSITIONS / AWARDS: No. 13, UK album chart; No. 3, French album chart; UK Silver disc

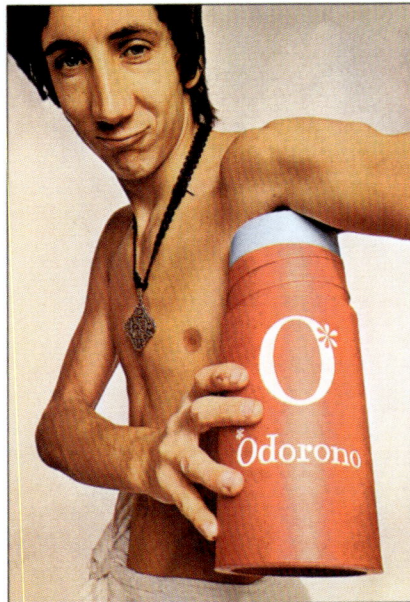

THE WHO SELL OUT

Replacing the stale smell of excess with the sweet smell of success, Peter Townshend, who, like nine out of ten stars, needs it. Face the music with Odorono, the all-day deodorant that turns perspiration into inspiration.

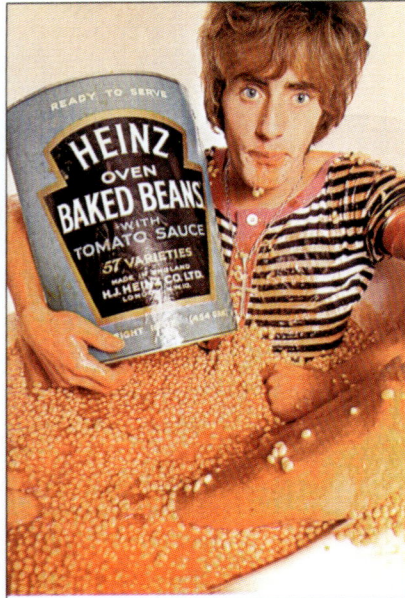

THE WHO SELL OUT

This way to a cowboy's breakfast. Daltrey rides again. Thinks: "Thanks to Heinz Baked Beans every day is a super day". Those who know how many beans make five get Heinz beans inside and outside at every opportunity. Get saucy.

ARMENIA CITY IN THE SKY

After the first of several jingles for Radio London throughout the album—a real-life pirate station that was launched in the wake of Radio Caroline's success—a psychedelic tour de force written by their friend, drummer Speedy Keen, who shares the vocals with Daltrey. Comparisons can certainly be drawn with The Beatles' "Lucy in the Sky with Diamonds," and other acid-trip evocations of the period.

HEINZ BAKED BEANS

In his autobiography, Pete Townshend says the fake jingles were trying to recreate the atmosphere of the surreal UK radio comedy from the fifties, *The Goon Show*— as Entwistle's energetic brass band arrangement demonstrates.

MARY ANNE WITH THE SHAKY HAND

Nearer than most Who offerings to the straightforward girl-adulation songs typical of the period, followed by a Moon drum break leading into a real-life ad for Premier Drums.

ODORONO

Though named for an actual product—the American deodorant Odo-Ro-No—the song comes over more as a conventional pop song, delivered by composer Townshend on lead vocal.

TATTOO

A gentle song by Townshend, sung by Daltrey; a "rite of passage" saga concerning two teenage brothers who get tattoos to prove their manhood, and the peer pressure on adolescents (and others) to conform.

OUR LOVE WAS

Another straightforward love song—"Our love was flying / Our love was soaring / Our love was shining / Like a summer morning"— with tightly arranged harmonies and a stand-out guitar solo from Townshend.

I CAN SEE FOR MILES

With its "psychedelic" message enhanced by swirling rhythms, complex overdubbed vocal harmonies, and shimmering instrumental effects, the track was a studio creation not easily adaptable for live performance. The single was a Top Ten hit on both sides of the Atlantic, but Townshend was nevertheless disappointed it never topped the charts, as he felt it should have done.

CAN'T REACH YOU

The second side of the original LP release cuts back on the use of commercials, real or contrived, and opens with a laid-back, melodic number in stark contrast to the hyper-intense "I Can See for Miles." On later editions of the album, the song is often titled "I Can't Reach You."

MEDAC

Written by John Entwistle, an amusing faux commercial for a cure for the skin complaint dreaded by every teenage boy, acne.

RELAX

Featuring Pete on Hammond organ, rising and falling in and out as the song progresses, and a two-chord stadium-rock guitar break halfway through, Townshend and Daltrey harmonize sleepily in this paean to drug-induced tranquility.

SILAS STINGY

Written in a style owing much to the English folk song tradition, this lilting tale of "Mingy Stingy," the "penny pinching" miser, is delivered by composer John Entwistle.

SUNRISE

Pete performing solo, singing the lead vocal on a delicate, folky ballad, accompanied by just his acoustic guitar. The last piece to be recorded for the album, on November 2, 1967.

RAEL (1 AND 2)

The mini-suite, or mini-opera as Townshend sometimes referred to it, was a five-and-a-half-minute precursor to The Who's next album and most ambitious project yet, *Tommy*. Daltrey's strong vocals backed with a marching beat lead to a complete change of melody halfway through, linked by guest Al Kooper's organ and Moon's explosive drumming.

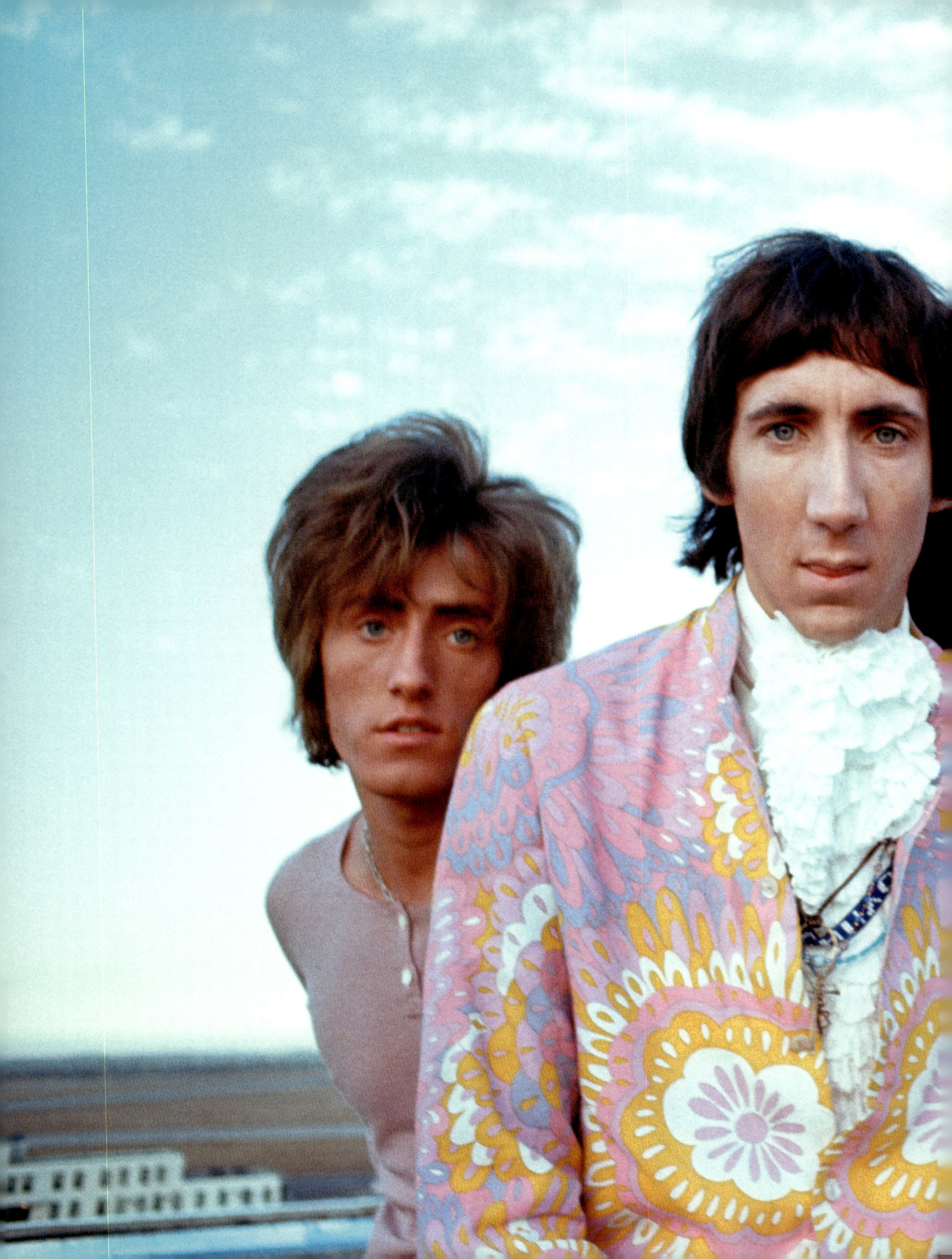

4 TOMMY

ken brodziak presents

THE WHO
THE SMALL FACES
PAUL JONES

supported by
THE QUESTIONS

SYDNEY STADIUM
JAN. 22 & 23
admission $3.50
$1.20

After half a dozen routine gigs around the UK, The Who kicked off 1968 with what would prove to be an ill-fated tour of Australia and New Zealand, top of the bill on a package show that included The Small Faces and ex-Manfred Mann vocalist Paul Jones. From the moment they arrived in Sydney on January 19, jet-lagged after a thirty-six-hour flight from London, things were bad tempered to say the least. An ill-advised press conference was the last thing the band needed after just stepping off the plane, and things seemed to get worse from there on.

UPS AND DOWNS

There were problems with a revolving stage in Sydney, resulting in police being called in after The Who and The Small Faces were accused of using obscene language. Then, on an internal flight between gigs, an altercation erupted when the English musicians were refused refreshments, resulting in the pilot radioing ahead and arranging for a police escort off the aircraft! And the Australian prime minister, John Gorton, actually contacted The Who by telegram, requesting that they never return to the country again. In the event, the band didn't revisit Australia for another thirty-six years, until 2004.

After Townshend had publicly announced that he would never visit Australia again anyway, the New Zealand leg of the tour was hardly an improvement, with wrangles over substandard PA systems, and house mikes being smashed to smithereens. Following their departure at the beginning of February, a local tabloid paper ranted about "the scruffiest bunch of Poms that ever milked money from this country's kids," calling them "unwashed, foul-smelling, booze-swilling no-hopers."

Later that month, The Who commenced their first North American tour as headliners, a six-week trek that started on February 21 at the Civic Auditorium,

PREVIOUS PAGES The Who, 1968. (L–R): Roger Daltrey, Pete Townshend, Keith Moon and John Entwistle.
LEFT The Who in concert at the Stadium in Sydney, January 22, 1968
ABOVE Concert poster from The Who's first Australian tour with Small Faces and Paul Jones, 1968

"Music can create fantastic high points in people's minds. We want to take those minds and bomb them open!"

PETE TOWNSHEND

San Jose, California, and ended triumphantly in Toronto, Canada, on April 7. Now they were among the elite of British bands making a big impact across the Atlantic, although Pete was dubious about the value of constantly touring coast-to-coast: "You just keep slogging away, travelling the highways and the freeways and the byways and the airways . . . You can't work, you can't think—your mind's blanked out." But with the band's finances being constantly on the brink of insolvency, the tours—though not huge moneymakers, after all expenses were deducted—were seen as an essential way to keep things afloat.

On May 22, The Who were back in the studio, recording what would be their next single release, "Dogs." But just two days before that, Pete Townshend got married to his long-time girlfriend Karen Astley, in a ceremony at Didcot Registry Office. It was the day after his twenty-third birthday. The couple moved into a large Georgian house in Twickenham, west London, and Kit Lambert was amused by the notion of the guitar-smashing rock 'n' roll wild man setting up a marital home in such a grand property, referring to the couple as "Lord and Lady Townshend."

The release of "Dogs" on June 14 would prove to be a serious disappointment for the band, only

LEFT Pete Townshend with his wife Karen Astley on their wedding day in 1968
OPPOSITE Pete Townshend, recording in his home studio in Twickenham, UK, 1969

reaching No. 25 in the UK chart. The flip side, "Call Me Lightning," had already been released in America as the A-side to "Dr. Jekyll and Mr. Hyde" back in March, where it also failed to make much of an impression—a definite letdown after the success of "I Can See for Miles."

There was another lackluster single when "Magic Bus" failed to make the Top Twenty on either side of the Atlantic. Written by Townshend back in 1965, it wasn't recorded until May 1968, and released in July in the US, but not until October in the UK—by which time the band were ensconced in the studio creating their most challenging album to date.

CONCEPT

Frustrated at their downturn in the singles charts, when not actually performing Townshend threw himself into the band's next project with a renewed urgency. He and Kit Lambert recognized that they needed something much more ambitious than a string of singles (however successful), followed by an obligatory album. Expanding the "mini-opera" concept that had featured on their last two albums—"A Quick One, While He's Away" from *A Quick One*, and "Rael" from *The Who Sell Out*—Pete began hinting that the next Who project would be an ambitious-sounding "rock opera."

He expanded fulsomely on the idea in a *New York Times* interview, in September 1968: "What we are going to try is opera, not something trashy like the pompous arty types do. They do fancy things because they can't play. We've done mini-operas, now we want a long thing around a theme—I've been thinking about a story about a blind, deaf kid—with dialogue, songs, and an incredible finale. I want to get into stuff that will leave the [guitar] smashing way, way behind. We'll be into impressionistic music, music like Wagner and Mahler, music that conjures up things more powerful than you can handle. Music can create fantastic high points in people's minds. We want to take those minds and bomb them open!"

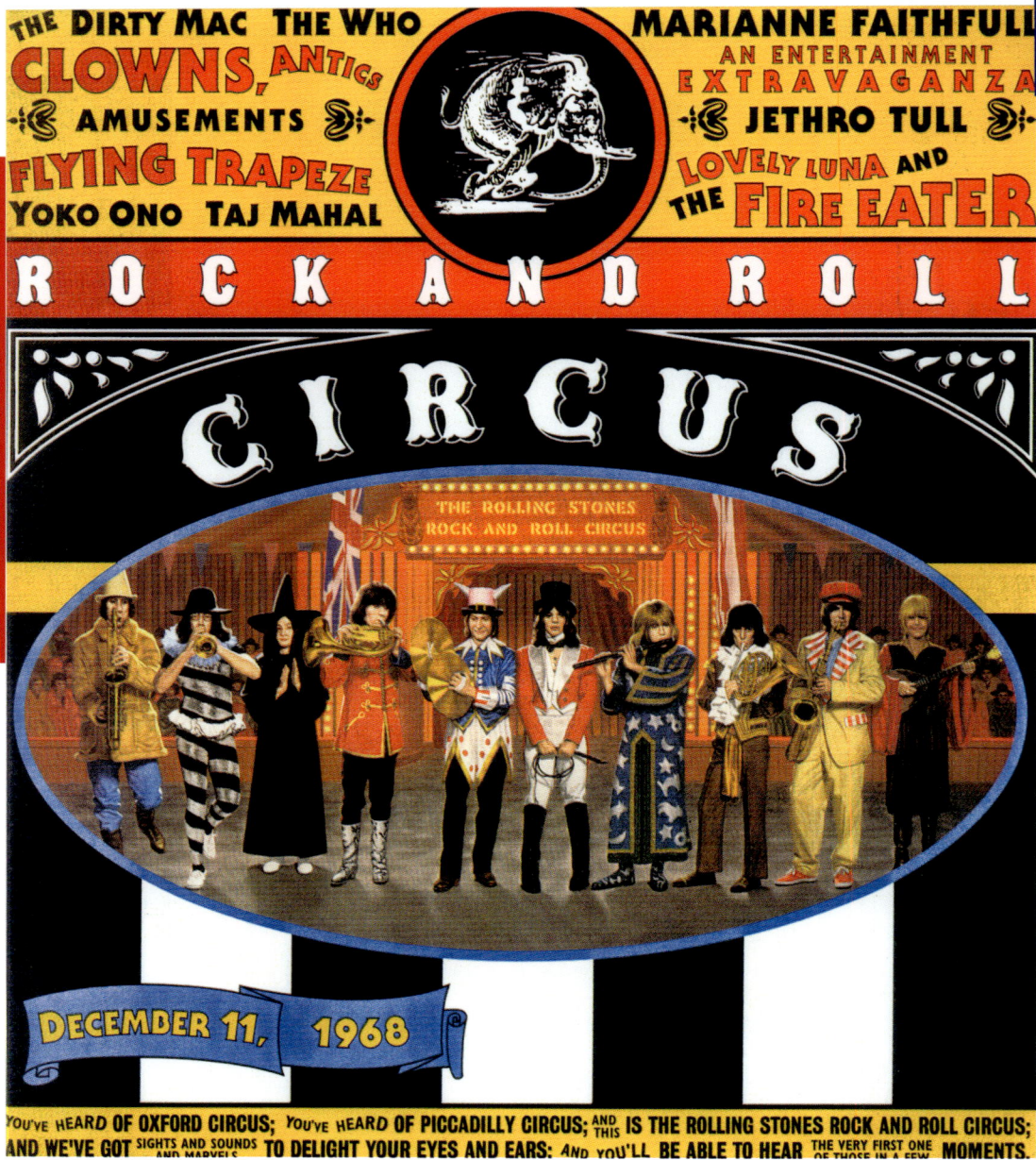

THE DIRTY MAC THE WHO MARIANNE FAITHFULL

CLOWNS, ANTICS AN ENTERTAINMENT EXTRAVAGANZA

AMUSEMENTS JETHRO TULL

FLYING TRAPEZE LOVELY LUNA AND THE FIRE EATER

YOKO ONO TAJ MAHAL

ROCK AND ROLL

CIRCUS

THE ROLLING STONES ROCK AND ROLL CIRCUS

DECEMBER 11, 1968

YOU'VE HEARD OF OXFORD CIRCUS; YOU'VE HEARD OF PICCADILLY CIRCUS; AND THIS IS THE ROLLING STONES ROCK AND ROLL CIRCUS; AND WE'VE GOT SIGHTS AND SOUNDS AND MARVELS TO DELIGHT YOUR EYES AND EARS; AND YOU'LL BE ABLE TO HEAR THE VERY FIRST ONE OF THOSE IN A FEW MOMENTS.

LEFT Poster for the 1996 film of *The Rolling Stones Rock and Roll Circus* originally staged on December 11,1968 RIGHT Mick Jagger chatting with Keith Moon and Pete Townshend, during filming of *The Rolling Stones Rock and Roll Circus* at Internel Studios in Wembley, west London

RECORDING

When recording began in September, at London's IBC Studios, Townshend had already outlined the plot in detail in a *Rolling Stone* interview, though little music had actually been written in advance. There were various working titles for the project, including "Deaf Dumb and Blind Boy" (which hinted at the final theme), "Amazing Journey," "Journey into Space," "The Brain Opera," and "Omnibus," with most material being brought in by Townshend as crude demo recordings, and developed by the group during lengthy sessions in the studio.

With Kit Lambert in the production chair and engineer Damon Lyon-Shaw by his side, the sessions were often arduous affairs, Daltrey later commenting that they probably spent more time talking and sorting out arrangements than actually recording any music. The songs were recorded on state-of-the-art 8-track tape, giving the band ample opportunity for overdubbing, with Townshend adding both piano and organ on some tracks, and Entwistle contributing a part on French horn. Recording was originally scheduled to finish before the end of the year, with the band booked for tour dates, but the Christmas and New Year holiday season came and went with no sign of any finished product for an increasingly impatient record company.

One interruption to their schedule that made the rock history books, if nothing else, was *The Rolling*

Stones Rock and Roll Circus, filmed as a musical documentary with an array of rock stars as costumed participants, in front of an eight-hundred-strong invited audience. The "cast," as well as The Stones and The Who, included Eric Clapton, Jethro Tull, John Lennon, Yoko Ono, Marianne Faithfull, and bluesman Taj Mahal. The opening lineup parade was led, circus style, by clowns, acrobats, midgets, and a cowboy on horseback. The musicians trooped on, each playing an unlikely instrument, including Keith Richards on tuba, John Lennon on trumpet, and Pete Townshend on saxophone.

With just a ten-minute spot to fill, The Who—with the notion of "rock opera" very much on their collective mind—opted for their 1966 "mini-opera" "A Quick One, While He's Away." Eventually, director Michael Lindsay-Hogg edited the footage to a sixty-six-minute film, which was first seen nearly twenty-eight years later, at the New York Film festival in October 1996, followed by its TV premiere in December.

Into 1969, the group were block-booked into IBC to try to wrap things up. But with weekend gigs a necessity to pay the bills, and Townshend still coming up with new material (not to mention rerecording many of the songs), things dragged on and on through January and February, until a final completion date was set for the end of April. In the event, the actual recording was finally completed in early March, although mixing and mastering took the project beyond its April deadline. Further delays involving the cover artwork notwithstanding, *Tommy* (as Pete had eventually decided to call it) was released as a double album in the middle of May.

PACKAGING

Since The Beatles had pioneered rock album art with their extravagant gatefold sleeve for *Sgt. Pepper's Lonely Hearts Club Band* in 1967, the format for vinyl long-player packaging (CDs were still a decade-and-a-half away) had become increasingly ambitious—and *Tommy* was no exception. The sleeve art was by Mike McInnerney, a prominent counterculture designer and art director. It was based on the *Tommy* story, which itself was inspired by the teachings of Meher Baba, the Indian guru whose philosophy McInnerney had first introduced to Townshend some time earlier.

blind boy "breaking out of a certain restricted plane into freedom."

TRIUMPH

Tommy was an instant hit, making the No. 2 spot in the UK charts and No. 4 in the USA, where it sold nearly a quarter of a million copies in the first two weeks. Just three months after its American release, on August 18, 1969, the album was awarded its first Gold disc for sales of over half a million.

As a trailer to *Tommy*, early March saw the first single release from the album. "Pinball Wizard" would become the best-known song of the collection, making No. 4 in the UK chart. Its subsequent status as a genuine rock anthem was further enhanced by the band's live performances of the album, and in the later film version of *Tommy*—in which it was performed by Elton John—released six years later, in March 1975.

The critics, by 1969 an increasingly powerful lobby in rock journalism, were divided in their response to the new offering from The Who. Some felt the device of a severely disabled youth as "hero" was in dubious taste, and others said the storyline left them confused. But most acclaimed the musicianship of the band, and Pete Townshend's success in linking the songs musically while achieving a stand-alone quality for each track as individual pieces—a feature of the best popular opera, as some were quick to point out.

In the UK *Record Mirror*, Lon Goddard wrote: "They have managed to create a number of different moods throughout the opera and used all facets of the power spectrum, from the heaviest and loudest to the gentle and the subtle; in fact, all the ingredients needed to classify it a fine opera." And writing in the *Melody Maker*, Chris Welch concluded his review of the album: "At a time when pop is undergoing a period of heavy criticism, The Who's achievement is creating something worthwhile and valid, and should be acknowledged as an important facelift to the somewhat battered image of pop.

Meher Baba was among a number of Indian spiritual masters whose teaching caught on among young people in the West in the late sixties. Born in 1894, he maintained total silence from 1925 until the end of his life in 1969, communicating with his disciples via a unique sign language—a clear link to the *Tommy* storyline. Townshend would enthuse about Baba as his "avatar," without any evangelical urge to convert those around him: "The thing I tell people . . . is that nothing ostensibly changes when an individual hears about Baba and starts to devote time to thinking about him and his work. No all-pervading joy creeps into life, no formula for solving difficult problems."

The album package was in the form of a fold-out triptych cover, which included a booklet of abstract designs that followed the storyline, plus the lyrics to all the songs. The surrealist-looking blue-and-white front cover illustration depicted a web of clouds, with images of The Who seen within the spaces, depicting, as McInnerney saw it, the deaf, dumb, and

ABOVE LEFT Pete in London, 1969. The picture on the wall is of Indian spiritual master Meher Baba, whose teachings greatly influenced Townshend.
OPPOSITE The Who performing on the major UK pop music show, BBC TV's *Top of the Pops*, April, 1969

"At a time when pop is undergoing a period of heavy criticism, The Who's achievement is creating something worthwhile and valid, and should be acknowledged as an important facelift to the somewhat battered image of pop."

CHRIS WELCH, *MELODY MAKER*, MAY 1969

TOMMY

TRACK LIST (original vinyl edition)
[All songs written by Pete Townshend
except where indicated]

SIDE ONE
1. Overture
2. It's a Boy
3. 1921
4. Amazing Journey
5. Sparks
6. The Hawker [Sonny Boy Williamson II]

SIDE TWO
1. Christmas
2. Cousin Kevin [John Entwistle]
3. The Acid Queen
4. Underture

SIDE THREE
1. Do You Thinks It's Alright?
2. Fiddle About [John Entwistle]
3. Pinball Wizard
4. There's a Doctor
5. Go to the Mirror!
6. Tommy Can You Hear Me?
7. Smash the Mirror
8. Sensation

SIDE FOUR
1. Miracle Cure
2. Sally Simpson
3. I'm Free
4. Welcome
5. Tommy's Holiday Camp [Keith Moon]
6. We're Not Gonna Take It

RECORDED: September 19, 1968–March 7, 1969, IBC Studios, London
RELEASED: May 17, 1969 (US), May 23, 1969 (UK)
LABEL: Decca (US), Track (UK)
PRODUCER: Kit Lambert
PERSONNEL: Roger Daltrey (vocals, harmonica); Pete Townshend (vocals, guitar, piano, Hammond organ,
        banjo); John Entwistle (bass guitar, French horn, vocals); Keith Moon (drums, vocals)
CHART POSITIONS / AWARDS: No. 2, UK album chart; No. 4, US album chart; US Platinum disc x 3;
        Gold discs: UK, Italy, France

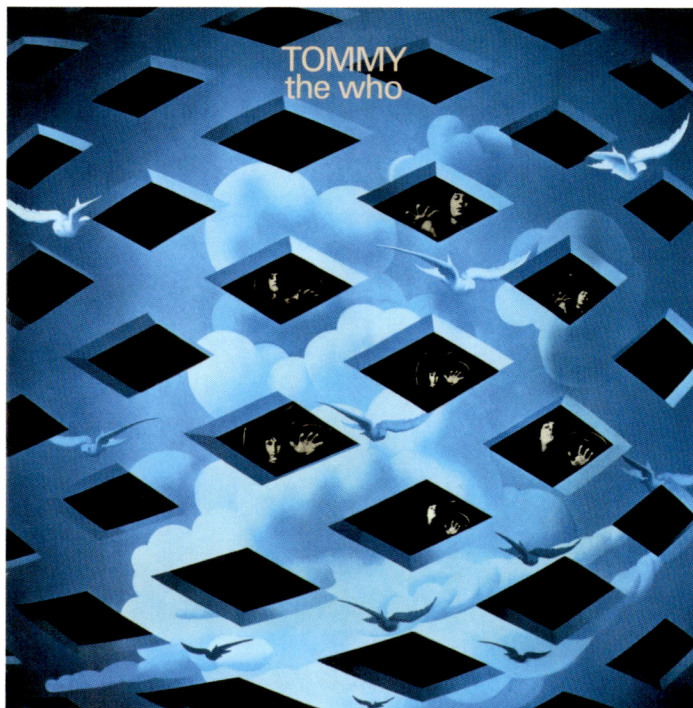

TRACK-BY-TRACK

OVERTURE
The opening track states the basic themes of the opera, with John Entwistle's French horn prominent, as we learn that a Captain Walker has gone missing during World War I.

IT'S A BOY
His widow gives birth to their son, Tommy, using the classic operatic form of a Greek chorus.

1921
Walker returns home, to find his wife making love to a new boyfriend. He shoots his rival, and Mrs Walker convinces her son that he saw and heard nothing, rendering the child deaf, dumb, and blind.

AMAZING JOURNEY
In an intensely lyrical song, Tommy learns to live his life by his sense of touch.

SPARKS
An instrumental "dream sequence."

THE HAWKER
A powerful rock treatment of the old blues "Eyesight to the Blind," as a charlatan doctor claims his wife can cure Tommy.

CHRISTMAS
A medium tempo song in which Tommy's father wonders whether his son will ever find religion.

COUSIN KEVIN
As his parents neglect him, Tommy is left with his sadistic cousin, the school bully.

THE ACID QUEEN
The Hawker's drug-fueled wife feeds Tommy with LSD, which leads into the next hallucinogenic "dream sequence" . . .

UNDERTURE
Another rock instrumental, with effective, tight drumming from Keith Moon.

DO YOU THINKS IT'S ALRIGHT?
A short chorus track, where Tommy is left with his drunken uncle . . .

FIDDLE ABOUT
. . . who rapes him, although the song has humorous overtones.

PINBALL WIZARD
The classic hit from the album, in which Tommy's disability develops his sense-of-touch skill on the pinball machine.

THERE'S A DOCTOR
The chorus continues with the story as Tommy visits a doctor, who says his problem is psychosomatic . . .

GO TO THE MIRROR!
. . . and finds the boy can also see himself in a mirror.

TOMMY CAN YOU HEAR ME?
Via the mirror, Tommy looks at his own reflection and begins to use it as a form of guru. But his parents are frustrated as he ignores them in favor of his own reflection.

SMASH THE MIRROR
His mother smashes the mirror, resulting in a rush of self-awareness in Tommy . . .

SENSATION
. . . and the realization that he can become a powerful religious leader, told in this haunting soliloquy.

MIRACLE CURE
A musical collage of newspaper headlines celebrating Tommy's sudden fame.

SALLY SIMPSON
The account of one of Tommy's devout followers, who is injured when storming the stage when he is giving a sermon.

I'M FREE
A deceptively simple song, in which Tommy rejoices in his newly acquired self-knowledge . . .

WELCOME
. . . and urges his growing band of followers to join him.

TOMMY'S HOLIDAY CAMP
As their numbers expand, bigger and bigger venues are needed for Tommy's huge congregations . . .

WE'RE NOT GONNA TAKE IT
. . . who eventually rebel, rejecting his teachings and leaving the camp, as he retreats back into his own state of self-awareness.

5 LIVE AT LEEDS

After some brief promotional events for the upcoming release of *Tommy*—including a live press preview of the entire album from the stage of Ronnie Scott's Club in London—on Sunday, May 9, 1969, The Who embarked on their most ambitious US tour yet.

FRONT LINE

The album shot up the American charts after its May 17 release, and the centerpiece of their performances would be *Tommy* in its entirety. From their first date at Detroit's Grande Ballroom, supported by Joe Cocker and The Grease Band, it was clear this was going to be on a whole new level compared to their previous North American visits.

The ongoing success of *Tommy*—shifting more than 200,000 copies in the first two weeks—catapulted them into the front line of UK touring bands, and as their trek came to an end in mid-June, another transatlantic date was being discussed.

The Who's agent in New York, Frank Barsalona, was enthusing about a festival gig in August that they should sign up for, insisting it could be important for them. Pete, who was anxious to spend more time with his wife and new baby—their daughter Emma had been born in the March—wasn't convinced the band should return to the US that quickly, but was outnumbered when it came down to it. The Who were booked for the date, which—though its proposed venue would change more than once—came to be known in the history books as Woodstock.

PREVIOUS PAGES The band pose for a feature in *Vogue* magazine, July 1969
LEFT The Who play Woodstock, New York, USA, August 16, 1969
ABOVE Pete and his wife Karen introduce their newborn baby daughter at Queen Charlotte's hospital, London, on March 30, 1969

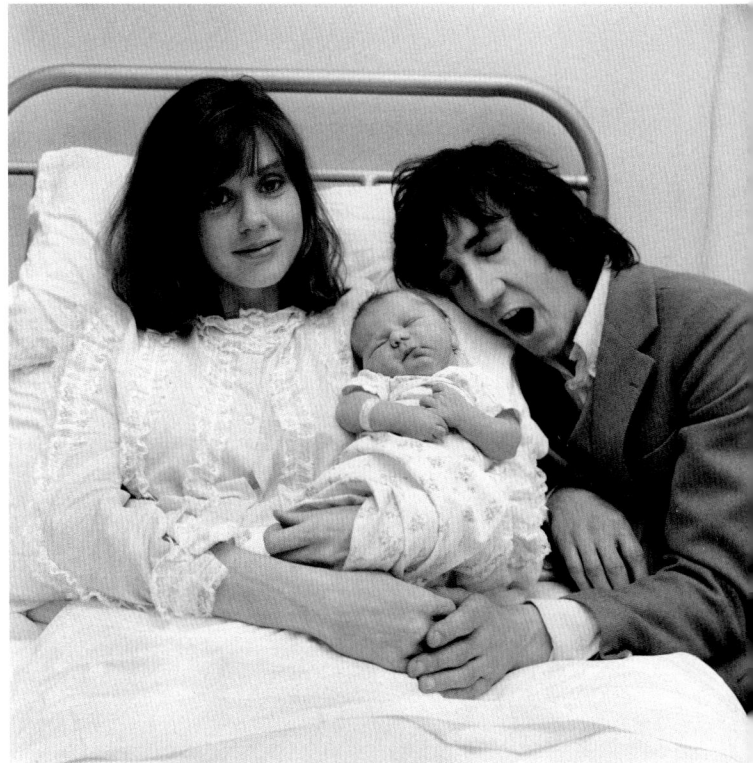

The band's first date back in Great Britain was a prestigious-sounding engagement at London's Royal Albert Hall on July 5. The final night in a week of "Pop Proms" concerts, it featured two shows with fifties rock legend Chuck Berry, who as a self-styled "king of rock 'n' roll" demanded the headline spot—as, of course, did The Who. A compromise trade-off was reached, with the American veteran closing the first concert, and The Who the second. In the event, a hard core of Berry's "Teddy Boy" fans, bent on causing trouble, disrupted The Who's first set, in scenes that reminded some of the mods-and-rockers bust-ups of the mid-sixties. For the second show, The Who managed to calm down even the die-hard rockers when they opened with two vintage-era anthems, Eddie Cochran's "Summertime Blues," and Johnny Kidd's "Shakin' All Over."

A string of regular rock circuit gigs followed through July and early August, including tried-and-tested venues such as Mother's Club in Birmingham, Hastings' Pier Ballroom, and the optimistically named Fillmore North (actually the Locarno Ballroom) in Sunderland. Then, on August 9, they topped the bill on the second night of the 9th annual Jazz and Blues Festival at Plumpton Racecourse, in Sussex.

As its name implied, the Festival had started life at the height of the early sixties jazz boom, "blues" being added as blues bands took over in many jazz venues, and the lineup giving way to a mix of rock, blues, and jazz (with rock now predominant) by the end of the decade. Headliners The Who followed a potpourri of acts including blues group Chicken Shack, jazz saxophonist John Surman, singer-songwriter Roy Harper, and the surreal rock-comedy act The Bonzo Dog Band, with whom Keith Moon had guested during their afternoon spot as "The Lone Arranger."

WOODSTOCK

The eclectic mix of styles and genres appearing throughout the Festival reflected the broad-based taste of audiences of the period—a diversity which would be demonstrated most famously in Bethel, a hundred miles upstate of New York City, just a week later.

As former standard-bearers of British Mod, and the personification of Pop-Art style—with some spectacular "auto-destruction" thrown in as an essential part of their stage presence—The Who's image and overall attitude never sat well with the peace-and-love spirit of the hippie counterculture, and this was never more evident than at Woodstock.

On Saturday, August 16, The Who flew by helicopter from New York City up to Bethel. The festival—billed as "three days of peace and music"—had been moved there after its original plan to be held in Woodstock itself, and subsequently at nearby Walkill, had been rejected by concerned locals, apprehensive of the "hippie invasion" being threatened via the media.

And in many respects they had good reason to be concerned. By the time The Who arrived on the Saturday, nearly half a million young people had massed on the site and thousands more were pouring

> ## "Everything and everyone was soaking wet. There were constant power cuts. People were climbing up on the stage, climbing up the lighting rigs."
>
> ROGER DALTREY

in by the hour. The band arrived at the nearby motel where most of the acts were billeted, then made their way to the festival site—first by car, then when that got bogged down in mud, the rest of the way on foot. Pete Townshend describes it vividly in his autobiography: "It took ninety minutes to drive two miles along a road so muddy that occasionally we needed to be pushed by passers-by. The road was littered with abandoned motorcycles and cars . . . it looked like a wartime flight."

The chaos was hardly better backstage. "Everything was breaking down," Roger Daltrey would recall, "Everything and everyone was soaking wet. There were constant power cuts. People were climbing up on the stage, climbing up the lighting rigs."

Even getting paid was a hassle. Seeing the mounting mayhem, The Who's team insisted on their fee being paid in cash before they played; when none was available, the festival organizers had to hire a helicopter to get the local bank manager out of bed, to open a time-locked safe and get the money.

The Who were scheduled to go on some time during the Saturday evening, but after interminable delays between each preceding performance—including The Grateful Dead, Janis Joplin, and Sly and the Family Stone—they took to the stage at 5am on the Sunday morning, heralding the dawn as the sun came up.

But the sheer energy of The Who's performance was guaranteed to awaken any slumberers in the vast gathering. A lengthy set consisted of nearly all the songs from *Tommy*, bookended by some usual crowd-the so-called "alternative society," and the basically down-to-earth stance of rock groups like The Who. Just as the band launched into "Acid Queen," the well-known politico-agitator Abbie Hoffman leapt onto the stage, grabbing the microphone and declaring "This is a crock of shit . . ." before launching into an appeal on behalf of fellow-activist John Sinclair who was in jail for a minor drug offence. Townshend was outraged, yelling at Hoffman to "Fuck off. Fuck off my fucking stage!" before hitting him across the head with his Gibson guitar, and kicking him off the stage, sending him reeling into the photographers' pit.

The incident grabbed the headlines, most in favor of Townshend's reaction, as *Variety* magazine reported: "During the explosive set by The Who, Yippie founder Abbie Hoffman grabbed a microphone onstage and began to complain about a friend's arrest. Guitarist Peter Townshend coldly clubbed him in the neck with his guitar and kicked him offstage. No one in the audience protested Townshend's actions."

And Pete himself remained unrepentant, his attitude to the "beautiful people" of Woodstock unchanged: "All these hippies wandering about thinking the world was going to be different from that day on. As a cynical English arsehole, I walked through it all and felt like spitting on the lot of them, trying to make them realize that nothing had changed and nothing was going to change. Not only that, what they thought was an alternative society was basically a field full of six-foot-deep mud laced with LSD. If that was the world they wanted to live in, then fuck the lot of them."

Their reception at Woodstock certainly guaranteed The Who's position as front-line superstars on the US rock circuit, a position enhanced on a worldwide scale in 1970 with the release of Michael Wadleigh's epic film of the event. The release of the movie, and the soundtrack triple album, established the legendary status of the festival, with The Who making one of the most spectacular appearances.

ISLE OF WIGHT

Two weeks after their appearance at Woodstock, on Saturday, August 30, 1969, The Who took the stage on the second day of what was being touted as "Britain's Woodstock." It was the second Isle of Wight Festival of Music, and the main focus of the event was the first public appearance in three years

Yippie (Youth International Party) founder, Abbie Hoffman, 1969

pleasers including "I Can't Explain," "Summertime Blues," and "My Generation."

Always skeptical about the hippie phenomenon, Townshend in particular went out of his way to appear at odds with the whole image of flower power, leaping about the stage in an all-white workman's boiler suit and Doc Martens boots. But despite Pete's misgivings, the self-styled "gathering of the tribes" at Woodstock took the band to its heart, its early-day performance being one of the best received of the entire festival.

One memorable incident did, however, illustrate the yawning gap between some of the attitudes of

Roger disembarking after The Who's precarious helicopter landing at the Isle of Wight Festival, August 30, 1969

"The huge downdraft flipped the plywood sheets in the air like bits of paper, threatening to decapitate onlookers. One struck the tail rotor blade, causing the craft to twist and falter. For a split second it looked like a crash landing . . ."

RAY FOULK,
ISLE OF WIGHT FESTIVAL ORGANIZER

of Bob Dylan, who with The Band was closing the festival the following evening.

Although they were headliners for the Saturday concert, The Who opted to appear during daylight—leaving the final spot for the Moody Blues—so they could actually land on the stage in a helicopter. Predictably, that wasn't allowed, so the band asked for a space to be made for the chopper to land as near to the stage as possible, marking it with a big letter "H" visible to the pilot. Half a dozen large plywood sheets were laid on the ground to form the "H," but when the helicopter descended, within twenty feet of the ground, disaster nearly occurred. Festival organizer Ray Foulk described what happened next: "The huge downdraft flipped the plywood sheets in the air like bits of paper, threatening to decapitate onlookers. One struck the tail rotor blade, causing the craft to twist and falter. For a split second it looked like a crash landing . . ." The band disembarked,

Live onstage at the Isle of Wight Festival, August 1969

shaken but unhurt, ran straight onto the stage, and launched into one of the best sets of their career.

As well as most of *Tommy*, the set that day included all the Who classics, including Mose Allison's "Young Man Blues," on which Pete played what one observer called "one of the best guitar solos in Who history." And unlike Woodstock, the Isle of Wight experience was a totally positive one for the band, as Townshend later confirmed: "What was incredible about the Isle of Wight thing was that The Who were totally and completely in control."

The rest of 1969 was taken up by consolidating their position as a truly world-class act, with concerts in the UK and Europe, plus another short visit to the United States. All of which featured *Tommy* almost in its entirety as the showpiece of their performances, to the point where the band were beginning to get frustrated that *Tommy* was sometimes being billed above them: It was often a case of "*Tommy* featuring The Who," rather than the other way round.

During the American visit, they played a six-night season at the Fillmore East in New York. Reviewing the October 20 opening night, the *New York Times* critic pointed out that, despite its grandiose description, *Tommy* was basically a rock concert by an established rock band: "*Tommy* is called a rock opera. But it is a rock opera for rock lovers, in the same way *Hair* is rock theater for theater lovers. In *Tommy* there is no action onstage, other than the normal motion of the members of The Who . . . Though *Tommy* is a complete story, with plot and all, it is rock music first."

TRAGEDY

On January 4, 1970, tragedy struck when Keith ran over and killed his chauffeur and minder, Neil Boland, in his Bentley. Keith, his wife Kim, and a group of friends had been drinking in the Red Lion pub in Hatfield, Hertfordshire; on the way out, they were followed by a gang of jeering youths, who started to kick and throw coins at the car. Boland was attacked by the twenty-strong mob as he got out of the car to chase them away, and in the fracas Moon drove the car at speed out of the pub car park, not realizing that Neil had fallen under the wheels.

Eventually, Keith was charged with drink-driving, but initially a charge of manslaughter had hung over his head. Years later, Roger Daltrey would reflect: "He didn't get away with it, not by any stretch. He was haunted by it, and his drinking just got worse and worse." And worse, in the case of Keith Moon, was pretty bad indeed.

Nicknamed "Moon the Loon" by the music press and in rock music circles generally, Keith was already notorious for his hell-raising antics, especially during The Who's on-the-road odysseys via backstage areas, tour buses, private planes, and hotel suites. It was Moon who perfected the use of cherry bombs, Moon who once drove a limousine into a swimming pool, and Moon who personified the stereotypical rock star hurling TV sets out of hotel windows. Collectively, The Who were considered just about the biggest risk by hotel chains worldwide—their bills to cover damage were often a serious element in the final expenses line in their tour accounts—but it was Keith Moon, time after time, who was mischief-maker in chief.

Recording sessions scheduled for immediately after the fatal accident were shelved temporarily, and resumed two weeks later when the band went into the studio to record "The Seeker." The song described a desperate character who, though ostensibly tough and ruthless to his fellow human beings, is inwardly seeking redemption of some kind. When it was released in March '70, the single's modest sales figures—making No. 19 in the UK charts, and only No. 44 in America—came as a disappointment to Townshend: "It was meant to bridge the gap between the old Who sound and the new Who sound. It was the first record in the limbo after *Tommy* and it excited us all."

LEEDS

Prior to the release of "The Seeker," however, a Who milestone was already in the pipeline. Even before the release of *Tommy*, rumors began to circulate in the music business—initiated by Pete, as he'd later admit—that a live album was in the offing. The group's soundman, Bob Pridden, had been recording various live performances over the preceding months, partly

in response to the increasing number of bootlegs in circulation. But when it came to sifting through recordings of no less than thirty-eight concerts, a new taping of specific shows seemed the easier answer.

In his autobiography Pete Townshend recalls, with much regret in hindsight, how he instructed Pridden to destroy the previous live recordings, before they selected two venues for concerts to be taped. The selected venues were the Refectory at Leeds University, on February 14—Valentine's Day—and the City Hall, in nearby Hull, on the following night.

It transpired that the bass guitar wasn't fully recorded at Hull, so the resulting album was just from the first concert. Simply entitled *Live at Leeds* and released on May 23, 1970, it has since been rated as one of the best live rock albums ever. Urgent and direct, it captures The Who in onstage performance, which could never be reflected in quite the same way via the more sterile atmosphere of a recording studio.

The cover, a plain brown cardboard affair not unlike the make-do packaging of a typical bootleg, was in direct contrast to the flamboyant psychedelia of *Tommy*. There was also a collection of facsimile Who memorabilia, carefully listed by Richard Green in his *New Musical Express* review: "One old Marquee poster, an ancient group photo, a letter cancelling a gig, a contract for the Woodstock Festival for twelve thousand five hundred dollars, a payment sheet, two date sheets, a letter from EMI about the High Numbers, a shot of Pete in action, the words of 'My Generation' with recording notes, a delivery note from Brock's Fireworks, and a notice about county court proceedings."

The album, which made the Top Ten in half a dozen countries, including No. 2 in Canada, No. 3 in the UK, and No. 4 in the US, was critically acclaimed as widely as its predecessor. For the *Record Mirror*, Rob Partridge called it "Quite simply, one of the great rock albums," while in the *New York Times*, Nik Cohn declared it to be "The best live rock album ever made."

Pete cuts an energetic figure onstage at The Who's legendary *Live at Leeds* show, February 14, 1970

LIVE AT LEEDS

TRACK LIST (original vinyl edition)
[All songs written by Pete Townshend except where indicated]

SIDE ONE
1. Young Man Blues [Mose Allison]
2. Substitute
3. Summertime Blues [Jerry Capehart, Eddie Cochran]
4. Shakin' All Over [Johnny Kidd]

SIDE TWO
1. My Generation
2. Magic Bus

RECORDED: February 14, 1970, University of Leeds Refectory, Leeds, UK
RELEASED: May 23, 1970
LABEL: Track, Polydor
PRODUCER: Kit Lambert, The Who
PERSONNEL: Roger Daltrey (vocals, harmonica); Pete Townshend (guitar, vocals);
                        John Entwistle (bass guitar, vocals); Keith Moon (drums, vocals)
CHART POSITIONS / AWARDS: No. 3, UK album chart; No. 4, US album chart; US Platinum disc x 2;
                        UK Gold disc

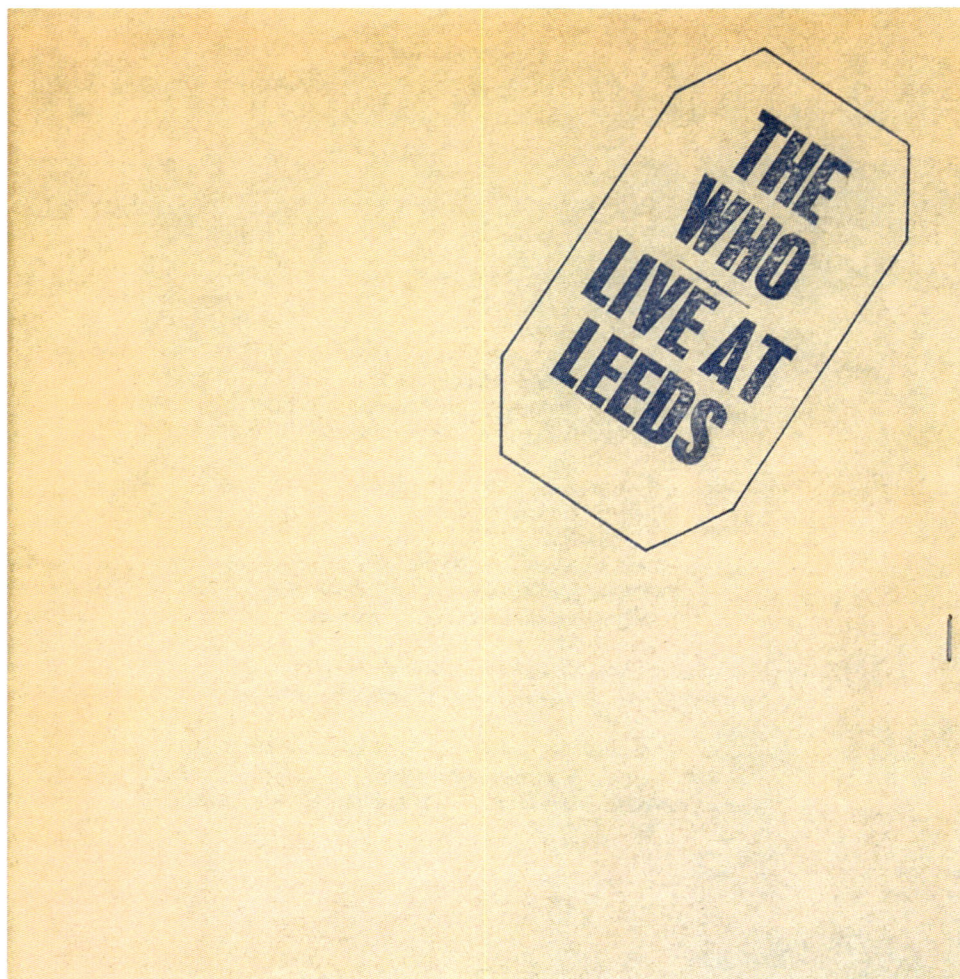

YOUNG MAN BLUES
Originally a cool piece of laid-back blues whimsy by pianist/vocalist Mose Allison from 1957, this powerful rendition by Daltrey had been part of The Who's live set since 1968.

SUBSTITUTE
At just over two minutes, a dynamic version of the 1966 single.

SUMMERTIME BLUES
Another regular from their live shows, the Eddie Cochran rock 'n' roll classic from 1958 reworked in true Who style, with John Entwistle interjecting the catch lines—such as "No dice son, you gotta work late"—at the end of each verse.

SHAKIN' ALL OVER
A four-minute workout on the vintage UK rocker, originally by one of Townshend's heroes, Johnny Kidd and the Pirates.

MY GENERATION
An extended, fifteen-minute version of their most iconic hit, including some crowd-pleasing jamming, and quotes from various other numbers including "See Me, Feel Me," and "Sparks," both from *Tommy*.

MAGIC BUS
At six minutes, with Daltrey playing harmonica and an extended ending, this is a longer and certainly more dynamic version than the single.

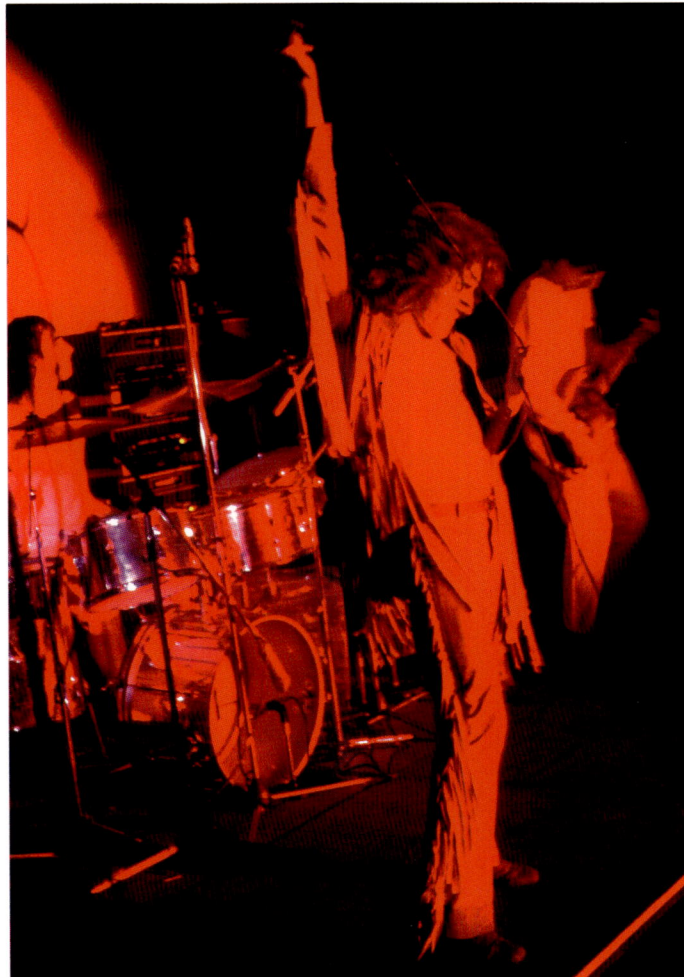

> "The best live rock album ever made."
>
> NIK COHN, *NEW YORK TIMES*, MAY 1970

Roger performing in the UK, at Leeds University, on February 14, 1970

6 WHO'S NEXT

After the universal success of *Live at Leeds*, the overwhelming feeling in the Who camp was that the next big project had to be a follow-up to *Tommy*— not a sequel of any sort, but something with an equally ambitious vision. Meanwhile, with the band in a position to make a real profit on it for the first time, another American tour was lined up starting the beginning of June, 1970.

SOMETHING IN THE AIR

Promoter Bill Graham had arranged for the opening concerts to be two shows in one evening at New York's smart Metropolitan Opera House, newly opened just three years earlier after moving from its traditional home on Broadway. This was the first time a rock band had played at the premier venue for classical music, and around eight thousand tickets grossing a total of $55,000 were snapped up within eight hours of going on sale. To ensure that genuine Who fans had an greater chance of attending than the Met's usual crowd, the tickets were only available at Graham's Fillmore East, located on the then still run-down Lower East Side.

The tour lasted just a month, taking in some of the biggest venues The Who had yet played. With crowds of up to thirty thousand greeting them in huge sports arenas across the United States, apart from major festivals it was the first real experience of "stadium rock" for the band. And while the band were finishing the US dates, Track Records decided (against the

band's better judgment) to release "Summertime Blues" as a single. From *Live at Leeds*, it was their first single to feature a live recording, so was regarded as something of a gamble; and the group's instincts were proven right, when it only managed to peak at No. 38 in the UK, and No. 27 in America.

Back in the UK in early July, Pete resumed work on a project he'd been developing spasmodically for almost a year—the album *Hollywood Dream*, by his pet protégés Thunderclap Newman. Formed by Townshend in 1969 as a showcase for Speedy Keen (who had written "Armenia City in the Sky" for *The Who Sell Out*), the three-piece group consisted of Keen on vocals, guitar, and drums, guitarist Jimmy McCulloch, and pianist Andy "Thunderclap" Newman.

PREVIOUS PAGES Keith Moon, during a performance of The Who's celebrated rock opera, "Tommy", at the Metropolitan Opera House, New York, on June 7, 1970
LEFT The Who, 1970. (L–R): Pete Townshend, John Entwistle, Keith Moon (top), and Roger Daltrey
RIGHT Pete Townshend protégés Thunderclap Newman pictured in 1969. (L–R): Jim Avery, Jack McCulloch, Jimmy McCulloch, Andy Newman, and John `Speedy" Keen.

Released in May 1969, their Townshend-produced single "Something in the Air" was a huge hit that summer, spending three weeks at the top of the UK chart, and with its reference to "the revolution's here" was one of the anthemic records of the era. Pete completed production on the album through July, with an eventual release earmarked for October.

The highpoint for The Who that summer was undoubtedly the third Isle of Wight Festival (and the second for the band), a marathon production which built on the success of the previous year's "Bob Dylan" event. It would be hard to decide who merited headlining, with a spectacular lineup of over forty acts that also included Joni Mitchell, Miles Davis, The Doors, Leonard Cohen, and Jimi Hendrix. The Who were billed as joint headliners with The Doors, for the Saturday night.

With The Doors not opening their set until just past midnight, The Who eventually got onstage at two in the morning, as DJ Jeff Dexter announced, "Ladies and gentlemen, a nice rock 'n' roll band from Shepherd's Bush, London . . . the 'Ooo!" The crowd was estimated at well over half a million, and Pete immediately put them at ease with some tongue-in-cheek repartee aimed at the political factions (Jean-Jaques Lebel and his Situationist group from Paris, among others) who had been agitating for the "liberation" of the festival all day: "We come 'ome and find ourselves playing to a load of fuckin' foreigners causing trouble."

They launched into "I Can't Explain," followed by all the usual favorites, a big chunk of *Tommy*, and, an exhausting two hours later, the inevitable "My Generation." Most observers, and The Who themselves in retrospect, agreed that they should have finished there, on a high, but for some reason they segued into "Magic Bus" and a faltering ending when Roger kept on singing as the band brought the number to a close. As Pete would write in *Melody Maker* the following week: "We ended once and it was perfect. Then for some reason, Roger kept on singing. Well, the group can't walk off, so we had to go on . . . You very much have to play the end of an act right. It's probably far more important than the rest of it put together."

LIFEHOUSE

Two weeks later The Who were making a short tour of Germany, Holland, and Denmark, followed by UK dates through October on which they were supported by The James Gang, the American group whose leader, Joe Walsh, had become a good friend of the band. But right through this period, Pete Townshend's overriding preoccupation was developing his next project, which was still very much in the theoretical stage.

After the American tour in the summer, the band had realized that *Tommy* was becoming a burden. Not so much performing it night after night—it was, after all, just a series of songs, like the rest of their repertoire, with all the variations that that offered—but the expectations it aroused in sections of their audience. There was a newly acquired post-*Tommy* fan base, who had only really latched on to the band in the wake of the album's runaway success, to whom that was what The Who were all about. Particularly in America, where fans tended to take these things more seriously, the content of *Tommy* had become a thing of almost mystic significance. "I am not bored with playing it," Keith Moon would comment at the time, "I am bored fucking talking about it."

Pete's ideas for a new project began to coalesce, as he intimated in the second of a series of monthly columns he wrote in *Melody Maker*: "There's a note, a musical note, that builds the basis of existence somehow . . ." It all sounded a bit vague, but the essence of what he had in mind was set in a dystopian Britain of the not-too-distant future. The country has suffered an apocalyptic disaster—maybe natural, maybe man-made—from which emerges a society in which diversions like music are banned.

Everyone wears "experience suits," linked electronically to a central "Grid," and through which the government transmits virtual "experiences" to the entire populace.

Sounding scarily familiar now, with its intimations of the Internet, social networking, virtual reality—and possibly global pandemic—at the time it was the stuff of pure science fiction.

The hero of the plot was Bobby, who takes over the Grid and uses it to induce the liberating state of rock 'n' roll music, freeing everyone from tyranny and lifting them to a higher plane. Heady ideas, which Pete envisaged being presented as an audience-participating live show involving the then-new technology of synthesized music, plus a proposed movie of the project, making it a truly multimedia experience. Called *Lifehouse*, the idea—despite some resistance from the rest of The Who, who didn't quite get it at first—was developed to the point where rehearsals were underway at London's Young Vic Theatre, starting in November 1970.

The idea was that the Young Vic would be the ongoing venue for a series of *Lifehouse* workshops, developing the concept live. By February 1971, Pete had produced a series of demos of the music, and the workshops were ready to start in earnest. But then things stuttered to a halt, as it became clear that nothing was developing beyond Pete's extravagant ideas, and the practical realities of the situation kicked in as the project was gradually wound down.

In the meantime, there had been a milestone of sorts on December 20, 1970, when The Who played *Tommy* in its entirety for the final time (apart from reunions decades later), at London's Roundhouse. Support acts on the charity performance included America, Patto, a fifty-piece Salvation Army choir singing Christmas carols, and a relative newcomer, Elton John.

Despite his ambitions for *Lifehouse* as a theatrical event grinding to a halt—although *Lifehouse* concerts at the Young Vic would be staged intermittently until the end of April—Pete Townshend at least had the satisfaction of having written some worthwhile material. With that in mind, Kit Lambert booked the band into the Record Plant studios in New York, commencing March 15—with himself in the production chair—to at least make *Lifehouse* a viable conceptual successor to *Tommy* as an album.

The numbers they were recording had all been tried out live during the Young Vic concerts, including "Won't Get Fooled Again," "Getting in Tune," "Behind Blue Eyes," and "Baba O'Riley," but the New York sessions were far from satisfactory. Kit Lambert had acquired a serious heroin habit, which was getting to the stage where it interfered with his ability to actually produce the recordings. After a frustrating week at the Record Plant, Pete decided to call it a day, and the band returned to England.

Initially, the idea was to mix and do overdubs on the material already laid down in New York, but it was clear Lambert wasn't up to the job. So Glyn Johns—whose track record as producer or engineer included albums by The Rolling Stones, Led Zeppelin, and

British stage director Frank Dunlop, (L) with Pete Townshend (R), at the Young Vic Theatre, London, UK, February 10, 1971

The Small Faces—was recruited to sort things out. Talking to *ZigZag* magazine, Pete explained: "So he listened to it and said it was great . . . But if we started again, he could do better." Johns's intervention came at a fortuitous time, not just for the band, but for Townshend in particular, who was suffering something near to a nervous breakdown after the traumas surrounding his commitment to *Lifehouse* and its subsequent abandonment.

ABOVE John Entwistle, 1971
OPPOSITE Roger Daltrey and Heather Taylor, 1971

So through April to June 1971, at both Olympic Studios in Barnes, south-west London, and the Rolling Stones Mobile Studio parked outside Mick Jagger's house in rural Hampshire, Johns and The Who rerecorded all the *Lifehouse* material for what would be their next album.

WHO'S NEXT

Meanwhile, John Entwistle—allegedly frustrated at not having enough of his own material featured on The Who's albums—released *Smash Your Head Against the Wall*, the first solo album from a member of the group. He'd finished recording it in January 1971, with a release in May. Prior to the LP hitting the shops, a single featuring two of the tracks ("I Believe In Everything" backed with "My Size") was released, on John's insistence, on April Fools' Day. Neither

single nor album did spectacularly well, but John had made his point, and in the process produced some interesting tracks that would not have otherwise emerged. Produced by Entwistle, it was the first recording involving (as engineer) Roy Thomas Baker, who went on to produce for Queen—including their iconic "Bohemian Rhapsody"—among many others.

While John was briefly basking in the spotlight of his solo enterprise, the group as an entity embarked on a series of "secret" dates around the UK, with little advance publicity and a cut-price ticket charge of fifty pence. They were trying out the ex-*Lifehouse* material that was now destined for their next album release, preceded on June 21 by the single "Won't Get Fooled Again," which climbed to No. 9 in the UK charts and No. 15 in the United States.

The song, describing a point in *Lifehouse* where the main characters have gone, leaving the government and army to fight it out between themselves, was Pete's warning against backing any cause blindly, in spite of the popular appeal of "revolution" among young people at the time. Townshend described it as

"A song against the revolution, because the revolution is only a revolution in the long run, and a lot of people are going to get hurt."

Reaction to the new material as performed on the mini-tour augured well for the forthcoming album. Chris Charlesworth's review in the *Melody Maker* was typical: "Mountains may tumble and fall, supergroups come and go, but the Who will always be with us. And while they are they continue to wear the crown of the most exciting live band in existence."

At the end of July—just two weeks after Roger Daltrey had married his long-standing girlfriend Heather Taylor—The Who set off on their first North American tour of 1971. It was timed perfectly for the release of the new album, now called *Who's Next*, two weeks into August. The album was almost universally well received, with critics and public welcoming the fresh new sounds of an invigorated band.

Enhanced by the use of state-of-the-art synthesizer technology, the new material was nevertheless highly accessible—a balance many bands failed to achieve, and Pete was anxious to maintain: "The technology is beginning to overtake the musician. The infinite possibilities presented by technologies makes me want to capture the present in a far more simple way."

In New York, *The Village Voice* called it "The best hard rock album in years," while in *Rolling Stone*, John Mendelsohn's somewhat circumspect review rated it as "intelligently conceived, superbly performed, brilliantly produced, and sometimes even exciting." It was the band's first album to top the UK charts, at the same time making the No. 4 spot in the US.

In retrospect, *Who's Next* has often been rated as the band's best-ever album—as one online review stated simply: "Perhaps THE most complete rock album in history, *Who's Next* has just about everything a classic rock fan can want in an album."

WHO'S NEXT

TRACK LIST (original vinyl edition)
[All songs written by Pete Townshend except where indicated]

SIDE ONE
1. Baba O'Riley
2. Bargain
3. Love Ain't for Keeping
4. My Wife [John Entwistle]
5. The Song Is Over

SIDE TWO
1. Getting in Tune
2. Going Mobile
3. Behind Blue Eyes
4. Won't Get Fooled Again

RECORDED: April–June 1971, Olympic Studios, London; Stargroves, East Woodhay, Hampshire (Rolling Stones Mobile Studio)
RELEASED: August 14, 1971
LABEL: Track
PRODUCER: The Who, Glyn Johns
EXECUTIVE PRODUCER: Chris Stamp, Kit Lambert
PERSONNEL: Roger Daltrey (vocals); Pete Townshend (guitar, VCS3, organ, synthesizer, piano, vocals); John Entwistle (bass guitar, brass, piano, vocals); Keith Moon (drums, percussion); Nicky Hopkins (piano, "The Song Is Over," "Getting in Tune"); Dave Arbus (violin, "Baba O'Riley")
CHART POSITIONS / AWARDS: No. 1, UK album chart; No. 4, US album chart; US Platinum disc x 3; UK Platinum disc; Gold disc, Italy

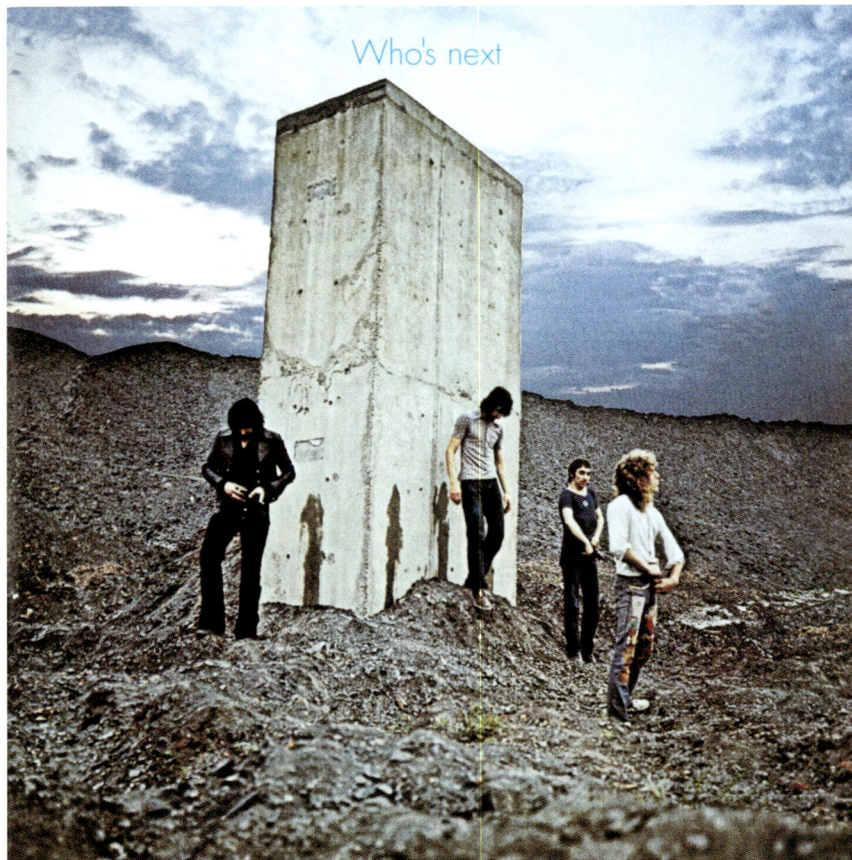

BABA O'RILEY

From the repetitive opening riff—Pete's organ fed through a VCS3 synthesizer—it's clear this is going to be something totally different from The Who. The name comes from Pete's guru, Meher Baba, and the avant-garde musician Terry Riley, the violin solo from guest Dave Arbus.

BARGAIN

Immediately recognizable as a typical Who song, with Daltrey in full voice, and Townshend again using (but never overusing) the synth to great effect.

LOVE AIN'T FOR KEEPING

A country-ish rocker, with great harmony background vocals, and Pete showing skilled restraint on the acoustic guitar breaks.

MY WIFE

The only non-Townshend song on the album, a John Entwistle composition with the bass player delivering the lead vocal and doubling on brass instruments.

THE SONG IS OVER

Townshend and Daltrey sharing the vocals, Pete the balladeer and Roger the preacher. Nicky Hopkins adds some essential piano.

GETTING IN TUNE

The second track featuring Nicky Hopkins on piano, this was originally recorded at the New York *Lifehouse* sessions as "I'm In Tune."

GOING MOBILE

An on-the-road "easy rider" theme typical of its time ("I'm an air-conditioned gypsy"), with bass and drums carrying all before them, and a great synth break.

BEHIND BLUE EYES

A majestic production, the drama lifting verse by verse, the light-and-shade dynamics of Pete's arrangements (and Glyn Johns's production) paying dividends throughout.

WON'T GET FOOLED AGAIN

As on the album's opener, a repeated synth figure takes us into classic Who chord-crashing on the closer, an eight-and-a-half-minute version of the chart single, with organ and drums "trading licks" to great effect.

"Perhaps THE most complete rock album in history, *Who's Next* has just about everything a classic rock fan can want in an album."

CLASSIC ROCK REVIEW, FEBRUARY 28, 2011

7 QUADROPHENIA

With their first US trip of 1971 over, The Who's first UK date of fall 1971 was a charity concert called "Goodbye Summer." Promoted by Ron and Ray Foulk, who had staged the Isle of Wight festivals in 1968, '69, and '70, it was in aid of the Bangladesh Relief Fund. The Who had attended the hugely successful Concert for Bangladesh organized by George Harrison on August 1, at New York's Madison Square Garden, and were keen to support the cause.

The all-day show was held at the Oval cricket ground in south London on September 18, and was headlined by The Who in front of 35,000 fans. The lineup also featured Mott the Hoople, Lindisfarne, Cochise, The Grease Band, Quintessence, America, Eugene Wallace, Atomic Rooster, and The Who's chums The Faces. The concert raised an estimated £18,000 after all expenses had been covered.

MEATY, BEATY, BIG, AND BOUNCY

A string of UK dates followed, and although they were primarily to promote *Who's Next*, in the event the gigs were also a useful plug for the band's forthcoming "greatest hits" compilation, which was set for release at the end of October. It was originally planned to call the album *The Who Looks Back*, but Kit Lambert felt it sounded like the band were all dead!

Called *Meaty Beaty Big and Bouncy*, the album was named for the four members of the band: "Meaty" was Daltrey, who looked quite muscular; "Beaty" was Moon, the drummer; "Big" was well-built Entwistle; and "Bouncy" was the onstage athletic Townshend. Selected by Pete, the fourteen tracks were a perfect cross section of their back catalog, with vintage (and later) Who represented by a string of classics including

PREVIOUS PAGES Live onstage at the Oval cricket ground, London, September 18, 1971
LEFT Live onstage at the Fête de l'Humanité, Île-de-France, Paris, September 9, 1972

"I Can't Explain," "Happy Jack," "I Can See for Miles," "Pinball Wizard," "Pictures of Lily," "Substitute," and of course "My Generation."

Despite some critics bemoaning the fact that the selection didn't delve into unissued or barely remembered rarities from The Who's archive (it was, after all, marketed as a "greatest hits" collection), the compilation did well in the charts. It got to No. 9 in the UK, and No. 11 in the US, where it was awarded a Platinum disc.

October also saw the release of the first of three non-album singles from the cancelled *Lifehouse*, Pete Townshend's "Let's See Action," with John Entwistle's "When I Was a Boy" on the B-side. Pete's demo version also appeared on his *Who Came First* collection the following year. Also released as a single in several other countries, but not the USA, "Let's See Action" reached No. 16 in the British chart.

The penultimate dates on the British tour were three consecutive nights from November 4, as the grand opening of the Rainbow Theatre in Finsbury Park, north London. The spectacular art deco building, which dated from 1930, had previously been the Astoria cinema. Doubling as a live concert venue, it had played host to dozens of jazz and rock greats over the years, including Louis Armstrong, Count Basie, Ray Charles, The Beatles, and, in February 1966, The Who. For the next decade the Rainbow became a premier music venue on the UK circuit, with names as varied as James Brown, David Bowie, Van Morrison, and The Osmonds all gracing its stage, before it closed in December 1981.

The second leg of The Who's lengthy US tour began on November 20, at the Charlotte Coliseum, in North Carolina, taking them on the road through till mid-December. After that it was mutually agreed that the band would do no further touring for a while, taking a much-needed, lengthy break. And for Pete that meant a chance to start thinking about the next album.

> "At the time I was still very doubtful about bringing in the synthesizer. I felt that, with a lot of songs, we'd end up spending so much time creating these piddly one-note noises that it would've been better just doing it on guitar."

ROGER DALTREY

ROCK IS DEAD

While the band were still on tour in the United States, Pete had been developing the idea of their next project. Initially, it was an idea for a film and album, conceived by Townshend in collaboration with Chris Stamp and the writer/critic Nik Cohn. It even had a working title, *Rock Is Dead—Long Live Rock!*

The core of the idea was that each member would write and oversee one side each of a double-disc album. Meanwhile, the film treatment that Cohn and Stamp had been working on—*Rock Is Dead (Rock Lives)*—involved a documentary about the band that would study the very existence of rock music and its function in society. As Cohn put it in the treatment for the project, the band are: ". . . a metaphor for rock in general—their public, and their context, and their time . . . to catch The Who, and, by doing so, catch the essence of Rock itself."

Through the spring of 1972, tracks were laid down at Olympic Studios, produced by The Who and with Glyn Johns as associate producer. Nothing further transpired, however; Townshend was dissatisfied with

LEFT AND OPPOSITE The Who performing at the opening of the Rainbow Theatre in London, November 1971

the way the focus (or lack of focus) of the project was going, and in June decided to call it a day. The tracks already recorded would eventually end up either as singles, or on the 1974 outtakes album, *Odds & Sods*, or on the band's next album, which wouldn't appear until October 1973.

The first track from the aborted sessions to appear as a single was "Join Together," recorded on May 22 and released on June 16. Originally intended for the *Lifehouse* album, after that the song appeared on the working track list for *Rock Is Dead—Long Live Rock*, until that too was abandoned. Roger Daltrey, while thinking it was a good single, was initially dubious about the use of synthesizer: "At the time I was still very doubtful about bringing in the synthesizer. I felt that, with a lot of songs, we'd end up spending so much time creating these piddly one-note noises that it would've been better just doing it on guitar." The single made the British Top Ten at No. 9, and No. 17 in the US.

Early in August the band began their only live dates in 1972, on a month-long tour of Europe, taking in Germany, Belgium, Holland, Sweden, Denmark, Switzerland, Austria, France, and Italy. The French dates included one of the band's biggest-ever audiences, at the Fête de l'Humanité in Paris. The "workers' festival" was organized to raise funds for the French Communist Party, and over 400,000 people watched The Who, supported by Country Joe McDonald.

WHO CAME FIRST

Throughout The Who's self-imposed furlough, Pete Townshend had been working on his own solo project, an album purely in tribute to Meher Baba. He had already taken part with other artists in two albums dedicated to the guru, small privately distributed limited edition releases—*Happy Birthday* and *I Am*—but this would be his first "official" solo album.

Playing on the old "chicken or the egg" question, the album was titled *Who Came First*, with its cover

LEFT John Entwistle with his band performing material from his third solo album *Rigor Mortis Sets In* on the BBC music program *The Old Grey Whistle Test*, London, May 21, 1973. (L–R): Tony Ashton, Eddie Jones, John Entwistle, and Graham Deakin.
RIGHT Roger Daltrey lifts up Keith Moon during a stage version of *Tommy* at the Rainbow Theatre, London, December 9, 1972. Others appearing included Steve Winwood (behind Daltrey and Moon), Peter Sellers (second right), and conductor David Measham (far right)

picturing Townshend in trademark boiler suit and Dr. Martens boots, appearing to be standing on a bed of eggs. The track listing included unused demos from the *Lifehouse* sessions, and some songs from the limited edition Baba tributes. Apart from just two tracks involving other musicians—Ronnie Lane, Caleb Quaye, and Billy Nicholls—it was a genuinely solo effort by Pete, who was playing guitar, keyboards, bass, drums, synthesizer, and harmonica at his home studio. He also did all the production, mixing, and engineering in what he described as "one ginormous ego trip . . ." Released at the end of September 1972, the album managed a modest No. 30 in the UK chart.

With no Who album as such on the horizon, the next solo effort coming close on the heels of *Who Came First* was John Entwistle's second collection under his own name, *Whistle Rymes*. The album title came from the frequent misspelling of John's surname, and featured guitar contributions from Peter Frampton (best known for his work with The Herd and then Humble Pie) and Jimmy McCulloch, who had played with Pete Townshend's hit-making group Thunderclap Newman.

Around the time of the November release of *Whistle Rymes*, John was back in the studio completing his third solo album, *Rigor Mortis Sets In*, which would hit the shops in the following May. It featured covers of three vintage rock 'n' roll songs—"Mr. Bass Man," "Hound Dog," and "Lucille"—and Entwistle originals in a similar vein. The lineup included sax man Howie

Casey, a Liverpool veteran who, like Jimmy McCulloch from the previous Entwistle album, toured and recorded with Paul McCartney's Wings.

Recorded in May 1972, at the same sessions that produced The Who's previous single "Join Together"—both initially destined for the abandoned *Lifehouse* album—"Relay" was released in America on November 25, and a month later in the UK. Backed with the Keith Moon song "Waspman," it made the Top Forty on both sides of the Atlantic, reaching No. 21 in the UK, and No. 39 on the *Billboard* chart.

TOMMY ON STAGE

The end of November also saw the American release (with the UK ten days later) of an ambitious version of *Tommy*, produced by Lou Reizner with orchestral backing by the London Symphony Orchestra and the English Chamber Choir. The lineup was exceptional, to say the least, with an all-star cast that included Steve Winwood as Tommy's father, Richie Havens as the Hawker, Ringo Starr as Uncle Ernie, actor Richard Harris as the Doctor, and Rod Stewart as "a local lad"; plus Townshend and Daltrey, as the Narrator and Tommy, respectively. The original plan was to have Rod Stewart singing the title role, but as Daltrey and Townshend got more involved in the project, Stewart's part was cut back to singing "Pinball Wizard." The double album was a significant success, selling over 400,000 copies (and earning a Gold disc) in the US in its first week.

More challenging in many ways was Reizner's plan to stage the production as a live concert at London's Royal Albert Hall. Unfortunately, the Albert Hall management did not consider the event suitable for the venue, apparently because they didn't agree that *Tommy* was a proper opera, as Reizner would recall: "We sent them the libretto, an acetate, [orchestra conductor] Measham sent a letter. We told them Princess Margaret would attend, and the reply was 'She's no reference, she associates with the Rolling Stones.'"

The location was switched to the Rainbow Theatre at fairly short notice (with only time for one complete day of rehearsals), and two sell-out shows were staged on December 9, in aid of the Stars Organisation for Spastics. Due to prior commitments, Ringo Starr's Uncle Ernie was played by Keith Moon, and Richard Harris's role as the Doctor was covered by Peter

Sellers. Despite some reviews panning the show due to the lack of solid rehearsal time, it was a huge success, raising nearly £20,000 for the charity.

DALTREY

Early in 1973, with The Who on another prolonged sabbatical, Roger Daltrey began recording a solo album. He had recruited the early-sixties pop idol Adam Faith to produce it, and Faith in turn brought in a budding new singer-songwriter named Leo Sayer to contribute some original songs. Daltrey was determined that the pop-oriented recordings would sound nothing like The Who, if only to signal that he had a musical identity outside of the band.

When it was released on April 20, 1973, the eponymously titled *Daltrey* did better than many might have anticipated, at one point selling over forty thousand copies a day. Though not greeted with

overt enthusiasm by many critics, the collection made it to No. 6 in the UK, a better chart performance than any of the earlier Who solo efforts.

One bone of contention as far as Roger was concerned was the lack of enthusiasm for the project on the part of the Who management team, Kit Lambert and Chris Stamp. According to Daltrey, they (and the record label Track) deliberately undersold it in America, afraid that a hit would lead to him leaving the band and going solo permanently. They needn't have worried: "I didn't care about any of that. I've always had people telling me I should go solo, but I didn't want to be a solo singer. I didn't want to do a Rod Stewart."

It wasn't the first time that Daltrey had misgivings about Lambert and Stamp's management. The previous year he had an audit done of the band's finances, and found them seriously wanting. It transpired that the pair, by this time both with a serious heroin addiction, were milking off money from the band's finances with no record of where it had gone.

By the time the band were back in the studio in mid-1973, Pete Townshend's patience with Lambert in particular was tested to the limit. "By the end of the second week I had had enough. Kit had been distracting the recording process, erasing tapes while I was out of the room, and I just snapped. Close to punching Kit, I just sacked him instead."

Daltrey was the first to formally engage Bill Curbishley—who as an employee at Track Records knew The Who, Stamp, and Lambert well—as his manager, in late 1972, followed by the rest of the band a year or so later. At the time of writing, after a long career in management representing, among others, Judas Priest, Robert Plant, and Jimmy Page, Curbishley continues to enjoy a close association with The Who on a personal and professional level.

QUADROPHENIA

The Who's return to the recording studio at the end of May was in a newly built (in fact still incomplete) state-of-the-art facility, Ramport Studios, that the group had converted from an old church hall in London's

LEFT Roger Daltrey recording in his home studio, Holmshurst Manor, Burwash, East Sussex, November 23, 1972
ABOVE John Entwistle (L) at Ramport Studios, Battersea, London, in June, 1974. The studio was owned by The Who.

Battersea, just south of the River Thames. In fact the first sessions took place in Ronnie Lane's Mobile Studio, while a 16-track control desk was still being fitted at Ramport.

The theme of the new album, which Pete had been working on for several months off and on, was based on the Mod culture that The Who had nurtured—and, arguably, had nurtured The Who—in the mid-sixties. The central character, Jimmy, struggles to find spiritual salvation via four different elements, the "quadrophenia" of the title, reflecting each of The Who's separate personalities in specific musical themes. Roger was the "Helpless Dancer," John the romantic ("Is It Me?"), Keith what Townshend described as the "bloody lunatic" ("Bell Boy"), and Pete the self-confessed hypocrite in "Love, Reign o'er Me."

The storyline was set against the seaside clashes between Mods and Rockers, which Townshend had witnessed at first hand in Brighton in 1964. A disillusioned Jimmy, after going through meaningless jobs, losing his girlfriend, and smashing up his scooter, returns to Brighton, the scene of his bygone glory days, only to find his former Mod compatriot now reduced to a servile job as a hotel bellboy. Jimmy ends up on a rock out in the sea—contemplating suicide, or redemption? Townshend leaves us to decide—or as he put it: "I realised I had no right to decide whether or not Jimmy should end his own life. I let Jimmy decide for himself."

Part of Pete's ambition for the album was to have it recorded in four-channel quadraphonic sound, a new but short-lived format for domestic record playing, that never took off in the way stereo sound had, a decade-and-a-half earlier. As well as tackling the technical complexity of quadraphonic recording, Townshend spent weeks through the summer undertaking field recordings for a variety of sound effects, ranging from thunderclaps and rainstorms to bird calls, brass bands, train whistles, and the omnipresent sound of the sea.

ABOVE The Mods versus Rockers clashes of the mid-sixties provided inspiration for the storyline of *Quadrophenia*. This was at Margate on May 17, 1964.
RIGHT Roger and Pete perform live onstage at the Lyceum Theatre in London during The Who's *Quadrophenia* tour on November 11, 1973

> "You get the sneaking feeling that Pete Townshend has tried to out-Tommy *Tommy* and gone sailing right over the top."

CHARLES SHAAR MURRAY, *CREEM*, JANUARY 1974

As the vast majority of the public never acquired quadraphonic sound systems, the album release was in conventional stereo. Released on October 26, it was well received by the rock press cognoscenti, though some were not as adulatory as they were about *Tommy*. Even skeptics like Charles Shaar Murray confessed that the album succeeded where they thought it might fail: "You get the sneaking feeling that Pete Townshend has tried to out-Tommy *Tommy* and gone sailing right over the top . . ." conceding "Suddenly you realize that Pete hasn't blown it after all. Face it, he very rarely does. *Quadrophenia* is both less and more ambitious than its notorious predecessor."

The album was preceded by a single taken from it, "5:15," which was released on October 5 in the UK, climbing to No. 20 in the charts. *Quadrophenia* was denied the No. 1 spot in the UK chart by David Bowie's *Pinups*, while in the US it similarly hit No. 2, prevented from topping that chart by Elton John's *Goodbye Yellow Brick Road*.

QUADROPHENIA

TRACK LIST (original vinyl edition)
[All songs written by Pete Townshend
except where indicated]

SIDE ONE
1. I Am the Sea
2. The Real Me
3. Quadrophenia
4. Cut My Hair
5. The Punk and the Godfather

SIDE TWO
1. I'm One
2. The Dirty Jobs

3. Helpless Dancer
4. Is It in My Head?
5. I've Had Enough

SIDE THREE
1. 5:15
2. Sea and Sand
3. Drowned
4. Bell Boy

SIDE FOUR
1. Doctor Jimmy
2. The Rock
3. Love, Reign o'er Me

RECORDED: May–June 1972, May–September 1973, Olympic Studios, London; Ramport Studios, London; Ronnie Lane's Mobile Studio (LMS)
RELEASED: October 26, 1973
LABEL: Track
PRODUCER: The Who, Glyn Johns
EXECUTIVE PRODUCER: Chris Stamp, Kit Lambert
PERSONNEL: Roger Daltrey (vocals); Pete Townshend (guitar, keyboards, banjo, cello, vocals); John Entwistle (bass guitar, French horn, vocals); Keith Moon (drums, percussion, vocals); Chris Stainton (piano, "The Dirty Jobs", "5:15," "Drowned"); Jon Curle (voice on "Cut My Hair")
CHART POSITIONS / AWARDS: No. 2, UK album chart; No. 2, US album chart; US Platinum disc; Gold discs: UK, France

TRACK-BY-TRACK

I AM THE SEA
One of Pete Townshend's "field recordings" brings us into an eerie introduction to the saga, with Daltrey's voice faint amid the sounds of the sea.

THE REAL ME
Roger and John rampant on a riff-driven piece of classic Who, the impressive bass part apparently recorded in one take.

QUADROPHENIA
A six-minute synth-dominated instrumental that, as the title track, serves as an alternative introduction, in effect an overture to the whole work.

CUT MY HAIR
The first song with a narrative aspect, with reference to Mod fashions, Townshend's vocals are phased into a radio broadcast reporting the Brighton beach riots between Mods and Rockers.

THE PUNK AND THE GODFATHER
Titled "The Punk Meets the Godfather" on the American pressing of the album. Dramatic rock which confirms Moon's contribution as the essence of The Who's sound.

I'M ONE
A lilting country-flavored ballad with Pete singing lead, the first-person lyric of the hero admitting that all he has had positive in his life has been the Mod ethos of his teenage years.

THE DIRTY JOBS
Daltrey at his expressive best, and one of the key lyrics in the entire album: "I'm getting put down / I'm getting pushed round / I'm being beaten every day. My life's fading / But things are changing / I'm not gonna sit and weep again," ending with crowd noises, thunderstorms, and fairground sound effects.

HELPLESS DANCER
The first of the four themes directly associated with a member of The Who, this is Roger as the once-optimistic young man, unable to control his destiny: "You realize that all along / Something in us going wrong . . ." It ends with a brief extract from the original recording of "The Kids Are Alright."

IS IT IN MY HEAD?
Roger delivers with consummate skill, and Pete and John help out on the chorus harmonies. Another classic evocation of teen angst from Townshend.

I'VE HAD ENOUGH
A song of varying phases and moods, including a string-effect hint of what becomes Pete's closer for the entire album, "Love, Reign o'er Me."

5:15
Some great arrangements with horns (courtesy of Entwistle), and a repeated piano figure by guest player Chris Stainton, taking us on the train journey from London to Brighton.

SEA AND SAND
More sea sounds, as Jimmy reflects on his affinity with the sea and sand rather than the stifling realities of his life back in the metropolis.

DROWNED
The oldest song in the collection, originally written in 1970 as a tribute to Meher Baba. It features Keith Moon at his spectacular best with some great percussive links between Daltrey's vocal statements, and brief but inspired horn punctuations.

BELL BOY
Keith's theme number, it's the story of Jimmy's former Mod hero—"I remember him from those crazy days"—who has sold out to be a servile bellboy at a local hotel. Some humorous vocals from Moon top off the cautionary tale to perfection.

DOCTOR JIMMY
Again the multiple personalities of Jimmy ("Doctor Jimmy and Mr Jim" referencing *Dr. Jekyll and Mr. Hyde*) are addressed, with John's theme "Is It Me?" running throughout a hugely successful multi-layered composition.

THE ROCK
At over six minutes, another lengthy instrumental which serves as a final reprise of much of what has gone before.

LOVE, REIGN O'ER ME
The final statement, and Pete's theme of redemption and self-discovery during Jimmy's self-isolation on a rock out in the sea. Many critics felt this was one of Daltrey's best studio performances of his career.

8 THE WHO BY NUMBERS

The weekend of the UK release of *Quadrophenia*, on October 26, 1973, saw The Who embark on a short British tour to promote the album. Even before the first date, it was clear things were not going to run smoothly.

QUAD ON STAGE

Pete had suggested they add Joe Cocker's keyboard man Chris Stainton (who had played on the album) as part of the touring lineup, but after some vociferous objection to the idea from Roger, Townshend agreed to a compromise, which involved backing tapes of all the keyboard and synthesizer parts. This in itself proved more difficult than he imagined, and things came to a head during rehearsals at Shepperton Studios when an argument between Roger and Pete escalated into an actual fight. Townshend hit Daltrey on the shoulder with his guitar, and Daltrey responded with a punch that landed Pete in hospital with temporary amnesia.

The pressure was on. For three shows at London's Lyceum Theatre from Sunday November 11, an estimated twenty thousand fans stood in line over the previous weekend for just nine thousand tickets. The "Fallout Shelter" tour, as it was dubbed, commenced on Sunday, October 28 at Trentham Gardens, Stoke-on-Trent, and it quickly became clear that Pete's ambition for a "quadraphonic" in-the-round experience was creating more problems alongside those of the backing tapes: "Our quadrophonic sound system was tricky too. In almost all of the smaller UK halls it was difficult to find space for the two rear speaker systems. They needed to be hung

high up, and it wasn't always possible to get them set up correctly before our time ran out."

The low point of the short British tour was certainly in Newcastle, where at the first concert, at the Odeon Cinema, Pete—after screaming at their soundman Bob Pridden onstage—demolished the amps and some of the backing tapes, before storming off. The band quickly followed him, somewhat nonplussed, before *Quadrophenia* was cancelled in favor of an "oldies" set—culminating in Pete destroying a precious Les Paul guitar, and Keith overturning his entire kit. Townshend would subsequently admit that his frustration was genuine, rather than part of the old Who stage act. In a 2008 article in *The Independent*, the concert was in a list of "The Worst Gigs of All Time" under the subhead "The Who go tape loopy."

And things didn't get any better when the North American leg of the tour commenced in front of a crowd of fourteen thousand at the Cow Palace in Daly City, just south of San Francisco, on November 20. During "Won't Get Fooled Again" Keith Moon collapsed at his drum kit; after a short break the band resumed with a revived Moon, only for the drummer to flake out again during "Magic Bus." This time Pete realized there was something seriously wrong, but rather than cancelling the rest of the performance asked if there was a drummer ("I mean somebody good") in the house.

Up stepped nineteen-year-old Scot Halpin, who accompanied the band for the rest of the show in jamming versions of the R&B standards "Smokestack Lightning," segueing into "Spoonful," then "Naked Eye." Backstage following the gig, The Who gave Halpin a tour jacket, which he later said was stolen right after the concert! Halpin would comment on The Who's stamina, telling *Rolling Stone* "I only played three numbers and I was dead." It transpired that Keith, by this stage of his career even more heavily

PREVIOUS PAGES Keith Moon reaches out to an audience member at the Lyceum Theatre in London, during the *Quadrophenia* show, November 11, 1973
LEFT Keith and Pete, as energetic as ever, onstage at the Odeon in Newcastle, as part of The Who's 1973 UK *Quadrophenia* tour

ABOVE Keith Moon pictured at home in Los Angeles, California, in 1974
RIGHT Atwood Stadium in Flint, Michigan on August 23, 1967. The Moon "Loonacy" era has its origins in this night, which saw Moon arrested after driving a car into a hotel swimming pool following a party to celebrate his twenty-first birthday.

into booze or drugs of one kind or another, had taken a potentially lethal dose of brandy and animal tranquilizer pills.

MOONACY

More mayhem followed, particularly in Montreal, Canada, where the band caused so much damage to a hotel room that they ended up spending time in the local jail. The carnage began when Moon, having spilled some ketchup from the lavish room service on offer, decided to make it an abstract "painting," by using the frame of a valuable work on the wall. After kicking the original canvas out of the frame, more destruction ensued as Pete and Keith rammed a marble coffee table through a wall, before hurling it through a window, followed by a TV set being thrown into the swimming pool, and so on.

The hotel management called the "Mounties" (Royal Canadian Mounted Police), who rounded up sixteen of the party, including Moon, Townshend, and Entwistle—with Daltrey having slept through it all! After seven hours, and a $6,000 cash reimbursement for the damage caused, the band and entourage were released, fulfilling their final three dates of the tour in Boston, Philadelphia, and Largo, Maryland.

The Montreal incident was possibly the most extreme example of riotous behavior by The Who, but certainly not unique. It could be said that they created the template for on-the-road excess that became almost the norm for successful rock bands in the seventies, and the ringleader of these orgies of destruction was usually Keith Moon.

From the early days of their touring career, particularly on trips across the United States, Moon was notorious for hotel vandalism, especially involving a predilection for cherry bombs—small, highly explosive fireworks. His habit, often when the band had just checked into a hostelry, was to see how much damage he could do to the en suite toilet facility.

"One day I was in Keith's room," Townshend would recall, ". . . and I said, 'Could I use your bog?' and he smiled and said, 'Sure.' I went in there and there was no toilet, just sort of an S bend, and I thought 'Christ, what happened?' He said, 'Well this cherry bomb was about to go off in me hand and I threw it down the toilet to stop it going off.' So I said, 'Are they that powerful?' and he said, 'Yeah, it's incredible!' So I said, 'How many of 'em have you got?' with fear in me eyes. He laughed and said, 'Five hundred,' and

British director Ken Russell filming Roger Daltrey in *Tommy*, on the Marlborough Downs, UK, 1974

a car into a hotel swimming pool. It was during the band's first full US tour, in 1967, when they were playing support to Herman's Hermits. The location was the Holiday Inn in Flint, Michigan, on the occasion of Keith's twenty-first birthday on August 23.

The story has taken on a number of versions in its repetition, with the car involved varying from a Rolls Royce to a Bentley to a Cadillac. But the most reputable account—if indeed any should be taken as definitive fact—cites the vehicle as a Lincoln Continental, backed up on more than one occasion by Moon himself: "Half-a-dozen cars were parked around this swimming pool. I ran out, jumped into the first car I came to, which was a brand new Lincoln Continental. It was parked on a slight hill, and when I took the handbrake off it started to roll, and it smashed straight through this pool-surround fence, and the whole Lincoln Continental went into the swimming pool—with me in it." Whatever the veracity of recollections of the party, The Who were banned from the Holiday Inn chain for life—which nevertheless failed to deter them from further hotel havoc over the years.

Back in London after the *Quadrophenia* tour, the band prepared themselves for the "Who's Christmas Party," four consecutive dates at the Sundown, Edmonton, running through the week before Christmas. This time, to avoid the rush for tickets that the Lyceum shows experienced earlier in the year, booking was only available by mail application. As Pete Townshend recalled in his autobiography, although the shows went down well, the reviews were, as he put it, ". . . beginning to get rather picky; some were just bad. Compared to other bands we were still good, but we were going off the boil." Part of the reason, he concluded, was that for a solid three years *Tommy* had been the essential part of their stage performances that earned them constant good notices: "*Quadrophenia* had failed to replace *Tommy* as the backbone of our live show."

TOMMY, THE MOVIE

Just before the Christmas concerts, Lou Reizner once again presented *Tommy* as a stage production at the Rainbow Theatre. Running for two nights, this time the only member of The Who involved was Roger Daltrey, with an all-star lineup that included David Essex

opened up a case full to the top with cherry bombs. And of course from that moment on we got thrown out of every hotel we ever stayed in."

The most legendary, and oft-repeated, example of Moon "loonacy" was the instance when he drove

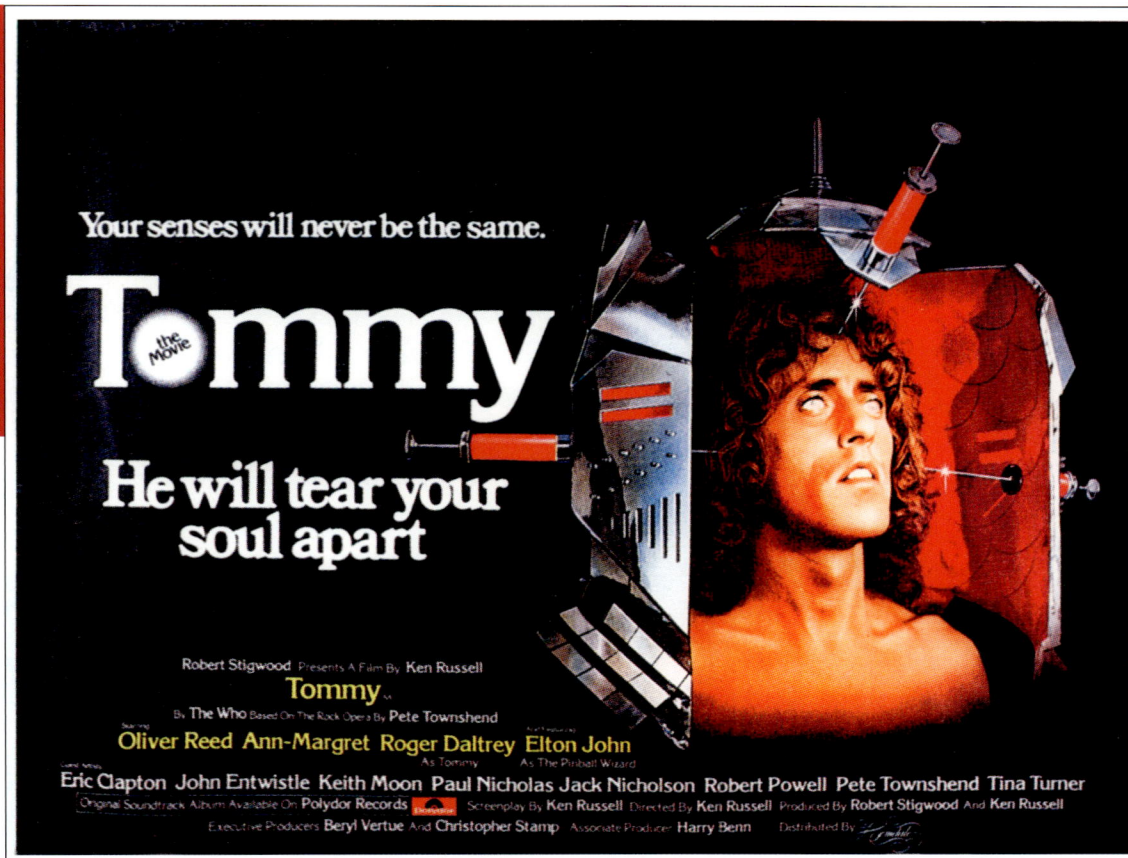

Your senses will never be the same.

Tommy
the movie

He will tear your soul apart

Robert Stigwood Presents A Film By Ken Russell

TOMMY M.

By The Who Based On The Rock Opera By Pete Townshend

Starring

Oliver Reed Ann-Margret Roger Daltrey Elton John
As Tommy   As The Pinball Wizard

Eric Clapton John Entwistle Keith Moon Paul Nicholas Jack Nicholson Robert Powell Pete Townshend Tina Turner

Original Soundtrack Album Available On Polydor Records   Screenplay By Ken Russell   Directed By Ken Russell   Produced By Robert Stigwood And Ken Russell

Executive Producers Beryl Vertue And Christopher Stamp   Associate Producer Harry Benn   Distributed By

Lobby card
for the movie
Tommy, 1975

(Narrator), Elkie Brooks (Mother), and Roy Wood as the "Local Lad." In the first-night audience, as well as Townshend and Moon, was the celebrated film director Ken Russell, who had recently begun working on a movie version of *Tommy*.

The idea of adapting the rock opera for the big screen had been first mooted by Chris Stamp in 1973, getting Robert Stigwood—who had a long-standing relationship with The Who—committed as producer. Stigwood engaged Russell on the basis of the director's critically acclaimed TV documentaries about classical composers—of which Townshend was also a fan—and hit movies including 1969's Oscar-winning *Women in Love*, and the 1970 horror film *The Devils*.

Before shooting began on the film, Russell insisted there would be no scripted dialogue, with the soundtrack featuring just music throughout. With that in mind, Pete agreed to be musical director, and from early January worked at Ramport Studios, alongside John Entwistle as associate musical director, creating

a brand-new score for the project. From early January, an array of musical talent was engaged on the soundtrack, including Ron Wood, Eric Clapton, Nicky Hopkins, and Chris Stainton.

In addition, various actors involved had to record their parts—something of a worry for Pete in the case of stars like Oliver Reed (playing Tommy's "uncle") and Jack Nicholson (the Doctor), who to his knowledge had never sung professionally before. As it turned out, both Reed and Nicholson rose to the occasion magnificently. Pete was also dubious about Ann-Margret (as Tommy's mother), the Swedish-born pop singer whose main claim to fame was having worked with Elvis on *Viva Las Vegas*; but she too, as a Hollywood professional, was well suited to the task in hand. The more music-based members of the cast were easier for Pete to work with, including Tina Turner as the Acid Queen, and Elton John as the Pinball Wizard. Plus of course there was Roger, who was well used to the role of Tommy.

LEFT Pete Townshend's first solo gig at the Roundhouse in London, April 14, 1974
RIGHT John Entwistle rehearsing with his band The Ox at Shepperton Studios, London, 1973

FEW AND FAR BETWEEN

The recording and filming of *Tommy* took up a big portion of 1974, with principal photography not completed until the end of August. Actual gigs by the Who, as a consequence, were few and far between.

During the initial recording sessions for *Tommy*, before any filming took place, the band did a handful of gigs in France, including a newly opened venue, the Parc des Expositions in Paris on February 10. Other than that, the odd solo venture was the only activity through the early months of the year.

Keith Moon was busy filming in *Stardust*, reprising his role as drummer J.D. Clover with Jim MacLaine and the Stray Cats, the fictional rock group led by David Essex in the hugely successful 1973 film *That'll Be the Day*. Pete Townshend, meanwhile, played his first solo concert on April 14, at the Roundhouse in London's Chalk Farm. The concert was a benefit for a community play center for local kids, and Pete agreed to take part after the original headliner, Tim Hardin, pulled out. Accompanied by a rhythm box, a keyboard, two tape decks, and two effects boxes, he ran through an hour's set that included Hardin's "If I Were a Carpenter," Bob Dylan's "Girl from the North Country," Jimmy Reed's "Big Boss Man," and a handful of Who favorites including "Pinball Wizard," "See Me, Feel Me," and, inevitably, "My Generation."

The day before Pete's twenty-ninth birthday, on Saturday, May 18, The Who played a "Summer of '74" concert at The Valley, home of Charlton Athletic Football Club, in south-east London. The band helped select the support acts for the eleven-hour gig, who included Lindisfarne, Bad Company, Humble Pie, and Lou Reed. An estimated eighty thousand fans eventually squeezed into the fifty-thousand-capacity stadium. And the following Wednesday, the band played a private "thank you" date at Portsmouth Polytechnic, for the 1,500 students who had worked on the *Tommy* movie as extras, plus all the cast and crew on the film. Townshend would subsequently rate the performance as one of their best ever: "Roger was especially good; during filming he had worked out consistently and was in great physical shape. As usual, he gave the show his all."

The only other gigs that summer were four nights at New York's Madison Square Garden. A total of 84,000 tickets were sold in just three days prior to the shows, which were staged between Monday, 10 and Friday, 14 June. "Whomania" was rampant across New York City, buoyed up by frantic attention from local radio stations, but the shows were uninspiring in many ways.

There were still recurring sound problems, even though songs from *Quadrophenia* were kept to a minimum, and as Townshend pointed out, with so many fans being "regulars" to their NYC shows over the years, it was easy for the band to slip into the trap of just going through the motions: "We decided to include some of the old stuff because we felt initially that a good five or six thousand of the front row seats at the Garden would be old Who devotees who enjoy the old stuff. And I think they did. It was easy to remember how to play the old songs 'cos we played

them that many times before. I just picked up the guitar and they seemed to come out."

Disappointment with the New York performances was a key factor in Pete's decision to quit touring for the immediate future, and in the event the band would not appear onstage again for fifteen months.

ODDS AND SODS

In the fall of 1973, in response to the increasing number of bootlegs appearing, John Entwistle began to compile an official collection of outtakes and other studio rarities by The Who. By July 1974 he had completed the remixing and mastering of the album, which was released as *Odds & Sods* at the beginning of October.

Entwistle and John Alcock, the producer of his solo albums, collected enough material for two LPs. As John explained to *Rolling Stone* writer Chet Flippo: "I tried to arrange it like a parallel sort of Who career—what singles we might have released, and what album tracks we might have released." The eleven tracks included "I'm the Face," the adaptation of Slim Harpo's "I Got Love If You Want It" which was the band's very first single when they were calling themselves The High Numbers; "Little Billy," which Pete Townshend wrote for

the American Cancer Society but was never released; "Glow Girl, " originally intended as a follow-up single to 1967's "I Can See for Miles," and "Put the Money Down," "Too Much of Anything," and "Pure and Easy," all leftovers from the ill-fated *Lifehouse* project.

Considering the slightly obscure nature of some of the material, the album was surprisingly successful on release, making No. 15 in the US charts and No. 10 in the UK, and went down well with the rock press. Ken Barnes, in *Phonograph Record*, called it "Nothing short of a dream come true," concluding his fulsome review: "Perhaps The Who should consider releasing an *Odds & Sods*-type album as an annual event—it would make the wait between new albums a lot easier to take, and would free some of the most fascinating vault material in existence."

While John Entwistle was completing work on *Odds & Sods*, he was also finishing his fourth solo album, which would appear in February 1975. Titled *Mad Dog*, it was credited to John Entwistle's Ox, a lineup of seventeen studio players that actually went out on the road at the end of 1974 as a four-piece consisting of Entwistle, Robert A. Johnson on guitar, Mike Deacon (keyboards), and drummer Graham Deakin. The live tour, performing dates in both the UK and United

States, was a loss-maker from the start, with a string of poorly supported gigs into late March 1975.

March 1975 also saw the one and only solo album by Keith Moon. Produced during Moon's period of excessive partying in Los Angeles, *Two Sides of the Moon* was a financial and artistic disaster. Despite an all-star lineup which included, on various tracks, Ringo Starr, Harry Nilsson, Joe Walsh, Ronnie Wood, John Sebastian, and Kenney Jones, the ill-conceived collection of covers featured Moon mainly as a vocalist, playing drums on just three tracks. Chart-wise it sank without trace, peaking at No. 155 in the *Billboard* 200, and making no impression at all in the UK listings.

The much-anticipated movie of *Tommy* was launched with a world premiere in New York on March 18, 1975, followed by a West Coast premiere the next evening, and a European premiere at London's Leicester Square Theatre on the 26th. The star-studded guest lists across the three events included, as well as all the cast, Paul and Linda McCartney, Dean Martin, Ryan O'Neal, Lulu, David Essex, Rod Stewart, and Britt Ekland. The film's first week in London set an all-time house record of nearly £27,000, and the film went on to be a box office hit across the world, with receipts of $27 million in the US by August, and over $1 million in France alone.

Most of the critics loved it, with *Variety* calling it "Spectacular in every way . . . The production is magnificent, the multi-track sound [a custom-built system trade-named Quintophonic] terrific, the casting and acting great, and the name cameos most showmanly." Subsequently, Ann-Margret earned a Golden Globe Award for her performance as Tommy's mother, and was also nominated for an Oscar for Best Actress. Pete Townshend also gained an Oscar nomination for his role in scoring and adapting the music. And at the First Annual Rock Music Awards, held in Santa Monica on August 9, *Tommy* received the award for "Best Rock Movie or Theatrical Production."

The European premiere of the movie version of *Tommy*, held in London on March 26, 1975. Elton John is pictured, (center), with his long-time collaborator, musician Davey Johnstone (back, right) and their guests.

BY NUMBERS

While the band was enjoying the favorable attention promoted by the *Tommy* movie, a month after the film premiered studio sessions were at last starting on their next album. For the fans it had been a long time coming. Roger, somewhat disenchanted with The Who, had been busying himself for his next solo release, *Ride a Rock Horse*, and another movie with Ken Russell, *Lisztomania*; John had taken to the road, with less than universal acclaim, with his own outfit Ox; Keith, spending more and more time in L.A., had been distracted by various film projects, and at other times was only just holding it together in the face of increasing drink and drugs indulgence; and Pete was now, at last, concentrating his mind on a new album.

For the album, Pete recruited the services of Glyn Johns, who they had worked so successfully with in 1971 on *Who's Next*. The entire project was very much Townshend-driven; the songs, all but one Pete's originals, were by and large introspective pieces which he had laid down as backing tracks, initially at home as demos on 16-track tape, with John and Keith contributing when available, plus Nicky Hopkins on piano; Roger then provided the vocals solo. There was a general apathy on the part of all four that resulted in sessions that—in Pete's own words—"dragged on and on."

Townshend confessed he felt detached from his own songs, and therefore the record as a whole, suffering writer's block and bouts of depression. His self-doubt was compounded by the fact that on May 19 he celebrated his thirtieth birthday, just when he felt the future of the most important facet of his life—The Who—was in doubt.

Differences within the band became more public, particularly those between Pete and Roger, who

at this point fundamentally disagreed on the future of the group. In an interview for the *New Musical Express*, Pete said he was depressed by the fact that the last time The Who toured he felt they were going through the motions: ". . . for the sake of the die-hard fans, copying what the Who used to be." Responding, Roger went on the defensive, claiming that Townshend had often ruined shows by being drunk onstage.

In retrospect, Daltrey would assess their differences more benignly: "Pete kept saying we were a nostalgia act. He said he hated touring . . . I couldn't sit on my arse and live off royalties. I had a young family and two kids elsewhere to support. But that wasn't the only reason I wanted to keep going. You have to tour. If you don't tour, you're dead."

Consequently, the impending success or failure of the new album—titled *The Who by Numbers*, with "drawing by numbers" portraits of all four created for the cover illustration by John Entwistle—could well have determined the future survival of the band.

Fortuitously, the album was more enthusiastically received than Townshend might have expected, gaining some good press reviews, including *Rolling Stone*'s verdict: "They may have made their greatest album . . . but only time will tell." Sales-wise, it peaked at No. 7 in the UK chart and No. 8 in America, gaining Gold and Platinum discs, respectively. And "Squeeze Box," the only the single from the album, not only made the bestsellers in the US and UK, but became the band's only international No. 1 when it topped the chart in Canada.

LEFT Poster for *Lisztomania*, starring Roger Daltrey, 1975
BELOW Roger and Keith following a performance with The Who at Leicester's Granby Halls, UK, October 18, 1975

THE WHO BY NUMBERS

TRACK LIST (original vinyl edition)
[All songs written by Pete Townshend except where indicated]

SIDE ONE
1. Slip Kid
2. However Much I Booze
3. Squeeze Box
4. Dreaming from the Waist
5. Imagine a Man

SIDE TWO
1. Success Story [John Entwistle]
2. They Are All in Love
3. Blue, Red and Grey
4. How Many Friends
5. In a Hand or a Face

RECORDED: April–June 12, 1975, Shepperton Studios, England, using Ronnie Lane's Mobile Studio (LMS)
RELEASED: October 3, 1975 (UK), October 25, 1975 (US)
LABEL: Polydor / MCA
PRODUCER: Glyn Johns
PERSONNEL: Roger Daltrey (vocals); Pete Townshend (guitar, ukulele, banjo, mandolin, accordion, vocals); John Entwistle (bass guitar, French horn, trumpet, vocals); Keith Moon (drums); Nicky Hopkins (piano)
CHART POSITIONS / AWARDS: No. 7, UK album chart; No. 8, US album chart; US Platinum disc; UK Gold disc

SLIP KID
A solid opener with alternating vocals from Pete and Roger, and some neat piano from guest Nicky Hopkins. Lyrically it's a (autobiographical?) warning for any youngsters with starry-eyed illusions about making it in the music business. Originally intended as part of the *Lifehouse* project

HOWEVER MUCH I BOOZE
More self-analysis by Townshend, with a deceptively cheery melody given the dark subject matter, and written, according to Pete, on the night he gave up drinking. Roger Daltrey refused to sing the lead vocal, as he didn't want to be identified with what was Townshend's personal problem.

SQUEEZE BOX
Encouraged by Ronnie Lane, who said it sounded like "a crazy Country and Western polka," Pete recorded this using guitars, banjo, mandolin, and accordion. "Squeeze Box" is a nickname for an accordion, but in the context of this song sexual innuendo is never far away. The song was originally written for a Who TV special, which never materialized, featuring a hundred topless women playing accordions!

DREAMING FROM THE WAIST
With a bass solo that smacks of pure virtuosity, this is a tale of sexual frustration. It was originally called "Control Myself," perhaps a more accurate title for a song addressing Townshend's angst at approaching middle age.

IMAGINE A MAN
A dramatic offering, with some finger pickin' guitar from Townshend, exploring the thorny themes of marital breakdown and impotence. Daltrey's soaring vocals hint at the ballad artistry of McCartney at his best.

SUCCESS STORY
John Entwistle's only writing contribution to the album, from its solid intro, his own sardonic reflections on rock 'n' roll stardom: "Get a big flashy car / And a house for my Mum / The big break better happen soon / 'Cause I'm pushing twenty-one."

THEY ARE ALL IN LOVE
More warning signals about the music business, with a Celtic-rock feel plus effective (as ever) piano from Nicky Hopkins.

BLUE, RED AND GREY
Initially recorded solo by Pete (featured on vocals and ukulele) at his home studio, with Entwistle's brass arrangements overdubbed. Townshend would recall how it was Glyn Johns who wanted this upbeat splash of optimism on the album, despite Pete's objection that it was just personal reflections not worthy of release.

HOW MANY FRIENDS
Another cynical view of life in the fast track of the music world, beautifully delivered by Daltrey against a majestic backing of guitar and piano.

IN A HAND OR A FACE
Trademark Who, with Moon rampaging round the drum kit, incisive guitar, and a repeated chorus line—"I am going round and round"—reminiscent of their "I Can See for Miles" classic sound.

9 WHO ARE YOU

The long-awaited return of the band to the live stage began the same day as the UK release of *The Who by Numbers*, on Friday, October 3, 1975. Modestly titled "The Greatest Rock and Roll Band in the World," the tour began with two warm-up shows in Stafford, followed by nine more concerts in Manchester, Glasgow, Leicester, and London's Wembley Empire Pool. The tour, with European and American dates following the UK gigs, would mark a spectacular return to form for the band, and break various venue attendance records in the process.

Reviews were generally ecstatic: "Who gigs are made of moments like these . . ." wrote Andy Childs in *ZigZag* ". . . and on both occasions that I saw them, on the first night at Stafford and the last night at Wembley, they left me elated, my head reeling with so much great rock music and so many dynamic images."

But despite the euphoria among fans and critics, changes were in the air, altering the musical landscape in which The Who and their contemporaries had comfortably operated for a decade. On November 6, while The Who wound up their short European tour with two concerts in Ludwigshafen, Germany, a ramshackle quartet were making their debut, supporting the pub rock group Bazooka Joe at London's St Martin's School of Art. The band—whose brief set of covers that night included The Who's "Substitute"—called themselves The Sex Pistols.

RECORD BREAKERS

The North American tour—which would last until mid-December and resume in the spring of 1976—kicked off in front of a crowd of eighteen thousand at the Summit Arena in Houston, Texas. Riding high on the chart success of both *The Who by Numbers* and "Squeeze Box" in the US album and singles listings, the band seemingly could do no wrong. As if to prove the point, on December 6 they attracted the largest ever audience for an indoor rock concert, when 78,000 fans packed the Silverdome in Pontiac, Michigan, with the concert grossing over half a million dollars.

Partly in response to the excess demand for tickets for the October UK dates, when the band returned to England they staged three concerts just before Christmas at London's Hammersmith Odeon. Billed as "Merry Christmas From the 'Orrrible 'Ooo," they featured spectacular effects including balloons and fake snow descending on the audience, and Keith Moon descending to his drum kit via a winch.

But despite his energetic devil-may-care attitude, playing up to his "Moon the Loon" image for all it was worth, Keith's problems with drink and drugs were actually getting worse. Early in January he was taken to hospital after suffering an epileptic seizure, as a result of alcohol withdrawal. A press release insisted it was merely a case of food poisoning, but those around him were increasingly worried that Moon was on a downward spiral that nobody, least of all Keith himself, seemed able to halt.

When the second leg of the US tour began on March 9, 1976, the opening show in Boston had to be abandoned after just two numbers when Keith collapsed over his drum kit. This time there was no stand-in drummer called up from the audience; as Moon was rushed to the Massachusetts General Hospital, a replacement concert was promised for the end of the tour. Again the PR machine swung into action, saying it was a case of flu, but the actual cause was a potentially lethal mixture of brandy and barbiturates. After gigs in twelve cities across the

PREVIOUS PAGES The Who wave to their fans after performing onstage at Wembley Empire Pool in London, October 1975
LEFT The band onstage at Ahoy in Rotterdam, Netherlands, on October 27, 1975

length and breadth of the country, the tour closed on the first day of April with the rescheduled Boston Garden concert.

Another record was broken at the end of May when, at the first of three "The Who Put the Boot In" UK shows (all staged in football stadiums), The Who earned a place in the *Guinness Book of Records* as the World's Loudest Pop Group when the decibel reading hit 120. The concert was a return to the Charlton football ground, The Valley, where they'd played two years before at the "Summer of '74" concert.

Despite constant pouring rain, and some ugly crowd violence, it didn't put off over fifty thousand fans from enjoying themselves, with the band rising magnificently to the occasion—as Barbara Charone described eloquently in *Sounds*: "Charlton was one of those infrequent magical moments that happen in rock 'n' roll. Charlton *was* ugly and seedy, wet and dirty. Stripped of any surface glamour, Charlton was the supreme test. How many other bands could make 50,000 kids forget that they'd been standing in a steady downpour for over five hours? How many other bands would bounce onstage, slipping on the wet surface, rain hurled in their faces?"

The other two "Put the Boot In" concerts were at the Celtic football ground in Glasgow, and Vetch

ABOVE The Who at Madison Square Garden in New York on March 11, 1976. This show had been planned for March 10, but was put back a day after Keith Moon's collapse at his drumkit.
RIGHT The Who, May 3, 1976 at Charlton Athletic's football ground in London. The performance entered the *Guinness Book of Records* as the loudest concert ever, with the sound level at 120 decibels from a distance of 50 meters.

Field, then the home of Swansea City, in South Wales. A special train was arranged from London for the latter gig, for Charlton ticket holders who had been refused admission because of overcrowding, and a spate of ticket forgeries!

The band resumed their American trek with a four-date "American Whirlwind Tour" at the beginning of August, taking in cities missed on the itinerary in March. This visit was also marred by Keith Moon's increasingly shaky health. After the final date, in Miami, Moon collapsed at his hotel, spending eight days in hospital due to nervous exhaustion. After the incident he said: "I was drinking two bottles of brandy a day, champagne and wine at night. My doctor told me if I didn't stop, I'd be dead in three months."

"I was drinking two bottles of brandy a day, champagne and wine at night. My doctor told me if I didn't stop, I'd be dead in three months."

KEITH MOON

With a trademark leap, Pete Townshend at the Alameda County Stadium, in Oakland, California; October 9, 1976

And in October, the final leg of the year-long North American tour covered ten concerts in nine cities, finishing in Toronto on the 21st, in front of a crowd of twenty thousand. Although disenchanted with the way the band had been playing over the past year, Townshend would recall how "The last show of the tour . . . was a triumph: we were astounded how we had bounced back." He also remembered: "Keith seemed fit again, and played brilliantly." It would be, however, the last gig Keith Moon ever played with The Who before a paying audience.

PUNK!

While The Who—once working-class heroes as the standard-bearers of mid-sixties Mod—were jetting across America from one hotel suite to the next, a new generation of musical rebels were galvanizing the youth of mid-seventies Britain. Through 1976 a new wave of "punk" bands (the name appropriated from a similar trend already thriving in New York) had emerged on the live club circuit, playing high-energy pared-down rock, where sheer enthusiasm often took the place of any technical expertise. Indeed, many of these new groups celebrated the fact that all you needed to perform was a two-chord guitar tune and a very fast drummer, decrying the "dinosaurs" of mainstream rock, in the hierarchy of which The Who were firmly established alongside Led Zeppelin, The Rolling Stones, and so on.

By the end of the year, punk was dominating the UK music press, led by bands like The Damned (who were the first to release a single, in October '76), The Clash, and most notoriously The Sex Pistols. And the Pistols grabbed the national tabloid headlines as well, following an expletive-heavy TV interview, just as their debut "Anarchy in the UK" was released.

CARRYING ON

Despite the upheaval caused by the punk groups, for The Who things carried on regardless, as if operating in some parallel, bygone universe where nothing had changed.

While they were still in North America, a "greatest hits" compilation, *The Story of The Who*, appeared. Though incomplete in many ways due to the rights issues on some of their recordings, it rose to No. 2 in the UK album chart. As John Entwistle observed, "I

The sleeve for the 1977 *Rough Mix* album from Pete Townshend and Ronnie Lane

think it caters to the new breed of fan who hasn't got the old material."

Then on their return, in November, Roger began work on his third solo collection, *One of the Boys*, which featured a spectacular list of guest guitarists including Eric Clapton, Alvin Lee, Hank Marvin, and Mick Ronson. There was also a new song contributed by Paul McCartney, and appearances by both John Entwistle and Keith Moon. Nevertheless, when it appeared in May 1977 sales didn't match the stellar lineup, making the No. 45 and No. 46 spot in the UK and US, respectively.

And at the same time, sessions were underway for *Rough Mix*, Pete Townshend's collaboration with Faces' bass player Ronnie Lane. Pete and Ronnie had struck up something of a special bond over the years, not least because of a mutual attachment to the teachings of Meher Baba. As with Roger's solo outing, the album, produced by Glyn Johns, had a strong cast of supporting players such as Charlie Watts, saxophonist Mel Collins, and Eric Clapton—plus, helping out on the horn section, John Entwistle. Released in September 1977, it failed to make a huge impression chart-wise, just making the Top 50 on both sides of the Atlantic.

Pete decided that The Who would not tour again for the next few months at least, against the wishes of John and Keith, who felt live gigs were the lifeblood of the band—although the latter's physical condition was a growing cause of concern. And, perhaps because he also had a solo project underway, Roger was for once in complete agreement with Pete over the immediate future of the group.

WHEELING AND DEALING

It was the financial future of The Who, and particularly Pete's stake in that future, that was the focus of a crucial meeting set up to sort out the long-standing issues between the band and their former managers Chris Stamp and Kit Lambert. The meeting, on January 20, 1977, was attended by Stamp, Pete, Pete's attorney Sam Sylvester, his UK publisher from Essex Music, David Platz, and—to Pete's surprise—the American publisher and business manager Allen Klein.

Klein had a fearsome reputation in the rock business, having been controversially involved with both The Beatles and Rolling Stones at crucial points in their careers. At the meeting, held in Platz's office in London's Soho, it transpired—and it was the first time Townshend had any knowledge of it—that Klein actually owned shares in his American publishing. Consequently, any settlement negotiated would include wheeler-dealer Klein as an interested party.

Although Pete came away from the eleven-hour meeting with a settlement of over a million pounds—and more direct control over his back catalog—he was less than satisfied that as part of the deal, Klein would get a percentage of any future royalties he earned from songwriting.

All Townshend wanted to do when the meeting wound up was to drown his sorrows. Although he now had a fat check in his pocket—for earnings that Klein had frozen, though were rightfully Pete's all along—he felt his ongoing disillusion with the music business was even more vindicated. With Chris Stamp in tow, he decided to make for the Speakeasy, a fashionable late-night haunt favored by the rock fraternity.

It wasn't long before Pete, by this time well inebriated, came across two of the Sex Pistols, drummer Paul Cook and guitarist Steve Jones.

> ## "I was screaming at them. If you wanna take over, come and fucking take over."
>
> PETE TOWNSHEND

RIGHT Steve Jones and Paul Cook of punk rock band The Sex Pistols in 1976

Mistaking Cook for the Pistols' vocalist Johnny Rotten, Townshend started screaming at the two punks about the corrupt state of the music business. "I was screaming at them," Pete would recall, "'If you wanna take over, come and fucking take over.'" According to Jones, "We were all a bit tipsy, but he was going up to people screaming 'Who are you? Who the fuck are ya?'"

To Pete's surprise, the two Pistols turned out to be big fans; indeed, The Who were among a small number of established rock names that the punk movement approved of. Continuing his tirade, nevertheless, Pete took out the publishing check, rumored to be for over half a million pounds, and ripped it up in front of his two new-found admirers. Lurching into the night, Townshend woke up next morning and immediately

wrote "Who Are You," recalling both his outburst at the Speakeasy, and his latest experience of the murky workings of the music industry.

THE KIDS ARE ALRIGHT

Apart from various promotional appearances plugging their individual projects, there was little group activity by the band until the summer of 1977, when production started on the Who documentary movie *The Kids Are Alright*, which had been in development since 1975. Shooting began in July at Shepperton film studios (which the band had recently acquired), with cameos of the four arriving on the set individually, then moved to L.A. for a week to film "Keith at home" sequences, the drummer now living in a luxurious house near Malibu Beach.

The "rockumentary" was directed by Jeff Stein, an American admirer of the band who had no previous film experience as such. Using archive gig footage, promo films, TV performances, and interviews, from as early as 1964, Stein put together a collage of the band's career, spending over two years sourcing material from the UK, Europe, and America. Memorable live clips included sequences from their appearances at the Monterey and Woodstock festivals.

In order to include essential songs that were not available, fresh performances were arranged to be included in the movie. The first of these, at the Gaumont State Cinema in Kilburn, London, in December 1977, was considered inadequate for purpose, with Moon's performance in particular definitely below par. The drummer was clearly overweight, and in a debilitating

The Who

state due to seemingly non-stop indulgence of drink and drugs.

A second show, before an invited audience at Shepperton Studios in May 1978, provided the required footage—specifically of "Baba O'Riley" and "Won't Get Fooled Again." The Shepperton performance would be the last time Keith Moon appeared with The Who. Critically applauded, the film premiered at the Cannes Film Festival on May 14, 1979. A soundtrack album, released the following month, reached No. 8 in the US *Billboard* chart.

WHO ARE YOU

With rehearsals already underway at the band's Ramport Studios, recording of The Who's next album, *Who Are You*, began in earnest in January 1978. However, the production was beset by delays from the start.

Early on, Pete sustained an injury to his hand, which prevented him from playing for a month; Roger had a throat infection which required surgery; and Keith's physical condition, and his actual playing, was getting worse. And John "Rabbit" Bundrick, the keyboard player booked for some of the sessions, fell out of a taxi door as he arrived at the studio, breaking his arm. He was replaced by ex-Zombies Rod Argent for the recording.

On one track, "Music Must Change," Moon was unable to play in the required 6/8 time, so the drum track was replaced by sound effects of footsteps and cymbal crashes. Out of sheer frustration, Daltrey, Entwistle, and Townshend all considered sacking Keith, but as there was no heavy touring in the immediate future, they were willing to give him another chance to straighten himself out.

Produced by Glyn Johns and Jon Astley (brother of Pete's then wife, Karen Astley), on its release on Friday, August 18, 1977 *Who Are You* was greeted with mixed views from the critics, but was a sure success with record buyers. Earning two Platinum discs in America, it reached No. 2 in the chart; in the UK it made Gold at No. 6; and it was also awarded two Platinum discs in Canada for sales of over 200,000.

John Entwistle being filmed for *The Kids Are Alright* at his Gloucestershire home in the UK

TRAGEDY

Three weeks before the album was released, on Saturday, July 29, Peter Meaden, the original publicist and mentor for The Who, died aged thirty-six at his parents' home in north London, from an overdose of barbiturates. He had been addicted to drugs, alongside a serious problem with alcohol, for some time.

As well as being a tireless evangelist for Mod in the mid-sixties—he was often referred to as "The Modfather" because of his trendsetting influence—

his role as co-manager of The Who, albeit under the alternative name of The High Numbers, was crucial in them being identified as *the* Mod band. Pete Townshend in particular appreciated the part Meaden had played in the band's genesis, and had been privately helping him out financially over the years.

And tragedy would strike again, even more traumatically for the band, when Keith Moon was found dead in his London flat on Thursday, September 7, just three weeks after *Who Are You* was released. The evening before, Keith and his Swedish girlfriend

LEFT Keith Moon at the British premiere of *The Buddy Holly Story* on September 6, 1978 with girlfriend Annette Walter-Lax, the evening before he died
ABOVE Roger Daltrey talking with Bill Wyman of The Rolling Stones at Keith Moon's Funeral, Golders Green Crematorium, north London, on September 13, 1978

"We are more determined than ever to carry on . . . although no human being can ever take his place."

PETE TOWNSHEND

Annette Walter-Lax had attended a preview of the movie *The Buddy Holly Story*, as guests of Paul and Linda McCartney. They dined with the McCartneys at the fashionable restaurant/cocktail bar Peppermint Park, then returned home to their apartment at 9 Curzon Place in upmarket Mayfair.

The flat was rented from the singer Harry Nilsson, who said he felt a little nervous about letting it to Moon as the Mamas and Papas' Mama Cass had died there four years earlier, and he thought it might be cursed. Pete Townshend had lent Keith the money to rent it: "We wanted him to come home, all of us . . . he wanted to come home, but he had no money . . ." He told Nilsson there was nothing to worry about: "I assured him that lightning wouldn't strike the same place twice."

Having taken a number of sedatives, Keith fell asleep while they were watching a movie in bed. He awoke next morning, insisting that Annette cook his usual steak breakfast, then fell asleep again after taking more tablets. When Walter-Lax tried to stir him again, at around three-thirty in the afternoon, Moon was unconscious; unable to wake him, she called an ambulance, and he was dead on arrival at the Middlesex Hospital. It transpired Keith had taken a total of thirty-two pills, a fatal dose of the drug clomethiazole (also known as Heminevrin), which ironically he had been prescribed to help in alcohol withdrawal. An expert would later write in the UK *Sunday Times* that, considering his tendency to take all things in excess, Moon should never have been given the drug in the first place.

Keith was cremated on September 13, 1978 at Golders Green Crematorium, where his ashes were scattered in the Garden of Remembrance. The private ceremony was attended by, as well as family and his three colleagues in The Who, Rolling Stones Charlie Watts and Bill Wyman, Eric Clapton, and other musical friends; and floral tributes were received from an array of rock music celebrities including ex-Beatles, Led Zeppelin, the Moody Blues, David Bowie, and Fleetwood Mac.

The Who would, of course, continue after a lengthy break, making their first stage appearance after Moon's death in May 1979, with Kenney Jones on drums. In a press statement after their drummer's death, however, Pete Townshend wrote that "We are more determined than ever to carry on . . . although no human being can ever take his place."

WHO ARE YOU

TRACK LIST (original vinyl edition)
[All songs written by Pete Townshend except where indicated]

SIDE ONE
1. New Song
2. Had Enough [John Entwistle]
3. 905 [John Entwistle]
4. Sister Disco
5. Music Must Change

SIDE TWO
1. Trick of the Light [John Entwistle]
2. Guitar and Pen
3. Love Is Coming Down
4. Who Are You

RECORDED: September 1977–April 1978, Ramport Studios, London; Olympic Studios, London; RAK Studios, London; Eel Pie Studios, London
RELEASED: August 18, 1978
LABEL: Polydor / MCA
PRODUCER: Glyn Johns, Jon Astley
PERSONNEL: Roger Daltrey (vocals, percussion); Pete Townshend (guitars, piano, synthesizer, ukulele, banjo, vocals); John Entwistle (bass guitar, brass, synthesizer, vocals); Keith Moon (drums, percussion); Rod Argent (synthesizer, piano, keyboards); Andy Fairweather Low (vocals); Billy Nicholls (vocals); Michael Nicholls (vocals)
CHART POSITIONS / AWARDS: No. 6, UK album chart; No. 2, US album chart; US Platinum disc x 2; UK Gold disc; Canada Platinum disc x 2

NEW SONG
Townshend's heartfelt statement about FM radio expecting artists to clone "the same old song" based on their previous hit. Heavier on synth than The Who has sounded before.

HAD ENOUGH
John Entwistle's synth-driven melody rattles along, typically punctuated with trademark Moon fills. With a full string orchestration arranged by co-producer Jon Astley's father Edwin, it was also released on the double-A-side title-song single.

905
Another Entwistle composition; a country feel combined with techy sounds. Synth and acoustic guitar combine to create an other-worldly soundscape, part of an unfinished rock opera by John. A later promo video included stills from the 1984 movie of George Orwell's *1984*.

SISTER DISCO
Crashing guitar echoes vintage-era Who, although connected by some frantic synthesized string effects. Daltrey and Townshend share lead vocals in a nod to the seventies disco craze.

MUSIC MUST CHANGE
The dramatic number that signaled Keith Moon's deterioration once and for all, when he was unable to get to grips with the not-terribly-tricky 6/8 time signature. The drum part was left out in favor of cymbals and footsteps.

TRICK OF THE LIGHT
The third song penned by Entwistle, and one of his most stridently successful compositions with The Who. It's the nearest to a basic rocker on the album, with Daltrey in dynamic mode and Moon energetically on form.

GUITAR AND PEN
One of several songs which revisit ideas first explored in Pete's aborted *Lifehouse* project. Plenty of synth action, alongside Rod Argent's classy piano contributions.

LOVE IS COMING DOWN
A complex ballad with sophisticated string arrangements and some call-and-response vocals. It's another confessional from Pete Townshend: "Hope I don't sound / As immature as I feel," yet again questioning his emotional situation—"I'm not a loser / But did I really win?"

WHO ARE YOU
The nearest thing on the album to a traditional Who number. Daltrey's vocals are in full stride, Moon punctuates perfectly, and there are some delicate intervals in the middle bridge. A great closer, which hit the singles chart on both sides of the Atlantic.

10 FACE DANCES

With their public announcement that the band would carry on, made right after the death of Keith Moon—the very next day in fact—The Who were now in the position of having to find a new drummer, to replace the arguably irreplaceable Moon. As Roger Daltrey would later recall: "We wanted the spirit of the group to which Keith contributed so much to go on. We were in a daze of course, but those weren't just platitudes. We meant it."

There was a uniform consensus among the three remaining members that as Keith's talent and musical style was indeed unique, there was no point in looking for a straight substitute. If the band was to continue, it would have to be a different group, a genuinely new version of The Who. As Bill Marshall put it in The Who: The Official History, "To be The Who, but The Who Mark II."

THE WHO MARK II

Pete Townshend had already made his mind up who he would offer the drumming job to, when Phil Collins offered his services: "I knew he would make a great drummer for us, but he was building a solo career, and was still touring and recording with Genesis . . . But I wanted Kenney Jones. He was my friend, I had worked with him quite a bit." The Who knew Kenney well, through his time with that other archetypal Mod band of the mid-sixties, The Small Faces, and later their Rod Stewart-fronted spin-off, The Faces. Plus, he had played with Roger, Pete, and John on the Tommy movie soundtrack. And by ironic coincidence, he was with Keith on the last night before he died, as a guest of Paul McCartney at the Buddy Holly film party.

The final decision about a new drummer didn't come easily, however. Roger for one wasn't convinced that

PREVIOUS PAGES The Who with new drummer Kenney Jones (far right) in Cannes, France on May 15, 1979
LEFT Quadrophenia poster, 1979

Jones was necessarily the best choice, the drummer's straightforward (but rhythmically reliable) style seeming the opposite to Moon's often unpredictable dynamic. And Pete didn't reach his decision without some serious consideration, as he explained in the Melody Maker a few weeks after Keith's death: "Roger and I have really got to get together and thrash out . . . not a compromise, but what is really gonna work. And if we can't do it so that it will work, then we should knock it on the head."

After some exhaustive rehearsals, Kenney Jones was officially offered the job as The Who's new drummer in November 1978. He felt as ambivalent as the other three about his taking over Moon's vacant drum stool: "I still feel a bit weird about joining The Who, because Keith is dead. If Keith had left the band, and then they asked me, I'd be fine. But Keith is gone, and I miss him. If only I could reverse this situation and not be in his seat, I would."

Also involved in rehearsals after Keith's passing was John "Rabbit" Bundrick, the American keyboard player who had been earmarked for the Who Are You sessions, but had to be replaced after he broke his arm getting out of a taxi at the door of the studio. He would join the group as an unofficial member, gigging with them from 1979 until 1981, and playing on their next album, Face Dances.

The Who, with their new lineup, returned to live performance on May 2, 1979, at a sell-out gig at London's Rainbow Theatre. At the time, elements of the punk scene had morphed into a "Mod Revival," spearheaded by avowed Who fans The Jam. It was an angle not to be ignored in the Melody Maker review of the concert, headlined "The Who: The Mod Revival, Yes." The piece acknowledged that the new members were still fitting in, but writer Mark Williams came away full of optimism for the future of the reconstituted group, concluding: "The Who have not let finesse get the better of them.

"The Who have not let finesse get the better of them. They've retained the sense of mischief that some feared would die with Keith Moon."

MARK WILLIAMS, *MELODY MAKER*

They've retained the sense of mischief that some feared would die with Keith Moon, and that was possibly the best news of Wednesday evening."

THE BIG SCREEN

The band's next live appearance was in France, at the Cannes Film Festival on May 14, coinciding with the showing of the Who documentary *The Kids Are Alright*. The film went on general release in cinemas the following month, alongside the soundtrack album, which did particularly well in America.

BELOW The Who, Cannes, France in 1979
RIGHT Pete Townshend (R) with Phil Daniels on the set of *Quadrophenia*, 1979

As the critic Charles Shaar Murray dramatically argued, reviewing the soundtrack album in the *NME*, after *Tommy* turned The Who into an archetypal stadium band, to retain whatever "street credibility" they might have with the younger post-punk audience, they had to delve into their Mod roots and aspirations: "In the case of The Who it appears that—ever since the arrival of the deaf dumb and blind meal ticket that gave them true megabankable stadium status in the States—they have had to hark back to the Mod era, almost as if—like vampires—they needed to maintain contact with their native soil or else rot where they stood."

And The Who maintained an even higher Mod-inspired profile on the big screen in August 1979, with the release of the film version of *Quadrophenia*. Based on the plot of the band's "rock opera," production had started at the end of September 1978, just three weeks after the death of Keith Moon. It was the feature-film debut for director Franc Roddam, and directly involved Pete Townshend, who contributed to the screenplay, even though the band as such never appeared in the movie. And Roger and John were also on hand for "technical advice" during shooting. The film was almost cancelled after Moon's death, but the producers (Roy Baird and The Who's manager Bill Curbishley, under the production company banner of The Who Films) managed to keep the idea afloat despite the shock of the tragedy.

Phil Daniels played the lead part of Jimmy, a London teenager who seeks a way out of his boring

nine-to-five job via the Mod subculture. Riding his scooter down to Brighton for a holiday weekend, he gets embroiled in the pitched beach battles between Mods and rival Rockers. He also meets a girl, Steph (Leslie Ash), who he becomes involved with, and the flamboyant Ace Face (Sting) who all the local Mods seem to look up to. After being arrested and fined, Jimmy returns to London, only to find Steph is now with his friend Dave. Meanwhile, his mother kicks him out after finding his stash of amphetamine pills, and the last straw is when his prized Lambretta scooter is wrecked in a crash.

Depressed, he returns to Brighton to relive past glories, only to find his "hero" Ace Face works as a menial hotel bellboy. In desperation, Jimmy steals Ace's scooter and speeds along the precarious cliff edge at Beachy Head. In an ambiguous ending, to the backing of "Love Reign o'er Me," we see the scooter smashing onto the rocks below, but it's not clear whether Jimmy has actually committed suicide, or just destroyed the scooter, the emblem of all things Mod.

The Who's music is evident throughout, with remixed versions of songs from the original *Quadrophenia* album, plus two numbers recorded after Keith's death with Kenney Jones on drums, "Get Out and Stay Out" and "Joker James." There are also several visual references to The Who in the movie, including a TV clip of them playing "Anyway, Anyhow, Anywhere" on *Ready, Steady, Go!*, and pictures of the band and the famous "Maximum R&B" poster in Jimmy's bedroom.

The Sex Pistols' Johnny Rotten (John Lydon) had originally been considered for the part of Jimmy, but given Lydon's high profile as the front man of the UK's most notorious punk group, the lesser-known Phil Daniels was the prefect choice. And coinciding with the "Mod Revival," the movie was well timed—had it appeared earlier in the seventies, for instance, it would have just seemed outdated. It was a huge success, both with the critics and at the box office, and remains a classic evocation of a key period in British youth culture.

ON THE ROAD AGAIN

Two days after the release of the *Quadrophenia* movie, on August 18, 1979, The Who made their biggest-ever UK appearance at Wembley Stadium in London. They headed a mixed-bag bill including Australian hard-rockers AC/DC, and punk stars The Stranglers, in front of a crowd estimated at nearly eighty thousand. Not all the reviewers were as enamored with the band's performance as their fans, however, several echoing Harry Docherty's sentiments in the *NME*: "The move into cinema is more worthy of their energies—and probably more exciting for them—at this stage in their career, and is certainly much more interesting than watching them wearily re-wash their old linen in public."

Nevertheless, attendance records were being broken in Britain, France, and Germany; at the Zeppelinfeld in Nuremburg, they played to a capacity crowd of 65,000. And once again America beckoned, with a tour heralded by five consecutive sold-out nights at New York's Madison Square Garden. After some more UK dates (two in Brighton and two in Stafford), the US tour proper began on November 30, in Detroit, Michigan.

It was just three nights into the tour when disaster struck. The venue was the Riverfront Coliseum in Cincinnati, and it was first-come-first-served "festival" seating for the best front-row seats. According to reports, before the concert some fans outside mistook The Who's sound-check for the show opener, and rushed for the entrance doors. Only three doors of eleven were already open, and in the ensuing melee, eleven fans died in the crush.

Bill Curbishley, the promoters, and civic authorities decided that the show should go on, through fear of more crowd problems if it was cancelled, and agreed not to tell the band until after the concert. The Who came off the stage euphoric after a good set, only to be told then what had happened. "We decided not to tell you," Curbishley explained to a stunned group. "The crowd couldn't be allowed to leave the building while security was still dealing with the trouble outside." The next evening, opening their show in Buffalo, New York, Roger told the crowd that the band had ". . . lost a lot of family last night, and this show's for them."

The thirteen-date tour wound up at the Capital Center in Landover, Maryland, on December 17. It would be The Who's last gig until the end of March 1980, apart from a concert at London's Hammersmith Odeon on December 28 as part of the Concerts for the People of Kampuchea. The four-concert event was organized by Paul McCartney and United

ABOVE The band during another American tour, September 1979, with Kenney Jones behind the drum kit
RIGHT Stouffer's Hotel, Cincinnati, December 4, 1979: Roger Daltrey (L) and John Entwistle (R) prepare to leave the hotel after learning of the eleven concert goers who were crushed to death in a stampede at The Who's show the previous night at the Riverfront Coliseum.

Nations secretary-general Kurt Waldheim, in aid of the victims of the war in Cambodia. High-profile names performing across the four nights included Queen, The Clash, Elvis Costello, and McCartney's band Wings. On the final night McCartney presented a thirty-strong all-star group dubbed the Rockestra, which included, from The Who, Pete Townshend and Kenney Jones.

In the meantime, between touring, from 1978 Pete Townshend had been writing and recording tracks for his second solo album, *Empty Glass*, which was released in April 1980. His work on the album was during a period when The Who's career, after enjoying a revival, was thrown into disarray by the death of Keith Moon and the subsequent upheaval of finding a new drummer.

The album was also written against the personal backdrop of Townshend's struggles at that time, including alcohol, drug abuse, marital problems, and of course the loss of Moon. The album, with a lineup that included Kenney Jones and "honorary" Who member John Bundrick, was greeted by some reviewers as the Who album that could have been,

but never was. Released on April 21, 1980, *Empty Glass* made No. 11 in the UK album charts, and No. 5 in the *Billboard* 200.

Another major solo project was Roger's lead part in the movie *McVicar*, based on the memoir of John McVicar, a notorious UK armed robber once described by London's Metropolitan Police as "Public Enemy Number One." The film follows McVicar's time in prison, his escape and return to crime, and subsequent recapture, after which he educates himself, gains a degree, and writes the best-selling book *McVicar by Himself*. Like *Quadrophenia*, the film was produced by Bill Curbishley and Roy Baird (plus Roger Daltrey) as The Who Films Ltd.

There was also a soundtrack album from the film, released shortly before the movie in June 1980. Featuring all four members of The Who (and "Rabbit" Bundrick) alongside a dozen or so other musicians, it was Roger's best-selling solo collection.

After a three-month break at the beginning of 1980, at the end of March The Who went on the road again with a handful of European dates followed by another major US and Canadian tour. Split in two

LEFT The Charity Concert for the People of Kampuchea, Hammersmith Odeon, London, 1979. Front row, (L–R): Pete Townshend, Denny Laine, Bruce Thomas, Ronnie Lane, and Dave Edmunds.

RIGHT *Empty Glass*, the 1980 solo album by Pete Townshend

BELOW Roger Daltrey (far right) pictured with John McVicar (far left) and co-star Adam Faith (second left). Daltrey played the title role of McVicar in the 1980 film of the same name.

LEFT Daltrey and Entwistle at the Oakland Coliseum in April 1980, Oakland, California RIGHT One of many US dates during the latter end of 1979

parts, the North American itinerary stretched from mid-April to mid-July, after which the band got down to some serious studio time in preparation for their long-awaited next album release.

FACE DANCES

American Bill Szymczyk, who had worked with Joe Walsh, B.B. King, The Eagles, and many others, was recruited to produce the new album, which would be the band's first US release with Warner Brothers. Work began at Odyssey Studios in London in July 1980, after some test sessions there in March. It was the first of two albums to feature Kenney Jones on drums, and Townshend was likewise pleased with the contribution of John Bundrick (the other "new", though unofficial, Who member) throughout. And in his autobiography, Pete also described how Szymczyk was something of a perfectionist: "Bill was methodical in his work, always shooting three complete takes of each track so he could cut the best parts together if he needed to." It was a smooth, no-flaws approach that did, however, strip The Who's performance of some of its characteristic edge.

In preparation for the first release by the "Mark II" Who, Pete recruited his friend Peter Blake, the British Pop Art pioneer, to design a cover. It would be the first such commission for Blake since his memorable sleeve

work for the Beatles' *Sgt. Pepper*, back in 1967. Blake in turn invited sixteen eminent UK artists to contribute a picture of a member of the band, four pictures of each musician. The result—which included portraits by David Hockney, Allen Jones, Joe Tilson, Patrick Procktor, and Blake himself—was certainly the most ambitious sleeve concept for a Who album to date.

There were some mixed reviews, including a major thumbs-down in *Rolling Stone*, which described the album as feeling "scattershot, centerless." What many critics seemed to agree on, was that the album worked best when considered as a follow-up to Pete's solo effort *Empty Glass*. But while his highly personalized, often introspective, lyrics worked perfectly in the context of the "Pete" album, they didn't come over as easily when voiced by a second party, Roger Daltrey. Indeed, Townshend would later admit that he had been keeping some of his best songs for his solo efforts, the next of which—*All the Best Cowboys Have Chinese Eyes*—would appear in 1982.

Nevertheless, *Face Dances* hit the No. 4 spot in the *Billboard* album chart, and No. 2 in the UK. It also rendered a big hit in the single "You Better You Bet," which made the *Billboard* Hot 100 at No. 18, and the British singles list at No. 9.

FACE DANCES

TRACK LIST (original vinyl edition)
[All songs written by Pete Townshend except where indicated]

SIDE ONE
1. You Better You Bet
2. Don't Let Go the Coat
3. Cache Cache
4. The Quiet One [John Entwistle]
5. Did You Steal My Money

SIDE TWO
1. How Can You Do It Alone
2. Daily Records
3. You [John Entwistle]
4. Another Tricky Day

RECORDED: July–December 1980, Odyssey Studios, London
RELEASED: March 16, 1981
LABEL: Polydor / Warner Bros
PRODUCER: Bill Szymczyk
PERSONNEL: Roger Daltrey (vocals); Pete Townshend (guitars, keyboards, vocals); John Entwistle (bass guitar, vocals); Kenney Jones (drums); John "Rabbit" Bundrick (keyboards)
CHART POSITIONS / AWARDS: No. 2, UK album chart; No. 4, US album chart; No. 1, Canadian album chart; US Platinum disc; UK Silver disc

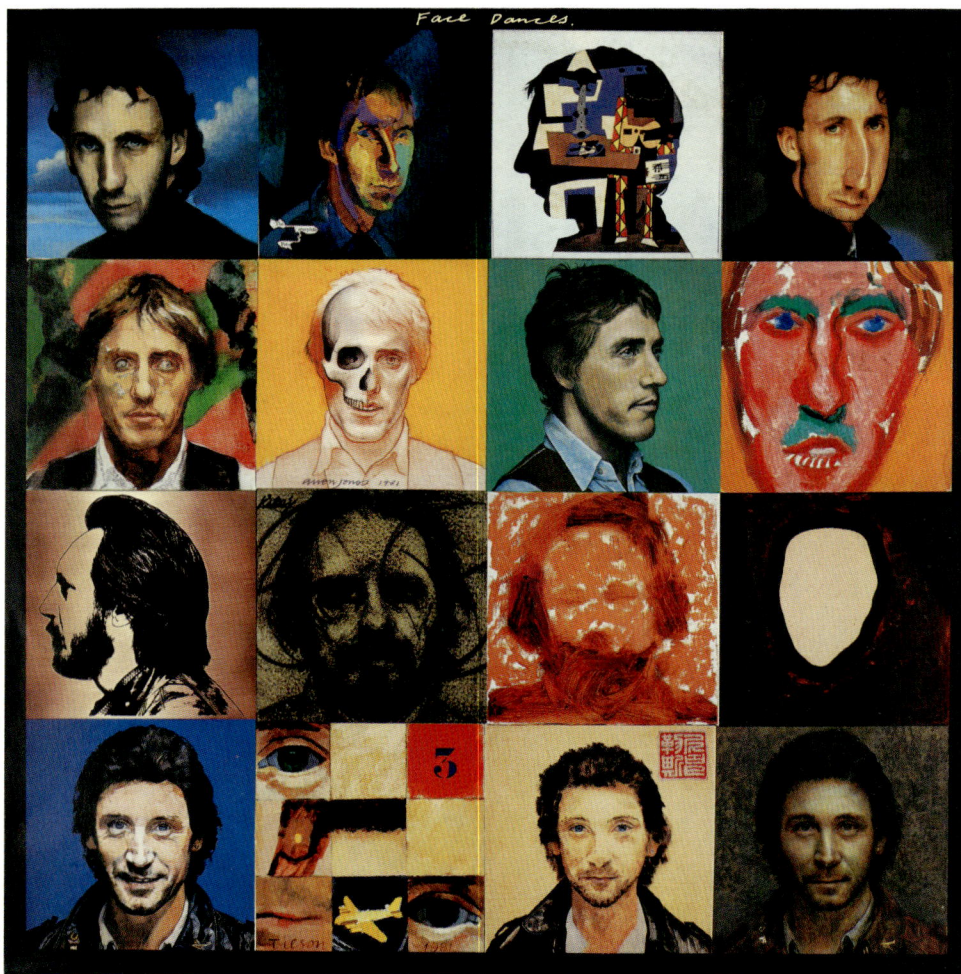

YOU BETTER YOU BET

After the opening keyboards and doo-wop-inspired backing vocals, Daltrey—his voice in punk mode at times—delivers a minor Who classic, which remained in their repertoire for all their subsequent tours over the years. The obvious choice for the album's key single release.

DON'T LET GO THE COAT

With lyrics based in part on the teachings of Meher Baba, an example of "Roger sings Pete" that is perhaps a little too smooth around the edges, right down to the seamless fade-out ending.

CACHE CACHE

Written right after Townshend's brief two-day retirement from the music scene in March 1980 when, in his own words, he absconded during a European tour and spent his time living like a tramp in Berne, Switzerland. The title is French for hide-and-seek, which is precisely what he was playing. He ended up in a (fortunately empty) bear pit, before being rescued and flown back to Vienna for The Who's gig that night.

THE QUIET ONE

One of two songs by John Entwistle, his throaty vocals fitting perfectly into the heavy-metal-influenced backing, all in stark contrast to the presumption in the title.

DID YOU STEAL MY MONEY

Written by Pete on discovering he had been ripped off by a girl, after an evening encounter in Tempe, Arizona: "Did you search me / Did you turn me over / While I cold turkeyed / On the sofa." Again, a slicker production than usually associated with The Who.

HOW CAN YOU DO IT ALONE

A weirdly melodramatic narrative that focuses on a teenager's angst, after being caught stealing a girlie magazine. Delivered energetically by Daltrey via a stomping, jaunty tune that belies the intended seriousness of the lyric.

DAILY RECORDS

A love song with touches of Latin American in the chord changes. Uncharacteristic of The Who, or Townshend for that matter, with some of the "observational" lyrics bordering on the sycophantic: "I look at baggy suits and leather capped with puke / I look at Richmond married couples denim look / I watch my kids grow up and ridicule the bunch / When you are eleven the whole world's out to lunch".

YOU

The second Entwistle offering, but this time sung by Roger Daltrey. Again, as with "The Quiet One," the song doesn't have the sharp cutting edge of sardonic humor that usually characterizes the bass player's compositions.

ANOTHER TRICKY DAY

Voted No. 48 in "The Who's 50 Greatest Songs" in *Rolling Stone* magazine, the dynamics are near perfect in a complex tune that Daltrey handles with consummate skill, and characteristic assurance. A great finisher, celebrating music itself as a panacea to life's problems with the iconic one-liner "Rock and roll will never die."

11 IT'S HARD

Prior to the release of *Face Dances* on March 16, 1981, The Who had undertaken their biggest ever tour of the UK, lasting from the end of January to mid-March. As well as Kenney Jones and "Rabbit" Bundrick in their respective roles, another recent modification to the lineup was Roger Daltrey playing guitar, something that hadn't been featured onstage since the days of The Detours. Twenty-six dates criss-crossed the UK, followed by a pan-European TV broadcast live from the stage of the Grugahalle in Essen, Germany. That would be the last concert appearance by the band for a full eighteen months.

HIATUS

Ten days after the German gig, Pete Townshend was in New York, recording some demos for his next solo album, when the word came through that Kit Lambert had died. It was devastating news for Pete, Roger, and John, who had lost Peter Meaden, Keith Moon, and now another key figure in the band's history, all within the space of three years. Lambert had apparently been drinking heavily in El Sombrero, a well-known gay nightclub in London, and died later after falling down stairs and suffering a cerebral hemorrhage at his mother's home. His life had been plagued by a serious heroin addiction for some years, and many (including Townshend) believed the hemorrhage was related to a beating he'd received earlier from a drug dealer, over an unpaid debt.

A major factor in The Who's lengthy hiatus would be Townshend's own battle with addictions. Though never all-consuming, as they had become in the case of Keith Moon—although ironically it was an overdose of drugs designed to aid alcohol withdrawal that proved fatal for the drummer—Pete realized things would only get worse if he did nothing about it. In September 1981, Townshend suggested to Bill Curbishley that he needed some time off, and his manager agreed, writing to him: "I think you need a complete break of two or three months . . . no dope, no booze . . . no London or New York "

Of course, it didn't work out as straightforward as that. Proposed tour dates through fall and winter were put on hold, and any sessions toward a new album postponed indefinitely, likewise the work initiated on Pete's next solo project. But although by the end of 1981 he hadn't tasted alcohol for a couple of months, Townshend was still indulging in cocaine and heroin, and certainly not avoiding the nightlife in London, New York, or elsewhere.

Early in 1982, Pete called the addiction therapist Meg Patterson, who he had known since 1974 when she helped Eric Clapton, then struggling with a heroin habit. Patterson administered her controlled withdrawal system known as NET (Neuro-Electric Therapy) from her base in California. Pete spent a month being treated by Meg and her husband, George, who talked him though the hardest times: "I spent five days climbing the walls . . . my rehab had taken thirty days, and I was clean at last."

Meanwhile, the bouts of severe depression that Pete had been suffering through 1981 were not helped by discontent in the Who camp itself. After *Face Dances*, it emerged that Roger was not happy with Kenney Jones as their drummer, claiming he couldn't work with him, and blaming him for what he saw as the shortcomings of the album, an overall lack of the traditional "Who" dynamic. Kenney on the other hand felt that one problem was Pete keeping the best songs for his solo projects, while John placed the blame for an overall blandness in the production

PREVIOUS PAGES The Who, 1981. (L–R): Pete, Roger, Kenney and John.
LEFT Pete Townshend, 1982. Townshend suffered severe bouts of depression through much of 1981 and 1982, due in part to his own addiction battles.

firmly at the door of producer Bill Szymczyk. And on the general topic of touring, Pete felt the band should cut back in favor of the recording studio, while John and Roger were adamant in the opposite view; to them, as it had been to Keith Moon, live performance was the lifeblood of The Who, and as long as the band existed, it always would be.

From the fall of 1981 and into the spring of 1982, Townshend had been working spasmodically on his third solo album. Produced by Chris Thomas, who had also produced Pete's previous album, *Empty Glass*, it was recorded at three separate studios around London—Townshend's own studio Eel Pie (formerly Oceanic), AIR, and Wessex. Although Kenney Jones, for one, felt Pete was keeping the best songs for his solo endeavors, most of the songs were complex to the point of being pretentious at times, and certainly not suitable material for The Who. Even the title, *All the Best Cowboys Have Chinese Eyes*, seemed deliberately obscure—Townshend explained it as referring (in an analogy that wouldn't be acceptable these days) to Western movie heroes like Clint Eastwood and John Wayne having "eyes like slits."

IT'S HARD

Pete's album was released in June 1982, just as The Who were back in the studio to finally lay down completed tracks for their long-awaited tenth studio album, *It's Hard*. With live dates having been deferred for over a year, the record company were pushing for a new album to appear ahead of a return to the road in September 1982. As a consequence, the tracks were recorded very quickly, with the entire album completed in less than a month, at producer Glyn Johns's home studio Turn Up-Down. Roger Daltrey for one, wanted to hold back the tracks, which he didn't feel were properly finished, but with Warner Brothers in the US breathing down their necks for "product," the band were forced to release it.

Although all the group were dissatisfied with the album in one way or another, it garnered a mixed reception. Aided no doubt by the tour that followed immediately after its release, it made a respectable showing on the album charts on both sides of the Atlantic. And to the surprise of many, particularly in the Who camp, it received a five-star top rating in *Rolling Stone* from critic Parke Puterbaugh, who called it "A strong affirmation of this band's ability to reach millions with powerful rock & roll and trenchant, galvanizing politics."

LEFT Kenney Jones, 1982. Roger Daltrey was reportedly unhappy with Jones as their drummer, citing a lack of "Who" dynamic.
BELOW The Who were pulling in different directions. Townshend wanted to take time off from touring, while Daltrey and Entwistle felt that live performance was the lifeblood of the band.

"A strong affirmation of this band's ability to reach millions with powerful rock & roll and trenchant, galvanizing politics."

PARKE PUTERBAUGH, *ROLLING STONE* REVIEW OF *IT'S HARD*, SEPTEMBER 30, 1982

IT'S HARD

TRACK LIST (original vinyl edition)
[All songs written by Pete Townshend except where indicated]

SIDE ONE
1. Athena
2. It's Your Turn [John Entwistle]
3. Cooks County
4. It's Hard
5. Dangerous [John Entwistle]
6. Eminence Front

SIDE TWO
1. I've Known No War
2. One Life's Enough
3. One at a Time [John Entwistle]
4. Why Did I Fall for That
5. A Man Is a Man
6. Cry If You Want

RECORDED: June 1982, Turn Up-Down Studio, Surrey, England
RELEASED: September 4, 1982
LABEL: Polydor / Warner Bros
PRODUCER: Glyn Johns
PERSONNEL: Roger Daltrey (vocals, guitar); Pete Townshend (guitars, keyboards, vocals); John Entwistle (bass guitar, vocals); Kenney Jones (drums); Andy Fairweather Low (guitar); Tim Gorman (keyboards)
CHART POSITIONS / AWARDS: No. 8, US album chart; No. 11, UK album chart; No. 3, Canadian album chart; Gold discs: US, Canada

TRACK-BY-TRACK

ATHENA
An autobiographical piece from Townshend, written after he met the actress Theresa Russell, who he admitted he immediately fell for in a big way. Unfortunately for Pete, Ms Russell—at the time engaged to film director Nicolas Roeg—didn't reciprocate his advances. An up-tempo, fun number that belies the composer's disappointment at the time, it made No. 28 in the US singles chart, and No. 40 in the UK.

IT'S YOUR TURN
Written by John Entwistle, featuring a rhythm guitar part by guest Andy Fairweather Low, who also comes in briefly on harmony vocals.

COOKS COUNTY
One of the more overtly political songs on the album—"People are suffering / Say it again / People are hungry / Say it again"— written by Townshend after seeing a shocking television documentary on Chicago's Cook County Hospital. An effectively repetitive guitar riff keeps the whole thing coasting along, with Kenney Jones showing where economy counts.

IT'S HARD
The title track, but one of the least distinguished on the album, with a soft rock sound untypical of The Who at any time in their career. Another example of Pete bemoaning his own situation rather than, as in much of his earlier work, that of less privileged members of his fan base. The lyrics were originally presented to the rest of the band as a demo for a song called "Popular" for *Face Dances*, but they rejected it then and were not much keener on it this time round.

DANGEROUS
Another Entwistle track, this was the first song from *It's Hard* to be added to the band's live set. With constant throbbing guitar holding it all together, broken only by an instrumental bridge, a strident crowd-pleaser in classic Who mold.

EMINENCE FRONT
A rare example of The Who dipping their toes into funk. Singing the lead vocals, at Glyn Johns's insistence, Townshend described this as being particularly radio-friendly. With a repetitive synth figure running throughout, and introduced by a Townshend solo which he varied nightly, the song became a regular fixture in the band's live set. Roger Daltrey, who was dubious about the album as a whole, felt this and the final track were the only songs really worthy of release. Tim Gorman guests on keyboards.

I'VE KNOWN NO WAR
Nothing less than a warning of the horrors of a nuclear holocaust, from the perspective of a pacifist protester: "I'll never know war / And if I ever know it / The glimpse will be short / Fireball in the sky." Daltrey's delivery is nothing short of heartfelt, and Townshend's guitar parts sound similarly inspired.

ONE LIFE'S ENOUGH
A gently paced love ballad, which Pete originally wrote with himself in mind as vocalist. But Roger carries it off with an assured sensitivity. Another stand-out track.

ONE AT A TIME
The third Entwistle entry, and a truly rocking one, with tremendous drumming from Kenney Jones—justifying once and for all (although this would be his final album with The Who) his position in the band.

WHY DID I FALL FOR THAT
Another anti-war lyric from Townshend. Rather busy on the arrangements, but the lyrics—"The streets of the future littered with remains / Of both the fools and all the so-called brains"—come over effectively enough, ending with a nice old-fashioned fade-out of the title line.

A MAN IS A MAN
With a plodding arrangement, the whole pace of the song comes over as somewhat lugubrious—an accusation that can rarely be made about anything by The Who.

CRY IF YOU WANT
A tour de force for a closer. Daltrey handles Townshend's stream-of-consciousness lyrics—a swirling, exclamatory sermon, casting doubt on the former certainties of arrogant youth—with superhuman gusto. The band attack our ears as if it's the last number they'll ever play, with machine-gun powered vocals, scintillating guitar, powerhouse bass parts, and driving, commanding percussion.

12 WHO'S LAST

For the moment at least, *It's Hard* would be The Who's swansong as far as studio albums were concerned, as would the follow-up tour organized to promote it. Townshend was adamant it would be their last concert trek for a long time, if not forever.

FAREWELL

John Entwistle, on the other hand, was firm in his view that if The Who stopped touring, he would find some other outfit to keep on the road: "I'm not prepared to just carry on doing albums," he told *Rolling Stone*. "If the touring isn't there, then I'd rather get my own thing together, which involves touring as well."

But Roger Daltrey, who with Entwistle had resisted Townshend's plans for a "studio only" strategy, would nevertheless claim that he agreed with Pete about future touring, if only to save Pete from himself: "Pete's drinking got very bad by '82. That's why I stopped the band. Two bottles of brandy a day and who knows whatever else. It was going to kill him. And I didn't want to kill Pete Townshend." So the dates they were about to embark on, in September 1982, were billed as a "farewell tour." To all intents and purposes, that made the impending termination of The Who official.

The tour kicked off on home territory with two dates at the huge National Exhibition Centre in Birmingham on September 10 and 11, before opening in North America at Largo, Maryland on September 22. For most of the concerts—which included two dates at Shea Stadium in Queens, New York City—the UK punk band The Clash played support. The tour, one

of the biggest moneymakers of the band's career, wound up three months later on December 17, the second of two nights at the Maple Leaf Gardens in Toronto, Canada. Nailing their rock 'n' roll credentials firmly to the mast, that final show opened with "My Generation," and closed with "Twist and Shout."

TERMINATION

Through 1983, Pete Townshend spent most of his time on various projects other than the now-stagnant Who. While in New York during the farewell tour, in October 1982, he had been offered a job as an acquisitions editor at the prestigious UK publisher Faber and Faber. Once the tour was over, Townshend relished the role. He had been involved in book publishing since 1977 when he had set up Eel Pie Books, and also opened the Magic Bus bookshop in Richmond, south-west London. And he had been working on a collection of short stories and poetry since 1979, which would be published by Faber in 1985 as *Horse's Neck*.

PREVIOUS PAGES The Who, playing a UK date in 1982
LEFT Pete Townshend during the eighties, pictured outside his bookshop, Magic Bus, in Richmond-Upon-Thames, London
ABOVE RIGHT Pete with British punk star Joe Strummer of The Clash (who were supporting The Who), before their show on October 13, 1982, at Shea Stadium in Flushing, New York

"Pete's drinking got very bad by '82. That's why I stopped the band. Two bottles of brandy a day and who knows whatever else. It was going to kill him. And I didn't want to kill Pete Townshend."

ROGER DALTREY

His appointment at Faber, looking after a list of titles focused on "popular arts," was formally announced at a press conference early in 1983. "I think [Faber boss] Matthew Evans wanted a bit of 'fun,'" Townshend later told the *Sunday Times*. "Some of the excitement that was going on elsewhere in the publishing industry; the growth of interest in the popular arts, youth culture—terrible phrase—contemporary things. What I did not want to be was just the man who dealt with all the pop music stuff."

Pete hadn't abandoned The Who altogether, however. In April 1983 he released *Scoop*, a compilation double album of twenty-five demos of both released and unreleased Who material, and demos of brand new songs. One track, "Unused Piano: '*Quadrophenia*,'" would be nominated for a Grammy award for Best Rock Instrumental, the following January.

Townshend said he still wanted the band to continue as a studio outfit, while turning their back on touring—much as The Beatles had done in September 1966, after their final tour of the United States. And there was added pressure for him to write material for another Who album, to fulfill a contractual obligation to Warner Brothers. But in the event, Pete found himself unable to produce the songs required—his songwriting had simply "dried up" as far as The Who was concerned.

Early in December 1983, Townshend came to an arrangement with the record company that terminated their contract, in exchange for an undisclosed sum of money being returned from advances already paid. And on December 16, at a specially convened press conference, he announced his decision to leave the band, effectively bringing The Who to an end. A statement to the press read: "I will not be making any more records with The Who. It's already been stated that our tour of America in 1982 was our last, and I can now add that I will not perform live again anywhere in the world with The Who."

Though anticipated in many respects, the announcement—issued via The Who's press agent Keith Altham—nevertheless came as a shock to Daltrey, Entwistle, and Jones, who were seemingly not consulted. An angry Roger Daltrey issued his own reaction, telling the press sarcastically: "It was a wonderful Christmas present."

EXTRACURRICULAR

Roger, in the meantime, had been busy with his own extracurricular activities outside the orbit of The Who. On October 29 he appeared in a BBC TV production of the eighteenth-century opera *The Beggar's Opera*, in the lead role as the robber Macheath. And the following month, the BBC began shooting *A Comedy of Errors* by William Shakespeare, with Daltrey playing the dual comic roles of the Dromio twins.

Then on November 14, the *New York Times* reported that Roger was soon to be directing a movie based on the lives of the notorious London gangsters the Kray twins. The film never came to fruition, mainly, according to Daltrey, because it was with the risky involvement of the Krays themselves, though by this time they were both serving long sentences in prison: "This other production team popped up and I was glad to let them have it. I just didn't want it in my life any more. It felt too dangerous."

Stage, film, or television projects not withstanding, Roger also filled the vacuum left by the defunct Who with another solo album, his fifth. The title—*Parting Should Be Painless*—was a clear reference to Townshend's departure, and the subsequent breakup of The Who. Though none of them self-penned, the choice of songs—from various writers including Bryan Ferry, and The Eurythmics—gave a strong autobiographical pitch to the album. Daltrey also stressed that musically it represented the kind of direction he wanted The Who to go in, had Pete not pulled the plug on the band.

Roger Daltrey on set of *The Beggar's Opera*, 1983. Daltrey had taken a variety of film and TV roles to fill the vaccuum left by The Who.

WHO'S LAST

Toward the end of 1984, a double live album of The Who was released. The original version, which was being compiled by John Entwistle, began with recordings from a mid-seventies concert and continued up to the 1982 farewell tour. However, the record company, MCA, didn't approve of John's choices, wanting them to focus more on The Who's best-known hits. John subsequently gave up on the project, and the collection was assembled somewhat hastily by Dave "Cy" Langston. All the tracks now featured were from concerts on the farewell tour, and the album was appropriately titled as *Who's Last*: At the time of its release, it was indeed considered to be the last album of the band.

The album was greeted with almost universal derision from the rock music press. Most of the performances were acknowledged as below par compared to the studio originals, or indeed the earlier concert versions on *Live at Leeds*. It's worth remembering that at the time, the 1970 Leeds release was the only other live (non-bootleg) Who album on the market, except for soundtrack performances from *Woodstock* and *The Kids Are Alright*. Many reviews considered the release opportunistic, though not all going as far as Kurt Loder in *Rolling Stone*, who concluded his scathing attack: "I can't think of another band as committed and allegedly idealistic as the Who that has ended its career on so sour and sickening a note."

And the fans certainly stayed away in droves, the collection only making a modest showing sales-wise—a telling response, especially considering the album was being touted by the record company as a "farewell" souvenir of the band. Many of the performances of classic songs are lackluster and uninspired, the band often sounding like they are merely going through the motions, as if anticipating their imminent retirement. But in retrospect, the album does represent an essential moment in The Who's history, at a time when indeed there seemed to be no future for the group.

LEFT John Entwistle, 1982
ABOVE The Who performing at JFK Stadium in Philadelphia, on September 25, 1982 as part of their "farewell" tour

WHO'S LAST

TRACK LIST (original vinyl edition)
[All songs written by Pete Townshend
except where indicated]

SIDE ONE
1. My Generation
2. I Can't Explain
3. Substitute
4. Behind Blue Eyes
5. Baba O'Riley

SIDE TWO
1. Boris the Spider [John Entwistle]
2. Who Are You

3. Pinball Wizard
4. See Me Feel Me / Listening to You

SIDE THREE
1. Love, Reign o'er Me
2. Long Live Rock
3. Reprise
4. Won't Get Fooled Again

SIDE FOUR
1. Doctor Jimmy
2. Magic Bus
3. Summertime Blues [Eddie Cochran, Jerry Capehart]
4. Twist and Shout [Phil Medley, Bert Russell]

RECORDED: October 10, 20, 27 and December 14, 1982, "farewell" US tour
RELEASED: November 1984 (US), December 1984 (UK)
LABEL: MCA
PRODUCER: Dave Langston
PERSONNEL: Roger Daltrey (vocals, guitar, harmonica); Pete Townshend (guitar, vocals); John Entwistle
(bass guitar, vocals); Kenney Jones (drums); Tim Gorman (piano, keyboards, synthesizer, vocals)
CHART POSITIONS / AWARDS: No. 48, UK album chart; No. 81, US album chart

MY GENERATION
Like most of the album, this was recorded at the Richfield Coliseum in Cleveland Ohio on December 14, 1982. It's certainly "Who by numbers" time, with all the components there, but sounding like a highly efficient tribute band.

I CAN'T EXPLAIN
Daltrey's delivery is uncharacteristically stilted, with Kenney Jones's drum breaks lacking the fiery unpredictability of Keith Moon.

SUBSTITUTE
Recorded earlier in the tour, at the Jack Murphy Stadium in San Diego, California, on October 27. After realizing any of this collection isn't going to be quintessential Who, the listener can settle back and enjoy some acceptable versions of classics—but who wants just "acceptable" from The Who?

BEHIND BLUE EYES
This is the earliest recording featured from the tour, from an October 10 concert at the Brendan Byrne Arena in East Rutherford, New Jersey. The majestic ballad from *Who's Next* seems to come to a perfunctory halt, even though it's actually of a similar three-and-a-half minutes' duration as the original.

BABA O'RILEY
Even the opening synth riff sounds thin here—partly to do with the mix as much as the performance—and Roger's voice seems to be straining at the edges.

BORIS THE SPIDER
As with much of the album, the whole band sound listless, rushing through the much-loved Entwistle song as if they can't wait to get off the stage.

WHO ARE YOU
The only song from later than 1973, even though the band played some good picks from *It's Hard* throughout the tour.

PINBALL WIZARD
Something of a shambles, with Daltrey rushing the words out, and Pete crashing through the guitar parts like the heavy metal player he clearly wasn't. Only Entwistle seems in a solid groove, and that's largely lost in the mix.

SEE ME FEEL ME / LISTENING TO YOU
The ecstatic applause as the song opens shows how the vast crowds were wowed enough by just seeing The Who in person, especially as it was being promoted as their last-ever tour. A rather stodgy version of the *Tommy* anthem.

LOVE, REIGN O'ER ME
Daltrey's voice couldn't have really sounded this unconvincing. Once again, the mix has a lot to answer for.

LONG LIVE ROCK
The Who in Status Quo territory. Entwistle tries to keep it solid, while Pete plays it safe with some predictable riffing, and Tim Gorman's keyboards give it the boogie lift it sorely needs.

REPRISE
Pete suddenly lights up with his own brand of guitar boogie, an out-and-out flag-waver that segues as an up-tempo encore to the previous track.

WON'T GET FOOLED AGAIN
Pete Townshend manages to force his way through, despite an appalling job at the mixing desk.

DOCTOR JIMMY
From *Quadrophenia*, another messy version that begs for the discipline and controlled mixing of the recording studio.

MAGIC BUS
Along with the next track, this was recorded at the Kingdome, Seattle Washington on October 20. Townshend's call-and-response vocals seem out of synch, and the "Bo Diddley" beat doesn't come over as potently as it should here.

SUMMERTIME BLUES
Over the years, one of The Who's consistently successful attempts at an oldies cover, this rendition of Eddie Cochran's standby comes across as adequate, but again disappointing. For once, Kenney Jones's drumming rises to the occasion.

TWIST AND SHOUT
The only recorded version of The Who's cover of the old soul classic made famous by the Isley Brothers and The Beatles—with Daltrey's vocals a bit too close to Lennon for comfort—"Twist and Shout" was released simultaneously as a single, with this album's version of "I Can't Explain" on the flip side. Perhaps not surprisingly, the single did no better than the album.

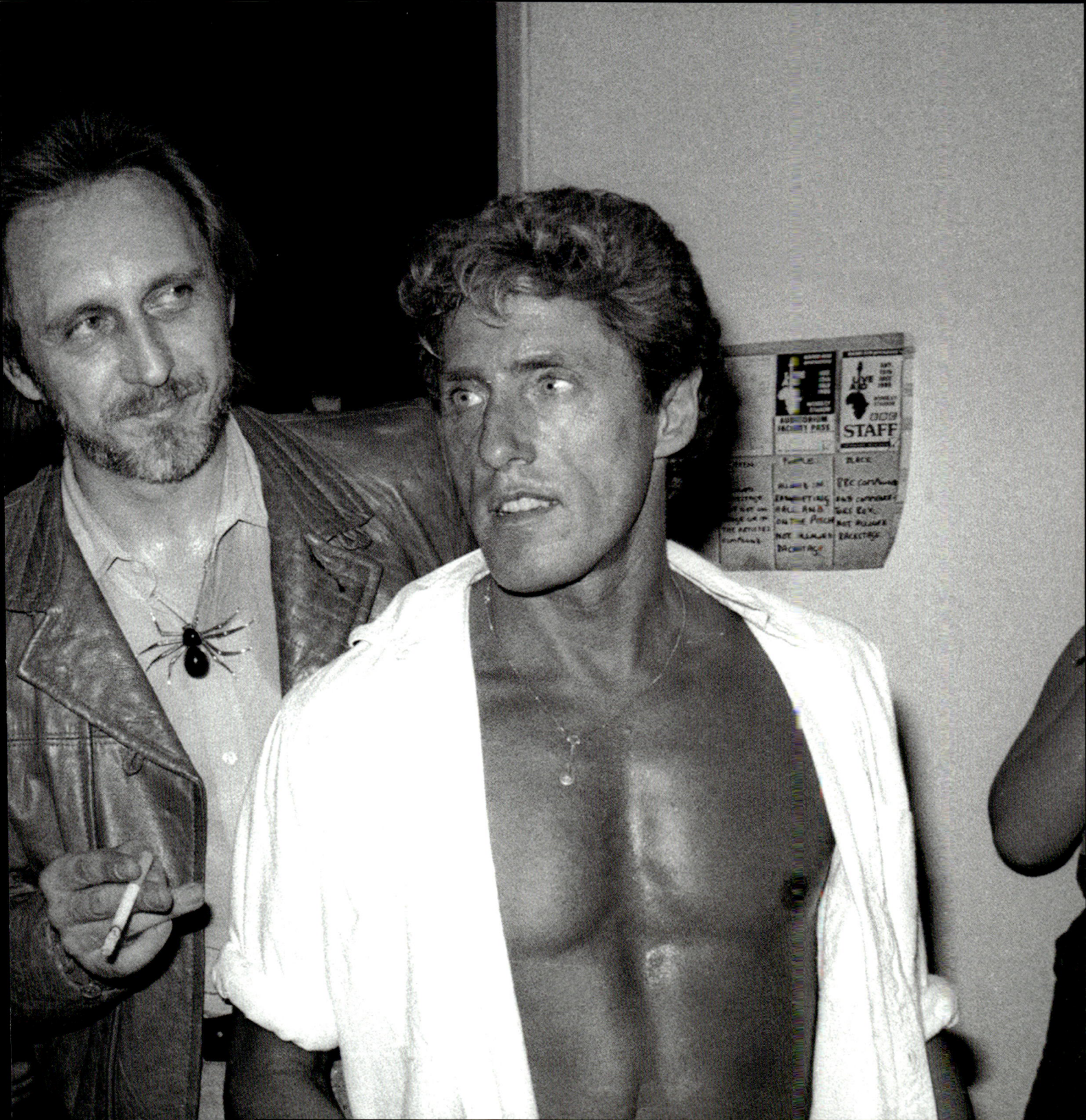

13 JOIN TOGETHER

Despite their 1982 North American trek being their "farewell" tour, and the subsequent 1984 album actually being titled *Who's Last*, it was not the end of the story for The Who. Within eight months of the ill-received release, the band were reunited onstage once more, for the now-historic Live Aid concert in July 1985. And at the end of the decade, in 1989, the band got together for a reunion tour marking the twenty-fifth anniversary of The Who, commemorated for posterity in the double-CD *Join Together* released in March 1990.

LIVE AID

In the spring of 1985, Pete Townshend—along with a host of other big music names—got "the call" from Bob Geldof, lead singer with the Irish punk band The Boomtown Rats.

The previous Christmas, Geldof, and Midge Ure of Ultravox, had organized Band Aid, a supergroup of mainly UK and Irish pop stars singing a charity single in aid of the victims of famine in Ethiopia: "Do They Know It's Christmas" shot to the top of the charts in thirteen countries, and at the time was the fastest-selling single in UK chart history.

Inspired by Band Aid's success, Geldof and Ure decided to hold a marathon benefit show, which they dubbed Live Aid, simultaneously in London and the United States, and contacted just about every rock superstar on the planet with a view to taking part. There was no arguing with Geldof's style of persuasion: "If The Who appear we know we will get an additional million pounds of revenue," he told Pete. "Every pound we make will save a life. Do the fucking maths. And do the fucking show."

PREVIOUS PAGES The Who after their Live Aid appearance, July 13, 1985
LEFT Roger and Pete onstage at the Live Aid concert

On July 13, 1985, and broadcast live around the world, the two concerts were held simultaneously at Wembley Stadium in London, and the John F. Kennedy Stadium in Philadelphia. Because of the live TV factor, a seamless timetable was essential, with acts allowed twenty minutes or so, and alternating (taking into account the time difference) between the UK and US concerts. Introduced by actor Jack Nicholson at the JFK stadium, and DJ Tommy Vance at Wembley, The Who went onstage in London at precisely 7.59pm local UK time, sandwiched between The Pretenders' and Santana's sets from Philadelphia.

Their opening was delayed by an embarrassing minute or so, over a problem with John Entwistle's bass, then as they launched into "My Generation" the broadcast sound cut off due to a fuse blowing on the TV feed. Roger had got as far as "Why don't you all fade . . ." when the TV audio failed, only returning during the last verse of the next number, "Pinball Wizard." The broadcast apart, all sounded fine onstage as the band played on. "Love, Reign o'er Me" was next, the short set ending with a nine-and-a-half minute rough-at-the-edges version of "Won't Get Fooled Again." And Pete Townshend was in the final encore lineup at the end of the concert, when he and Paul McCartney lifted a triumphant Bob Geldof on their shoulders. It would be another three years before Pete, Roger, John, and Kenney performed together again.

BONUS

Given the fact that The Who were now a defunct entity, the latter half of 1985 was something of a bonus season for their fans, with solo projects from Daltrey and Townshend being followed at the end of November with a compilation of rare tracks by the band.

In September 1985, Roger Daltrey would release what he considered probably his best solo album

UNDER A RAGING MOON ■ ROGER DALTREY

LEFT Pete Townshend, 1985, in his role on the editorial team at Faber and Faber RIGHT Roger Daltrey's 1985 album *Under a Raging Moon*, dedicated to Keith Moon

yet, *Under a Raging Moon*. Dedicated to the memory of Keith Moon, the title track—written by John Parr and Julia Downes—was certainly the most heartfelt. Appearing as the final track on the album, the song featured no less than seven drummers, including Queen's Roger Taylor, Cozy Powell, Stewart Copeland of The Police, and Ringo Starr's son Zak—who went on to be the regular drummer for later manifestations of The Who. In fact John Entwistle had wanted to play the Moon tribute at Live Aid, but Townshend wouldn't agree, and later the bass player recorded it for his solo live album *Left for Live*, which appeared in 1999.

Pete Townshend released his fourth solo album in November. *White City: A Novel* fell somewhere between a concept album and the "rock opera" idiom that Pete had long flirted with. The songs were based on a story narrative that accompanied the album, set in a downtrodden housing estate in White City, west London, not far from Townshend's home district of Acton. The largely doom-laden lyrics addressed the social issues produced by urban decay, each song a platform for Pete's moral concerns that were not as easily expressed in the setting of The Who's music.

Produced by Chris Thomas, who had also produced Townshend's *Empty Glass* and *All the Best Cowboys Have Chinese Eyes*, the album featured an array of eminent names in a session capacity, including "Rabbit" Bundrick, familiar to all Who fans, Simon Phillips (who would go on to replace Kenney Jones on drums in the next lineup of the band), drummer Clem Burke of Blondie fame, and Pink Floyd's Dave Gilmour on guitar. The work was also the basis for a sixty-minute film, *White City: The Music Movie*, directed by Richard Lowenstein and starring Pete Townshend and Frances Barber, released on video simultaneously with the album.

November 30, 1985 saw the release of *Who's Missing*, a collection of obscure or unreleased tracks spanning the band's career from 1965 to 1971. Highlights included a live version of Townshend's "Bargain" from *Who's Next*, a little-known Daltrey song "Here for More," and covers of various 1960s R&B songs. These included "Barbara Anne" (made famous by The Beach Boys), James Brown's "Shout and Shimmy," and "Lubie (Come Back Home)," recorded by The Who in 1965, a cover of "Louie, Go Home" by Paul Revere and the Raiders. A second volume, *Two's Missing*, would be released in April 1987.

Two days later, on December 2, 1985, Roger Daltrey embarked on his first solo tour of the United States—a short affair which he would later admit that, compared to touring with The Who, was not an altogether satisfactory exercise.

of covers including the Elvis Presley-Big Boy Crudup classic "That's All Right Mama," Robert Parker's "Barefootin'," and (perhaps most surprisingly) "Boogie Stop Shuffle," and "Oh Lord, Don't Let Them Drop That Atomic Bomb on Me," both by the great jazz bassist and composer Charles Mingus. After working on the album—which was envisaged as a video-stage musical—for a couple of months, Pete discarded the idea in favor of developing the *Iron Man* project.

A UK newspaper carried a story in June 1986 that Roger Daltrey was thinking about emigrating to Australia, the singer being quoted that he felt England was "going down the tubes." In the event, he never left Britain. Like Townshend (and indeed John Entwistle), Daltrey allied himself to various causes and charities. In October he and his band performed at a concert at London's Adelphi Theatre, in support of the Standing Conference on Drug Abuse, to establish and run drug rehab centers.

It was announced that The Who were planning a one-off "reunion" concert during December, at London's Marquee Club, scene of some of their earliest triumphs. Manager Bill Curbishley then jumped the gun somewhat, when he went on to book the band into some US dates—when Townshend heard about it, he pulled The Who out of the Marquee appearance. But the year ended with a personal positive for Pete, when Virgin signed him to a contract for the *Iron Man* project.

In March 1987, Townshend released the second volume of his demo recordings, *Another Scoop*, a companion to the first collection, *Scoop*, of 1983. Of twenty-seven songs, just one was not a Townshend original—Cole Porter's 1935 classic "Begin the Beguine."

And on April 1, John Entwistle acted as musical director for an AIDS benefit concert at London's Wembley Stadium for World AIDS Day. With an all-star lineup that included George Michael, Elton John, Boy George, and Meat Loaf, John played bass behind some of the acts. The concert was released as a hugely successful video, *Stand By Me: AIDS Day Benefit*.

June '87 saw the release of Roger Daltrey's seventh solo album, *Can't Wait to See the Movie*. Greeted by mainly negative reviews, the album failed to make any impact, although a single from it, "Hearts of Fire" backed with "Lover's Storm," did make the UK chart at No. 88.

STOP-START

Much of 1986 through 1988 was a stop-start period for the ex-Who, particularly Pete. He was forging ahead with his job at the publishers Faber and Faber, and musical ventures were seeming more and more like the sideline rather than vice versa. Early in 1986 he had proposed making the poet Ted Hughes's children's book *The Iron Man* into a stage musical, much as Andrew Lloyd Webber had turned another Faber book, T. S. Eliot's *Old Possum's Book of Practical Cats*, into the highly successful musical *Cats*.

Then in April, Townshend came up with a preliminary track listing for his next solo album. With the working title *Beguines, Tangos and Love*, it was to feature, alongside new songs from Pete, an array

Pete Townshend threw a huge upmarket benefit ball on October 20, in aid of his Double "O" Charity, to fund treatment clinics and rehabilitation centers for people with serious drug and alcohol problems. At £100 a ticket, the event's 150 guests included Bill Wyman, Midge Ure, Steve Winwood, Simon Phillips,

OPPOSITE Pete Townshend, promoting his 1985 album and film *White City: The Music Movie*
ABOVE John Entwistle performs a solo show at The Channel in Boston, USA, on November 19, 1987

and Dire Straits' Mark Knopfer. Pete and Dire Straits put on a one-hour show, with a mix of originals and oldies including "That's All Right Mama," "No Face, No Name, No Number," and 'Barefootin'."

John Entwistle, as eager as Townshend or Daltrey to forge a musical career outside the omnipresent shadow of The Who, made his first post-Who solo appearances in the United States in November 1987. He was backed by Rat Race Choir, a rock group from Westchester, New York, founded and led by drummer Steve Luongo.

REUNION

Not for the first time, in February 1988, *Rolling Stone* reported on rumors that The Who were to get together again, for an American tour in the upcoming summer. Though that was not to be, the story was not without foundation, and as a prelude to future collaborations, on February 8, the band assembled to receive a Lifetime Achievement Award from the British Phonographic Industry. The occasion was the annual Brit Awards ceremony, televised live from London's Royal Albert Hall; The Who's perfunctory set of "My Generation" and "Who Are You" was faded out after the start of "Substitute," due to the show overrunning. It would be the last time until 2014 that Kenney Jones appeared with the band.

As if to hint furthermore at some upcoming Who revival, at the end of February, a rerelease of "My Generation," with "Substitute" on the B-side, hit the UK charts, peaking at No. 68. And on March 2, the band assembled at the Marquee Club to promote a "greatest hits" album, *Who's Better, Who's Best*. Subtitled *This Is The Very Best of The Who*, the collection really was just that, making it to No. 10 in the UK chart and gaining a Silver disc in the process.

Through the rest of 1988, John Entwistle was the only ex-Who member who seemed to be relishing performing live, with yet another North American tour of small club venues. Playing mainly material from his unreleased album *The Rock*—which didn't finally appear until 1996—as the John Entwistle Band, he took in dates in the US and Canada from late June into early August.

Through the closing months of 1988, there would be further evidence that Townshend, Daltrey, and

Entwistle were in a collaborative mood, when Roger and John put the finishing touches to their contribution to Pete's *Iron Man* project.

Featuring Townshend, Daltrey, and others (including R&B legends John Lee Hooker and Nina Simone) in "character" roles, the three Who survivors played together on two tracks, "Dig" and Arthur Brown's "Fire." Entitled *The Iron Man: The Musical by Pete Townshend*, the album would eventually appear in late June 1989, by which time The Who had indeed reunited, for their twenty-fifth anniversary "The Kids Are Alright" tour.

OPPOSITE The Who at the Brit Awards, London, 1988
ABOVE Simon Phillips behind the drums for The Who, 1989

ANNIVERSARY

For the quarter-century anniversary, The Who put together a show involving two acts and an intermission. The first half consisted of music from *Tommy*, the second a run-through of some hits, a few rarities, and some Townshend solo songs. For the tour The Who—with Simon Phillips on drums—were augmented by "Rabbit" Bundrick on keyboards, percussionist Jody Linscott, guitarist Steve "Boltz" Bolton, plus a five-piece horn section and three backup vocalists.

Beginning with a New York warm-up show on June 21, the tour took in forty-three dates through the US and Canada, ending at the Dallas Cotton Bowl on September 3, 1989. During the tour there were special performances in New York and Los Angeles entirely dedicated to *Tommy*, at which a variety of guests appeared including Phil Collins, Billy Idol,

Steve Winwood, and Elton John. Not all the reviews were comfortable with the expanded lineup, feeling the spectacular production was a step too far from The Who's basic rock 'n' roll band stance.

The band repeated the formula for ten shows in the UK, including two special *Tommy* concerts at the Albert Hall which featured guest appearances by Winwood, Idol, Collins, and the American vocalist Patti LaBelle.

To top off their anniversary year, in January 1990, The Who were inducted into the Rock and Roll Hall of Fame in a ceremony at New York's Waldorf Astoria Hotel. The induction was conducted by U2 front man Bono, and Keith Moon was represented by his twenty-three-year-old daughter, Mandy, who announced that her daddy couldn't be there partly because he had been banned from the hotel! With Pete playing acoustic guitar, The Who ended the proceedings with a run-through of "Substitute," Won't Get Fooled Again," and "Pinball Wizard."

To mark the twenty-fifth anniversary once and for all, in March 1990, The Who released a three-album (or two-CD) box-set souvenir of the "Kids Are Alright" tour, entitled *Join Together*. Taking the format of the touring shows, the album was divided between a live version of *Tommy*, and a collection of former hits and new material. All of the *Tommy* tracks were recorded either at the Universal Amphitheatre in Los Angeles or New York's Radio City Music Hall, the rest from various other shows across six venues during the tour. The album was dedicated to Keith Moon.

Critical response to the album was muted, and reservations about it weren't restricted to members of the rock press. In June 1990, Pete Townshend dismissed the album almost out of hand: "I didn't pick the title, cover or collection of songs," he told *Musician* magazine, "And I wouldn't be hurt if a Who fan told me they weren't going to buy it."

OPPOSITE The charity concert of *Tommy* at the Royal Albert Hall, London, with Billy Idol flanked by Roger and Pete; October 31, 1989
BELOW Pete and Roger onstage during the Rock and Roll Hall of Fame induction ceremony at the Waldorf Astoria, New York City January 17, 1990

JOIN TOGETHER

TRACK LIST
[All songs written by Pete Townshend except where indicated]

CD ONE
1. Overture / It's a Boy
2. 1921
3. Amazing Journey
4. Sparks
5. Eyesight to the Blind (The Hawker) [Sonny Boy Williamson II]
6. Christmas
7. Cousin Kevin [John Entwistle]
8. The Acid Queen
9. Pinball Wizard
10. Do You Think It's Alright?
11. Fiddle About [John Entwistle]
12. There's a Doctor
13. Go to the Mirror!
14. Smash the Mirror
15. Tommy Can You Hear Me?
16. I'm Free
17. Miracle Cure
18. Sally Simpson
19. Sensation
20. Tommy's Holiday Camp [Keith Moon]
21. We're Not Gonna Take It

CD TWO
1. Eminence Front
2. Face the Face
3. Dig
4. I Can See for Miles
5. A Little Is Enough
6. 5:15
7. Love, Reign o'er Me
8. Trick of the Light
9. Rough Boys
10. Join Together
11. You Better You Bet
12. Behind Blue Eyes
13. Won't Get Fooled Again

RECORDED: June 27, August 24, 1989, twenty-fifth anniversary US tour
RELEASED: March 1990
LABEL: Virgin
PRODUCER: Bob Clearmountain, Clive Franks, Billy Nicholls
PERSONNEL: Roger Daltrey (vocals, guitars, harmonica, tambourine); Pete Townshend (guitars, vocals); John Entwistle (bass guitar, vocals); Simon Phillips (drums); Steve "Boltz" Bolton (guitar); John "Rabbit" Bundrick (keyboards); Billy Nicholls (backing vocals); Cleveland Watkiss (backing vocals); Chyna Gordon (backing vocals); Simon Clarke (alto sax, baritone sax); Simon Gardner (trumpet); Roddy Lorimer (trumpet); Tim Sanders (tenor sax); Neil Sidwell (trombone); Jody Linscott (percussion)
CHART POSITIONS / AWARDS: No. 59, UK album chart; No. 180, US album chart

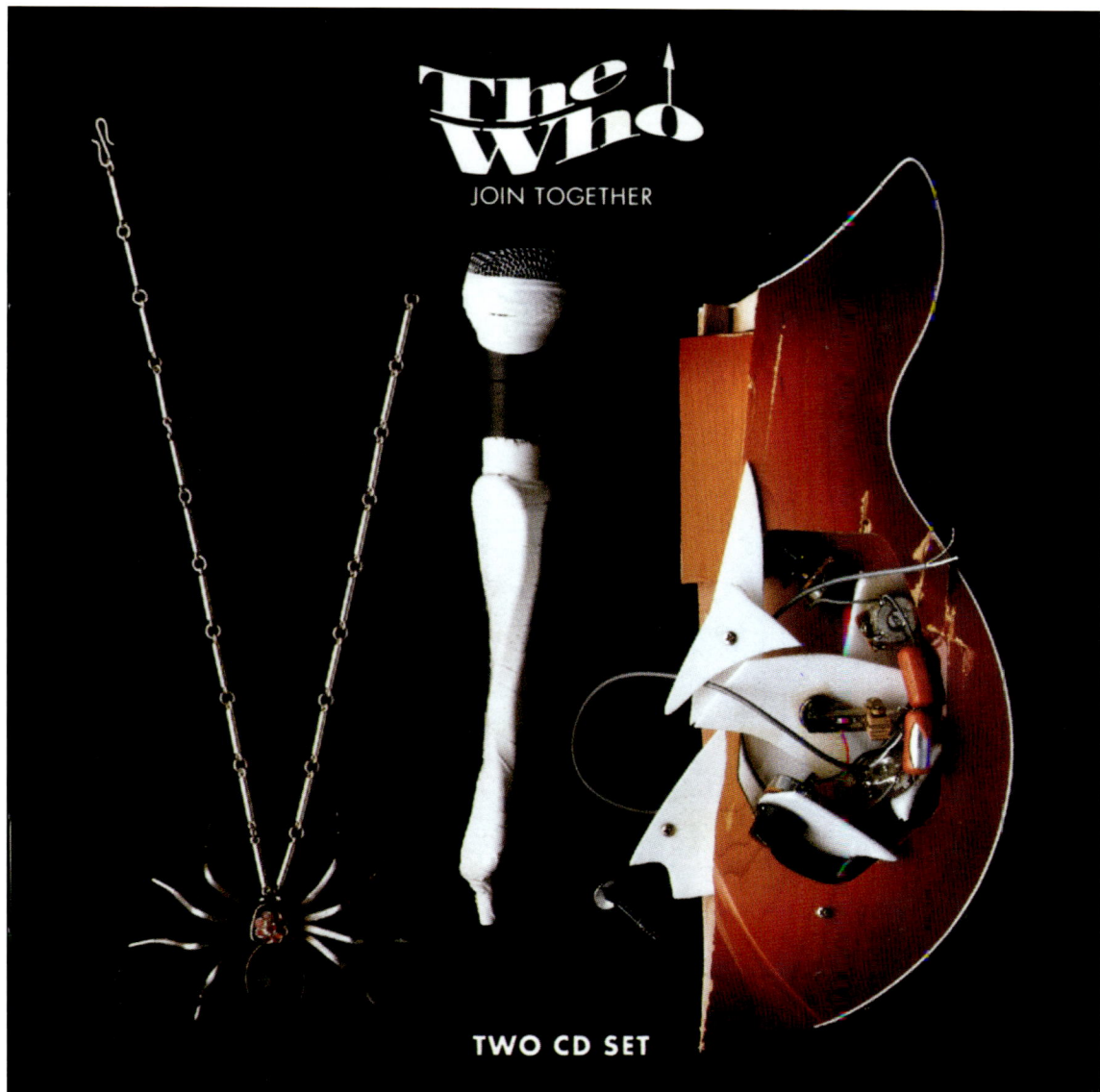

The Who
JOIN TOGETHER

TWO CD SET

"I didn't pick the title, cover or collection of songs. And I wouldn't be hurt if a Who fan told me they weren't going to buy it."

PETE TOWNSHEND ON *JOIN TOGETHER*

OVERTURE / IT'S A BOY
Recorded August 24, 1989, Universal Amphitheatre, Los Angeles. A dramatic opener that augers well for the rest of the album, instrumentally impressive with the horns and backing voices . . . but really The Who? Segues into "It's a Boy" from the backing chorus.

1921
Recorded August 24, 1989, Universal Amphitheatre, Los Angeles. The "operatic" element takes over . . . this is, after all, the live version of *Tommy*.

AMAZING JOURNEY
Recorded August 24, 1989, Universal Amphitheatre, Los Angeles. Drummer Simon Phillips is impressive throughout the song.

SPARKS
Recorded August 24, 1989, Universal Amphitheatre, Los Angeles. More guitar and keyboard fireworks, for a five-minute instrumental: *Rolling Stone* once described the original as "Wagnerian."

EYESIGHT TO THE BLIND (THE HAWKER)
Recorded June 27, 1989, Radio City Music Hall, New York City. Daltrey in blues-shouting home territory, but certainly the studio version does the Sonny Boy Williamson song more justice.

CHRISTMAS
Recorded August 24, 1989, Universal Amphitheatre, Los Angeles. "Tommy can you hear me . . ." Roger pleads mid-song, the audience are loving it.

COUSIN KEVIN
Recorded June 27, 1989, Radio City Music Hall, New York City. Entwistle's sinister lyrics get rather dissipated in the stagey chorus setting.

THE ACID QUEEN
Recorded June 27, 1989, Radio City Music Hall, New York City. Despite some energetic drumming holding everything together, a bit of a plodder . . . and the instrumental break halfway was obviously better to see live than just listen to.

PINBALL WIZARD
Recorded June 27, 1989, Radio City Music Hall, New York City. The best-known song from *Tommy*, greeted by huge applause from the New York audience before it even takes off. Actually benefits from the added instrumentation and voices in the live context.

DO YOU THINK IT'S ALRIGHT?
Recorded June 27, 1989, Radio City Music Hall, New York City. The twenty seconds-plus intro to more Entwistle weirdness . . .

FIDDLE ABOUT
Recorded June 27, 1989, Radio City Music Hall, New York City. The awkward, staccato treatment matches the uncomfortable subject matter.

THERE'S A DOCTOR
Recorded August 24, 1989, Universal Amphitheatre, Los Angeles. Another quickie link, this time with call-and-response vocals. Barely worth being presented as a separate track.

GO TO THE MIRROR!
Recorded August 24, 1989, Universal Amphitheatre, Los Angeles. "See me, feel me, touch me . . ." The essence of *Tommy*, the grand treatment sounds justified here.

SMASH THE MIRROR
Recorded August 24, 1989, Universal Amphitheatre, Los Angeles. Soulful delivery, albeit operatic at times . . . and all in just over a minute.

TOMMY CAN YOU HEAR ME?
Recorded August 24, 1989, Universal Amphitheatre, Los Angeles. Another anthem that sums up *Tommy*, though less than a minute this time.

I'M FREE
Recorded August 24, 1989, Universal Amphitheatre, Los Angeles. Third in a line of shorties, a soaring guitar break carries everything into a "Pinball" outro riff.

MIRACLE CURE
Recorded August 24, 1989, Universal Amphitheatre, Los Angeles. "Extra extra, read all about it . . ."

SALLY SIMPSON
Recorded August 24, 1989, Universal Amphitheatre, Los Angeles. Back to single-length songs, critics described the horn-led backing and general slickness as "The Who on ice."

SENSATION
Recorded August 24, 1989, Universal Amphitheatre, Los Angeles. "I am the light" . . . the heartfelt soliloquy, coming later than on the studio album.

TOMMY'S HOLIDAY CAMP
Recorded June 27, 1989, Radio City Music Hall, New York City. Keith Moon's take on cockney music-hall jollity, that before *Tommy* would have been lost on an American audience.

WE'RE NOT GONNA TAKE IT
Recorded August 24, 1989, Universal Amphitheatre, Los Angeles. A full-on finale to the first half of the tour set-list, ending Disc One in the CD package.

EMINENCE FRONT
Recorded July 27, 1989, Carter-Finley Stadium, Raleigh, North Carolina. The longish synth and guitar intro was obviously more impactful when witnessed live, taking us into funk territory with the repeated figure and horn statements.

FACE THE FACE
Recorded August 22, 1989, Jack Murphy Stadium, San Diego, California. From Pete's *White City* album. After a jaunty intro from backing singer Chyna Gordon and company, the feel of a jam session with a horn-led buildup and trombone solo is nearer to regular jazz than anything normally expected from The Who.

DIG
Recorded August 24, 1989, Universal Amphitheatre, Los Angeles. One of two songs performed by The Who on Pete's *Iron Man* album.

I CAN SEE FOR MILES
Recorded August 24, 1989, Universal Amphitheatre in Los Angeles. A true Who classic, but one which they found difficult to play as a four-piece as it originally required two guitars. Here the problem's solved, and more so.

A LITTLE IS ENOUGH
Recorded July 25, 1989, Pontiac Silverdome, Pontiac, Michigan. From Pete Townshend's 1980 album *Empty Glass*, with some flashy horn parts and distinctive synth solo.

5:15
Recorded July 27, 1989, Carter-Finley Stadium, Raleigh, North Carolina. Daltrey's in tough voice with a favorite from *Quadrophenia*. John Entwistle did the horn arrangements on the original, and possibly here.

LOVE, REIGN O'ER ME
Recorded August 24, 1989, Universal Amphitheatre, Los Angeles. Bundrick's piano brings things in majestically, waiting for the crowd to recognize the tune. Again, the horns and voices (not to mention the ending) are a bit over the top.

TRICK OF THE LIGHT
Recorded August 18, 1989, BC Place, Vancouver, Canada. The only track recorded at a Canadian date of the tour. John Entwistle's song from 1978's *Who Are You*. On a couple of dates at the start of the tour, Pete played electric guitar on this, before reverting to acoustic for the rest of the trek.

ROUGH BOYS
Recorded July 29, 1989, Tampa Stadium, Tampa, Florida. The first time on record for a rousing Who version of this Pete Townshend solo song—another that had appeared first on *Empty Glass*.

JOIN TOGETHER
Recorded August 22, 1989, Jack Murphy Stadium, San Diego, California. A throbbing intro with harmonica and what sounds like a jaw harp, a Who soul-stirrer originally released as a single in 1972, having been part of the aborted *Lifehouse* project.

YOU BETTER YOU BET
Recorded August 22, 1989, Jack Murphy Stadium, San Diego, California. On a song originally recorded in November 1980 for *Face Dances*, Daltrey's vocal here veers toward the mannerisms of late-seventies punk.

BEHIND BLUE EYES
Recorded August 24, 1989, Universal Amphitheatre, Los Angeles. In complete contrast to the last track, this was the second single to be released from *Who's Next* in 1971. A great vocal from Roger, and some fine acoustic guitar from Pete.

WON'T GET FOOLED AGAIN
Recorded July 25, 1989, Pontiac Silverdome, Pontiac, Michigan. Stirringly anthemic, as all the best Who songs tend to be, and a perfectly rousing version, with strident horns adding to the richness. But as with most of the selections on the album, the question is, does the extra musical weight add or distract from the essential Who at the core of all this?

14 BBC SESSIONS

Into the nineties, The Who—which now basically consisted of Townshend, Daltrey, and Entwistle—was still a highly temporary affair, despite the euphoria of many fans at the prospect of a reunion generated by the "Kids Are Alright" tour. Kenney Jones had now left the fold; Simon Phillips was never considered in more than an honorary session-player capacity; and the preoccupations of Pete, Roger, and John were focused in the main on their non-Who activities.

PREOCCUPATIONS

John Entwistle took off on yet another tour in the fall of 1990, this time with a potential "supergroup" lineup modestly calling themselves The Best. The group featured former Nice keyboard man Keith Emerson, ex-James Gang and Eagles guitarist Joe Walsh, Jeff Baxter from Steely Dan and the Doobie Brothers, Simon Phillips on drums who had already worked alongside John on The Who's previous tour, and the relatively unknown Rick Livingstone sharing lead vocals with Entwistle and Walsh.

One of the shortest-lived supergroups in the history of rock music, The Best played just a handful of dates in Japan and Hawaii, before retiring from the scene due to Joe Walsh's "personal problems." It was, however, the first time that a member of The Who had played in Japan, marked by a show in Yokohama that was broadcast on local TV, and later released on DVD.

Roger Daltrey, still seemingly as involved in the movie business as the music business, co-produced and starred in *Buddy's Song*, which opened in London

early in 1991. In the film, based on the novel of the same name by Nigel Hinton, Roger played a middle-aged rocker whose son has aspirations to making it in pop music. The son was played by singer Chesney Hawkes—in real life the son of "Chip" Hawkes, of the sixties band The Tremeloes—who had a No. 1 UK hit with a song from the movie, "The One and Only."

In July 1991, Pete, Roger and John agreed to contribute a song to the Elton John tribute album, *Two Rooms: Celebrating the Songs of Elton John & Bernie Taupin*. Their cover of "Saturday Night's Alright for Fighting"—on which Daltrey and Entwistle recorded their parts separately from Townshend—would be the last time John appeared on a recording by The Who.

TOMMY, THE MUSICAL

Despite them not being a formal unit, The Who's profile—and that of Pete Townshend in particular—was to the fore again with the opening of the stage musical *The Who's Tommy*, which Pete wrote with

PREVIOUS PAGES Into the nineties. The Who now basically consisted of Townshend, Daltrey, and Entwistle.
LEFT The Who's *Tommy*, the musical, opens at London's Shaftsbury Theatre, March 1996. (L–R): Pete Townshend, actor Paul Keating, who played the title role, and singer Kim Wilde who played Mrs Walker.
ABOVE RIGHT Roger Daltrey with Chesney Hawkes in the film *Buddy's Song*, 1991. Daltrey portrays Hawkes' father in the film.

Des McAnuff. The premiere was at the La Jolla Playhouse in San Diego, California; situated on the campus of the University of California, the Playhouse is a not-for-profit professional theater founded in 1947 by the Hollywood actors Gregory Peck, Dorothy McGuire, and Mel Ferrer. To support the Playhouse's work in providing educational opportunities in theater arts, on Pete's suggestion the opening night on July 1, 1992 was a benefit for the theater and the Nordoff Robbins Music Therapy Foundation.

After rave local reviews and a hugely successful run, the show opened on Broadway with previews from March 29, 1993 at the St. James Theatre, officially starting on April 22. Produced by George Martin, it ran for 899 performances before closing in June 1995, earning Pete both a Tony and an Olivier Award. That was followed by a successful run in Canada in 1995, and then London's West End, where it played at the Shaftesbury Theatre from March 1996 through to February 1997.

Not long after the Broadway opening of *The Who's Tommy*, early in June 1993, Pete released what would be his final solo album (up to the time of writing) of new original material. Another concept album, *Psychoderelict* leaned more toward the structure of a radio play, with lots of dialogue, rather than the "rock opera" concept of previous ventures. Critical reaction was mixed, to say the least: *New Musical Express* thought it was "dazzlingly ambitious," while *Rolling Stone* described the storyline—about a sixties rock musician accused of involvement with an underage girl—as full of "cliché and bombast." The album failed to chart in the UK, and only made No. 118 in the American listings.

TOGETHER AGAIN?

The next time The Who actually got together again, though hardly as a performing unit, was on February 23 and 24, 1994, when Roger Daltrey—who was turning fifty the following week—organized two concerts at New York's Carnegie Hall.

LEFT Pete with Tommy Hilfiger holding a T-shirt designed by Hilfiger promoting the *Psychoderelict* album
RIGHT The finale of "Daltrey Sings Townshend" at Carnegie Hall, February 24, 1994. The lineup included Daltrey (far left), Linda Perry (second left), Jon Bon Jovi (fourth left), Alice Cooper (fourth right), Sinéad O'Connor (second right), and Townshend, (far right).

Billed as "Daltrey Sings Townshend: A Celebration," the shows were an all-star performance of Pete's songs, backed by a full orchestra conducted by Michael Kamen. Contributors included Lou Reed singing "Now and Then," Alice Cooper with "I'm a Boy," and The Spin Doctors performing "I Can't Explain." John Entwistle joined Roger on his performances, but Pete sang his two numbers—"And I Moved" and "Who Are You"—without either of his old colleagues. The three original members of The Who only appeared together onstage for a grand finale, with all the other guests, for "Join Together."

Townshend confirmed his distancing from any reformation of The Who, when he declined Roger's invitation to take a version of the "Daltrey Sings Townshend" show on the road. So Roger assembled a ten-piece band for what was billed as a solo US tour, including Pete's brother Simon on guitar, John on bass, "Rabbit" Bundrick on keyboards, and Zak Starkey on drums. Plus, local symphony orchestras were hired on a venue-to-venue basis, to reproduce the Carnegie Hall experience as near as possible.

QUADROPHENIA LIVE

Hardly viable financially, the tour was concluded earlier than planned. But the highlight of the concerts, an abridged version of *Quadrophenia*, attracted enough attention to the songs from Pete's rock opera to inspire a major tour of the work in 1996. This would be the catalyst for The Who, with Townshend, Daltrey, and Entwistle, to reunite onstage once again.

Rumors of the rift between Townshend and Daltrey were often exaggerated, borne out by the pair being seen together at the London opening of the *Tommy* musical in March '96. So it didn't come as a complete surprise when it was announced that there would be (as it was billed on the posters) "Pete Townshend's Premiere of *Quadrophenia* with All-Star Cast," featuring Pete, Roger, and John—in effect, with Zak Starkey on drums, The Who.

LEFT The Who Performing *Quadrophenia* at Earls Court in London, in 1996
ABOVE Roger Daltrey at the "Masters of Music" concert in London's Hyde Park, June 29, 1996. His Mod-style eye-patch covers a black eye, sustained after Gary Glitter accidentally hit him in the eye with a mike stand during rehearsals.

The occasion, on June 29, was a huge "Masters of Music" concert in London's Hyde Park, also featuring Eric Clapton, Bob Dylan, and Alanis Morissette, in aid of the Prince's Trust charity. It was the first time the work had been played in its entirety since 1973, and it included Phil Daniels (from the *Quadrophenia* movie) as narrator, Adrian Edmondson as the Bell Boy, and Stephen Fry as the Hotel Manager.

Due to his recurring hearing problems, Pete only played acoustic guitar and piano, leaving the electric guitar to Pink Floyd's Dave Gilmour. And Roger appeared wearing a Mod-style eye-patch, after Gary Glitter (who was playing the Godfather) swung a mike stand around during rehearsals, hitting Daltrey in the face and injuring his eye socket.

The success of the Hyde Park show, despite some technical hitches, prompted a six-night run at Madison Square Garden in New York in July, followed by a full North American trek through the fall, with the band now officially billed as The Who. Then, after sell-out dates in the UK, in the spring of 1997, the show took in thirteen cities across continental Europe. As a third visit of the *Quadrophenia* extravaganza took the entourage across the United States through the summer, Pete had started introducing the electric guitar to his performances once more. To many fans, this signaled the possibility of a return of a basic Who lineup—and they were right, though it would be another year before it actually happened. Meantime, through 1998, those same fans had to be satisfied with separate tours by all three principals.

FORAYS

Roger Daltrey toured the UK, Europe, and America with the British Rock Symphony, a package that included Alice Cooper, Procol Harum's Gary Brooker, and vocalist Darlene Love, covering hits by the likes of Led Zeppelin, The Beatles, The Rolling Stones, and of course The Who. The lineup also included Simon Townshend on guitar and Zak Starkey on drums.

John took to the road once again with The John Entwistle Band, on a "Left for Dead—the Sequel" tour, which reprised his 1996 trip of the same name with Godfrey Townsend on guitar and Gordon Cotton on keyboards. After a February one-off at the House of Blues in L.A., they criss-crossed the US between mid-June and mid-November.

And Pete, too, made some short sharp forays into the gigging arena with three US concerts in August, using a modified amplifier to play more electric guitar again while not damaging his hearing. The band comprised Jody Linscott on percussion, Jon Carin on keyboards, Peter Hope-Evans on harmonica, bass player Chucho Merchán, and Tracey Langran on guitar and vocals.

Pete's band, minus Ms Linscott, assembled again for two dates in England in November, at the

ABOVE John Entwistle and Roger Daltrey pictured with Robert Plant (L) at Hyde Park in London, 1996. Daltrey's black eye is evident.
LEFT Pete onstage for *Quadrophenia*, at the Hans-Martin-Schleyer Halle, Stuttgart, Germany, May 5, 1997

Shepherd's Bush Empire in London, and a benefit for a theater group in Cornwall. And the night before the Shepherd's Bush gig, Pete played at London's Sound Republic at a "Rock the Dock" benefit for Liverpool dockers who had lost their jobs. Pete played a seven-song set completely solo, on piano and guitar, before being joined for "Magic Bus" by Steve Cradock from Ocean Colour Scene, and Noel Gallagher of Oasis.

MILLENNIAL

Early in 1999, the BBC approached Pete Townshend with a view to reviving his *Lifehouse* project, but redeveloped with writer Jeff Young as a radio play. Aimed to coincide with the coming millennial celebrations at the end of the year, Pete embraced the idea enthusiastically. But by the time the play was recorded in the summer, he had agreed with manager Bill Curbishley to something of greater significance to The Who and their followers—nothing less than the long-hoped-for reunion of the five-piece band.

The impetus came from Curbishley, who in late May had written a letter to Pete expressing concern over John Entwistle's situation with regard to his finances. In a word, the bass player was broke. His various touring enterprises had sunk him heavily into debt—often against advances from record companies—and his bank was offering no more loans or overdrafts. He was even having to sell old guitars to keep afloat.

Curbishley put it to Townshend that one way to help Entwistle was with a short tour by The Who. Pete immediately agreed, as did Roger, and the first shows were announced by Pete on July 28, to take place at Chicago's House of Blues in November. Expecting another large conglomerate, fans were delighted when at a preliminary date on October 29, at the MGM Grand Garden Arena in Las Vegas, just the five-piece Who—with "Rabbit" Bundrick on keyboards and Zak Starkey on drums—took the stage. Two gigs at Neil Young's Bridge School Benefit in California followed,

LEFT November 10, 1998: Pete in Truro, Cornwall with guitarist Tracey Langran (L) and bass player Chucho Merchán RIGHT John Entwistle at home in Gloucestershire, UK, 1997

before the much-anticipated two nights at the House of Blues in Chicago, on November 12 and 13.

Back in the UK, on December 3, Pete enjoyed the first airing of his *Lifehouse* play on the BBC's "highbrow" channel, Radio 3. Then, heading for the millennial New Year, on December 22 and 23, the five-piece Who played two Christmas charity shows at the Shepherd's Bush Empire. Critics were delighted, drawing comparisons with the lineup of the band of the sixties and seventies.

THE BBC SESSIONS

Into the twenty-first century, and as if to celebrate the classic early years of The Who, in February 2000, *BBC Sessions* was released. With all twenty-six tracks presented in chronological order (except one, the third track, being misplaced), the album represented a unique collection of previously unreleased versions of favorite Who songs, recorded for radio and TV broadcasts between 1965 and 1973. Plus the band contributed special Radio 1 jingles, based on their songs, of which just two appeared on the album.

Due to requirements by the Musicians' Union and its "needle time" agreements with the BBC, restricting the number of records played, appearing on radio or TV in the sixties and seventies meant bands having to make fresh "live" recordings for broadcasts. Stripped of studio effects and complex production, the result often provided an insight into a rock group's genuine musical abilities. In some cases, The Who (like many other bands) would get round this by submitting remixed studio tapes, over which Roger would sing a fresh vocal.

Upon its release, *BBC Sessions* did surprisingly well, given that most of the numbers had not only appeared in their original form on various compilations, but also on innumerable official (and bootleg) live albums. It spent just two weeks in the UK album chart, reaching No. 24.

BELOW John Entwistle, Zak Starkey, Pete Townshend, John "Rabbit" Bundrick, and Roger Daltrey of The Who, 1999

BBC SESSIONS

TRACK LIST
[All songs written by Pete Townshend except where indicated]

1. My Generation (BBC Radio 1 Jingle)
2. Anyway, Anyhow, Anywhere [Pete Townshend, Roger Daltrey]
3. Good Lovin' [Rudy Clark Arthur Resnick]
4. Just You and Me, Darling [James Brown]
5. Leaving Here [Holland-Dozier-Holland]
6. My Generation
7. The Good's Gone
8. La-La-La-Lies
9. Substitute
10. Man with Money [Don Everly, Phil Everly]
11. Dancing in the Street [William "Mickey" Stevenson, Marvin Gay, Ivy Joe Hunter]
12. Disguises
13. I'm a Boy
14. Run Run Run
15. Boris the Spider [John Entwistle]
16. Happy Jack
17. See My Way [Roger Daltrey]
18. Pictures of Lily
19. A Quick One (While He's Away)
20. Substitute (Version 2)
21. The Seeker
22. I'm Free
23. Shakin' All Over / Spoonful [Johnny Kidd / Willie Dixon]
24. Relay
25. Long Live Rock
26. Boris the Spider (Radio 1 Jingle) [John Entwistle]

RECORDED: 1965–1973, Aeolian Hall, London; BBC Playhouse Theatre, London; De Lane Lea Studios, London; IBC Studios, London; BBC Television Centre, Wood Lane, London
RELEASED: February 15, 2000
LABEL: Polydor
PRODUCER: Michael Appleton, Bernie Andrews, Bill Bebb, Jimmy Grant, Bev Phillips, Brian Willey, Paul Williams
PERSONNEL: Roger Daltrey (vocals, harmonica, tambourine); Pete Townshend (guitars, vocals); John Entwistle (bass guitar, vocals); Keith Moon (drums, percussion, vocals)
CHART POSITIONS / AWARDS: No. 24, UK album chart

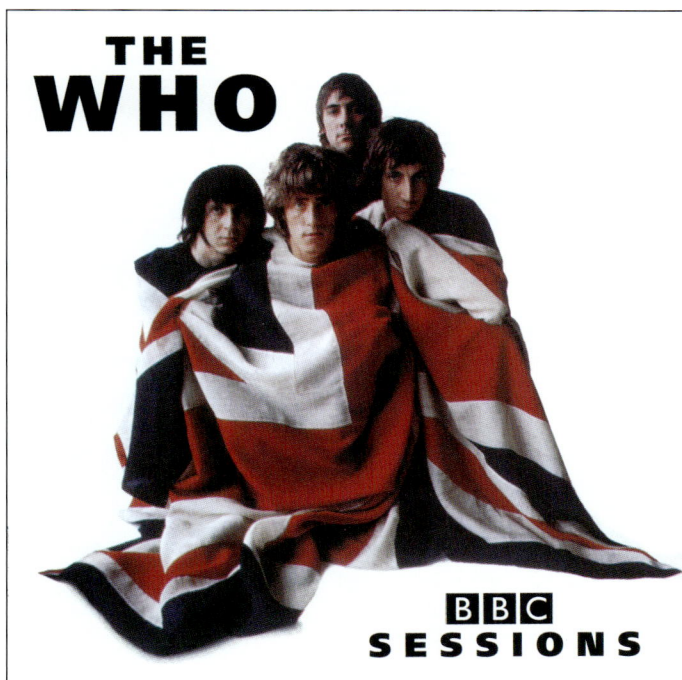

MY GENERATION (BBC RADIO 1 JINGLE)
Broadcast on *Top Gear*, October 15, 1967.
The album intros with a jingle for Radio 1,
based on their most recognizable song—
"Talking 'bout my favorite station . . ."

ANYWAY, ANYHOW, ANYWHERE
Broadcast on *Saturday Club*, May 29, 1965.
A great version with a fantastic solo. Roger
Daltrey would later comment that he
reckoned it better than the single.

GOOD LOVIN'
Broadcast on *Top Gear*, June 19, 1965.
A previously unreleased cover of the
Olympics' single, which reached No. 81 in the
US charts; a year later, The Rascals' version
hit the No. 1 spot. Jolly sixties R&B-pop,
inoffensive and suitably catchy.

JUST YOU AND ME, DARLING
Broadcast on *Saturday Club*, May 29, 1965.
Some great blues shouting from Roger,
though a weak solo from Pete. A not-heard-
before take on the James Brown original.

LEAVING HERE
Broadcast on *Saturday Club*, May 29, 1965.
Lots of echo gives it that "live" sound. This
early Motown hit by Eddie Holland was
originally recorded (but never released) by
The Who as The High Numbers.

MY GENERATION
Broadcast on *Saturday Club*, November 27,
1965. It was their current hit when this was
taped for the BBC's *Saturday Club*. Echo-
laden handclaps and a lengthy climax add to
the excitement!

THE GOOD'S GONE
Broadcast on *Saturday Club*, November 27,
1965. The BBC's Brian Matthew announcing
The Who as a "pop art group" says it all. A
bit lugubrious by The Who's standards, it
has to be said, but the feedback guitar break
sounds adventurous—in a mid-sixties kind
of way.

LA-LA-LA-LIES
Broadcast on *Saturday Club*, November 27,
1965. The backing vocals, a bit tricky at
the best of times, are impressive given the
"live" context.

SUBSTITUTE
Broadcast on *Saturday Club*, March 19, 1966.
Recorded in March 1966, a good up-tempo
version of their current hit. Moon's drumming,
though to the back of the mix, sounds
potentially explosive.

MAN WITH MONEY
Broadcast on *Saturday Club*, March 19, 1966.
The song, originally the flip side to the Everly
Brothers' 1965 hit "Love Is Strange," was part
of The Who's stage set at the time of the BBC
recording in March 1966.

DANCING IN THE STREET
Broadcast on *Saturday Club*, March 19, 1966.
Another commendable cover version, this
time the Motown standard made famous
by Martha and the Vandellas. Initially quite
laid-back, until Pete's distortion-heavy guitar
fade-out.

DISGUISES
Broadcast on *Saturday Club*, September 17,
1966. In September 1966, another hint at
psychedelic influences creeping into The
Who's repertoire. Brian Matthew's brief chat
with Pete follows the take.

I'M A BOY
Broadcast on *Saturday Club*, September 17,
1966. A straightforward delivery of the band's
current single, released in August 1966.

RUN RUN RUN
Broadcast on *Saturday Club*, January 21,
1967. Another cheerful introduction from
Saturday Club compere Brian Matthew, into
a confident version of the song, with a much
longer guitar solo than that on the original.

BORIS THE SPIDER
Broadcast on *Saturday Club*, January 21,
1967. John has fun reproducing his "Boris"
vocals, with lots of echo for the radio
listeners. Matthew quizzes Pete about
guitar smashing before going into the
next number . . .

HAPPY JACK
Broadcast on *Saturday Club*, January 21, 1967.
A virtually faultless version, with some
powerful drumming from Moon and
precise vocals.

SEE MY WAY
Broadcast on *Saturday Club*, January 21, 1967. Again, a great version of a track from their current *Quick One* album.

PICTURES OF LILY
Broadcast on *Top Gear*, October 15, 1967. Differs from the single version in that a Hammond organ has been added, played, one assumes, by Pete Townshend.

A QUICK ONE (WHILE HE'S AWAY)
Broadcast on *Top Gear*, October 15, 1967. A good live rendition, considering the tightness in the vocal harmonies required.

SUBSTITUTE (VERSION 2)
Broadcast on the *Dave Lee Travis Show*, April 19, 1970; the *Johnnie Walker Show*, May 25, 1970; the *Dave Symonds Show*, May 25, 1970. Keith counts in this alternative version, quite different from the longer, earlier recording in the collection.

THE SEEKER
Broadcast on the *Dave Lee Travis Show*, April 19, 1970; the *Johnnie Walker Show*, May 25, 1970; the *Dave Symonds Show*, May 25, 1970. A light, but highly effective performance of the current single, introduced by the Radio 1 DJ Dave Lee Travis.

I'M FREE
Broadcast on the *Dave Lee Travis Show*, April 19, 1970; the *Johnnie Walker Show*, May 25, 1970; the *Dave Symonds Show*, May 25, 1970. Another take for the *Dave Lee Travis Show*, recorded in April 1970. Similar (possibly the same?) backing vocals as the original *Tommy* recording.

SHAKIN' ALL OVER / SPOONFUL
Broadcast on the *Dave Lee Travis Show*, April 19, 1970; the *Johnnie Walker Show*, May 25, 1970; the *Dave Symonds Show*, May 25, 1970. A concert favorite with audiences, also heard in a live version on *Live at Leeds*, the Johnny Kidd crowd-pleaser segues into the Willie Dixon R&B standard "Spoonful."

RELAY
Broadcast on *The Old Grey Whistle Test*, January 30, 1973. "Whisperin'" Bob Harris intros this one, recorded for BBC TV's *Old Grey Whistle Test* in January 1973.

LONG LIVE ROCK
Broadcast on *The Old Grey Whistle Test*, January 30, 1973. Some crowd-pleasing rock 'n' roll sentiments, reminiscent of a Chuck Berry anthem, another for the influential *Old Grey Whistle Test* TV show.

BORIS THE SPIDER (RADIO 1 JINGLE)
Broadcast on *Top Gear*, October 15, 1967. Jingle time again for the Radio 1 audience, this time a very brief announcement by John in his "Boris" voice.

15 ENDLESS WIRE

ENDLESS WIRE

When the first decade of the new millennium dawned, The Who hadn't made a studio album for over seventeen years, and it would be another seven before the next one appeared. Those opening years of the twenty-first century would prove traumatic on many levels—for The Who themselves, and indeed for the world at large—before *Endless Wire* was released in October 2006.

INSPIRATION

The success of the fresh-sounding five-piece, that had delighted fans and critics in the handful of gigs in America and the UK at the end of 1999, proved to be the first real inspiration in years for Pete, Roger, and John to get together once more on a regular basis as The Who.

But ahead of any new dates by the revived Who, Pete enthusiastically revisited his once-abandoned *Lifehouse* project, with the release of *Lifehouse Chronicles* in February 2000. The massive six-CD box set included demos and alternative recordings of songs relating to the rock opera, plus the 1999 *Lifehouse* radio play.

"And still *Lifehouse* rolls on," wrote Gavin Martin in *Uncut* magazine: "Whether the play clarifies the concepts enough for Townshend's original plan for a movie remains to be seen. What's certain is that the best music here reaffirms his position as one of rock's true visionaries." The release was followed by two performances of the work at the Sadler's Wells Theatre in London, with a now-familiar Townshend lineup that included Chucho Merchán on bass, percussionist Jody Linscott, and Peter Hope-Evans on harmonica.

PREVIOUS PAGES October 2000, during four consecutive nights at New York's Madison Square Garden
LEFT October 20, 2001: Pete with The Who at "The Concert for New York City" organized by Sir Paul McCartney, following the September 11 attacks in 2001

"**Whether the play clarifies the concepts enough for Townshend's original plan for a movie remains to be seen. What's certain is that the best music here reaffirms his position as one of rock's true visionaries.**"

GAVIN MARTIN REVIEWING *THE LIFEHOUSE CHRONICLES, UNCUT, JANUARY 2000*

The Who, with "Rabbit" on keyboards, and Zak Starkey once more behind the drum kit, kicked off a US tour in June. It culminated, after twenty-three concerts, in four sell-out nights at Madison Square Garden at the beginning of October. Reviews were generally very favorable, encouraging Roger, in particular, to push for a new album of Who material.

An eleven-date British tour followed, climaxed on November 27 with an all-star charity show at the Royal Albert Hall in London, in aid of the Teenage Cancer Trust. Guest appearances included Paul Weller, Pearl Jam's Eddie Vedder, Noel Gallagher, Stereophonics' Kelly Jones, Bryan Adams, and violinist Nigel Kennedy.

And early in 2001, The Who were honored with a Grammy Lifetime Achievement Award by the US

LEFT Roger (L) and John (R) rehearsing with The Who at the Sanctuary Recording Studios in London, on June 15, 2002 RIGHT Pete and Roger among the mourners at at the funeral of John Entwistle, held on July 10, 2002 at St Edward's Church, Stow-on-the-Wold, Gloucestershire

National Academy of Recording Arts and Sciences. John Entwistle accepted the award on behalf of the band, at an untelevised ceremony the night before the actual Grammy broadcast from the Staples Center, Los Angeles.

CALAMITY

But the next time The Who convened as a group would be under the long shadow of the terrorist attacks on the United States of September 11, 2001. An all-star benefit for the victims of the tragedy, and in particular the families of police and firefighters who lost their lives, was staged at Madison Square Garden on October 20. Billed as "The Concert for New York City," the event was organized by Paul McCartney, and featured a host of UK and US names including David Bowie, Elton John, Eric Clapton, Mick Jagger, Keith Richards, Bon Jovi, Billy Joel, and Destiny's Child.

Up until The Who's set, all the musical tributes had been deliberately restrained, seemingly appropriate to the occasion. Roger had suggested to the band that they follow suit, but Pete insisted they should just be The Who and play accordingly. While not trying to, The Who stole the show.

A sensational four-song set followed, concluding with "Won't Get Fooled Again" played against the backdrop of the Twin Towers destroyed in the 9/11 calamity. The band's delivery was angry and heartfelt, rousing a similar reaction in the audience, as firefighters and police began pumping their fists in the air. The change in the atmosphere was palpable, the mood shifting from sorrow to one of anger and pride, and all agreed The Who were responsible for lifting the crowd's spirits from mourning to defiance.

AGONY

Just a year after the New York concert, The Who would once more be visited by a tragedy, this time much closer to home.

Early in 2002, at the end of January, the band played three warm-up concerts in preparation for two charity dates at the Royal Albert Hall on February 7 and 8. The charity was again the Teenage Cancer Trust, which Roger had become personally involved with, going on to organize a similar benefit every year. The two sell-out gigs were part of five days of concerts also involving Marti Pellow from Wet Wet Wet, Oasis, and a Paul Weller lineup that included

Jimmy Page and Robert Plant. The two Albert Hall dates, which were filmed, would be the last gigs John Entwistle played with The Who.

Over the first half of the year, plans were put in place for a full North American tour, and in June the band gathered at Pete's Eel Pie studio in Twickenham, west London, for rehearsals. The publicity surrounding the upcoming tour was huge, with the first date being set for June 28 in Las Vegas.

On June 26, John Entwistle stayed at the Hard Rock Hotel in Las Vegas, and after drinking in the bar with friends, retired to Suite 658 with Alycen Rowse, a local dancer who John knew from previous visits to the city. The next morning Rowse awoke to find John dead in bed next to her; the subsequent report by the Clark County Medical Examiner determined the cause of death as a heart attack, brought on by an intake of cocaine.

Roger and Pete were devastated, and after cancelling the first two nights of the tour, had to decide whether to carry on. They chose to continue, which came as a shock to many fans and observers, but Pete and Roger both hoped it was a move John would have supported, especially considering the

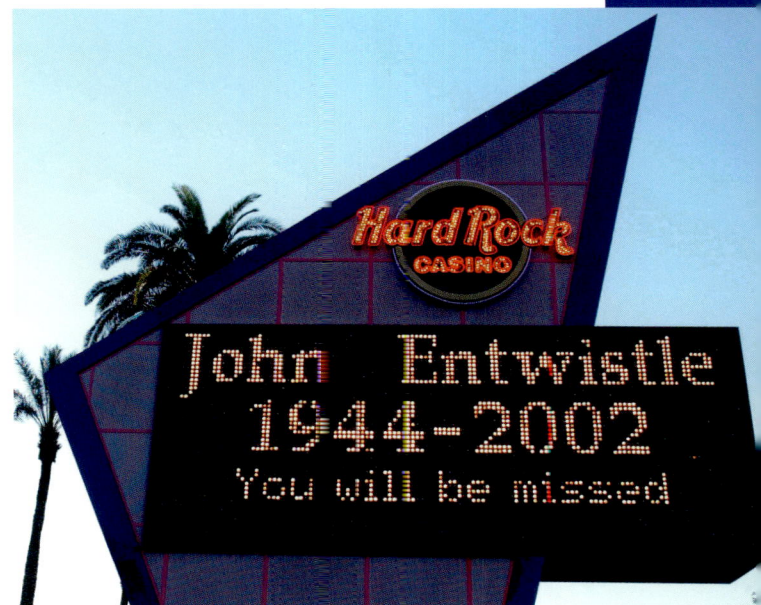

A tribute to John Entwistle who died in his hotel room at the Hard Rock Hotel & Casino in Las Vegas on June 27, 2002—just one day before The Who was to begin their North American tour

> "I simply believe we have a duty to go on, to ourselves, ticket buyers, promoters, big and little people."

PETE TOWNSHEND FOLLOWING
JOHN ENTWISTLE'S DEATH

number of people who had time and money—indeed their livelihoods—invested in the tour. "I don't feel I know for certain that John would have wanted us to go on," Pete wrote online. "I simply believe we have a duty to go on, to ourselves, ticket buyers, promoters, big and little people." And almost immediately, John's son, Christopher, issued a statement supporting the decision to carry on.

The Who began their tour on July 1 at the Hollywood Bowl, with the lineup completed by Pino Palladino (who had worked with Pete on various projects including *White City* and *Psychoderelict*) on bass, John Bundrick, Zak Starkey, and Pete's brother Simon on guitar and backup vocals.

There was a break in the schedule after four dates, during which John's funeral took place at St Edward's Church in Stow-on-the-Wold, Gloucestershire, near his home. Pete and John flew back for the ceremony, which was also attended by their former drummer Kenney Jones.

LEFT The Who onstage during the first concert of the "Teenage Cancer Trust: The Who & Friends Live At The Royal Albert Hall 2004" series, at the Royal Albert Hall on March 29, 2004

BELOW Sydney
Entertainment Centre,
Australia, July 28, 2004.
(L–R): Simon Townshend,
Roger Daltrey, Pete
Townshend, Pino Palladino,
Zak Starkey, and John
"Rabbit" Bundrick.

The tour resumed on July 26, and carried on through August, ending on September 26 in Toronto, Canada. The loss of John seemed to enthuse Roger and Pete—now dubbed "The Two" by fans—with their initial agony followed by a commitment in his honor, producing sensational performances that promised that the power of The Who would continue. The loss of John also focused Pete on considering his long and sometimes rocky relationship with Roger. With all its ups and downs, the dynamic the two had developed would continue, even after the loss of key participants Moon and Entwistle—resulting in an album of new songs, although that was still another four years down the road.

SCANDAL

Early in 2003, a press-conducted scandal erupted that nearly wrecked Pete's career. An international FBI sting of child pornography websites cited a "famous British rock star" among seven thousand potential offenders who had used such sites, and Pete admitted he had used his credit card to access one site, then reporting his findings to anti-child-pornography agencies. He was questioned, and his computers were seized by the police, whose thorough examination over four long months confirmed Pete's explanation in every detail.

Nevertheless, though not charged, he was given the choice of a "caution" and being placed on a list of low-key sex offenders for five years, or taking the case to court. Exhausted by the four months of tabloid press harassment and mental stress, which he managed to survive with the support of many friends in the music business, Pete opted for the caution, as opposed to legal action which would have been likely to drag on for years.

THEN AND NOW

During the hiatus that was 2003, in June, the band released their seventh official live album, *Live at the Royal Albert Hall*. A three-CD release, the first two discs were recorded at the Teenage Cancer Trust concert of November 27, 2000, and included the guest contributions of Paul Weller, Eddie Vedder, Noel Gallagher, Kelly Jones, Bryan Adams, and Nigel Kennedy. Disc Three featured four numbers recorded at the Albert Hall on February 8, 2002: "I'm Free," "I Don't Even Know Myself," "Summertime Blues," and "Young Man Blues." They would be the last recordings of John Entwistle with The Who.

The Forum in London's Kentish Town was the venue for The Who's return to the live stage once again. With the same personnel that had completed the 2002 tour after John's death—Pete, Roger, Zak, Pino (his first UK gigs with the band), "Rabbit," and Simon—they played three nights over March 22 to 25, 2004, followed by a Teenage Cancer Trust benefit at the Albert Hall on the 29th. Their return to the rock 'n' roll fray was greeted ecstatically by fans, with a review in *The Guardian* concluding: "The Who, it seems, still have the power to move an audience in ways far beyond the standard reverence afforded heritage rock acts."

The day after the Albert Hall concert saw the release of a major "greatest hits" singles compilation, with the addition of two new songs—their first studio tracks in thirteen years. Entitled *The Who: Then and Now*, the album concluded with the two new items, "Real Good Looking Boy," a tribute to Elvis Presley, and "Old Red Wine," a tribute to John Entwistle. Greg Lake played bass on the Elvis number, Pino Palladino on the tribute to John. The album proved to be one of The Who's most successful releases in many years, hitting the No. 5 spot in the UK album chart.

And as a counterpart to *Then and Now*, in April 2004, the band released *The 1st Singles Box*, a UK-only boxed collection of twelve CDs. Each disc contained just two tracks, representing the A and B side of the original singles. Again, the two new songs that had appeared on *Then and Now* concluded the set, as the final "single." A vinyl edition was also produced, with the twelve singles in the "authentic" 7-inch, 45-rpm format.

THE WORLD

In May, the six-piece Who kicked off what amounted to their first "world" (or at least trans-global) tour, with two dates in New York either side of a gig in Boston. June saw three big appearances in Britain, at Cardiff's International Arena, the National Indoor Arena in Birmingham, and the Isle of Wight Festival. Then in July, concerts in Yokohama and Osaka took them to Japan for the first time in the history of the band. And, thirty-six years after their previous debacle there, they played three dates in Australia,

before two August appearances in Hawaii, and two more back on the US mainland.

A landmark year for the rejuvenated band, 2004 ended with Roger Daltrey being awarded a CBE (Commander of the British Empire) in the Queen's annual New Year's Honours List, for his charity work with the Teenage Cancer Trust.

WHO ARE TWO

There were few live appearances by The Who in 2005—only two dates in all, the first featuring the duo of Roger and Pete, the second just two numbers by a full lineup.

The Daltrey-Townshend date—their first as a duet—was on June 13 at the Gotham Hall in New York City. Playing in aid of the Four Seasons of Hope children's charity, they were accompanied on keyboards by Jon Carin, who had worked with The Who on both the *Quadophenia* live dates and the "Daltrey Sings Townshend" tour.

Then on July 2, a full band played a two-song set—"Who Are You" and "Won't Get Fooled Again"—as part of Bob Geldof's Live 8 concert. Like 1985's Live Aid, the star-studded benefit, staged in London's Hyde Park, was in aid of famine relief. The lineup of Pete, Roger, "Rabbit," and Simon was supported on this occasion by Damon Minchella on bass and Steve White on drums, both from Paul Weller's band.

ENDLESS WIRE

But meanwhile, on the recording front things were developing toward a new Who album. Immersing himself in the new technology, Pete had started a blog to serialize a novella, *The Boy Who Heard Music*. Written as a sequel to 1993's *Psychoderelict*, it developed into a mini-opera *Wire & Glass*, which in turn served as the basis for much of The Who's next studio project, *Endless Wire*.

Pete premiered some of the songs on Rachel Fuller's webcast show, *In The Attic*. Musician and singer-songwriter Fuller, by this time Townshend's partner, had been involved with Pete (who had separated from his wife, Karen, in 1994) since late 1997.

LEFT Roger Daltrey holds his CBE medal up as he is driven away from Buckingham Palace, London on February 9, 2005. Roger was awarded the Commander of the British Empire honor for his services to music, the entertainment industry, and charity. BELOW Roger and Pete with The Who at Live 8, at London's Hyde Park on July 2, 2005

Then, in the summer of 2006, a full-blown tour was announced, supporting the forthcoming album. First there was a charity gig at Knebworth House in rural Hertfordshire, followed by a return to the refectory at Leeds University on June 17, where the legendary *Live at Leeds* album was recorded in 1970. That was followed by a major tour of UK and European concerts through June and July. An EP of six tracks from the forthcoming album, *Wire & Glass*, was released on July 17, followed by a further tour—taking in eighteen

BELOW Pete Townshend and Rachel Fuller during an Attic Jam on November 7, 2006 at the Hotel Cafe in Los Angeles
BOTTOM RIGHT The Who, June 17, 2006. The band return to the refectory at Leeds University in the UK, where the legendary *Live at Leeds* album was recorded in 1970.

concerts through the US and Canada—before *Endless Wire* hit the shops at the end of October.

Produced through 2005 at Pete's home studio and his Eel Pie Oceanic studio, and completed in May 2006, it was The Who's first album of new studio material since *It's Hard* in 1982. With nineteen songs in all, *Endless Wire* was a return to the ambitious concept album that The Who had made their own through *Tommy* and *Quadrophenia*. At its heart, the second part of the album—the *Wire & Glass* mini-opera—marked Pete's addressing once again themes explored in those works, and in his partly realized *Lifehouse* project.

The album was generally well received in the music press, with *Rolling Stone* giving it four out of five stars: "Daltrey and Townshend have made a record as brazen in its way and right for its day as *The Who Sell Out* and *Tommy* were in theirs." And it went down well with the record-buying public, making the Top Ten albums in the United States and UK, at No. 9 and No. 7, respectively.

"Daltrey and Townshend have made a record as brazen in its way and right for its day as *The Who Sell Out* and *Tommy* were in theirs."

ROLLING STONE

ENDLESS WIRE

TRACK LIST
[All songs written by Pete Townshend
except where indicated]

1. Fragments [Pete Townshend, Lawrence Ball]
2. A Man in a Purple Dress
3. Mike Post Theme
4. In the Ether
5. Black Widow's Eyes
6. Two Thousand Years
7. God Speaks of Marty Robbins
8. It's Not Enough
   [Pete Townshend, Rachel Fuller]
9. You Stand by Me

Wire & Glass: A Mini-Opera
10. Sound Round
11. Pick Up the Peace
12. Unholy Trinity
13. rilby's Piano
14. Endless Wire
15. Fragments of Fragments [Pete Townshend, Lawrence Ball]
16. We Got a Hit
17. They Made My Dreams Come True
18. Mirror Door
19. Tea & Theatre

RECORDED: December 2004–May 2006, Pete Townshend's home studio, London;
Eel Pie Oceanic Studios, London
RELEASED: October 30, 2006
LABEL: Polydor, Universal Republic
PRODUCER: Pete Townshend (with Bob Pridden and Billy Nicholls for Roger Daltrey's vocals only)
PERSONNEL: Pete Townshend (guitars, bass guitar, drums, piano, keyboards, violin, banjo, mandolin, drum machine, vocals); Roger Daltrey (vocals); John "Rabbit" Bundrick (Hammond organ, vocals); Pino Palladino (bass guitar); Zak Starkey (drums); Lawrence Ball (electronic music); Ellen Blair (viola); Jolyon Dixon (acoustic guitar); Rachel Fuller (keyboards); Peter Huntington (drums); Gill Morley (violin); Vicky Matthews (cello); Brian Wright (violin); Stuart Ross (bass guitar); Simon Townshend (vocals); Billy Nicholls (vocals)
CHART POSITIONS / AWARDS: No. 7, US album chart; No. 9, UK album chart

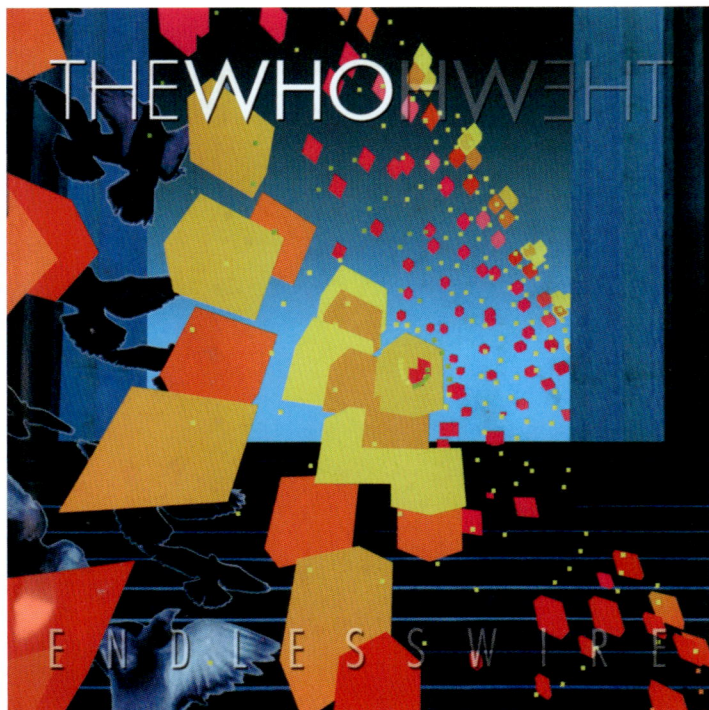

FRAGMENTS

Based on the experiments of its co-composer, Lawrence Ball, in Pete's novella *The Boy Who Heard Music*, this is the first big hit for fictitious narrator Ray High and his band The Glass Household. The opening synthesizer riff recalls the similar intro to "Baba O'Riley."

A MAN IN A PURPLE DRESS

Pete's simple acoustic guitar backs Roger in a powerful ballad. A critique of religious leaders inspired by watching Mel Gibson's *The Passion of the Christ*, and written, tellingly, after Pete's traumatic brush with the law (and the tabloid press) over child pornography investigations.

MIKE POST THEME

A dynamic though understated unleashing of electric Townshend, who programed a drum machine and also played drums live on the track.

IN THE ETHER

An odd one, with Pete coming on with a growling delivery which—especially against the "background" piano—can only remind us of the master of barfly balladry, Tom Waits. In his autobiography, Pete described it as "A song for the voice of an old man, a ghost, singing from beyond reality."

BLACK WIDOW'S EYES

Although the structure calls for some old-school Who dynamics, Pete's acoustic guitar smooths any rough edges. From the title, it was presumably written about his unrequited infatuation with the actress Theresa Russell in the early eighties—Russell went on to play one of her most memorable roles in the 1987 psycho-thriller of the same name.

TWO THOUSAND YEARS

Townshend plucks various stringed instruments—guitar, banjo, mandolin, even a touch of violin—in this piece of folksy nonsense.

GOD SPEAKS OF MARTY ROBBINS

Pete is self-accompanied on acoustic guitar, and as archetypal singer-songwriter he's a long way from windmilling guitar hero. A delicate paean to a country music legend.

IT'S NOT ENOUGH

As he explained at the time of the album's release, the lyrics represent Townshend's reflections on French New Wave cinema. A gentle rocker, written with his girlfriend Rachel Fuller, who also plays keyboards on the track.

YOU STAND BY ME

At a minute-and-a-half, a teasingly short folky. Again, it's just Pete alone with his acoustic.

SOUND ROUND

Allegedly first written for *Who's Next* (1971) but not recorded, it's the first short, sharp salvo in the *Wire & Glass* mini-opera. Some terrific drumming from Pete Huntington leaves you wanting more.

PICK UP THE PEACE

Almost a trademark Who rocker—Daltrey in full flight, the backing rampant—again, the short duration is underselling the product.

UNHOLY TRINITY

Some hints at country sounds here, with an effective vocal backed by some down-home banjo and barroom piano.

TRILBY'S PIANO

With its easy-listening string arrangements maybe a bit too "song from the shows" for many Who fans, but it's Pete's heartfelt dedication to his muse and inspiration, and indeed worthy collaborator, Rachel Fuller.

ENDLESS WIRE

The title track refers to the global wire network envisioned in *The Boy Who Heard Music*, predating much that has since developed on the Internet. A strange arrangement of acoustic guitars and piano, and a world-weary delivery from Townshend.

FRAGMENTS OF FRAGMENTS

More tricky electronics from Pete and his techy cohort Lawrence Ball.

WE GOT A HIT

An old-fashioned sounding Who rocker, with lots of harmony vocal responses—"Good news, we got a hit"—to Roger's palpable enthusiasm.

THEY MADE MY DREAMS COME TRUE

On another brief acoustic outing, Pete delivers a forceful vocal with some Dylanesque tinges, although frustratingly short and sweet.

MIRROR DOOR

Prereleased for radio play before the *Wire & Glass* EP, then remixed by Pete adding the echo touches to Roger's vocals. It imagines a place where musicians meet after their death, comparing notes. Among the deceased mentioned, alongside Elvis and Buddy Holly, is Doris Day—it was only after the sessions that it was pointed out to Pete that she was still alive!

TEA & THEATRE

With its dramatic chords and riveting vocals, certainly the most haunting song on the collection. And the most poignant, given the past memories of The Who that it evokes.

16 QUADROPHENIA LIVE IN LONDON

QUADROPHENIA LIVE IN LONDON

The tour supporting *Endless Wire*, which had commenced in the summer of 2006 prior to the album's October 30 release, signaled Pete and Roger's renewed enthusiasm for performing in public. The coming months through 2007, 2008, and into 2009 were dominated by live appearances—at festivals, in special high-profile charity events, and simply on the road.

ENDLESS TOUR

The North American *Endless Wire* dates resumed at the Hollywood Bowl on November 4, and continued with hardly a break until mid-December, resuming again in February 2007 for another fourteen concerts. That leg of the tour concluded at the end of March, followed by an Albert Hall date for the Teenage Cancer Trust; although Roger organized the concerts in aid of the charity, The Who did not always appear, but when they did it was usually a memorable performance.

The European dates of the tour began in Lisbon on May 16, and continued until July 9 in Helsinki, Finland, interrupted by a few UK and Irish concerts, including The Who's first-ever appearance at the Glastonbury Festival. By 2007, the annual gathering had evolved from a hippy "alternative" event in 1970, to the leading UK festival of its kind.

Every year, a major name would occupy the coveted headline spot on the Pyramid stage on the Sunday night, and this year it fell to The Who to provide a fitting climax to the four-day festival. Despite torrential rain and the trademark muddy conditions associated with outdoor rock fests in the UK, the band out on an amazing show with eleven numbers spanning their career, followed by no less than six encore songs.

PREVIOUS PAGES The Who taking control on the Pyramid Stage at Glastonbury, June 24, 2007
LEFT Roger Daltrey launches the Teenage Cancer Trust competition to win The Magic Bus, a unique 1965 VW Camper van, on April 8, 2008 outside the Royal Albert Hall in London

other things, was an enduring symbol of the youth movement of the sixties, especially as typical "hippy" transport from the early festival days of Monterey and Woodstock. The Who entertained the crowd—not all dedicated rock fans by any means—with an eighteen-song set that inevitably included "Magic Bus." And Pete recalled how, in their early days, the band traveled from gig to gig in the iconic VW T1 version of the bus.

AMAZING JOURNEY

Early in November, Pete and Roger were present at the premiere of *Amazing Journey: The Story of The Who*, an ambitious four-hour documentary covering the entire history of the band, directed by Murray Lerner and Paul Crowder. The film featured new interviews with Townshend and Daltrey, plus contributions from Kenney Jones and the late John Entwistle. Built around rare photographs and archive footage of The Who—including the 1970 Leeds University concert, and a 1964 gig as The High Numbers at the Railway Hotel—the film included exclusive interviews with, among others, Sting, Noel Gallagher, Eddie Vedder, and ex-Sex Pistol Steve Jones. It went on to be nominated for a Grammy award in 2009.

And, now they were once more on something of a roll, The Who's amazing journey was nowhere near over. During the 2008 Teenage Cancer Trust concerts at the Royal Albert Hall in April, The Who's contribution was to close the week-long event with a rare six-number acoustic set from Roger and Pete. Then, after two July dates on the US West Coast—one the VH1 Rock Honors Tribute honoring The Who with Foo Fighters, Flaming Lips, and Incubus, the other a private party at the E3 video games event—they were off again in October on yet another international campaign.

Ten American dates were followed in November by five shows in Japan, including two concerts in the famous Budokan arena in Tokyo. And the year was completed with three appearances at London's Indigo O2, over the week before Christmas.

Earlier that month, on December 8, The Who, in the person of Townshend and Daltrey, were included in the annual Kennedy Center Honors, when US President George W. Bush presented the awards to outstanding contributors in the performing arts. The other honorees

Embracing Pete at the end of their show, Roger shouted to the crowd: "It may be muddy, it may be wet, but you were fantastic!"

When the tour finally wound up in Helsinki, it had lasted off and on for over a year. For many of the dates, Pete's partner Rachel Fuller came along, doing her *In the Attic* live webcasts from the shows. She also took the opportunity to stage "Attic Jam" concerts while on the road, small acoustic events with various guest artists—including Pete of course—usually put together with her assistant Carrie Cooke. The first "Attic Jam" had been held in October 2005 at the Bedford Arms in London, followed by the "Basement Jam" in December, which was streamed live from Townshend's Oceanic Studios. On the American sections of the tour, "Attic Jam" events were held in small venues in Chicago, Los Angeles, and New York City, and at the South by Southwest festival in Austin, Texas.

There was only one other gig by The Who in 2007, and a bizarrely unusual one at that. The occasion, on October 6, was a gathering of forty thousand people in Hanover, Germany, celebrating the sixtieth anniversary of the Volkswagen "Bulli" minibus. The organizers acknowledged that the minibus, among

alongside Pete and Roger were actor Morgan Freeman, country singer George Jones, vocalist Barbra Streisand, and choreographer Twyla Tharp.

For fans "down under," The Who's shows in March 2009 were long awaited. The six gigs in Australia and one in New Zealand were the first proper tour in that part

LEFT The 31st Annual Kennedy Center Honors, December 6, 2008 in Washington DC. Honorees included Roger Daltrey and Pete Townshend, alongside country music singer George Jones (back row, right), dancer and choreographer Twyla Tharp (front row, left), actor Morgan Freeman (front row, center) and actress and singer Barbra Streisand (front row, right).
ABOVE Pete (R) and Roger perform live onstage with The Who at the Brisbane Entertainment Centre on March 24, 2009 in Brisbane, Australia. The show was one of six forming the first proper tour in that part of the world for over forty years; the lengthy gap largely due to the band's infamous confrontations with the authorities on their first visit in 1968.

of the world for over forty years, after some infamous confrontations with the authorities back in 1968.

Other than that, it was private pursuits for the rest of the year, except for the almost-obligatory Teenage Cancer Trust show. Even when the full band couldn't be mustered for the occasion, organizer Roger Daltrey was anxious that The Who should be represented somehow. The concert at London's Emirates Stadium in May featured another pared-down set from Pete and Roger, with some modest backing from Simon Townshend, backing vocalist Billy Nicholls, and bass player Danny Thompson.

NEW GROUND

A new compilation album, *Greatest Hits Live*, broke new ground for The Who, when in January 2010 it was initially released solely on the iTunes Store digital service, followed by a "hard copy" CD in March. The twenty-two tracks spanned the band's entire career, recorded live between 1965 and 2009.

And there was a new ground of another kind in February 2010, when the band played the half-time set at the Super Bowl National Football League finals in Miami, Florida. A time-honored tradition since the late sixties, the spot had been graced previously by, among others, Bruce Springsteen, Paul McCartney, and The Rolling Stones. For their short set, the six-piece Who played a medley of hits comprising "Pinball Wizard," "Baba O'Riley," "Who Are You," "See Me Feel Me," and "Won't Get Fooled Again"—all incomplete versions, with no breaks. Reviewing the short performance, the *New York Times* captured the image of the now-ageing rockers: "Townshend, in a porkpie hat and shades with a black suit hanging off his lanky frame, was grizzled. Daltrey, in a striped neo-Mod jacket and a scarf, revealed a voice that was raspy and thick."

At the end of March, The Who reconvened yet again at the Royal Albert Hall, as part of ten concerts for the Teenage Cancer Trust. What made this particular show a landmark was that it entailed a new live performance of *Quadrophenia* in its entirety, with guests Tom Meighan of Kasabian as Ace Face, and Pearl Jam's Eddie Vedder as the Godfather.

There was a plan to take the rock opera on the road, with various guests involved, but that ambition

was put on hold when Pete had a return bout of the tinnitus that had been plaguing him off and on for some years. The hearing complaint dated back to the mid-seventies, and was clearly linked to Pete's constant exposure to the loud amplification of The Who's music.

The tour, entitled "Quadrophenia and More," would eventually begin with a concert in Sunrise, Florida, in November 2012, but in the meantime it was Roger Daltrey who carried the Who flag for most of 2011 and 2012. The gigs for the full Who lineup were few and far between. In fact in 2011 that amounted to just one appearance; another cancer charity benefit, this time for Killing Cancer, on January 13 at London's Hammersmith Apollo. The Who played four numbers, on a bill that also included Richard Hawley, Bryan Adams, Debbie Harry, and Jeff Beck. Daltrey also contributed an acoustic set backed by guest folk musicians.

And for the rest of the year Roger fronted his own band. With Simon Townshend, Jon Button (and later James Hunting) on bass, drummer Scott Devours, Loren Gold on keyboards, and Frank Simes on guitar, he toured the UK, North America, and—into the spring of 2012—Europe and Japan.

QUADROPHENIA AND MORE
Before the "Quadrophenia and More" tour kicked off, The Who played a short medley of three songs—"Baba O'Riley," "See Me Feel Me," and "My Generation"— as the final act at the closing ceremony of the 2012 Olympic Games in London, on August 12.

LEFT Roger and Pete at the Super Bowl XLIV Halftime Press Conference at Broward County Convention Center on February 4, 2010 in Fort Lauderdale, Florida
ABOVE Pete Townshend performs during A Concert For Killing Cancer at Hammersmith Apollo on January 13, 2011 in London

LEFT Roger (L) and Pete perform during the closing ceremony of the London 2012 Olympic Games at the Olympic Stadium on August 12

The concept of the tour was ambitious, with the live band playing in front of huge images drawn from their musical history, and even two sequences of Moon and Entwistle synched to play along with the group onstage. Plus there was a running montage of archive footage evoking the previous half-century of cultural history that was the background to The Who, cut in with sequences of them performing over the years.

The opening tour date in Florida, on November 1, heralded twenty-two concerts in the US and Canada, with keyboard players John Corey, Loren Gold, and Frank Simes (the latter two having played on Daltrey's tour dates), Pino Palladino once more on bass, and Zak Starkey on drums. Plus there were two horn sections, led by Greg Miller and Reggie Grisham. After a break over Christmas and New Year, the trek continued through February 2013, finishing up at Madison Square Garden.

During the pre-Christmas dates, on November 25, 2012, news came through of the death of their former manager alongside Kit Lambert, Chris Stamp, at the age of seventy. In later life he had become a psychodrama therapist, based in New York; he died of cancer at Mount Sinai Hospital, NYC. The following year a documentary film was made about his career in rock with Kit Lambert, *Lambert & Stamp*. Directed by James D. Cooper, it had its world premiere at the Sundance Film Festival in January 2014.

Following the US dates, the "Quadrophenia and More" tour resumed in June 2013, with appearances across the UK—plus Amsterdam and Paris—culminating at London's Wembley Arena on July 8. For this last leg of the tour, Zak Starkey—having pulled a tendon at the end of the February dates—was replaced by Scott Devours. In his autobiography, Roger recalled how the eminent classicist Mary Beard had congratulated them on the archival montage, after the Wembley show: "She said we'd encapsulated the late 20th-century period perfectly. An A+ from a proper academic. That really made me happy."

This final concert would be recorded, and released more or less in its entirety on June 9, 2014, as the album *Quadrophenia Live in London*. The audio CD was reasonably well received, but the DVD released on the same day—the next best thing to seeing the concert, with its amazing visual effects, live—went straight in at No. 1 on the *Billboard* Music Video Sales chart.

TOP RIGHT Roger and Pete perform at "12-12-12," a concert benefiting The Robin Hood Relief Fund to aid the victims of Hurricane Sandy, at Madison Square Garden on December 12, 2012
RIGHT The Who at the 02 Arena in London, on June 15, 2013

QUADROPHENIA LIVE IN LONDON

TRACK LIST
[All songs written by Pete Townshend)

1. I Am the Sea
2. The Real Me
3. Quadrophenia
4. Cut My Hair
5. The Punk and the Godfather
6. I'm One
7. The Dirty Jobs
8. Helpless Dancer (Roger's theme)
9. Is It in My Head?
10. I've Had Enough
11. 5:15
12. Sea and Sand
13. Drowned
14. Bell Boy (Keith's theme)
15. Doctor Jimmy (containing "Is It Me?" John's theme)
16. The Rock
17. Love, Reign o'er Me (Pete's theme)
18. Who Are You
19. You Better You Bet
20. Pinball Wizard
21. Baba O'Riley
22. Won't Get Fooled Again
23. Tea & Theatre

RECORDED: July 8, 2013, Wembley Arena, London
RELEASED: June 9, 2014
LABEL: Universal Music
PRODUCER: Pete Townshend
PERSONNEL: Pete Townshend (guitars, vocals); Roger Daltrey (vocals, tambourine, harmonica, acoustic guitar); Pino Palladino (bass guitar); Simon Townshend (guitar, vocals); Frank Simes (keyboards, vocals); Scott Devours (drums, percussion); John Corey (piano, keyboards, vocals); Loren Gold (keyboards, vocals); Dylan Hart (horns); Reggie Grisham (horns) Plus: John Entwistle (bass solo on "5:15," via video recording); Keith Moon (vocals on "Bell Boy," via live show recorded May 18, 1974, The Valley, Charlton, London)
CHART POSITIONS / AWARDS: No. 28, UK album chart; No. 118, US album chart

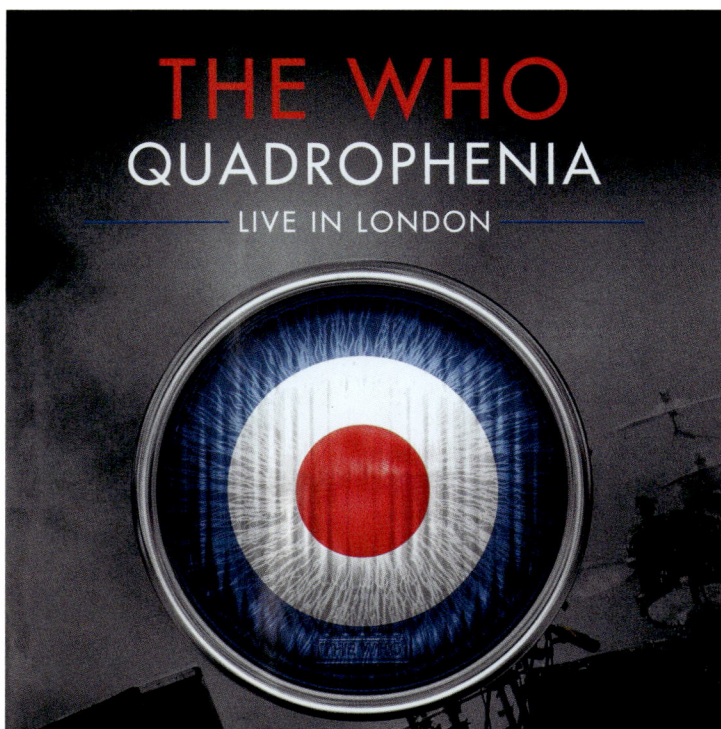

I AM THE SEA
As on the original album, an impressionistic evocation of the sounds of the sea.

THE REAL ME
Daltrey's voice is in fine fettle on a raucous union with Pete's belligerent rhythm and lead guitar.

QUADROPHENIA
The rousing instrumental led by Pete, and enhanced here with the full backing of the horn section et al. As seen on the DVD, the performance was backed with wartime and post-war time footage evoking the England that The Who were born into, segueing visually into their teenage years of Elvis, the Cold War, and the birth of the swinging sixties.

CUT MY HAIR
The first song of the "opera" with a narrative thrust; on the studio album it merged into radio broadcasts reporting the "Mods versus Rockers" riots on Brighton beach.

THE PUNK AND THE GODFATHER
As Roger gets into his stride, his voice seems to strengthen on this, a mini-drama in itself.

I'M ONE
Pete's acoustic stab at a country-style number, with acoustic finger-picking to match, and some appropriate harmonica from Roger.

THE DIRTY JOBS
A neat lead vocal from Pete's little brother, Simon, hitting some spots his big bro' probably can't manage any more. He contributes the lead guitar too.

HELPLESS DANCER (ROGER'S THEME)
A cry of desperation on the part of Roger's character in the opera, the once-ebullient teenager now out of control of his future.

IS IT IN MY HEAD?
An anguished delivery of the angst-driven ballad, leading to . . .

I'VE HAD ENOUGH
. . . which one reviewer called "the darkest point in the show."

5:15
A sensational bit of trickery, the extended version of the number has a spliced-in virtual bass solo from the late John Entwistle that sounds like he's actually there.

SEA AND SAND
Roger and Pete share the vocals on the evocative melody, and there's some sturdy drumming from Scott Devours.

DROWNED
Pete's vocals, as ever, are impressive—complemented by some rousing harmonica from Roger.

BELL BOY (KEITH'S THEME)
Keith appeared on the stage back screen, the live band synching in with the video shot at The Valley, the Charlton Athletic football ground, on May 18, 1974. A tear-jerker for many in the audience.

DOCTOR JIMMY
The band, with horn section (in all, over a dozen musicians onstage), does musical justice to the multilayered song, which includes "Is It Me?"—John's theme.

THE ROCK
The horns provide an uplifting intro to another extensive instrumental.

LOVE, REIGN O'ER ME (PETE'S THEME)
A dramatic piano introduces Roger, his voice still strident, bringing the rock opera to a climactic ending.

WHO ARE YOU
The first of the "bonus" encore items, slightly rough at the edges compared to the original.

YOU BETTER YOU BET
Townshend described this as "just a pop song," but what a pop song! An upbeat winner, with Roger's enthusiastic delivery punctuated with harmonies right where they count.

PINBALL WIZARD
By this time, the band could have been in danger of going through the motions, but as always it's one of The Who's most reliable crowd pleasers.

BABA O'RILEY
Reacting to the instantly recognizable intro, the crowd are on their feet before the number gets underway. Roger at his rampant best, with Pete filling in the bridge passage—where the audience join him singing along with "It's only teenage wasteland."

WON'T GET FOOLED AGAIN
Drummer Scott Devours, by this time a seasoned Who veteran, what with the just-ended tour, and a year or so with Roger's band as well, proves his credentials in this blistering version of the Who standard.

TEA & THEATRE
A straightforward, no-frills closer, from 2006's *Endless Wire*. Pete's acoustic guitar is sparse and effective against Roger's heartfelt delivery. A mellow ending to what was obviously a landmark evening for all present.

17 WHO

Prior to the release of *Quadrophenia Live* in June 2014, Pete Townshend told *Billboard* magazine on April 16 that The Who were embarking on a tour to mark their fiftieth anniversary. And the plan was more formally announced at the end of June, at a press conference held at Ronnie Scott's Jazz Club in London. Roger commented that the tour—called "The Who Hits 50!"—was "the beginning of the long goodbye," before he and Pete played a short acoustic set of "Substitute," "Bargain," "The Kids Are Alright," and "Won't Get Fooled Again." They also hinted there might be a new album in the offing, but that was still some considerable time in the future.

HITTING FIFTY

The week before the press conference, Pete and Roger had reunited with Kenney Jones for their first gig together since 1988. The occasion was a festival at the Hurtwood Park Polo Club, at a benefit gig for Prostate Cancer UK. The three fronted a ten-piece lineup for just five numbers, as the closing act on a bill that included Jeff Beck, Mick Hucknall, Procol Harum, and Mike Rutherford. The Who also joined in the all-star finale on the old Rolling Stones standby "It's Only Rock 'n Roll (But I Like It)."

At the beginning of September, Zak Starkey was welcomed back into the fold, when he appeared with the band filming at London's Porchester Hall, as part of a "Stand Up for Cancer" international telethon. They played just two abbreviated numbers in front of an invited audience of Who fans, a segued medley of "Baba O'Riley" and "See Me Feel Me."

PREVIOUS PAGES The Who Hits 50! tour launch at Ronnie Scott's Jazz Club in London, on June 30, 2014

LEFT The Who perform live onstage at the British Summertime Festival at London's Hyde Park on June 26, 2015. Daltrey and Townshend, both well into their mid-seventies, still serving up plenty of stamina and energy

Starkey was now back on a regular basis, kicking off on November 23 with a pre-tour appearance at the Abu Dhabi Formula One Grand Prix in the United Arab Emirates. The lineup would be the same as the tour proper, which commenced at the end of the month, with Pete, Roger, Zak, and Pino augmented by the three keyboards of Loren Gold, Frank Simes, and John Corey.

The UK leg of the anniversary tour, which began a week later, also had an album to promote. After the September release of their first single in a decade, "Be Lucky," a compilation, *The Who Hits 50!*, appeared at the end of October. Featuring two dozen singles from throughout their career, the original CD release peaked at No. 93 in the US *Billboard* chart, but fared better in the UK, where it made the No. 11 spot.

The tour was paused after a mid-December gig in Cardiff. Roger was suffering from a bad cold, but insisted on going on, straining nerves in his neck in the process, and his doctor insisted he take at least two months off. The UK dates resumed at the end of March 2015, with two previously cancelled London gigs at the O2 Arena, plus the annual Teenage Cancer Trust date at the Albert Hall. Then "The Who Hits 50!"

tour hit America, with twenty-one concerts taking them from mid-April in Tampa, Florida, to Forest Hills, New York, at the end of May.

After headlining in London's Hyde Park on June 26, two days later The Who made their second appearance as the closing act on Sunday night at Glastonbury. And immediately following Glastonbury, Pete declared in *Mojo* magazine: "I think The Who will stop after this year," but adding "I think Roger and I will do odd things together." Then in September, when some remaining US tour dates had to be cancelled on account of Roger coming down with viral meningitis, Townshend assured *The Guardian*: "We are rescheduling all the shows for next spring 2016. Once Roger is completely well, we will come back stronger than ever, and Roger and I will give you all a show to remember."

BACK TO THE WHO

Which of course they did, when the "Back to The Who Tour 51!" hit the road in North America, as a continuation of the previous outing. Twenty-nine dates from early March to the end of May took them

OPPOSITE The Who Hits 50! tour ticket

ABOVE Roger and Pete during Desert Trip at the Empire Polo Field, Indio, California, October 16, 2016

RIGHT Roger Daltrey looks out across the audience at Mediolanum Forum, Milan, Italy, September 19, 2016

across the US and Canada, followed by the Isle of Wight festival, some European dates, and another two US concerts—plus Mexico City—before they wound up at the Desert Trip festival in Indio, California, in October. Whichever way you read it, The Who were certainly back.

No sooner were the 2016 dates completed than, in November, the band announced that five UK dates for April 2017 would include a full live performance of *Tommy* in its entirety—the most comprehensive selection from the album presented in concert since 1989. The first two concerts were the regular Teenage Cancer Trust dates at the Albert Hall, then five more across the UK. Dubbed "2017 Tommy and More," the tour gigs featured selections from both *Tommy* and *Quadrophenia*, plus a good quota of other "greatest hits." The lineup for these dates, and those following through 2017, had one change in personnel, with Jon Button —who had played with Roger Daltrey's touring band in 2009—replacing Pino Palladino on bass.

The Who were back in North America in July, for what seemed once again like a regular commitment, with "The Who 2017" tour. That was followed in September by the band's first-ever tour of South America, with five concerts in São Paulo, Rio de Janeiro, and Porto Alegre in Brazil, Santiago in Chile, and the Argentinian capital, Buenos Aires.

WHO MINUS

Between the North and South America tours by The Who, Pete Townshend played five US dates with "Classic Quadrophenia." The project, which Pete had premiered at the Royal Albert Hall back in 2015, was a collaboration with his partner Rachel Fuller. With opera star Alfie Boe, erstwhile punk Billy Idol, and a full classical orchestra conducted by Robert Ziegler, the spectacular kicked off in Lenox, Massachusetts with the Boston Pops Orchestra, before visiting New York, Chicago, and Los Angeles.

Coming right in the middle of dates by The Who, it signaled that individual activities were still of equal importance to both Pete and Roger. And this was echoed immediately following the South American concerts, when Roger took the band—without Townshend—on a short "Who Hits, Who Rarities, and Solo Hits" tour of five dates in America and Canada.

In fact it was the band without Pete that represented any Who-related activity in 2018, as Roger fronted the

six-piece for some more transatlantic dates in March, followed by the Teenage Cancer Trust later in the month. Then in the summer he headed an orchestral version of *Tommy*—not unlike Pete's "Classic Quadrophenia"—across the US, with a different forty-five-piece orchestra (plus the Who band) at each venue, conducted by Keith Levenson.

Suddenly, Roger seemed to have assumed stewardship of The Who's legacy in Pete's absence, enthusing to the press: "For me, *Tommy* has always been all of us. You're Tommy, I'm Tommy. The other characters are different parts of our human makeup. We all have the potential to be Uncle Ernie, or spiteful cousin Kevin. We're all trying to get through this life the best we can. For a lot of it, we are deaf, dumb and blind. Hopefully, we end up with our eyes open."

LEFT Pete Townshend's "Classic Quadrophenia" concert, September 13, 2017, at The Rosemont Theatre, Chicago, with (L–R): Eddie Vedder, Alfie Boe, Billy Idol, and Pete Townshend ABOVE Pete Townshend pictured with members of the 48-piece orchestra at the Amalie Arena, Tampa Florida, on the second leg of The Who's Moving On! tour

MOVING ON

With Pete (voluntarily) out of the picture, the future of The Who as a Daltrey-Townshend unit looked in doubt once again. That was until January 2019, when the band announced there would be a full tour of the US and Canada—dubbed "Moving On!"—with a batch of dates in the spring then more in the fall. And it was also announced at the same time that The Who would be recording a brand new album in the coming months.

The first leg of "Moving On!" kicked off in early May, and wound up on June 1. For each concert The Who were accompanied by a full symphony orchestra, conducted by Keith Levenson, who had worked similarly with Roger Daltrey on *Tommy* the previous summer. And the album of Daltrey's *Tommy* exercise, *The Who's Tommy Orchestral*, was released in June to all-round acclaim, and, amazingly, shot to the No. 1 spot on *Billboard*'s Classical Music chart the week it was released.

July saw The Who, with the orchestral backing, gracing the stage at Wembley Stadium in London, topping a bill that included their friend Eddie Vedder, The Kaiser Chiefs, and vocalist Imelda May. During

> **"Thankfully, it's much too late for Daltrey and Townshend to die before they get old, so with *Who* they show that even in rock 'n' roll, it's possible to age both with grace and vigor and without abandoning purpose. Or lose the talent to make stirring, highly gratifying music."**
>
> *CHICAGO TRIBUNE,* DECEMBER 6, 2019

their set, Pete paid tribute to his long-standing guitar tech who had tragically died that week: "Some of you may already know that Alan Rogan passed away two days ago. He was my guitar tech for over forty years. He battled cancer and he finally lost his battle. He was a great guy and he was chipper and in high spirits until the end."

The "Moving On!" tour resumed on September 1 with a return date at Madison Square Garden. As on the first leg, many reviewers applauded the sheer stamina and energy of Daltrey and Townshend, now both well into their mid-seventies: "Partway through The Who's concert on September 1 at Madison Square Garden, Pete Townshend apologized for the band's rustiness," began one, "But the epic performance the group delivered over two and a half hours bristled with an urgency and rawness bands one-third his and Roger Daltrey's age would sell their souls for."

There was some concern when two shows had to be postponed on account of a pollen infection affecting Roger's voice, but all was well when the tour concluded in Pacific Palisades, California at the end of October. The final date was a "Backyard Benefit" for Teen Cancer America—a charity set up by Daltrey and Townshend in 2012—also featuring Kenny Loggins, Pink, and The Foo Fighters.

WHO, THE ALBUM

Meanwhile, the band's promise at the beginning of the year of a new album had indeed come to fruition.

In the January press release, Pete had predicted a mixed bag involving "dark ballads, heavy rock stuff, experimental electronica, sampled stuff, and Who-ish tunes that began with a guitar that goes yanga-dang." So in February 2019, Pete, his brother Simon, Pino Palladino, and Billy Nicholls had convened at British Grove Studios in Chiswick, west London, to start laying down tracks with producer Dave Sardy. And as with their most recent albums—bearing in mind the previous *Endless Wire* was thirteen years earlier—Townshend and Daltrey elected to record their parts separately. With the addition of various session players during the process, including no less than three guest drummers as well as Starkey, recording was completed at the end of August.

The December release of *Who* was greeted enthusiastically by press and public. There was a general consensus that both in terms of the actual songs and their performance, it was a return to form—without being deliberately retrospective in style, a resurgence of the Who dynamic of old. The review in the *Chicago Tribune* was typical of many when it concluded: "Thankfully, it's much too late for Daltrey and Townshend to die before they get old, so with *Who* they show that even in rock 'n' roll, it's possible to age both with grace and vigor and without abandoning purpose. Or lose the talent to make stirring, highly gratifying music."

Perhaps not surprisingly, many fans and critics paused to consider whether this would be the final

studio album from The Who; at the time of its release, Pete Townshend was seventy-four, and Roger Daltrey seventy-five. That prospect was reinforced by the spectacular cover artwork by Peter Blake (who had designed *Face Dances* back in 1981), which involved a series of images reflecting The Who's long career. A patchwork of twenty-two squares included a Royal Air Force roundel (The Who's famous "Mod" target symbol), a pinball machine, a *Quadrophenia*-style scooter, and an early inspiration, rhythm and blues icon Chuck Berry.

ABOVE Pete and Roger reveal The Who's latest album cover, designed by Sir Peter Blake, at the Pace Gallery in New York, September 12, 2019

Pete, too, addressed the issue of their mortality when the album was released: "Roger and I are both old men now, by any measure, so I've tried to stay away from romance, but also from nostalgia if I can. I didn't want to make anyone feel uncomfortable. Memories are OK, and some of the songs refer to the explosive state of things today."

Alongside a "Deluxe" edition that included three bonus tracks, sales-wise the release was a universal success. As well as going straight to the No. 2 position in both the US and Canada, and No. 3 in the UK, it reached the Top Fifty in at least thirteen other countries worldwide.

INTO THE TWENTIES

As the new decade opened, plans were being finalized for a resumption of touring, in support of the *Who* album. And nearer to home, Pete and Roger played two dates as The Who at the Pryzm nightclub in Kingston-upon-Thames, south-west London. The occasion was the fiftieth anniversary of their legendary appearance (and live recording) at Leeds University on February 14, 1970. Each night, February 12 and 14, the pair played two forty-minute shows backed by Simon Townshend, Billy Nicholls on backing vocals, Phil Spalding on bass, and Jody Linscott on percussion.

Tour dates for the UK and Ireland had already been set to commence on March 16 in Manchester, finishing on April 8 at London's Wembley Arena. All the dates were sold out, tickets having gone on sale six months earlier, but events that no one could have predicted brought everything to a halt.

With the onset of the worldwide coronavirus pandemic, all leisure activity of a "social" nature came to an immediate standstill, and it hit the music industry as hard as other sectors. As far as The Who were concerned, the scheduled 2020 UK tour was now marked in for a year later, in the spring of 2021. However, at the beginning of 2021, coronavirus rates in the UK soared, and the tour dates were ultimately cancelled.

FINALE

With the enforced furlough brought about by the pandemic, the definitively named *Who* could well have been the final album released by Townshend and Daltrey under the banner of The Who.

December 2020 marked fifty-five years since the release of the band's debut album, *My Generation*. The dynamic career of The Who, from the mid-sixties onwards, has encapsulated much of the history of post-fifties rock 'n' roll, often as a powerhouse for change in the music itself, and the fashions and tropes surrounding it.

It was The Who—as early as their brief incarnation as The High Numbers—who more than any other band personified Mod, from their first grass-roots fan following in west London, to Pete Townshend's ultimate homage in the form of the *Quadrophenia* saga on record, on the screen, and on the road.

Closely linked to their Mod image was Pete's art school background, and his consequent embracement of the Pop Art movement, utilizing the imagery of Union Jack flags, "target" roundels, and familiar symbols culled from advertising and comic books. Tellingly, the artwork for The Who's possibly final album *Who* was designed by the pioneer of British Pop Art, Sir Peter Blake.

Likewise the guitar-smashing and similar onstage mayhem, a trademark of The Who's performances for most of their career, Pete related back to the theories of "auto-destructive" art introduced to him by his college tutor Gustav Metzger. The implied violence, accompanied by unprecedented levels of volume, would be reflected in heavy metal and punk rock, which both emerged in the seventies.

The Who's introduction of radical guitar techniques, involving power chords and amplified feedback, would have a direct influence on Jimi Hendrix, Cream, and the later records of The Beatles—and the work of more experimental artists like Vanilla Fudge and Pink Floyd. And the band's adoption of synthesizers and other electronic advances has impacted on generations of rock styles, from New Wave to Brit Pop, Grunge to Alt Rock—from The Jam to Oasis, Nirvana, and The Killers.

Pete Townshend's breadth of vision was responsible for The Who's ventures into rock opera—*Tommy*, *Quadrophenia*, and the *Wire & Glass* "mini-opera" on their *Endless Wire* album. These landmark works, while seeming pretentious in their ambition, were nevertheless direct in their impact, like all good pop art should be.

With the death of Keith Moon, and later John Entwistle, there was a question mark over the future of the band. But it has endured, fronted by Pete Townshend and Roger Daltrey, with a variety of backing personnel. And the essence of The Who, embodied in the presence of its two prime architects, remains forever accessible in over half a century of recordings that make up the band's enduring legacy.

Pete and Roger at the unveiling of the founding stone of London's official Music Walk of Fame, at The Jazz Café, in Camden, London on November 19, 2019. The Music Walk of Fame commemorates the world's most extraordinary musicians, and when completed will feature over 400 artists. The Who were recipients of the first stone.

WHO

TRACK LIST
[All songs written by Pete Townshend except where noted)

1. All This Music Must Fade
2. Ball and Chain
3. I Don't Wanna Get Wise
4. Detour
5. Beads on One String (Pete Townshend, Josh Hunsaker)
6. Hero Ground Zero
7. Street Song
8. I'll Be Back

9. Break the News (Simon Townshend)
10. Rockin' in Rage
11. She Rocked My World

Bonus Tracks—Deluxe edition
12. This Gun Will Misfire
13. Got Nothing to Prove
14. Danny and My Ponies

RECORDED: February 3, 2019–August 2019, British Grove Studios, London; Metropolis Studios, London
RELEASED: December 6, 2019
LABEL: Polydor, Interscope
PRODUCER: Pete Townshend, Dave Sardy (with Bob Pridden and Dave Eringa for Roger Daltrey's vocals only)
PERSONNEL: Pete Townshend (guitars, vocals, harmonica, percussion, synthesizer, violin, cello, hurdy-gurdy); Roger Daltrey (vocals); Pino Palladino (bass guitar); Simon Townshend (percussion); Zak Starkey (drums); Dave Sardy (percussion, Mellotron, synthesizer); Joey Waronker (drums); Benmont Tench (organ, Mellotron); Gus Seyffert (bass); Carla Azar (drums); Matt Chamberlain (drums); Josh Tyrrell (handclaps); Rowan McIntosh (handclaps); Andrew Synowiec (acoustic guitar); Gordon Giltrap (acoustic guitar); Fergus Gerrand (percussion)
CHART POSITIONS / AWARDS: No. 2, US album chart; No. 2, UK album chart; No. 3, Canadian album chart

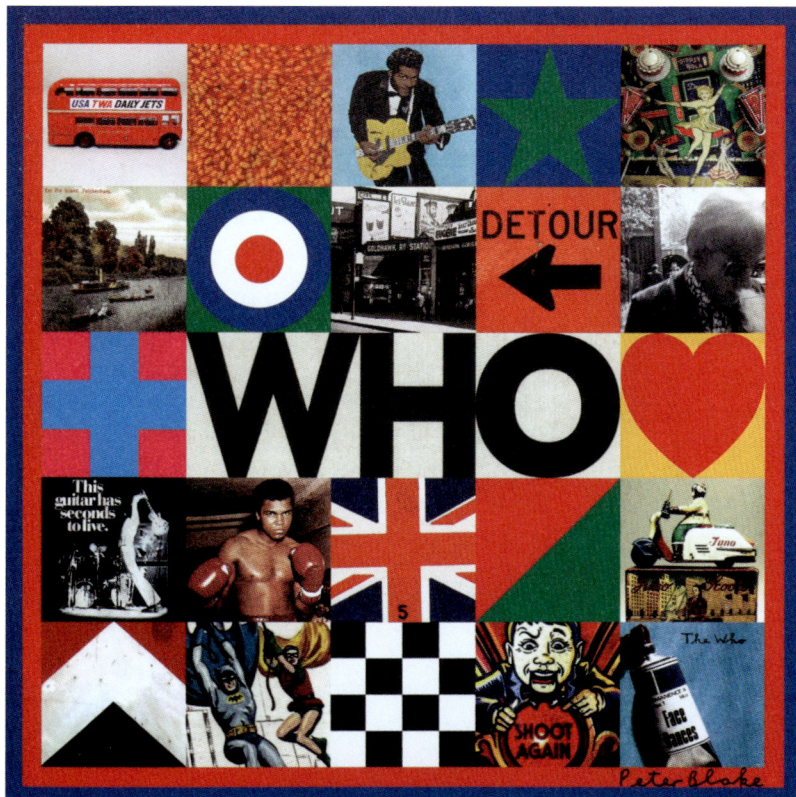

ALL THIS MUSIC MUST FADE
A dramatic opener, cross-referencing both the transience of pop music, and of the sometimes fraught relationship between Townshend and Daltrey.

BALL AND CHAIN
Pete Townshend's original version was written as "Guantanamo" in 2015, addressing the controversial American base in Cuba which was used to house suspected terrorists after 9/11. Proves Daltrey can sound as angry as ever, when he wants to.

I DON'T WANNA GET WISE
A biographical pitch, though not clear whether it's Pete or Roger talking—"Those snotty young kids were a standing success"— to their twenty-year-old past self.

DETOUR
A Bo-Diddley-style beat takes us through some funky changes, and by the synth fade-out it sounds like a sixties dance-floor anthem gone electronic.

BEADS ON ONE STRING
Pete collaborates with Josh Hunsaker, who composed the melody, on a ballad treatment sometimes verging on the bland. The title comes from a saying by Meher Baba, and the lyrics have an anti-war message with a spiritual slant: "I just know that we shame him / When we kill in his name."

HERO GROUND ZERO
Some trademark Townshend guitar bombast kicks off an otherwise reflective piece—"I was adopted by the angels / they said my future was postponed."

STREET SONG
Another sociopolitical slant, on a tub-thumping call to the barricades. A slight message delivered with over-the-top, grandiose arrangements.

I'LL BE BACK
The harmonica intro almost takes us into easy-listening land, with some lush strings behind Pete's relaxed vocals.

BREAK THE NEWS
Written by Simon Townshend, a slice of cute folk rock reminiscent of, if anything, Wings-era Paul McCartney.

ROCKIN' IN RAGE
Some strident, angry vocalizing from Roger Daltrey on a guitar-heavy rocker. "If I can't tell the truth for fear of being abused. . ."

SHE ROCKED MY WORLD
Over a Latin-tango rhythm, Roger growls the bitter-sweet lyrics with a pent-up, understated energy that rounds off the collection perfectly.

BONUS TRACKS—DELUXE EDITION

THIS GUN WILL MISFIRE
Flamenco-style guitar backing on a strident anti-war song, a rundown of the travails and contradictions of military hostilities.

GOT NOTHING TO PROVE
First recorded as a demo in 1966, the light melody line and inconsequential lyrics hark back to those more innocent days.

DANNY AND MY PONIES
More acoustic backing for a folky treatment addressing the eternal problem of homelessness: "Danny laid back and surveyed the view / A king on his bench, he was cold, he was blue."

DISCOGRAPHY

STUDIO ALBUMS

Title, followed by month/year of first release and UK/US variations

My Generation (December 1965; US: ***The Who Sings My Generation***, April 1966)

A Quick One (December 1966; US: ***Happy Jack***, May 1967)

The Who Sell Out (December 1967; US: January 1968)

Tommy (May 1969)

Who's Next (August 1971)

Quadrophenia (October 1973)

The Who by Numbers (October 1975)

Who Are You (August 1978)

Face Dances (March 1981)

It's Hard (September 1982)

Endless Wire (October 2006)

Who (December 2019)

LIVE ALBUMS

Live at Leeds (May 1970)

Who's Last (December 1984; US: November 1984)

Join Together (March 1990)

Live at Isle of Wight 1970 (October 1996)

BBC Sessions (February 2000)

The Blues to the Bush / 1999 (UK only, March 2000)

Live at the Royal Albert Hall (June 2003)

Live from Toronto (April 2006)

View from a Backstage Pass (October 2007)

Greatest Hits Live (January 2010)

Live at Hull 1970 (November 2012)

Quadrophenia Live in London (June 2014)

Live in Hyde Park (November 2015)

Live at the Isle of Wight 2004 (June 2017)

Tommy Live at the Royal Albert Hall (October 2017)

Live at the Fillmore East 1968 (April 2018)

Woodstock 1969 – Live & Remastered (February 2019)

COMPILATION ALBUMS

Magic Bus: The Who on Tour (September 1968)

Direct Hits (October 1968)

Meaty Beaty Big and Bouncy (October 1971)

Odds & Sods (September 1974)

The Story of The Who (September 1976)

Phases (May 1981)

Hooligans (October 1981)

Who's Greatest Hits (November 1983)

Rarities Vol. I (August 1983)

Rarities Vol. II (August 1983)

The Singles (October 1984)

Who's Missing (November 1985)

The Who Collection (December 1985)

Two's Missing (April 1987)

Who's Better, Who's Best (March 1988)

Thirty Years of Maximum R&B (July 1994)

My Generation: The Very Best of The Who (August 1996)

The Best of The Who (20th Century Masters: The Millennial Collection) (April 1999)

The Ultimate Collection (June 2002)

Then and Now (March 2004)

The 1st Singles Box (May 2004)

Greatest Hits (December 2009)

Greatest Hits & More (February 2010)

Icon (April 2011)

Icon 2 (April 2011)

Pinball Wizard: The Collection (May 2012)

The Who Hits 50! (October 2014)

SOUNDTRACKS

Tommy (March 1975)

The Kids Are Alright (June 1979)

Quadrophenia (October 1979)

Amazing Journey: The Story of The Who (US only, April 2008)

EXTENDED PLAY

Ready Steady Who (November 1966)

Tommy (November 1970)

This Is My Generation (March 1988)

Won't Get Fooled Again (August 1988)

My Generation (June 1996)

Wire & Glass (July 2006)

BIBLIOGRAPHY

Boyd, Joe, *White Bicycles: Making Music in the 1960s* (Serpent's Tail, 2006)

Daltrey, Roger, *Thanks a Lot Mr Kibblewhite: My Story* (Blink Publishing, 2018)

Denselow, Robin, *When the Music's Over: The Story of Political Pop* (Faber & Faber, 1989)

Evans, Mike, *The Art of British Rock* (Frances Lincoln, 2010)

Evans, Mike, and Kingsbury, Paul, *Woodstock: Three Days That Rocked the World* (Sterling, 2009)

Fletcher, Tony, *Dear Boy: The Life of Keith Moon* (Omnibus Press, 1998)

Foulk, Ray, *When the World Came to the Isle of Wight, Volume One: Stealing Dylan from Woodstock* (Medina Publishing, 2015)

Frith, Simon, and Horne, Howard, *Art into Pop* (Methuen, 1987)

Geldzahler, Henry, *Pop Art 1955–70* (International Culture Corporation Of Australia, 1985)

Grantley, Steve, and Parker, Alan, *The Who by Numbers: The Story of the Who Through Their Music* (Helter Skelter, 2010)

Hewison, Robert, *Too Much: Art and Society in the Sixties* (Methuen, 1986)

Hinton, Brian, *Message to Love: The Isle of Wight Festivals, 1968–70* (Castle Communications, 1995)

Marsh, Dave, *Before I Get Old: The Story of The Who* (Plexus, 1983)

Marshall, Ben, *The Who: The Official History* (Virgin Books, 2015)

Miles, Barry, *Hippie* (Cassell Illustrated. 2004)

Miles, Barry, *London Calling: A Countercultural History of London since 1945* (Atlantic Books, 2010)

Miller, James, *Almost Grown: The Rise of Rock* (Arrow Books, 2000)

Neill, Andy, and Kent, Matt, *Anyway Anyhow Anywhere* (Virgin Books, 2002)

Nuttall, Jeff, *Bomb Culture* (MacGibbon & Kee, 1968)

Rees, Paul, *The Ox: The Last of the Great Rock Stars* (Constable, 2020)

Sandbrook, Dominic, *White Heat: A History of Britain in the Swinging Sixties* (Little, Brown, 2006)

Savage, Jon, *1966: The Year the Decade Exploded* (Faber & Faber, 2015)

Townshend, Pete, *Who I Am* (HarperCollins, 2012)

Wilkerson, Mark, *Amazing Journey: The Life of Pete Townshend* (Omnibus, 2007)

OTHER REFERENCE SOURCES
Periodicals:

Beat Instrumental (UK), *Chicago Sun-Times* (US), *Chicago Tribune* (US), *Classic Rock* (UK), *Creem* (US), *Datebook* (US), *Disc* (UK), *Esquire* (US), *The Guardian* (UK), *The Independent* (UK), *Melody Maker* (UK), *Mojo* (UK), *Musician* (US), *New Musical Express* (UK), *New York Times* (US), *New Zealand Truth* (NZ), *Phonograph Record* (US), *Record Mirror* (UK), *Rolling Stone* (US), *San Francisco Chronicle* (US), *San Francisco Examiner* (US), *Sounds* (UK), *Sunday Times* (UK), *Time* (US), *Uncut* (UK), *Variety* (US), *The Village Voice* (US), *ZigZag* (UK)

Websites:

classicrockreview.com / discogs.com / highway81revisited.com / rocksbackpages.com / rollingstone.com / streetsyoucrossed.blogspot.com / thewho.com / thewho.net / thewholive.net / thewhothismonth.com

PICTURE CREDITS

T: TOP; B: BOTTOM; L: LEFT; R: RIGHT

ALAMY: Front cover, P112 Everett Collection Inc/Alamy Stock Photo P16, P17 Trinity Mirror/Mirrorpix/Alamy Stock Photo P18, P19, P26–27, P38–39, P52–53, P58, P79, P141T Pictorial Press Ltd/Alamy Stock Photo P73 David Hickes/ Alamy Stock Photo P82, P83 Gijsbert Hanekroot/Alamy Stock Photo P88 Philippe Gras/Le Pictorium P106 Rob Cousins/Alamy Stock Photo P123 sjvinyl/Alamy Stock Photo P129 A Images/Alamy Stock Photo P134 WORLD NORTHAL/ Album P169 CBW/ Alamy Stock Photo P201T Roger Donovan/Alamy Stock Photo P201 REUTERS/Alamy Stock Photo P224–225 PA Images/ Alamy Stock Photo P228 gbimages/Alamy Stock Photo P230 Paul Hennessy/Alamy Live New **GETTY IMAGES:** Endpapers, P104 Michael Ochs Archives/Getty Images P2, P118 Gijsbert Hanekroot/Redferns P10–11, P35 The Visualeyes Archive/ Redferns P14, Larry Ellis/Daily Express/Hulton Archive/ Getty Images P15, P20, P28, P33, P43, P57, P126–127 Chris Morphet/Redferns P21 Paul Popper/Popperfoto via Getty Images/Getty Images P22L, P55, P107 GAB Archive/Redferns P34 Rolls Press/Popperfoto via Getty Images/Getty Images P42 Jeff Hochberg/Bernie Walters/Getty Images P44 Paul Ryan/Michael Ochs Archives/Getty Images P46 Evening Standard/Getty Images P47 C Maher/Getty Images P48 Jeff Hochberg/Getty Images P49 CBS Photo Archive/Getty Images P54 Fairfax Media via Getty Images P56 Hulton Archive/Getty Images P59 David Cairns/Express/Getty Images P60, P67 Daily Mirror/Mirrorpix/Mirrorpix via Getty Images P61 Ivan Keeman/Redferns P64–65 Jack Robinson/ Hulton Archive/Getty Images P66 Archive Photos/Getty Images P70 Anwar Hussein/Getty Images P76–77, P139B Bettmann/Contributor P81 Evening Standard/Hulton Archive/ Getty Images P86–87, P90, P91, P92, P93, P94, P95, P116–117, P120–121, P139T, P143, P154–155 Michael Putland/Getty Images P96 Staff/Mirrorpix/Getty Images P97 David Redfern/ Redferns P100–101 David Warner Ellis/Redferns P102, P109 Ian Dickson/Redferns P105 Wilson Lindsay/Michael Ochs Archives/Getty Image P110–111 Graham Wood/Evening Standard/Hulton Archive/Getty Images P120T Richard E. Aaron/Redferns P122, P142 Ed Perlstein/Redferns/Getty Images P125 Jones/Evening Standard/Hulton Archive/ Getty Images P132–133 Daniel SIMON/Gamma-Rapho via Getty Images P148 Ron Burton/Mirrorpix/Getty Images P151 Clayton Call/Redferns P157 Ross Marino/Getty Images P160 George Rose/Getty Images P161, P173, P180–181, P185 Ebet Roberts/Redferns P166 Pete Still/Redferns P171 Suzanne Kreiter/The Boston Globe via Getty Image P182, P188 Dave Benett/Getty Images P183 Richard Blanshard/ Getty Images P186–187 Brian Rasic/Getty Images P189 Paul Bergen/Redferns P192 SGranitz/WireImage P196–197, P198, P218 KMazur/WireImage P202-203 Dave Hogan/Getty Images P204 Bob King/Redferns P206 Johnny Green-Royal Rota/Getty Images P207 Mick Hutson/Redferns P208 John Shearer/WireImage for The Friedman Gr P209 Terry George/ WireImage P212–213 Hayley Madden/Redferns P214–215 Dan Kitwood/Getty Images P216 Ron Sachs-Pool/Getty Images P217 Bradley Kanaris/Getty Images P219 Denis ORegan/ Getty Images

P220 Jeff J Mitchell/Getty Images P221T Larry Busacca/ Getty Images for Clear Channel P221B Matt Kent/WireImage P226–227 Neil Lupin/Redferns via Getty Images P229T Frazer Harrison/Getty Images P229B Francesco Castaldo\Archivio Francesco Castaldo\Mondadori via Getty Images P233 Theo Wargo/Getty Images for Polydor Records P235 Jeff Spicer/Getty Images **REX SHUTTERSTOCK:** P7 Luigi Villani/ Shutterstock P8-9, P22–23 Dezo Hoffman/Shutterstock P12 David Magnus/Shutterstock P30 Hugh Vanes/Shutterstock P31 ANL/Shutterstock P40, P75 Ray Stevenson/Shutterstock P45 Barry Peake P69 Charles Knoblock/AP/Shutterstock P71 John Selby/Shutterstock P78 Sharratt/Shutterstock P108 Andre Csillag/Shutterstock P113 Graham Wiltshire/ Shutterstock P128 Shutterstock P136, P140, P141B, P146–147, P172, P187R Richard Young/Shutterstock P137 Frank Connor/ Curbishley-Baird/Kobal/Shutterstock P150 Graham Wiltshire/ Shutterstock P156 Martyn Goddard P159 Sten Rosenlund/ Shutterstock P164–165, P174 Alan Davidson/Shutterstock P168 Martin Lawrence/Mail On Sunday/Shutterstock P170 lipo Mustp/Shutterstock P175 Ron Frehm/AP/Shutterstock P184 Justin Sutcliffe/AP/Shutterstock P190 John Bryson/ Shutterstock P191 Robert Judges/Shutterstock P200 Peter Simpson/Shutterstock P230 Invision/AP/Shutterstock

ALBUM COVERS: P24: David Wedgbury (cover photography) P36: Alan Aldridge (cover artwork), Richard Evans (design & art direction) P50: Richard Evans (design & art direction), David King & Roger Law (cover artwork), David Montgomery (cover photography) P62: Richard Evans (design & art direction), Michael McInnerney (cover artwork), Barrie Meller (original LP photography) P74: Richard Evans (design & art direction), Graphreaks (cover design) P84: Richard Evans (design & art direction), Kosh (cover design), Ethan A. Russell (cover photography) P98: Richard Evans (design & art direction), Graham Hughes (cover design & photography) P114: John Entwistle (cover drawing), Richard Evans (design & art direction) P130: Richard Evans (design & art direction), Terry O'Neill (cover photography), Bill Smith (original LP design) P144: Michael Andrews (paintings) Brian Aris (photography), Clive Barker (paintings, photography, paint-box bronze on rear cover), Peter Blake (cover design, concept, paintings), Patrick Caulfield (paintings), Gavin Cochrane (photography), Richard Evans (design), Richard Hamilton (paintings), David Hockney (paintings), Howard Hodgkin (paintings), David Inshaw (paintings), Bill Jacklin (paintings), Allen Jones (paintings), R. B. Kitaj (paintings),Tom Phillips (paintings), Patrick Procktor (paintings), Colin Self (paintings), Joe Tilson (paintings), David Tindle (paintings) P152: Graham Hughes (photography) P162: Bill Smith (cover design), Gavin Cochrane (photography) P177: Icon (design) P193: Andie Airfix at Satori (artwork & design), Art Kane © Art Kane Estate (photography) P210: Richard Evans (design & art direction), Dave Snowden & Lawrence Ball (Visual Harmony software) P222: Richard Evans (image & memorabilia), Bob Kelly (Mod headlight design), Ryan Rogers/Oddopolis (design), Vartan (art direction), Jeff Veitch (photography) P234: Peter Blake (design, art direction & cover artwork), Rick Guest (photography), Simon Halfon (design & art direction)